The DSM-5 Alternative Model for Personality Disorders

The DSM-5 Alternative Model for Personality Disorders reviews and advances this innovative and increasingly popular scheme for diagnosing and evaluating personality disorders. The authors identify the multiple clinical, theoretical, and research paradigms that co-exist in the Alternative Model for Personality Disorders (AMPD) and show how the model can aid the practicing mental health professional in evaluating and treating patients, as well as show its importance in stimulating research and theoretical understanding of this domain. This work explores and summarizes methods of personality assessment and psychiatric evaluation, research findings, and clinical applications of the AMPD, highlighting its usefulness to clinical teaching and supervision, forensic application, and current research. It is a go-to reference for experienced professionals and researchers, those who wish to learn this new diagnostic system, and for clinicians in training.

Christopher J. Hopwood is an associate professor of psychology at the University of California, Davis.

Abby L. Mulay is a postdoctoral fellow in clinical forensic psychology at the Medical University of South Carolina, Charleston.

Mark H. Waugh is a staff psychologist at the Oak Ridge National Laboratory, adjunct clinical and teaching faculty at the University of Tennessee, Knoxville, and is in private practice in Oak Ridge, Tennessee.

The DSM-5 Alternative Model for Personality Disorders

Integrating Multiple Paradigms of Personality Assessment

Edited by
Christopher J. Hopwood, Abby L. Mulay and Mark H. Waugh

Routledge
Taylor & Francis Group
NEW YORK AND LONDON

First published 2019
by Routledge
52 Vanderbilt Avenue, New York, NY 10017

and by Routledge
2 Park Square, Milton Park, Abingdon, Oxon OX14 4RN

Routledge is an imprint of the Taylor & Francis Group, an informa business

Library of Congress Cataloging in Publication Data
Names: Hopwood, Christopher J., 1976- editor. | Mulay, Abby L., editor. | Waugh, Mark H., editor.
Title: The DSM-5 alternative model for personality disorders : integrating multiple paradigms of personality assessment / edited by Christopher J. Hopwood, Abby L. Mulay, and Mark H. Waugh.
Description: New York, NY : Routledge, 2019. | Includes bibliographical references and index.
Identifiers: LCCN 2018044678 (print) | LCCN 2018045892 (ebook) | ISBN 9781315205076 (E-book) | ISBN 9781138693135 (hardback) | ISBN 9781138696327 (pbk.) | ISBN 9781315205076 (ebk.)
Subjects: | MESH: Diagnostic and statistical manual of mental disorders. 5th ed. | Personality Disorders--diagnosis | Personality Assessment | Models, Psychological
Classification: LCC RC473.P56 (ebook) | LCC RC473.P56 (print) | NLM WM 190 | DDC 616.85/81075--dc23
LC record available at https://lccn.loc.gov/2018044678

ISBN: 978-1-138-69313-5 (hbk)
ISBN: 978-1-138-69632-7 (pbk)
ISBN: 978-1-315-20507-6 (ebk)

Typeset in Times New Roman
by Taylor & Francis Books

Christopher J. Hopwood: I dedicate this book to my teachers, students, and patients. I am grateful to the DSM-5 Personality and Personality Disorders Work Group, whose Alternative Model has been a watershed in the mental health revolution that was a long time coming. Finally, it has been a privilege to work with Mark Waugh and Abby Mulay, whose clinical sensitivity, scholarship, and good nature largely explain any contribution this book might make in promoting a more holistic, integrative, and evidence-based conceptualization of people and their difficulties.

Abby L. Mulay: My journey to clinical psychology was nonlinear and required a little bit of faith in me by my mentors, so I dedicate this work to those who are willing to take a chance on the unexpected. I am grateful for the continued mentorship of Christopher J. Hopwood, Mark H. Waugh, and my graduate school advisor, Nicole M. Cain. I also dedicate this work to all of the patients/clients I have encountered as a therapist in criminal justice settings. Thank you for challenging me to grow as a therapist, demonstrating the healing power of humor, and inspiring hope in the recovery process.

Mark H. Waugh: I dedicate this book to many teachers. These include the guiding lights of Jane Loevinger and Paul Meehl, and the gifts of Roger Blashfield, Sidney Blatt, and many talented professors and supervisors too numerous to list. Beginnings include my physician-scientist father, William H. Waugh, my mother, Eileen G. Waugh, who "knew" people and opposed social injustice long before it was fashionable, and Virginia Forrest, who practiced what Donald Winnicott has to say about children. Presently, Lorrie G. Beevers and Michael J. O'Connell continue to teach me about people and life. Most important are my best teachers, the many patients who opened their selves to me and therein helped me to know more about being a person. Thank you.

Contents

Illustrations

Figures

Tables

Contributors

Jennifer L. Bishop, M.A. is a doctoral candidate in clinical psychology at the University of Tennessee, Knoxville and is currently on clinical internship at Cherokee Health Systems. Her clinical and research interests include behavioral medicine/health psychology, women's reproductive mental health, adolescent and adult development, psychological assessment, including personality assessment, and routine outcomes monitoring.

Roger K. Blashfield, Ph.D. is an academic clinical psychologist whose research area of interest is the classification of mental disorders. Students with whom he has worked include Mark Aldenderfer, Les Morey, Mark H. Waugh, Beth Flanagan, Jared Keeley, and Shannon Reynolds. He served on work groups for the *DSM-IV* and the *ICD-11*. Since retirement, he volunteers at the Hood River History Museum and assists the teaching of algebra in a local high school.

Nicole M. Cain, Ph.D. is Associate Professor of Clinical Psychology at Rutgers University in the Graduate School of Applied and Professional Psychology. She has previously been an Associate Professor at Long Island University, Brooklyn. Her research interests focus on understanding how personality pathology and interpersonal functioning impact diagnosis, psychotherapy process, and treatment outcome. She serves on the editorial boards of scientific journals focused on assessment and personality assessment.

Christopher J. Hopwood, Ph.D. is Associate Professor of Psychology at the University of California, Davis. He completed his doctoral training at Texas A&M University under the mentorship of Les Morey, and his internship at the Massachusetts General Hospital, Harvard Medical School with Mark Blais. Dr. Hopwood has served on the board of the North American Society for the Study of Personality Disorders, the Society for Interpersonal Theory and Research, and the Society for Personality Assessment, and has served as an Associate Editor for *Assessment*, the *Journal of Personality Assessment*, the *Journal of Personality Disorders*, and the *Journal of Personality and Social Psychology*. He has previously written or edited books on the Personality Assessment Inventory, personality disorder diagnosis, and multimethod clinical assessment. He is a licensed clinician and clinical supervisor; his research interests involve personality assessment and interpersonal processes.

Robert F. Krueger, Ph.D. is Distinguished McKnight University Professor at the University of Minnesota, USA. He completed his undergraduate and graduate work at the University of Wisconsin, Madison, and his clinical internship at Brown University. Professor Krueger's major interests lie at the intersection of research on psychopathology, personality, psychometrics, behavior genetics and physical health. He has received a number of awards, including the American Psychological Association's Award for Early Career Contributions and the Hoch Award from the American Psychopathological Association (APPA). He is currently Editor of the *Journal of Personality Disorders.*

Abby L. Mulay, Ph.D. is a postdoctoral fellow in clinical forensic psychology at the Medical University of South Carolina. She completed her clinical forensic psychology internship at the University of North Carolina School of Medicine/Federal Correctional Complex (Butner, NC) and obtained her Ph.D. in Clinical Psychology from Long Island University (Brooklyn Campus). Her clinical and research interests include personality assessment, forensic assessment, and treatment issues relevant to justice-involved individuals.

Aaron L. Pincus, Ph.D. received his B.S. in psychology from the University of California, Davis, his Masters in psychology from the University of California, Berkeley, and his Ph.D. in clinical psychology from the University of British Columbia. His research focuses on integrating personality, psychopathology, and psychotherapy from the perspective of Contemporary Integrative Interpersonal Theory. He is a Fellow of the Society for Personality Assessment and recipient of the Theodore Millon Award for contributions to personality psychology.

Michael J. Roche, Ph.D. is Assistant Professor of Psychology at Penn State Altoona. He completed his Ph.D. at the Pennsylvania State University, after finishing his pre-doctoral clinical internship at Massachusetts General Hospital, Harvard Medical School. Dr. Roche has published over 30 authored and co-authored articles and book chapters on the topics of personality, personality disorder, interpersonal processes, and experience sampling methodology. He serves as Consulting Editor for *Assessment* and is the Newsletter Editor for the Society for Interpersonal Theory and Research. He teaches undergraduate courses in clinical psychology and personality, advanced graduate courses on cognitive-behavioral and psychodynamic treatment techniques, and statistical workshops on advanced longitudinal data analysis.

Megan R. Schmidt, M.A. is a doctoral student in clinical psychology at the University of Tennessee. Her research interests include cognitive, personality, and situational risk factors for aggression.

Mark H. Waugh, Ph.D., ABPP is Staff Psychologist at the Oak Ridge National Laboratory, Adjunct Clinical and Teaching Faculty at the University of Tennessee (Knoxville), and in private practice in Oak Ridge, Tennessee. A Fellow in the Society for Personality Assessment, he graduated from the University of Florida and completed internship training at University of Texas Health Sciences Center at Dallas, and postdoctoral fellowship at Yale Psychiatric Institute. He has a long-standing clinical and scholarly interest in personality assessment, personality theory, and personality disorders (aka, what makes people tick).

Foreword

For over two centuries of modern scientific study, the nature of mental disorders has eluded clinicians, scientists, patients, family members, and society. There are four eras in the creation of classification systems designed to improve our understanding of psychopathology. Each of these four eras is described below.

One: The Pre-Historic Era

We open discussion of the Pre-Historic era with a story.

A young physician, having just finished medical school, returns home to join his father's medical practice. On his first day, the young doctor accompanies his father, an old country doctor. The young doctor eagerly hitches up the horse and buggy for a long day of making house calls.

At the first house call, they find a woman suffering bad chest pains. The old doctor begins his physical exam. After about three minutes, he rises, looks the woman in the eye, and says, "Madam, you need to give up everything associated with candy. If you give up everything associated with candy, you will feel much better."

Climbing back onto the horse and buggy, the young doctor turns to his father and asks, "Dad, how did you do that? I studied at one of the best medical schools in the country, and none of my professors could reach a diagnosis and tell a patient what to do in three minutes."

The old doctor replied, "Look, son, diagnosis is simple. We walked in the house and what did we see? Boxes of candy everywhere. There were even boxes of candy in the bathroom. This woman is overweight. I don't know precisely what is causing her chest pains, but if she stops eating candy and loses weight she will feel much better."

They proceed to the next house. Their next house call finds a man with a bad cough. The old doctor starts his exam. Again, after three minutes, he stops and says, "Sir, you need to give up everything associated with smoking. If you give up everything associated with smoking, you will feel much better." The two doctors leave.

Once more, the young doctor is impressed. The old doctor says, "Son, I told you that diagnosis is simple. When we walked in the house, the first thing I could smell was cigarette smoke. There were cartons of cigarettes all over the house. I don't know what is causing his cough, but cigarette smoking can only make it worse. He needs to stop smoking."

The next house call finds a woman with "sick headaches." The young doctor, eager to test his skills, asks if he can perform the examination. The old doctor is pleased. He nods affirmatively and steps aside to watch his son. After only three minutes, the young doctor stops, puts away his thermometer, and says, "Mam, you need to give up everything associated with religion. If you give up everything associated with religion, you will feel much better."

The physicians leave. Back in the buggy, the old doctor addresses his son. "I don't understand. I did not see anything in that house that suggests this woman has any interest in religion. There were no Bibles, no religious pictures, no quotations from Bible verses, and so forth. And, what does religion have to do with sick headaches, anyway?"

The young doctor smiles and says, "Dad, you told me that diagnosis was simple. You remember how nervous I was when I was starting the exam? I was so nervous I dropped the thermometer. Well, when I bent over to pick it up, I couldn't help but notice that under the bed was the preacher."

The *Pre-Historic Era* is so named because, from the perspective of many modern commentators on psychopathology, the writings and ideas from the era are viewed as too crude and uninteresting to be worth discussing in any detail. The Pre-Historic Era primarily covered the 19th Century. Prior to this time, the dominant views of mental disorders were framed in religious terms. At the start of the 1800s, a secular view of mental disorders began to form, stimulated by the Enlightenment and by the writings of two men who played important roles in the political revolutions in their country. Benjamin Rush was a signatory to the *Declaration of Independence* and wrote a book about mental disorders in which he discussed four families of psychopathology: mania, melancholia, paranoia and dementia. Phillipe Pinel was involved in the French Revolution. After the French Revolution, he became the head of all asylums in France. Pinel argued for a psychological treatment of the mentally ill, one that was strongly rooted in a humanistic approach to insanity. The writings of Pinel and Rush contributed to the development of the asylum movement in the United States. This reform, championed by Dorothea Dix and others, eventually resulted in virtually all states creating places of refuge to care for the mentally ill. The directors formed a national association and published a scientific journal (*American Journal of Insanity*). The physicians who cared for the mentally ill during the first half of the 19th Century were called *alienists,* a name derived from Pinel's writings and reflecting the idea that the task was to help patients deal with their mental alienation.

After the American Civil War, another group of physicians became important. They were known as *neurologists.* The neurologists, unlike the alienists who largely thought any classification of mental disorders was premature, emphasized identifying specific syndromes of psychopathology. The single most important category of mental illness during the second half of the 1800s was *dementia paralytica.* This disorder was more common in men and started with grandiose delusions. This mental change was followed by the development of motor paralysis, and it invariably led to death. This category accounted for 15% to 25% of patients in asylums. Two American neurologists, Dr. William Hammond (Surgeon General of the US Army during the Civil War) and Dr. Edmund Spitzka, wrote influential textbooks of psychopathology that detailed 30 to 35 different mental disorders.

Two: The Kraepelinian Era

The second era is named the Kraepelinian Era in recognition of the German psychiatrist whose writings initiated major changes in psychiatric classification. Prior to Kraepelin, the German physician with the greatest international recognition for writings on psychopathology was Richard von Krafft-Ebing. He, like Spitzka and Hammond, advocated a scientific, neurological approach to psychopathology. Krafft-Ebing later also wrote a book about unusual forms of sexual behavior. Krafft-Ebing's ideas set the stage for both Emile Kraepelin and Sigmund Freud. Kraepelin wrote the several editions of his influential textbooks between 1883 and 1926. His ideas were important because he emphasized a developmental view of psychopathology and because his writings about cases were strikingly clear, describing the behavior of patients in detail. Both Krafft-Ebing and Kraepelin were influenced by Wilhelm Wundt, an early German physician and philosopher who was the first person to call himself a psychologist. Wundt advocated experimental methods for the study of behavior.

Kraepelin was bold and re-organized thinking about the categories of mental disorders. In the sixth edition of his textbook on psychiatry, Kraepelin described two sister concepts: *dementia praecox* and *dementia paralytica.* Kraepelin also combined the concepts of mania, melancholia, and periodic insanity into one category which he called manic-depressive insanity (now known as bipolar disorder). Confirmation of the etiology of dementia paralytica was achieved just after the publication of Kraepelin's textbooks. The solution to this prevalent, well-known, and fatal mental disorder from the 19th Century stimulated the hope in psychiatry that a similar solution could be found for dementia praecox (schizophrenia).

Kraepelin was born in 1856 in central Europe, and in the same year in the same general area of Europe another influential neurologist was born: Sigmund Freud. Freud never achieved the status and acclaim that Kraepelin did in the form of professorships and professional recognition. Nonetheless, modern historians view Freud as one of two geniuses whose ideas had enormous influences on 20th Century culture (the other being Albert Einstein). Freud, partially building on the ideas of Krafft-Ebing, viewed sexuality as a primary influence on human behavior. He also emphasized the importance of psychological symbols, development, interpersonal relationships, and subjective experiences about which people might not be aware. Like the alienists of the Pre-Historic Era, Freud had relatively little use for classification which he regarded as an overly simplistic approach to understanding psychopathology.

The scientific solution to dementia paralytica was truly remarkable. In 1927, Austrian physician Julius Wagner-Jauregg, a friend of Sigmund Freud, was awarded the Nobel Prize in Medicine for showing the fatal progression of dementia paralytica could be stopped by giving patients malaria. In this treatment, the high fever killed the bacterial spirochetes (note: antibiotics had not yet been discovered). This achievement further reinforced the Kraepelinian idea that mental illness was a medical disease. Soon after Wagner-Jauregg's demonstration of the malaria cure, the organization of asylum directors in the United States renamed themselves the American Psychiatric Association in 1921. They emphasized their status as a recognized specialty of medicine. This new organization published a formal classification of mental disorders, the *Statistical Manual for the Use of Institutions for the Insane* (Committee on Statistics, American Medico-Psychological Association, 1918). Beginning with the NCMH's original 22 diagnoses, this system contained 73 diagnoses largely based on categories taken from Kraepelin's textbook editions. The *Statistical Manual* went through ten editions between 1921 and the end of World War II. After WWII, the *Statistical Manual* underwent a complete transformation, partially to incorporate the ideas of psychoanalysts and psychiatry's growing emphasis on outpatient practice. This new standardized classification was called the *Diagnostic and Statistical Manual of Mental Disorders* (DSM). The DSM used short, narrative intentional definitions of mental disorders.

Despite psychiatry's hopes that a solution to schizophrenia was on hand, as with dementia paralytica at the end of the Pre-Historic Era, a resolution was not forthcoming. Subsequently, comparative cross-national studies showed that the American use of the diagnosis of schizophrenia was overinclusive. Further empirical studies suggested that American psychiatrists lacked consistency in their diagnoses of all mental disorders. By the end of the Kraepelinian Era, the weak reliability of psychiatric diagnosis was seen as a major impediment to clinical success and to the scientific understanding of mental disorders.

Three: The DSM-III Era

The DSM-III era began in 1972 with a small, now classic paper published in the *Archives of General Psychiatry* (Feighner et al., 1972). This paper was written by a group of psychiatrists at Washington University in St. Louis. The paper argued there were 16 mental disorders which had sufficient evidence to support their validity. The paper further proposed a set of diagnostic criteria to be used for defining these disorders in research. This idea of using diagnostic criteria to define mental disorders was stimulated by earlier definitional achievements in research on rheumatology. In New York City, Robert Spitzer, a psychiatrist who had helped in the writing of the DSM-II and who proposed a compromise solution to the intense professional debate at the time about whether homosexuality was a mental disorder, realized the potential importance of the St. Louis group's ideas. Robert Spitzer had worked with a noted experimental psychopathologist and psychologist named Joseph Zubin, and Spitzer's research utilized factor analytic methods to study ways of measuring patients' symptoms. Spitzer and the St. Louis Group formed an alliance to create a revolutionary new way of classifying mental disorders that would utilize diagnostic criteria. This new system was the DSM-III.

The success of the DSM-III was almost instantaneous. Its publication earned the American Psychiatric Association so much money that it created a publication company from the revenue. The use of diagnostic criteria generated extraordinary attention. Numerous studies appeared concerning criticism and revision of the wording of the criteria, proposing additional categories with new criteria, and formal structured interviews to assess these criteria in patients were published. The accepted wisdom was that the "reliability problem" of psychiatry had been solved, even though the diagnostic practices of daily clinical work probably showed little change.

Following the DSM-III in 1980, the APA published a revision in 1987 (DSM-III-R), and another edition in 1994 (DSM-IV). The DSM-5 appeared in 2013. The number of mental disorder categories exploded across these editions, starting with 108 in the DSM-II, 303 in the DSM-III, 383 in the DSM-IV, and 541 in the DSM-5. Research funding and research publications typically relied on the post-DSM-III diagnostic criteria for defining groups of patients when studying mental disorders.

At this point, a new problem appeared. Patients who met the diagnostic criteria for a disorder often also the met the diagnostic criteria for another disorder. In fact, what became clear was that it was the unusual patient who met the criteria for one and only disorder. Instead, patients met criteria for several disorders, sometimes as many as a dozen. The "reliability problem" of the Kraepelinian Era was replaced by what has been called the "comorbidity problem" of the DSM-III Era.

Another less-recognized problem emerged in the DSM-III Era. This was the "validity problem." The original paper by the St. Louis group proposing diagnostic criteria said there were only 16 valid mental disorders with strong evidence for their existence as separate categories. When the explosion in the number of mental disorder categories occurred across the DSMs, critics complained about this growth. Spitzer responded with a well-known quotation: "Let a thousand flowers bloom, even if some of them are weeds" (see Blashfield & Fuller, 1996, p.7).

In the DSM-III Era, weeding has not been a priority. An example of this could be seen with the DSM-5: the committee charged with the classification of personality disorders initially wanted to delete all the categories in this section of the classification and replace them with a dimensional system. The justification for this was the comorbidity problem. One-quarter of the patients who met the criteria for at least one personality disorder also met the criteria for five or more personality disorders (the DSM-IV only recognized eleven personality disorder categories). This degree of diagnostic overlap suggests the descriptive validity of these categories was poor. However, the prospect of deleting personality disorder categories led to an intense outcry from many political constituencies associated with these disorders. As a result, the efforts of the DSM-5 work Group for personality disorders failed. No change was permitted. The personality disorder section of the DSM-5 was identical to the DSM-IV classification of these disorders.

Which returns us to the story that opened the discussion of the Pre-Historic Era. There are two lessons to be learned from that story.

First Lesson

What makes the story relevant is the cross-cutting of two paradigms from Era Two, the Kraepelinian Era. These two paradigms have often been regarded as conflicting with each other. These are the Kraepelinian emphasis on diagnosis, and the Freudian emphasis on sex (e.g., the preacher story). Understanding psychopathology will require the blending of multiple paradigms.

Second Lesson

Like the old doctor said, diagnosis is simple. Any topic that is simple, when analyzed carefully, becomes complex. Understanding mental disorders requires knowledge from many domains.

Four: The Future Era

Read on. The remainder of this book is about the Fourth Era.

Roger K. Blashfield, Ph.D.
Hood River, Oregon
Professor Emeritus, Auburn University

Preface

The *DSM-5* Alternative Model for Personality Disorders (AMPD) is a novel dimensional model for personality disorder (PD) diagnosis located in Section III of the *Diagnostic and Statistical Manual of Mental Disorders, Fifth Edition* (*DSM-5*; American Psychiatric Association [APA], 2013). This book examines the AMPD with respect to theory, research, and practice. In so doing, we offer an updating of and points of view on this important model for PD. We start from an assumption that echoes Dr. Roger Blashfield's words from the Foreword: "Any topic that is simple, when analyzed carefully, becomes complex. Understanding mental disorders requires knowledge from many domains." A model of PD must be simple enough to be practical, but must not ignore the complexity of the subject. To grapple with complexity requires many types of information and sources of knowledge. In this regard, analogy to the idea of scientific paradigms is helpful. The AMPD represents a paradigmatic shift from how PDs have traditionally been approached. Furthermore, a major theme of this book is that the AMPD connects with multiple paradigms of personality assessment. That is, many perspectives exist within the AMPD, each of which contributes to understanding people. A second assumption underlying our book is that the AMPD is an important step in the evolution of quantitative psychopathology.

We are honored to have Dr. Blashfield introduce our discussion because his book, *The classification of psychopathology: Neo-Kraepelinian and quantitative approaches* (Blashfield, 1984), was a major impetus to the field of quantitative psychopathology. His was not the first or only word on the subject, for like all great ideas, precedent can be found—for example, early sketches of psychopathological personality dimensions were offered by Theodule Ribot and by George Heymans who, inspired by Wundt, began to empirically map the domain. Kurt Schneider, who coined the term *endogenous depression* and famously described the "first-rank" symptoms of schizophrenia, also offered an early hybrid-dimensional scheme of PDs. The quantitative point of view saw substantial elaboration in the study of mental abilities as in, for example, Charles Spearman and the *general factor* (g) of intelligence. The quantitative contributions of Raymond B. Cattell,

Hans Eysenck, and Maurice Lorr to personality science and psychopathology are well-known. With a historian's eye, however, Dr. Blashfield pointed out that the American Catholic priest Thomas V. Moore predated these latter contributors with the first publication in 1930 of factor analysis applied to mental patients (Moore, 1930). The quantitative approach to psychopathology matured further through the work of Graham Foulds in psychiatric classification, Thomas Achenbach in child psychopathology, and Roy Grinker's empirical studies of dimensions of the borderline syndrome. More recently, W. John Livelsey and Thomas Widiger, to very selectively name but two of several key investigators, have greatly advanced contemporary dimensional approaches to PD. Underlying each of these aforementioned contributors is the quantitative-dimensional theme Dr. Blashfield articulated in 1984. We hope you will find our words on the subject worthwhile.

The book's chapters stand on their own. Each articulates important aspects of the AMPD and reflects the voice of the individual author. The chapters in some cases also offer ideas, observations, and extensions of the AMPD less readily accommodated in traditional journal outlets. This book grew out of a symposium given at the annual convention of the Society for Personality Assessment in Chicago, Illinois, in March 2016, by five authors contributing in the present volume (NMC, CJH, RFK, ALP, MHW). This resulted in an invitation from the publisher to develop a book-length statement. We expect readers of different backgrounds will find it useful: practitioners desiring to learn about the model, graduate students and early career mental health professionals, as well as established scholars, investigators, and practitioners who seek to understand and help those suffering from what we call disorders of personality.

For those less familiar with the AMPD, we briefly describe the model below and refer the reader to the *DSM-5* (2013), Section III AMPD for reference. It is important to have in mind some background and a basic understanding of the model in order to benefit from the material in the book.

In brief, diagnosis with the AMPD requires fulfilling seven criteria for PD. Criterion A refers to the individual's level of personality functioning. Using the Levels of Personality Functioning Scale (LPFS; Bender, Morey, & Skodol, 2011), individuals are evaluated in the domains of self (i.e., identity and self-direction) and interpersonal functioning (i.e., empathy and intimacy). Criterion B includes 25 maladaptive personality traits, which may be assessed by clinician ratings or other methods, including self-report formats. The 25 maladaptive personality traits are organized into the following five domains: negative affectivity, detachment, antagonism, disinhibition, and psychoticism. Criteria C and D include the pervasiveness and stability of the personality disturbance. Finally, Criteria E, F, and G cover differential diagnosis and possible alternative explanations for personality disturbance (e.g., substance use, medical conditions, or developmental stage).

We hope this book provides a useful framework for understanding, applying, and advancing this new diagnostic scheme. We also hope those who quest to understand and help persons in need will find the AMPD an exciting development.

1 Construct and Paradigm in the AMPD[1]

Mark H. Waugh

About 2,300 years ago, Theophrastus described 30 personality types. The depictions in Theophrastus' *Characters* (Bennett & Hammond, 1902), beginning with the duplicitous "Dissembler," to the cruel, antisocial "Vicious Man," are surprisingly modern. Theophrastus also notably contributed to the science of classification, but for botany, not psychiatric disorders. His organization of flora persisted until Carl Linnaeus developed a botanical taxonomy built on binomial nomenclature in 1753 (de Queiroz & Gauthier, 1994). The *Diagnostic and Statistical Manual of Mental Disorders, Fifth Edition* (DSM-5; APA, 2013) Alternative Model for Personality Disorders (AMPD) is a psychiatric nosology for personality disorders (PD) contained in an officially promulgated system for classifying mental disorders. Like the classifications of Theophrastus and Linnaeus, the AMPD embodies principles of taxonomy, and its nosology has its own binomial nomenclature. As Pincus (2011) stated, Criterion A may be likened to genus, and Criterion B to species of PD.

Classification is a human activity. We naturally categorize objects, tasks, and experiences. We find a task easy or difficult, feel that a new food is tasty or unpalatable, and regard a new acquaintance as a pleasant type of person or not. Similarly, natural categorization becomes formalized for objects of professional and scientific study such as medical conditions (e.g., *International Classification of Diseases-10*; ICD-10; WHO, 1992), chemical elements (e.g., the Periodic Table), and books (e.g., the Dewey Decimal System; Wiegand, 1998). Scientific taxonomy condenses and organizes information by certain principles. Classifications are human products. As such, they have complicated histories. This is the case for chemistry, biology, and medicine, as well as the mental health disciplines. Amongst others, Blashfield (1984), Berrios (1999), Millon (1994), and Kendler (2009) outline the history and many nuances within the classification of psychopathology and PD. They note the imprint of precedent and unarticulated assumptions are salient in classification. These perspectives, along with the notion of *paradigm* (Kuhn, 1962/2012), help us to take the measure of the AMPD.

A major theme of this book is that many models and methods apply in the scientific investigation of and in clinical practice with PDs. Wiggins

(2003) used the Kuhnian idea of paradigm to illustrate pluralism in personality assessment. Waugh and colleagues (2017) extended Wiggins' (2003) scheme to the AMPD, noting that multiple paradigms inhere within the AMPD. This is more than an academic observation. That is, the nature of people and of the enterprise of diagnostic nosology should inform our methods of assessment. Issues of measurement are very relevant to the AMPD. Advancing this idea in psychometrics, Loevinger (1993, p. 1) invoked Herman Melville and likened rigorous measurement of psychological concepts to a "white whale." For Loevinger (1993), pursuit of scientific understanding is guided by methods that conform to the nature of the object of the search (Loevinger, 1957). In other words, epistemology and ontology reciprocally inform each other. The elusive "whale" is unlikely to be found by a single method or a single model. Similarly, for PD, multiple conceptual and methodological approaches pertain.

As a point of departure, we start with Theophrastus' inventory of 30 "characters" and then quickly move the clock forward to Phillippe Pinel in the 18th Century. Pinel advanced the humanitarian treatment of the mentally ill, and he also established an early psychiatric nosology. This nosology was the first to describe a category for what we now call PD (*manie sans délire* [mania without delusion; at the time, mania referred to agitation, not psychosis]; Crocq, 2013). Psychiatric classifications evolve and reflect important scientific and sociological concerns of their times (Blashfield, Keeley, Flanagan, & Miles, 2014; Kendler, 2009). Contemporary conceptions of PD also are built from antecedent understandings. Sir Isaac Newton's aphorism about progress and standing on the shoulders of giants applies to the field of PD as well.

The genealogy of the AMPD Criterion B includes the lexical tradition. This derives from the early work of Allport and Odbert (1936) on trait names and Cattell's (1933) multivariate study of personality temperament. This path travels through the Big Five (Goldberg, 1993), alongside Five Factor Model (FFM) connections with PD (Widiger & Trull, 2007), to quantitative psychology (Achenbach, 1966; Blashfield, 1984; Krueger, 1999) and the trait-facets of Criterion B (Krueger & Markon, 2014). And if our lens is clear and strong, the tracings of Theophrastus appear within the lexical tradition.

Criterion A, level of personality impairment, starts with the notion of personality itself and emerges from concepts of constitution, self, and character (Berrios, 1996; Zachar, 2015). The ideas of self and character originated in art, literature, theater, and philosophy. Scientific psychology uses different terms and methods, but aspires to map the same terrain of personality, self, will, and consciousness (Gardner, 1992). Recognizing these shared goals underscores the wisdom of ensuring that both objective and subjective dimensions are included in a model of PD. Criterion A derives from psychodynamic, attachment, and social-developmental theory

(Bender, Morey, & Skodol, 2011) and schematizes PD functioning on a dimension of impairment. The broad purview of Criterion A is suggested in the metaphors McAdams (2015) uses to characterize personality within a life-history framework: actor, agent, and author. Actors *do*, agents exercise *will*, and authors *narrate*. These ideas are examined closely later in this chapter, but at this juncture, we note McAdams and Pals (2006) organized personality constructs into five broad heuristic domains. The three domains most relevant to PD are dispositional traits (e.g., psychometric traits), characteristic adaptations (e.g., contextualized, dynamic patterns of motivation and adapting), and narrative identity (e.g., development of a life story). The scope of Criterion A spans these domains and points to agentic and narrative aspects of PD.

Understanding PD must address subjectivity. Symptom checklists, structured interviews, psychophysiological, and pharmacogenetic assays provide important information and may further consistency of agreement in diagnoses of PD. But, these approaches are not sufficient for a comprehensive science of psychopathology (Jaspers, 1912/1968; Kendler, 2005; Marková & Berrios, 2009; Meehl, 1986). For this, a broader repertoire of concepts and methods is needed. This would span neuroscience and molecular psychiatry on one end, and range to the narrative domain and subjective experience of the person on the other end. Zachar and Kendler (2007) point out that any classification model that uses the idea of *self* must permit narrative models and narrative data. After all, the self (person) is the terrain of PD. The arts of Homer, Shakespeare, and Faulkner alongside the narrative psychological science of the individual life story (McAdams, 1993) speak to the nature of self and self-experience. Of course, this is not a new idea, as is found in the writings of William James (James, 1890/1950). But, how may the clinician or psychopathologist know another's subjectivity? The philosopher Nagel (1974, p. 435) asked "what is it like to be a bat," and concluded this seems an impossible quest. Indeed, the study of reflective functioning (RF) and mentalization (Fonagy et al., 1991), an important line of investigation in personality and PD, posits this is the case. Yet, we can infer others' mental states with degrees of confidence, aided by knowledge, experience, and empathy. Building on this idea, Fonagy, Luyten, and Allison (2015) theorized the common core of PD is a tacit, closed-off quality of personality functioning. This core reflects implicit distrust, a generalized foreclosure of normal, evolutionarily acquired processes of human social openness and reciprocity wherein we learn and grow from experiences with others. This closed-off quality underlies nosologically defined PD: the "…enduring pattern of inner experience and behavior…manifested in…cognition, affectivity, interpersonal functioning, (or) impulse control… (that) is inflexible and pervasive…" (DSM-5; APA, 2013, p. 646). Furthermore, this core of PD, often characterized as ego syntonic, is the "ground" of subjective experience, if considered within the Gestalt figure-ground heuristic. This existential ground is sometimes enacted in fears of rejection, loss, emptiness, attack, negation, shame, intimacy, or self-usurpation. As well, it may manifest in vulnerability to piercing emotional pain, a sense of falling apart, or de-stabilizing hypersensitivity to humiliation. To understand PD, this subjective side of experience must be coordinated with objective observation (Parnas, Sass, & Zahavi, 2012). Scientist and clinician alike seek to make sense of inferences about others' mental states, and many types of data and points of view are needed.

Kendler (2005; 2015) argued the path for the psychopathological scientist is different than the chemist, for example. The natural scientist operates within a correspondence theory of truth. This presumes a fixed and independent reality. In contrast, psychiatry and related disciplines cannot assume an independent reality (separate from "mind") because what psychiatry studies is composed of both third-person (objective) and first-person (subjective) points of view. Furthermore, to report a psychiatric symptom is *ipso facto* an interpretation of one's experience (even if "brain-based"), and this is communicated dialogically (Marková & Berrios, 2012). Given this territory, a coherence theory of truth is appropriate. This interpretive attitude is less ambitious, subject to revision, and offers working explanations of phenomena based on the standard of consistency, as opposed to a fully mind-independent reality. Extending this line of reasoning, Kendler (2015) concludes that psychological processes are nested within biological functions, and these (inseparable) domains act bi-directionally. Neither domain trumps the other's explanatory value (Kendler, 2008). Biological findings require back-translation into the psychological realm, and subjectivity is an emergent domain arising from biology. A similar if heuristic logic may be analogized to the personality scheme of McAdams and Pals (2006). Different realms of personality constructs are interwoven within the person, and they may benefit from different approaches to understanding. Neither trait, characteristic adaptation, or narrative identity provides sufficient explanation. Furthermore, it may be helpful to regard narrative identity, for example, as emerging from or "nested" within domains of characteristic adaptation and trait. A dispositional trait may lend itself to objective observation, but aspects of narrative identity less so. In sum, Kendler's (2015) explanatory pluralism and the ideas of McAdams and Pals (2006) can inform PD.

To the extent the AMPD aspires to model disorders of personality (self), it must efficiently organize PD constructs, inform science and practice, coordinate with an evidence base, and demonstrate clinical utility—and connect with the lived experience of patients. In discussing clinical utility, Mullins-Sweatt and Widiger (2009) emphasized that a diagnostic system should be easy to use, facilitate communication, and help in the treatment of patients. In other words, a PD nosology with clinical utility looks beyond documentation, description, and science. Optimally, it may help bring the person to life for the clinician, and it surely should not obstruct empathy. These aspirations are not contrary. Concern for subjectivity need not subvert methodological rigor (Rychlak, 1968; 1988) or a priority given to objectivity in psychiatric classification (Cooper, 2012). A robust PD model permits first-person experience (personhood) to be coordinated with the third-person perspectives important in professional work and scientific study. The project thus assumes intentionality and meaning. Parameters like situation, context, history, and random events also are admitted to the table. Such an ecumenical approach means our constructs and methods are proxies rather than statements of reality (Cronbach & Meehl, 1955; Kendler, 2015). Following this line of reasoning, our constructs (informed presumptions) become *open concepts* (Meehl, 1977). That is, our understandings are approximations, imprecise and provisional, representing our best efforts for the time.

This chapter discusses the AMPD with respect to these caveats and concerns. This involves brief review of the history and principles of psychiatric classification. In addition, ideas of scientific paradigm, metaphor, map, construct, and measurement are applied to PD. This examination concludes that the AMPD provides heuristic advantage for the scientist and the practitioner.

Paradigms and Psychiatric Classification

Kuhn (1962/2012) articulated the idea of paradigm as we commonly understand it. He described science as a discipline and mode of inquiry consisting of evolving patterns of interrelated assumptions, methods, and conclusions (paradigms). Paradigms determine standards, what counts as evidence, and what is considered acceptable to study. Thus, a paradigm is a template or lens through which objects of study are known. Since scientists are people and theories are human constructions, sociological and historical forces affect these templates. The Kuhnian paradigm is a powerful concept. It can be applied very broadly, like Foucault's notion of *epistemes* in history (Flynn, 1994). More narrowly, theories of personality (Loevinger, 1987), the field of personality assessment (Wiggins, 2003), and the discipline of psychiatry (Kendler, 2005) display paradigm dynamics. Implicit dynamics of paradigms also affect psychiatric classification (Blashfield et al., 2014).

Zachar and Kendler (2017) argue psychiatric nosology presently is facing a Kuhnian crisis of confidence, in large part generated by the emerging paradigm of dimensionalization of diagnosis. Concerns about the appropriateness of categorical classification for PD diagnosis are not new (e.g., Livesley, 1985; Livesley, 1991; Meehl, 1986; Widiger & Frances, 1985), but they now are changing the landscape of the field. To appreciate the significance of the dimensional paradigm, it is helpful to examine that which it seeks to model.

Psychiatric nosology is a branch of medical disease classification, and diseases traditionally have been understood as categorical entities. Consider neurosyphilis, a disease historically highly relevant to psychiatry. One either has or does not have this disease. There is a cause (i.e., the infectious bacterium *Treponema pallidum*) and, if the disease is not cured, it eventually produces the neuropsychiatric syndrome of general paresis. Philosophical, scientific, methodological, professional, and sociological assumptions accompany categorical diagnosis. In this example of neurosyphilis, assumptions include discrete class, organic etiology, natural course of illness, and belonging to the province of natural science.

The notion of discrete class assumes psychometric zones of rarity (Kendell & Jablensky, 2003). This means symptom variation shows a class (taxon) structure, not a continuous distribution on a dimension. It is important to note that categorical diagnosis itself is a paradigm. Traditional categorical diagnosis, as with disease and symptoms, has a specific organization to its classificatory elements and often an implied etiology. This is the idea of a *syndrome,* first articulated in Thomas Sydenham's 17th Century description of chorea (i.e., Saint Vitus' Dance; see Martino et al., 2005). A syndrome has a discrete structure and typically assumes a biological cause. Biological etiology is not necessary, however. A cause can be psychological. For example, a psychodynamic etiology is presumed in conversion hysteria. The syndrome concept works well with classic medical diseases (e.g., neurosyphilis, pneumonia), but less so for some illnesses such as hypertension (HTN). HTN has biological causes but fits better with a dimensional model, rather than a syndrome, because HTN represents a summary product of diverse biological processes construed on a gradient. Note, this conception is not simply a way to capitalize on the metric advantage of quantity compared to categorical measurement. Rather, the underlying processes are viewed as inherently dimensional. In the example of HTN, medical convention establishes threshold values for identification of disease presence, with the "category" of HTN serving as a convenient proxy for the underlying dimensional disease processes.

In terms of psychiatric disorders, most empirical studies (e.g., Caspi et al., 2014; Krueger, 1999) and theoretical analyses (Kendler, Zachar, & Craver, 2011; Zachar & Kendler, 2007) question the validity of categorical structure in psychiatric nosology. Research findings suggest psychopathology may include just a few categorical disorders such as autism, substance use, and schizotypy (Haslam, Holland, & Kuppens, 2012). In the realm of PD, categorical structure appears even less likely. The sole exception with some empirical support for a taxon structure is schizotypy (Lenzenweger, 2015; Meehl, 1962). An excellent empirical review is found in Haslam and colleagues (2012), and a thorough conceptual analysis in Meehl (1992). Regarding the issues of the metrics of psychopathology, some suggest the distinction between category and continuum itself may not be sharp and may also lie on a continuum (Borsboom et al., 2016).

The *medical model* is often implicitly assumed in traditional categorical diagnosis (syndrome). The medical model incorporates several philosophical assumptions with natural science, social, and professional implications

(Lilienfeld et al., 2015; Murphy, 2017). A strict or hard medical model is problematic for PD in several ways. These include socio-political and professional aspects of classification, some of which are discussed later. The medical model is problematic also in that cultural, social, normative, and agentic-constructivist concerns are intrinsic with ideas of the self and personality (Zachar & Kendler, 2007). A strict medical model with categorical-syndromic diagnosis fails to do justice to the subjective, constructivist, and nominalist aspects of PD. One classificatory remedy is to emphasize the pragmatic utility of diagnosis rather than assumptions of natural essence as implied in the medical model. This stance views PD as a *practical kind*, rather than a *natural kind*, which is the case in a mind-independent natural substance, entity, or condition (e.g., neurosyphilis; Zachar & Kendler, 2007).

Zachar and Kendler (2017) note that as psychiatric nosology moves closer to dimensionalization, scientific and professional debate intensifies, and fundamental assumptions of classification begin to shift. The DSM-5 (APA, 2013) aspired to increased dimensionalization of diagnosis (Regier, Narrow, Kuhl, & Kupfer, 2009), but implementation was limited, falling short of a full transdiagnostic reframing of nosology (e.g., Krueger & Eaton, 2015). The field of PD, however, has made substantial progress toward adopting a dimensional paradigm (Clark, 2007; Widiger & Trull, 2007), and one version is the AMPD. The limitation of categorical PD diagnosis is a major theme of this chapter (and book) to which we often return. Some of the challenges brought by changing nosological paradigms are seen in scholarly debate over the merits of a hybrid categorical-dimensional model versus full dimensionalization (see Herpertz et al., 2017; Hopwood et al., 2017). Some of these concerns are illustrated in the following clinical example.

The Case of Ellen West

Ellen West (pseudonym) was an early 20th Century woman who lives on in the annals of psychiatry. In part, this is because three major figures in psychiatry were involved in her care. Existential psychiatrist Ludwig Binswanger (1958) published a case history of his treatment of Ellen West approximately 20 years after her death by suicide. Psychopathologists Eugen Bleuler (who gave us the term *schizophrenia)* and Emil Kraepelin (whose ideas form the bases for modern DSMs) consulted on the care of Ellen West. The following psychiatric sketch of Ellen West was developed from the accounts given by Binswanger (1958), Ghaemi (2003), and others.

Ms. West, a Swiss woman of Jewish ancestry, developed psychiatric symptoms in late adolescence. As a child, she was "lively but headstrong… a violent child" who was Tom-boyish, a perfectionist in school, and often had feelings of "emptiness" (Binswanger, 1958, p. 238; subsequent quotations from same source). As she matured she feared gaining weight, and she later struggled with an eating disorder. She took thyroid pills, laxatives, and used excessive exercise to keep her weight down. Her moods were fickle and labile. She was energetic, very social, wrote poetry, and immersed herself in social welfare projects. Yet at other times she was anxious, afflicted with dark moods and self-criticism, and ruminated over her weight, leading to bouts of self-starvation. She felt great conflict over her romantic relationships and life roles, questioning her commitment to marriage, motherhood, and social activism (this must be understood in terms of the limited opportunities available to women at the time). Regarding a family history of psychiatric problems, reportedly both parents and one sibling suffered from anxiety and depression.

By her early 20s she was under psychiatric care, including stays in a sanitarium. At age 32, she began psychoanalysis. Reportedly, her social functioning improved, but her fear of being alone, dysphoria, and anorexia failed to abate. Her moods were labile, and she suffered intermittent thoughts of wanting to be dead. She reportedly courted death through risky behavior such by visiting an orphanage during an outbreak of scarlet fever and kissing the children in hopes of becoming ill. She rode horses recklessly at these times, and once she threw herself in front of a moving carriage.

She sought treatment with a second psychoanalyst but reportedly made little progress. She became very symptomatic and attempted suicide at least three times (once by jumping from the analyst's office window). Although hospitalized, lability, dysphoria, and anorexia persisted. Her psychoanalyst characterized her subjective states as empty, dead, and hollow—distinguishing these from the diagnosis of depression (Binswanger, 1958). Emil Kraepelin consulted on her case and diagnosed "melancholia" (p. 254). But her analyst disagreed and diagnosed "severe obsessive neurosis with manic-depressive oscillations (p. 260)," and he recommended outpatient treatment and returning to ordinary social engagements. She was discharged, but her course deteriorated. Her physician terminated the psychoanalysis (against the wishes of the analyst) and returned her to a sanitarium, at which time Binswanger assumed psychiatric care. He diagnosed "severe cyclothymic depression" (p. 261) as well as anxiety, suicidal wishes, and fear of gaining weight. Yet, despite the structured environment of the sanitarium, her functioning declined. Binswanger requested consultations from Bleuler and another unnamed foreign psychiatrist.

Bleuler diagnosed "unambiguous schizophrenia" (p. 265). The second psychiatrist differed, citing an absence of intellectual deterioration, then considered pathognomonic for schizophrenia, and he diagnosed "psychopathic constitution progressively unfolding" (p. 266). Parenthetically, note that the term *psychopathic* generally referred to "psychological" as opposed to "organic" etiology, anticipating the modern concept of PD (Berrios, 1996; Zachar, 2015). Supported by the opinions of Bleuler, Kraepelin, and others, Binswanger concluded Ellen West was a case of "schizophrenia simplex of a polymorphous form" (p. 364) and reasoned, along with consultants, her declining mental status constituted evidence she was untreatable. Drawing on his developing existentialist psychiatry (*dasiensanalyse*), Binswanger (1958, p. 363) considered her course an "emptying of the personality," supporting the diagnosis of schizophrenia despite absence of intellectual decline, thought blocking, hallucinations, and delusions. At the time, schizophrenia was considered a progressive and deteriorating disease, a form of dementia (i.e., *dementia praecox*). On these bases, Binswanger and others concluded that "no reliable treatment is possible" (p. 267), and he discharged her to return home, despite her stated intention to take her own life. Once home, her mood lifted, she busied herself writing letters, and began to eat with relish. But, three days later, she committed suicide with a fatal dose of poison. Writing an existential analysis of her case 20 years after her death, Binswanger (1958, p. 313) argued that her death represented an "act of authentic expression and freedom from imprisonment in the face of non-being."

Scholars have considered Ellen West from various psychological, psychiatric, and socio-political perspectives. These include eating disorder, feminist theory, death anxiety, and ethics of permitted suicide (e.g., Bray, 2001; Jackson, Davidson, Russell, & Vandereycken, 1990; Maltsberger, 1996; Stewart, 2012). Criticizing Binswanger's treatment of Ellen West, the humanistic psychologist Carl Rogers (1961) cited Binswanger's interest in authenticity and faulted him for not seeing her personhood.

In the present day, diagnoses of eating disorder, affective disorder, anxiety disorder, and PD might be considered for Ellen West, including the differential diagnosis of bipolar disorder. Her history shows significant signs of PD, including emotional lability, self-harm and suicidal behavior, chronic feelings of emptiness, risky behavior and impulsivity, anxiety and rumination, and identity conflicts. Notable also is the observation that her functioning apparently declined within (relatively unstructured) psychoanalyses and during lengthy residential treatments. Furthermore, her psychiatrists experienced her very differently, as reflected in divergent diagnoses. Patient characteristics and treatment outcomes like Ellen West were historically important in the development of the construct of borderline personality organization (Kernberg, 1967; Knight, 1953) and borderline personality disorder (Gunderson, 2009b).

Assuming her symptoms were not fully accounted for by affective and eating disorder, the AMPD Level of Personality Functioning Scale (LPFS) may be applied to Ellen West's history. Problems with her sense of self and regulation of emotion and self-esteem indicate significant impairment in the domain of Identity. In addition, erratic functioning and achievement suggest moderate impairment in Self-Direction. On these bases alone, Criterion A establishes the presence of PD (i.e., two or more ratings of moderate impairment). Regarding the pathological personality trait-facets of Criterion B, her history reveals significant emotional lability, anxiousness, depressivity, and rigid perfectionism. Impulsivity, risk taking, perseveration, withdrawal, separation insecurity, and anhedonia are also suggested (see Addendum A at the end of this chapter). Applying the hybrid categorical-dimensional algorithms of the AMPD, ratings on Criterion B trait-facets yield the diagnosis of *borderline PD* (6 of 7 criteria; ≥ 4 are required and must include impulsivity, risk taking, or hostility). Parenthetically, recent research suggests the trait-facets of anhedonia, perceptual dysregulation, and suspiciousness, along with a dimension of self-harm, are associated with categorical borderline PD (Bach & Sellbom, 2016; Evans & Simms, 2018). In terms of full dimensional diagnosis, Personality Disorder Trait-Specified (PD-TS) might be coded, listing the most prominent pathological personality trait domains or facets. For example, *PD-TS with negative affectivity* is the most general dimensional PD diagnosis for her case. Alternatively, to emphasize specific trait-facets, the diagnosis of *PD-TS with emotional lability, depressivity, and rigid perfectionism* could be used. Interestingly, this application of the AMPD to the historical data on Ellen West arrives at the same place as Ghaemi (2003) did using the DSM-IV (APA, 1994): the diagnosis of borderline PD.

We revisit the tragic life of Ellen West not to fault Binswanger, Kraepelin, Bleuler, and others. Her care should not be appraised by current standards and conceptions of psychopathology. After all, she received premier treatments of her age. Rather, our analysis illustrates the applicability of the AMPD and fact that paradigms in psychopathology evolve.

Diagnostic Paradigms Evolve

The case of Ellen West illustrates complexities of differential diagnosis for an individual patient, the relevance of different conceptions of psychopathology, and their time-bound nature. Ellen West's psychiatrists struggled with diagnoses varying between unambiguous schizophrenia, manic-depressive oscillations, obsessive neurosis, and psychopathic constitution, amongst others. These reflected emerging nosological concepts of schizophrenia, affective disorder, neurosis, and PD. They also represented differing paradigms of psychopathology. As noted, one of Ellen West's consultants was Emil Kraepelin whose many contributions to psychopathology included the classification of schizophrenia and manic-depression into separate diseases (Jablensky, 2007), a distinction that re-organized the nosology of the day The Kraepelinian conception was a medical disease model. Ellen West's other consultants saw neurosis, reflecting the psychoanalytic point of view, and of psychopathic constitution, a concept which anticipated PD and assumed psychological etiology but was not neurosis. With the benefit of the long view, however, the case of Ellen West reveals psychiatric classifications are not static (Blashfield et al., 2014). They reflect scientific priorities, sociological elements, and professional standards which compete for dominance in the field. In other words, Kuhnian paradigm dynamics are in play. In this regard, Kendler (2009) posed a provocative question: If one could rewind time and let scientific psychopathology re-evolve, would the outcome resemble our current views?

Kendler (2009; 2015) reasoned the major psychoses would re-emerge but many nosological constructs would not. To cite an egregious example, *drapetomania*, the condition that reportedly caused a Negro slave to want to escape slavery (Cartwright, 2004), would not be reconstituted. Likewise, homosexuality is no longer considered a mental disorder (Spitzer, 1981; see Zachar & Kendler, 2012). Psychiatric diagnoses are time-bounded, and they reflect sociological factors and values (Sadler, Hulgus, & Agich, 1994). Kendler (2015) opined many of our present psychiatric constructs ultimately may resemble *phlogiston* (i.e., the chemical theory that combustion involves the release of fire-like substances). In other words, our conceptions may be useful now, but they eventually yield to newer and presumably more productive views. In this regard, note that Kuhn (1962/2012, p. 12) reminded us, "all past beliefs about nature sooner or later turn out to be false."

For many years, PDs were understood through a religious-moral lens. This eventually was transformed by the metaphor of evolution in an approach known as degeneration theory. This was the view that PDs reflected a (Lamarckian) form of de-evolution such that over the generations, increasingly deteriorated psychiatric disease would emerge (Berrios, 1993; Zachar, 2015). In contrast, Schneider's (1958) formulation of psychopathic personalities drew on the idea of deviance from the norm, coupled with the notion that this caused suffering to the individual or to others. This rather modern conception, based on the metaphor of statistics, began to differentiate PD from the prevailing medical-psychiatric nosology. The statistical concepts of correlation and regression to the mean (Galton, 1888), and other advances in statistical methods, were appearing on the scene prior to Schneider's formulation. These set the stage for differential psychology, psychometrics, and the lexical hypothesis of trait theory (e.g., Allport & Odbert, 1936; Cattell, 1933). Underlying each of these evolving conceptions of PD were different metaphors. Relatedly, Loevinger (1987) observed that changing scientific metaphors were the background ideas around which major theories of personality developed.

The American Psychiatric Association's DSM arose in the wake of World War II. Pragmatics of tracking diagnoses for large numbers of military personnel required an organized, profession-wide effort. The DSM-I (APA, 1952) and DSM-II (APA, 1968) did not construe PD as a specific nosological category. This was consistent with psychodynamic thinking and the construct of neurosis, and it meant that many diagnoses contained elements of personality dynamics. But, the influence of the psychoanalytic paradigm in early DSMs has been overstated (Cooper & Blashfield, 2016). The diagnoses in the DSM-I and -II were defined by short descriptions resembling prototypes and generally reflected an eclectic psychiatry. PD was explicitly differentiated in the DSM-III (APA, 1980) by eliminating neurosis, adding a separate diagnostic axis for PD, and defining diagnoses by operationalized criteria. The DSM-III reflected the ascendant "neo-Kraepelinian" paradigm in psychiatry (Andreasen, 2006; Blashfield, 1984; Jablensky, 2007; Klerman, 1978). This trend favored ideas of organic cause, natural course, and progression of disease as found in Kraepelin's seminal classifications. It (supposedly) minimized theory, emphasized diagnostic reliability, and was descriptivist, congenial with a medically and biologically-oriented psychiatry. The DSM-III was built from the Research Diagnostic Criteria (RDC), promulgated as a model for psychiatric diagnosis (e.g., Feighner et al., 1972; Robins & Guze, 1970) and way to reclaim psychiatry's place in medicine. The separate axis for PD in the DSM-III was intended to highlight the importance of PD (Millon, 1983). Yet, how PD (Axis II) was diagnosed (or not) in clinical practice was often quite different than in research settings (Westen, 1997; Zimmerman & Mattia, 1999). Interestingly, research has shown that the operationalized criteria, set of PD categories, and clinician practices in diagnosing PDs have changed relatively little from the time of the DSM-III to the DSM-IV (Morey & Benson, 2016). Cooper (2015) refers to this as the "locked in" quality of the modern DSMs. Yet, as noted earlier, the hegemony of the DSM-III vision for PD diagnosis has now been challenged by the dimensional paradigm (e.g., Widiger & Trull, 2007), a shift comparable to a Kuhnian "crisis in confidence" (Zachar & Kendler, 2017).

The case of Ellen West reminds us to temper enthusiasm for our theories and approaches. The social and value dimensions of PD, not to mention dynamics of professional guilds and like-minded communities of researchers (Blashfield, 1984), mean a modicum of relativism, acceptance of culture-boundedness, and tentativeness are apropos.

Times eventually change and with them our understandings. Consider the previous example of neurosyphilis. Some readers may not realize the degree to which this disease, previously known as general paresis of the insane (GPI) or dementia paralytica, was formative to the field of psychopathology. Symptoms of syphilitic dementia were first described by Esquirol in the early 1800s (and formally identified as a disease syndrome in 1822 by Antoine Bayle [Kragh, 2010]), and estimates are that up to 20% of patients in asylums (i.e., psychiatric hospitals) in the 19th Century were afflicted with this mysterious, progressive, and fatal condition (Kragh, 2010). Its cause or specific etiology (Meehl, 1977) by *trepenema pallidum* was not understood until the early 20th Century. Early treatment called for inducement of malaria fever, a breakthrough that gave psychiatry its first Nobel Prize for Wagner-Jauregg in 1927. Only with the discovery of penicillin in the mid-20th Century was the disease effectively treated. This was a major triumph for medicine—and for psychiatry.

As noted by Blashfield (in the Foreword to this book), this success encouraged Kraepelinan ambitions to find the medical basis of schizophrenia and produced the RDC (see Feighner et al., 1972) and the DSM-III (APA, 1980). Contemporary psychiatry often cites the ideals of Engel's

(1977) biopsychosocial model but, in practice, pedagogy and scientific ambition generally reflect a psychopharmacological and neuropsychiatric paradigm (Andreasen, 2006). Practically speaking, the reigning paradigm is reductionistic. Although a medical model and natural kind conception of PD is problematic, PD nosology is not immune from disciplinary zeal, and of course, non-biological paradigms may dominate a field. To the extent PD is conceived and measured within a single lens, other images are eclipsed. In the past, psychiatry variously regarded GPI as caused by moral failure, alcoholism, behavioral excess, and by heredity. These very same causes have been championed for PD as well. Kendler (2009) and Blashfield et al., (2014) exposed the significant the role of historical contingency in our nosology. To accept time-bound relativism does not preclude scientific analysis (Meehl, 1986; Wakefield, 2006). On this matter, the psychopathologist Karl Jaspers (1913/1997; p. 605) recommended scientific humility:

> Such classification therefore has only a provisional value. It is a fiction which will discharge its function if it proves to be the most apt for the time. There is no "natural" schema which would accommodate every case.

This caution extends to the emerging paradigm of dimensionalization of diagnosis and the AMPD. We argue AMPD provides substantial scientific and professional advantages over traditional models of PD (Krueger, Hopwood, Wright, & Markon, 2014), but imagining where the science and treatment of psychopathology may go in 75 years, we know that the AMPD will not be the final word.

Paradigm and Explanation

The 19th Century philosopher Auguste Comte described the sciences as a hierarchy with mathematics at the base, ascending through astronomy, physics, chemistry, and biology to the apex of sociology. In Comte's pyramid, maximum generality occurs at the base, and its peak is the most complex. Comte's sociology reflects the social-human sciences, including psychiatry and psychology. Snow (1959) famously described the "two cultures" of the Sciences and the Humanities which represent two great traditions of intellectual discourse. More recently, Kagan (2009) explored the place of the social sciences (and psychology) in relation to the polarities of the sciences and the humanities. The author argued there now are "three cultures," which are the natural sciences, social sciences, and humanities. These cultures vary on multiple dimensions.

The Middle Ground

Kagan (2009) pointed out that each culture uses a different vocabulary, hindering communication across fields. The same term may be used with different meanings by natural scientists, social scientists, or scholars in the humanities—harkening to the proverbial "jingle fallacy" in psychology (Kelley, 1927) which refers to the confusion created when the same name is used for tests or measures of different constructs. Furthermore, Kagan (2009) noted that each of these cultures relates differently to history. The social sciences and humanities are affected by historical conditions, while the natural sciences are more connected to developments in technology. As noted earlier, historical currents have been important in psychiatric classification (Blashfield et al., 2014; Kendler, 2009).

Psychology and psychiatry straddle a middle ground between the natural/biological sciences and the humanities. This middle ground has long been a focus of philosophically informed psychology and psychiatry. The existential psychiatrist-philosopher Karl Jaspers (1913/1997), in *General Psychopathology*, specifically called for a *methodological pluralism*, in contrast to the Kraepelinian emphasis on organic disease conceptions of psychiatric disorder. Jaspers (1913/1997) described two major methods of psychiatry: the causal/objective/empirical (*Erklaren)* and subjective/interpretive (*Verstehen*). As suggested previously, the litmus test of Jasperian pluralism is necessary for useful conception of PD.

Paradigms

Kuhn's (1962/2012) central thesis is that science reflects sociological and historical dynamics. As formulated by Kuhn (1962/2012), a scientific paradigm prescribes what is acceptable to study, as well as what constitutes appropriate methods of analysis, relevant data, and rules for interpreting results. Paradigms are known by *exemplars*, examples of methods that are constitutive of the given point of view. The pendulum in the physics of classical mechanics and the theory of convergent evolution in biology are exemplars. The *Minnesota Multiphasic Personality Inventory* (Second Edition; MMPI-2; Hathaway et al., 1989) represents an exemplar of the empirical paradigm of personality assessment paradigm (Wiggins, 2003). The psychopharmacological paradigm of psychiatry also employs exemplars. Examples are the discovery that lithium carbonate could treat manic depression (Cade, 1949) and in 1952 that the drug chlorpromazine (Thorazine) could treat psychosis (Ban, 2007).

Paradigms of Personality Assessment

Wiggins (2003) used the notion of the Kuhnian paradigm to examine commonality and difference in major traditions of personality assessment. For Wiggins (2003, p. 4), paradigm refers to the "set of generally accepted beliefs or orienting attitudes within and against which personality tests are constructed, administered, and interpreted." Wiggins (2003) called attention to the major influence of one's educational experiences in developing paradigmatic affinity. The student or trainee is inculcated with the concepts and methods of assessment taught, valued, and practiced where trained. Paradigms define ranges and foci of convenience. Assessment communities, like Kuhnian scientific communities, generally speak the same vocabulary, find other paradigms problematic (incommensurable), and often share a similar educational pedigree. Wiggins (2003) identified five major paradigms of personality assessment. They are the *psychodynamic, personological, interpersonal, multivariate*, and *empirical*. These are now described.

The *psychodynamic* paradigm emphasizes intrapsychic conflict and the psychological unconscious. Historically, it has been associated with projective (performance) assessment methods such as the Rorschach Inkblot test, and the classic work of Rapaport, Schafer, and Gill (1946) represents an early exemplar. The metaphor of this paradigm is that things are not what they appear. The early psychoanalytic iceberg metaphor still applies—but must be reconfigured to reflect the *four psychologies* of the contemporary psychodynamic paradigm. These are drive theory, ego psychology, object relations/attachment, and self-psychology (Luyten, Mayes, Blatt, Target, & Fonagy, 2015). Thus, the metaphor that things are not what they appear spans inner conflict, self-agency and adaptation, templates of social relationships, and dynamics of self-functioning.

The *personological* paradigm derived from the case study of the individual and frequently makes use of qualitative inquiry and narrative data to study subjectivity and personal meaning (e.g., McAdams, 1995). The metaphor of this paradigm is story and personal narrative. Interpretive and narrative methods focus on phenomenology and subjective experience, and collaborative relationships are emphasized. The approach to assessment found in collaborative/therapeutic assessment (C/TA; Finn, 2007) represents a contemporary exemplar of the paradigm and reflects a general humanistic orientation (Finn & Tonsager, 2002).

The *interpersonal* paradigm derives from Sullivan's (1953/2013) interpersonal psychiatry and focuses on the dynamics of interpersonal (overt and internalized) interaction patterns. This paradigm is embodied in Leary's (1957) interpersonal circumplex approach (IPC). The IPC is an exemplar of the paradigm (Gurtman, 2009; Wiggins, 1996). Contemporary developments in this approach include Benjamin's (1996) structural analysis of social behavior (SASB) which has been applied extensively to PD (Benjamin, 1993; Pincus & Wiggins, 1990). Hopwood, Wright, Ansell, and Pincus (2013) articulated systematic connections between the AMPD and the interpersonal paradigm. The metaphor of this paradigm is the interpersonal field (Wiggins, 2003).

The *multivariate* paradigm evolved from the differential psychology and psychometric trait tradition. This paradigm is reflected in the Lexical Hypothesis (Cattell, 1943), the Big Five (Goldberg, 1993), and FFM approaches (Costa & McCrae, 1990). Furthermore, the paradigm is found in the expanding quantitative psychopathology movement (e.g., Krueger,

1999) and, to some extent, in the pathological personality traits of Criterion B in the AMPD. The metaphor of this paradigm is the matrix of correlation coefficients analyzed with multivariate methods such as factor analysis.

The *empirical* paradigm was influenced by the Kraepelinian tradition of psychiatric diagnostic categories. As noted, the MMPI-2 (Hathaway et al., 1989) is an exemplar instrument of the paradigm. However, other tests and measures including the Personality Assessment Inventory (PAI; Morey, 2007) also focus on psychiatric diagnosis. The empirical paradigm is not restricted to a categorical nosology. Dimensional constructs are also applicable. Furthermore, the term empirical does not signify it is the only paradigm that uses empirical methods. Rather, this refers to its historic focus on diagnostic variables, like with the MMPI-2, developed with the empirical criterion keying psychometric strategy (Meehl, 1945). It is important also to understand that procedures within the Rorschach Inkblot Method may reflect the empirical paradigm. This is seen in contemporary Rorschach systems such as the Comprehensive System (Exner, 2003) and Rorschach Performance System (RPAS; Meyer, Viglione, Mihura, Erard, & Erdberg, 2011), particularly in the case of diagnostically related index scores. The metaphor of the empirical paradigm may be the diagnostic construct, but it may be modeled with categorical, dimensional, or mixed classificatory structures. To the extent traditional categorical constructs are used, the metaphor of the syndrome applies. However, when diagnostic constructs are fully dimensionalized, the empirical and multivariate paradigms begin to converge. The multivariate and empirical paradigms are often descriptivist, but this is not a necessary property. For example, Meehl (1945) cited potential psychodynamic qualities within responses to self-report questionnaire items, and multivariate methods can be used within each of the Wiggins (2003) paradigms.

Metaphor

The cognitive-linguists tell us that metaphor orients, structures, and guides how we think (Lakoff & Johnson, 1980). Kuhn (1979) was explicit that metaphor plays a prefiguring role in scientific paradigms (see also Brown, T. L., 2003). Several examples illustrate this point. Consider the "Big Bang," "String Theory," and "Schrodinger's Cat" of physics. Darwinian evolution is a *blind watchmaker* (Dawkins, 1986), and Darwin used metaphors in composing the theory of evolution (e.g., *struggle for existence*; nature *selects*; Todes, 1987). Molecular biology and cognitive neuroscience draw on computing and information science (e.g., the genetic *code; messenger* RNA; *modularity*), and the cognitive paradigm in psychology is heir to the same metaphors. Metaphor is pervasive in medicine (Bleakley, 2017), affecting theory and how patients, physicians, medical scientists, and society relate to disease. Sontag (1978; 1989) explored this thesis with respect to tuberculosis (TB), cancer, and human immunodeficiency virus infection and acquired immune deficiency syndrome (HIV/AIDS). TB was known as *consumption*, a disease in which the body was slowly consumed. Cancer has often been described with spatial metaphors such as *invasion, spread*, and *terminal*, and its treatment framed as *war*. Importantly, metaphor imparts an interpretive frame, akin to an implicit Kuhnian (1962/2012) paradigm. To regard cancer as *invasion to be met with war* is not an empty figure of speech. Rather, a tacit dimension (Polanyi, 1952) frames oncology research, practice, and patient experience.

Psychiatry and psychology make abundant use of metaphor. Freud's psychoanalytic topographic model of mind (Strachey, 1953) uses the image of an iceberg, most of which is below the surface, to convey the idea of lack of conscious awareness. The steam engine became a metaphor for psychoanalytic drive theory, reflected in the terms cathexis and libido. The interpersonal paradigm of personality assessment is fashioned with the metaphor of the interpersonal *field*, borrowing from Michael Faraday's studies of electricity and James Clerk Maxwell's electromagnetic field theory (Wiggins, 2003). A currently popular metaphor construes depression as a *chemical imbalance*. This metaphor has implications that range from the ontology of sadness (Horwitz & Wakefield, 2007) to marketing efforts to prescribers and the public (France, Lysaker, & Robinson, 2007; Lacasse & Leo, 2005). The metaphor has an upside and a downside. Deacon and Baird (2009) showed that, to the extent people saw depression as a chemical imbalance, the stigma of mental disorder was reduced, but pessimism about recovery increased and the relevance of psychosocial intervention decreased. The chemical imbalance metaphor casts depression with an essentialist, causal, and categorical template. Essentialism is also very relevant to conceptions of PD as discussed shortly.

Metaphors likewise prefigure PD nosology, and the metaphors of the AMPD are discernible in the traditions and methods from which it derived. McAdams' (2015) metaphors of *actor, agent*, and *author* apply. Recall that Criterion A of the AMPD derives from psychodynamic, attachment, and social-cognitive developmental theories, which emphasize internality, formative relationships, and constructivism. In other words, the metaphors of *agent* and *author* are embodied. Criterion B stems from the lexical trait tradition, makes use of multivariate methods like factor analysis, and by emphasizing empirical description it builds on the metaphor of *actor*—whose behavior is observable. The AMPD also can be distinguished from traditional PD nosology by two other key metaphors. These are dimensionalization, as noted before, and the metaphor of a map.

Cartography, Construct Validity, and Psychometrics

Korzybski (1933) famously stated a map is not the territory. A map cannot be point-for-point with its referent; if so, it is of no use. A map must be abstracted and scaled in proportion to its referents, and this logic exists in psychiatric classification as well (Millon, 1991). A psychiatric nosology prioritizes certain features of human experience and behavior, codifies them, and develops a system to communicate this information. This is what cartography does for geographical terrain. Interestingly, psychiatric nosology and cartography have much in common.

Psychiatric classification, for Blashfield and Draguns (1976), is nomenclature which facilitates information retrieval, description, prediction, and concept formation. Mullins-Sweatt, Lengel, and DeShong (2016) argued that clinical utility is a fundamental quality of a diagnostic nosology, and this is composed of its ease of use, communication value, and contribution to treatment planning (Mullins-Sweatt & Widiger, 2009). Furthermore, this desideratum of clinical utility is separate but related to issues of construct validity. Returning to the ancient practice of cartography, mapmaking saw significant development in World War II (WWII) when Arthur Robinson of the Office of Strategic Services (OSS; now called the Central Intelligence Agency) combined art with geography in creating maps that emphasized purpose, utility, and communicative value (Wilford, 2001). The parameters valued in psychiatric nosology (e.g., representation of referent, utility, communication, and art) are not only similar to cartography, but also experienced significant advances during WWII. The Robinson projection was a new type of world map that revised the previous Mercator projection (Robinson, 1958; Robinson, 1979; Wilford, 2001). Dating from 1569, the Mercator was designed to aid European navigators in sea travel. But this map distorted visualization of the globe near the poles (e.g., Greenland is depicted as much larger than Africa, but is smaller). Robinson's interest was not sea travel, and he maximized aesthetic appeal and communication in this new strategy (Robinson, 1974) which became the basis of the world map used by the National Geographic Society for many years (Wilford, 2001). The Robinson projection shows its greatest fidelity in the temperate zone, where most of the world's land mass and people are located. Importantly, when two dimensions (world map) are used to depict a three-dimensional reference (the world), distortion is unavoidable. Certain foci are prioritized at the expense of others. Mapmaking and psychiatric nosology are very similar endeavors. Strategic decisions made by people determine what and how the subject is represented, and the criterion of utility is very important. The purposes and parameters determine utility, and what is considered useful changes over time.

Construct Validity

The representational dimension of cartography corresponds to validation in psychiatric classification (i.e., construct validity; Cronbach & Meehl, 1955; Loevinger, 1957). Classic statements of MacCorquodale and Meehl (1948) and Cronbach and Meehl (1955) on construct validity are explanations of map–territory relations. MacCorquodale and Meehl (1948) distinguished between an intervening variable (IV) and a hypothetical construct (HC). An IV is an operationalized concept that can be measured empirically. In contrast, a HC is abstract, tied to theory, and does not have a direct empirical referent. For example, to say "intelligence" is what intelligence tests measure implies it is an IV. But if "intelligence" is considered an abstract dimension composed of multiple cognitive abilities, it becomes a HC. The terms (concepts) "personality," "psychosis-proneness," and "separation anxiety" are HCs. In biology, "gene" and "immunity" are constructs, like "dark matter" in physics.

From this construct validity perspective, we may ask, is schizophrenia a HC? Is PD a HC or an IV? Operationally speaking, if a "schizophrenia test" defined schizophrenia, schizophrenia would be an IV. A construct validity point of view, in contrast, conceptualizes schizophrenia as a syndrome or set of psychopathological dimensions rather than a specific algorithm of diagnostic criteria or profile of neuropsychiatric measurements. Relatedly, Slaney and Garcia (2015) reviewed ambiguities with how the term *construct* is used in social sciences. They noted that at times use verges on objectification of the construct, a form of misplaced concreteness. In other words, if the hypothetical status is neglected, the construct becomes reified. Again, as Korzybski (1933) put it simply, a map is not the territory.

Note also that as MacCorquodale and Meehl (1948, p. 106) explored these issues, they used the word *metaphor*: "For a genuine intervening variable, there is no metaphor because all is merely shorthand summarization. For hypothetical constructs, there is a surplus meaning that is existential." This notion of *surplus meaning* casts diagnosis within the construct validity frame—as opposed to operational definitions. Morey (1991) elaborated the point that diagnoses are constructs, not just algorithms of diagnostic criteria, and that the surplus meanings can inform science and practice. Cronbach and Meehl (1955) developed the idea of the *nomological network* in construct validity. This refers to the set of meaningful connections between constructs which are inferable from analyses of empirical measurements. A corollary of this reasoning is that constructs inform theory, and theory informs constructs. Constructs are refined through empirical study, and the new understandings of constructs guide theory revision and its subsequent empirical tests. There is a reciprocal and iterating relationship between theory and data. Regarding psychiatric classification, however, the interests of construct validation are somewhat different than practical issues of prediction or the act of diagnostic identification which speak more to the clinical utility of a diagnostic system (Mullin-Sweatt & Widiger, 2009). These points are illustrated below with a construct with relevance to PDs.

Reflective functioning (RF) is a construct important in PDs. The Reflective Functioning Scale (RF; Fonagy, Steele, Steele, Moran, & Higgitt,

1991) was derived from attachment theory and research. RF references the broader concept of mentalization, the ability to make sense of mental states in self and others. The study of mentalization traces from early work on the theory of mind (ToM; Premack & Woodruff, 1978) and connects with the psychopathology of autistic spectrum disorders (Baron-Cohen, Leslie, & Frith, 1985). Mentalization also links to (constructs of) mindfulness, psychological mindedness, empathy, and affect consciousness (Choi-Kain & Gunderson, 2008). Drawing on attachment theory, ToM, and psychoanalytic developmental psychology, Fonagy, Gergely, Jurist, and Target (2005) formulated a model of PD with mentalization playing a central, organizing role. This model seeks to account for several psychopathologic observations, informs psychotherapy, and is positioned within the sociobiological theory of evolution (Fonagy, Luyten, & Allison, 2015). In other words, the construct of mentalization, measured with RF indicators (interviews, observation, self-report, etc.), exists within a nomological network that arose from and has been shaped through observation and theory across the fields of anthropology, biology, neuroscience, psychopathology, psychology, and psychotherapy. Moreover, RF was part of the conceptual heritage of the Level of Personality Functioning Scale (LPFS; Bender, Morey, & Skodol, 2011), the indicator for Criterion A of the AMPD. Diagnosis with the AMPD thus brings substantial surplus meanings (Morey, 1991), some of which involve the nomological network of RF. This is very different than contemporary criterion-based diagnosis.

Psychometrics

Blashfield and Livesley (1991) proposed that psychological tests could be considered a metaphor for psychiatric classification. Viewing symptoms as test items suggests this similarity. For example, diagnostic criteria, like test items, may be cumulated to generate scales, also known as criteria-based diagnoses. This permits analyses of psychometric reliability and validity. Likewise, classification systems use a test manual, the DSM. Continuing this metaphor, diagnostic efficiency statistics such as sensitivity and specificity resemble psychometric item analyses. Psychometric approaches like these appeared on the scene with the advent of the criterion-based diagnoses of the DSM-III (e.g., Grilo et al., 2001). The parallel to a psychological test, however, is approximate. For example, the categorical conceptualization of diagnoses in traditional psychiatric classification is less consistent with this metaphor compared to the dimensional approach. But, the AMPD moves closer to actualizing Blashfield and Livesley's (1991) metaphor. Criterion A of the AMPD, the LPFS, is a psychometric rating scale, and Criterion B may be assessed with the self- or informant-report forms of the Personality Inventory for the DSM-5 (PID-5; APA, 2013). These AMPD instruments share the metaphor by bridging classification and psychometric tests. This development is consistent with Markon's (2013) call for epistemological pluralism in psychiatric nosology. He argued psychiatric nosology could be scaffolded by psychological tests, and this would offer conceptual and methodological pluralism to the enterprise. Interestingly, recent DSMs have moved in this direction with the diagnoses of intellectual disability, learning disorder, and neurocognitive disorder, which are defined with reference to psychometrics.

A construct-based approach to PD diagnosis directs attention to the different ways diagnostic constructs may be modeled psychometrically. The underlying psychometric model within a nosology has important implications. A *formative* measure is comprised by its indicators (e.g., "…shorthand summarization…"; MacCorquodale & Meehl, 1948, p. 106). A classic example is the psychometric *index* of socioeconomic status (SES). SES is fully defined by income and education. A psychometric *scale*, in contrast, traditionally uses Classical Test Theory (CTT) of psychometrics and sees an underlying common cause or latent variable *reflected* in variation in indicators (e.g., test items, diagnostic criteria), representing the construct dimension. This measurement model values factor analytic-type procedures and is paradigmatic in the quantitative psychopathology approach to psychiatric classification. The Hierarchical Taxonomy of Psychopathology (HiTOP; Kotov et al., 2017) consortium of investigators exemplifies this approach. In the realm of PD, this is evidenced in the pathological personality traits of Criterion B (Krueger & Markon, 2014) as well as kindred FFM-based PD models (Bagby & Widiger, 2018) and the Computerized Adaptive Assessment of Personality Disorders (CAT-25; Simms and colleagues, 2011).

Network analysis is another way to model diagnostic systems. This approach challenges the CTT-based assumption of a latent variable generally adopted in quantitative psychopathology. In network approaches, symptoms are viewed in dynamic relation to one another and causally connected (Borsboom, 2008; Borsboom et al., 2011). For example, in network models, panic anxiety causes avoidant behavior. This contrasts with the view that panic and avoidance symptoms are reflections of an underlying latent dimension (panic disorder) as is construed in reflective measurement models. The network approach to personality and psychopathology is an emerging, complex area of investigation (McNally, 2016) as well as critical debate (Forbes, Wright, Markon, & Krueger, 2017; Guloksuz, Pries, & Van Os, 2017). Suggestive evidence for the validity of network-modeled psychiatric conditions has been found for posttraumatic stress disorder (PTSD) and possibly for major depression (e.g., Cramer et al., 2016). PD has been less studied from this perspective. However, Richetin, Preti, Costantini, and De Panfilis (2017) applied network analysis to borderline PD symptoms, and their results affirmed the central role of affective stability and identity problems in the disorder.

Because diagnostic systems can be conceptualized in terms of different psychometric models, it is important to be clear on the underlying model and its implications (Borsboom, 2008; Meehl, 1986; Nelson-Gray, 1991). This is particularly so for the prevailing DSM criterion-based approach to psychiatric diagnosis. Since the DSM-III, psychiatric nosology has followed the tacit psychometric model of formative measurement, like the indexing of SES. This is the case because diagnosis is wholly defined by indicators; no more, no less. Consider, for example, borderline PD. Presently, this diagnosis is defined by the presence of five or more of nine diagnostic criteria (which mathematically can be combined in 256 ways). If the diagnosis is wholly constituted by five or more "test items," this is no different than saying intelligence is what intelligence tests measure. Moreover, note there are several useful intelligence tests. Intelligence as defined by one test is not the same intelligence as defined by another. Extending this scenario, the many available intelligence tests thus produce multiple intelligences, so to speak. Similarly, the many ways borderline PD can be constituted from diagnostic criteria yield multiple borderline PDs (i.e., 256 ways). Zandersen, Henriksen, and Parnas (in press, 2018) indicted problematic issues such as this in their review of the modern history of borderline PD. That is, criteria-based diagnoses create conceptual problems.

With the DSM-III (APA, 1980) criterion-based approach, diagnosis became literalized and, in the process, the representational aspect of diagnosis was minimized. Traditional DSM diagnosis resembles a map scaled to a one-to-one correspondence of map and territory. How useful is this? This criterion-count approach of the DSM-III aspired to improve clinicians' agreement on diagnoses, but its success is debatable (Frances, 2012; Markon, 2013). If the interest is representation of a diagnostic construct with metaphor and surplus meanings, the modern DSM approach falls short. Ticking off criteria until the diagnosis is established at a cutpoint (e.g., five of nine criteria equals borderline PD; *quod erat demonstrantum*; QED), is a very different diagnostic endeavor than framing signs, symptoms, and subjectivity within parameters of context and dynamics of clinician-patient interaction. Rather, the criteria-count approach is a recipe for the slippery-slope to reification (Hyman, 2010). Reflexive application of criterion-based diagnosis collapses the scaling of the map to that of territory. The disutility of this approach is broad. The writer Borges (1946/1998, p. 325) cautioned in a 130-word short story, titled in pregnant irony "On Exactitude in Science," that "…the Art of Cartography attained such Perfection…and the Cartographers Guilds struck a Map of the Empire whose size was that of the Empire, and which coincided point for point with it…the following Generations…saw that that vast map was Useless… still today there are Tattered Ruins of that Map, inhabited by Animals and Beggars…." Note that this indictment is not just of reification but also disciplinary zeal, to which the long view of history is not kind.

The AMPD is a Map

In the AMPD, the coordinates of the map are Criterion A and Criterion B. These coordinates do not *constitute* PD, they *reflect* hypothetical constructs. These coordinates provide orientation to explore the territory of PD. They also connect to the nomological networks that span the traditions and science from which Criterion A and B were formulated. The AMPD cannot equally serve all audiences or stakeholders—no nosology can. But, it's pan-theoretic nature renders the AMPD a diagnostic heuristic, a very different type of psychiatric nosology.

In the 1940s and 1950s, the reigning paradigm in psychology was behaviorism. To this, the noted comparative psychologist Frank Beach wrote an essay with the clever title, "The snark was a boojum." Beach (1950) admonished the field of psychology for reflexive use of *Ratus norvegicus*, the white rat, analogizing to Lewis Carroll's (1876/1981) *The Hunting of the Snark* (Carroll et al., 1981).

Beach (1950) warned that a doctrinaire, single-method approach to understand animal behavior (i.e., the "snark") risked an unhappy ending for the field much like Carroll's character the Baker. In questing for the "snark," the Baker instead found the "boojum," resulting in him vanishing. Similarly, Andreasen (2006) warned the field of psychiatry of a possible silent spring if psychopathology were defined by (reified) DSM criteria, rather than by constructs with surplus meanings. Literal, criteria-bound PD nosology is Borges' *exactitude*, the proverbial white rat, and Carroll's boojum. Carroll's (1876/1981, p. 29) character the Bellman brandished his map (see Figure 1.1) and declared:

> What's the good of Mercator's North Poles and Equators,
> Tropics, Zones, and Meridian Lines?
> So the Bellman would cry: and the crew would reply
> "They are merely conventional signs!
> Other maps are such shapes, with their islands and capes!
> But we've got our brave Captain to thank"
> (So the crew would protest) "that he's bought us the best—
> A perfect and absolute blank!"

What's the point of a map, if there is no map–territory relation? This is what Berrios (1999) concludes from conceptual analysis of psychiatric classification. If nosology does not embody a nomological net, it remains a catalogue of descriptive and documentary functions. This is useful but limited. The AMPD aims higher: it imports multiple personality paradigms, is psychometrically congruent with its construct domains, and offers broad nomological nets for PD. In these ways, the AMPD may protect against paradigmatic myopia, otherwise known as the "boojum."

Figure 1.1. The Captain's Ocean Chart revealed by the Bellman in Lewis Carroll's (1876/1981) *The hunting of the snark: An agony in eight fits.* Plate 4, by Henry Holliday. Image in the public domain.

Pluralism

Pluralism is a major current in contemporary philosophy of science. Cartwright (1999; 2004) argued the universe cannot be understood with a unitary perspective. The objects of science cannot be apprehended by a single, privileged approach. Chang (2017) observed that natural sciences have drawn on multiple paradigms throughout their history. For example, the evolution of the thermometer followed the path of epistemic iteration, bootstrapping concept and method across inadequate, competing theories of temperature. Likewise, modern chemical theory and developments in physics are pluralistic. Chang (2017) pointed out modern physics has evolved through paradigms of electron theory, of the zoo of particle physics, to string theory, and to dark matter conceptions of nature. For Chang (2017) the bottom line is that monism does not work (Cartwright, 1999).

Chang (2017) applied philosophical pluralism to psychiatric classification. For Chang (2017), the epistemic iteration (progress) of a field benefits by multiple explanatory paradigms—and this is just as true for psychiatric nosology as chemistry. Specifically, Chang (2017) reasoned that different models of psychiatric disorders, such as those using latent variables (e.g., factor analysis) and network analysis (Borsboom & Cramer, 2013), may progress in parallel. Chang (2017) cited the epistemic value of the specific contrasting nosologies of the traditional DSM and the Research Domain Criteria (RDoC; Cuthbert & Insel, 2013). The value of pluralism is seen in fostering opportunity for improved measurement, construct differentiation, and discernment of different layers of meaning.

Construct and Method in PD

The "white whale" of rigorous psychometrics is a metaphor for the quest of construct validity (Loevinger, 1993). As Wiggins (2003) observed, the what, where, and with whom one trains significantly influences theoretical perspectives and practices. Clinicians and researchers are of course human; their theories and methods are influenced by factors other than the ontology of the subject. Predilections can privilege some clinical and investigatory methods—whether self-report, clinical observation, experimental, biological assays, pharmacogenetic testing, neuroimaging, and/or performance-based personality assessments. Favored approaches are not always determined by evidence or clinical utility, and choice of method makes a big difference. For example, Samuel, Sanislow, et al. (2013) showed that self-report, clinician ratings, and structured interview assessment of PD differ in predictive and incremental validity. Relatedly, Samuel and Bucher (2017) demonstrated that accuracy of PD assessment varies as a function of method measurement (e.g., free-form clinical ratings; structured interviews; self-report; categorical versus dimensional measurement; see also Gritti & Samuel, 2015). The generally accepted approach of diagnostic assessment by structured interview puts its own stamp on data also. Parnas and colleages (2012) argued this popular approach is an exemplar of the paradigm of descriptive psychopathology. If this is the sole lens through which psychopathology is viewed, it can eclipse relevant areas of patient subjectivity and introduce distorting experimenter effects (see also Zandersen et al., in press, 2018). In summary, method matters a great deal, a point inherent in the logic of construct validation.

Campbell and Fiske (1959) described the classic Multi-Trait Multi-Method Matrix (MTMM). This heuristic systematically compares type of construct and type of method for convergence and divergence. Loevinger (1957) developed a conception of construct validity which has three arms. Convergent and discriminant validation, such as by the MTMM, is an exemplar of the *external component* of construct validity. The *substantive component* of construct validity addresses concerns of content validity. The *structural component* considers inter-item relationships (e.g., internal consistency, factor dimensions) and the degree to which the assessment method conforms to the nature of the construct. This latter facet of structural validity is sometimes less appreciated. To examine PD within the lens of construct validity requires coordination of model and measure. To accomplish this, personality theory, science, and assessment provide guidance. This is a different posture than the modern DSMs which define PD by criteria and reflect the shadows of disease concepts and medical traditions. The schema provided by McAdams and Pals (2006) for personality theory and method is an illustrative way to situate PD construct validation.

McAdams and Pals (2006) organized personality science in five domains. They are: (1) evolutionary substrate of personality, (2) dispositional traits, (3) characteristic adaptations, (4) narrative identity, and (5) social surround. The three domains of relevance to construct validation in PD are traits, characteristic adaptations, and narrative identity. Note that other personality schemes have defined boundaries between traits and characteristic adaptations somewhat differently (e.g., DeYoung, 2015; Fleeson & Jayawickreme, 2015), but we use McAdams and Pals (2006) for illustration. *Dispositional traits* reflect the psychometric paradigm of differential psychology as exemplified in the Big Five and FFM approach to personality. This generally implies a descriptive approach to personality (Block, 2010; McAdams & Walden, 2010). *Characteristic adaptations* represent motives, styles of coping and defending, and modes of adaptations of the individual (in the context of dispositional traits and life circumstances). *Narrative identity* refers to the individual's life story, one's meaning-making efforts woven as narrative. As noted before, McAdams (2015) offered the metaphors of actor (traits), agent (characteristic adaptation), and author (narrative) to evoke these domains. McAdams and Pals (2006; 2007) furthermore argued these domains may be aligned with prototypical assessment approaches. They suggested dispositional traits are well-suited to the psychometrics of individual differences such as with self-report and informant-report methods. Characteristic adaptations emphasize stylistic and process aspects of behavior and thus suggest some advantage to performance assessment or experimental methods. Narrative identity might favor qualitative and narrative approaches to capture elements of subjectivity. The McAdams and Pals' (2006) taxonomy of personality schemes invites different measurement strategies for different constructs. However, this is not axiomatic. No method lays exclusive claim to a construct type. Rather, the point is subtler. Construct by method interactions, including potential implications for theory and practice, may be obscured if a single construct-type or method is preferred.

Methodological implications of different types of personality constructs have been systematically studied by Bornstein (2009; 2011). Bornstein (2009) described the *heteromethod convergent problem* of personality assessment. This refers to the conundrum that different types of measures of the same construct often do not strongly correlate. Bornstein (2009) has shown that different methods of assessment (e.g., self-report; free response [performance] measures) of the same construct diverge in part because they tap different psychological expressions or manifestations of the construct. Bornstein (2011) elaborated a strategy of *process dissociation*. This dissects the meaning of test scores by examining how expressions of a construct vary across multiple methods of assessment. Bornstein (2009) argued for matching of construct-level and method of analysis, noting that subjectivity and observable behavior are different psychological domains. Bornstein's (2009) pluralism resembles McAdams and Pals' (2006) suggestion that some types of measurement may be particularly apt for some personality dimensions. This pluralism is consistent with the emphasis on fidelity of method in Loevinger's (1957) structural component of construct validity.

There is no royal road to the construct. For example, Cattell (1988) described the *data box*, a way of picturing relationships between Life (L), Test (T), and Questionnaire (Q) data across persons and occasions. A basic message of the data box is that there are many methods of measurement, and they provide different types of information. Self-report, informant report, performance assessment, experimental data, life history variables, psychophysiological data, genetic assays, and structured and semi-structured interviews are vantage points which may converge to varying degrees. Furthermore, the degree of convergence and divergence is information. It is not sufficient to view PD through a single lens such as the structured interview. This harkens to the disciplinary continuum described by Kagan (2009) and our placement of PD in the middle ground, bridging both behavior genetics and patient subjectivity. Echoing Jaspers (1957/1997), Bornstein (2009; p. 7) stated:

> The contrasting goals of physicists (discovery of meaning through objective analysis), artists (creation of meaning through subjective experience), and psychologists (who seek a middle ground, blending subjectivity and objectivity to enhance therapeutic effectiveness and scientific rigor) make the possibility of productive interchange especially promising.

Categorization, Essentialism, and Prototypes

Zachar and Kendler (2007) described six overlapping conceptual dimensions of psychiatric diagnostic categories. They are: *essentialism* versus *nominalism, objectivism* versus *evaluativism, causalism* versus *descriptivism, internalism* versus *externalism, entity* versus *agent*, and *category* versus *continua*. Space does not permit a full elaboration of these dimensions but note Zachar and Kendler's (2007) conclusion that the medical model of traditional psychiatric diagnosis is inescapably essentialist. *Essentialism* refers to the assumption of an underlying deep structure that is real, natural, and material. This type of construct is sometimes referred to as a *natural kind*. Examples include quartz, the brain, clouds, and pine trees. In the realm of personality and PD, however, essentialism creates problems. Zachar and Kendler (2007) point out that PD generally is viewed with terms that are more nominalist (i.e., our diagnoses are conventions, not real things in nature), evaluative (value judgments are unavoidable in PD), and internalist (the seat of PD is in the individual). This point of view renders the hard medical model much less applicable to PD and suggests use of diagnostic constructs that amalgamate conventions, description, values, notions of self-agency, and utility. This is known as a *practical kind*.

PD models, however, vary on these conceptual dimensions of diagnosis. When genetics, neurobiology, or psychodynamics are emphasized in PD, a degree of causalism is invoked. To view borderline PD as a classic syndrome construes it as an entity. As such, it draws on the essentialism and causalism of the affective neuroscience of separation distress (Panksepp, 2004), the notion of hyperbolic temperament (Zanarini & Frankenburg, 1997), and/or the psychological axis of abandonment anxiety (Masterson, 1981) as well as the assumed taxon structure. But, these conceptual dimensions do not have to be organized in the categorical classificatory structure of a syndrome. Neurobiological, genetic, and epidemiological approaches to nosology increasingly use dimensional models (Jablensky, 2016; see also Cloninger's [1987; 2000] psychobiological dimensional model of PD). In addition, regarding PDs as syndromes risks underemphasizing constructivist and narrative elements points of view. This occurs in part due to the cognitive predilections of clinicians and researchers.

Cognitive psychology has studied attributions people apply in personality traits, PDs, and clinical diagnoses. The work of Ahn, Flanagan, Marsh, and Sanislow (2006) is instructive: they examined essentialism in clinicians' views of medical and psychiatric disorders and found that medical disorders, relative to mental, were regarded as more essentialist. Within psychiatric disorders, PDs and adjustment disorders were the least essentialist. However, one third of the clinicians viewed mental disorders as categorical in nature. Haslam and Ernst (2002) also showed that people were predisposed to view mental disorders as discrete and with an essentialist template. Relatedly, Giffin, Wilkenfeld, and Lombrozo (2017) documented that people preferred to use labels (i.e., category names) in explaining the behavior of people. Importantly, the use of category names was felt to be cognitively satisfying and was linked to causalist beliefs. Thus, although PD is viewed as less compatible with categorical and essentialist assumptions, clinicians often organize diagnoses categorically (like in the traditional DSM). Moreover, to think categorically encourages essentialism, a point of view contrary to PD. Interestingly, Kim and Ahn (2002) showed that clinicians tacitly use causal theories of mental disorders when making DSM diagnoses—as opposed to following criteria-count diagnostic algorithms.

Similar concerns apply in the realm of personality traits. Haslam, Bastian, and Bissett (2004) studied dimensions of essentialism in personality traits. They found that essentialist thinking was associated with trait attributions. For example, traits were judged to be more discrete, biological, inherent, and helpful in describing others. Furthermore, they found that personality traits were considered relatively less useful in informing how to relate and interact with others. This cognitive bias with trait attribution can be connected to Zimmermann and colleagues' (2015) thoughts on distinctions between Criterion A and B of the AMPD. From their factor analytic study of the elements of the AMPD, Zimmermann and colleagues suggested Criterion A may *explain* the *how* of PD behavior, whereas Criterion B may reference *expressions* of the *what* of PD behavior. Haslam and colleagues' (2004) finding that traits are helpful in describing behavior resembles the notion that Criterion B captures *expressions* of behavior (Zimmermann et al., 2015). But, traits were found to be less helpful in guiding interactions with others, an observation that suggests the idea that traits are less *explanatory* of the *how* of others' behavior. To the extent trait attributions lend themselves to biological and inherent implications of essentialism, it is important to be mindful of this essentialist versus nominalist dimension when assessing the pathological personality traits of Criterion B.

In further study of essentialism in categorization, Kim, Johnson, Ahn, and Knobe (2017) showed that the degree of abstraction used in framing categories of behavior (e.g., traits or disorders) is directly associated with essentialist thinking. When more abstract, general descriptors are used, people are inclined to attribute biological causes. But, if the same behavior is framed in a concrete and particularized way (e.g., Joe acted in such and such a manner), people tend to assume psychological and intentional causes. Following this line of reasoning suggests that to the extent the AMPD draws on agentic constructs and narrative methods, essentialism in PD diagnosis may be reduced. This harkens to Schafer's (1980) challenge to psychoanalysis. Schafer (1980), a psychoanalyst, critiqued the prevailing psychoanalytic drive-theory of the times and argued for action-language based on verbs and adverbs, rather than nouns (e.g., to say one acted unwittingly, rather than acting out unconscious drives). This action language advances self-agency and it resonates with McAdams' (2015) personality construct metaphors of *agent* and *author*.

Understanding PD requires a degree of essentialism. However, essentialism applies to the personality or PD construct, not the cognitive predilection of the clinician. Essentialism in personality and PD is quite basic. For example, the early descriptions of Theophrastus (Bennett & Hammond, 1902) and

Galen's humoral theory (Crocq, 2013) were built on the idea of psychobiological temperament. Temperament remains figural in personality and PD theory as seen in Rutter (1987), Cloninger, Svrakic, and Przybeck (1993), and Clark (2005). The McAdams and Pals (2006) schematization places temperament within the construct level of dispositional traits. In addition, PD has been conceptualized within neurobehavioral dimensions (Depue & Lenzenweger, 2001), neurotransmitter systems (Cloninger, 1987), and with reference to specific biosocial dimensions of personality like sensation-seeking or risk-taking (White and colleagues, 1994; Zuckerman & Kuhlman, 2000). Behavior genetic findings are associated with PD (e.g., Livesley, Jang, & Vernon, 1998; Paris, 1993; Plomin, Owen, & McGuffin, 1994; South et al., 2017). The venerable trait tradition was influenced by psychobiological ideas of Eysenck (1963), and the prominent Big Five personality theories connect to neuroscience (e.g., DeYoung, 2015). Similarly, Crowell, Beauchaine, and Linehan (2009) formulate borderline PD as a biosocial disorder of emotional dysregulation. The construct of borderline PD hyperbolic temperament (e.g., Zanarini & Frankenburg 1997) has neurobiological referents (Stanley, Perez-Rodriguez, Labouliere, & Roose, in press, 2018). Millon (1994; 2016) formulated his conception of PD within evolutionary theory. Wakefield's (2006) concept of harmful dysfunction in PD also is developed with reference to evolutionary theory. The premature closing down of normal processes of social learning (epistemic petrification), considered by Fonagy and colleagues (2015) to be the common core of PD, is construed as an evolutionarily human (mal-) adaption. In short, PD spans the middle ground (Kagan, 2009) between the neurobiological and the narrative-psychological bookends of the explanatory spectrum. Like Jaspers (1913/1997), Markova and Berrios (2012) argued psychopathology must use hybrid concepts that bridge neurobiology and the interpretive realm (see also Kendler, 2008). In the AMPD, Criterion B, the pathological personality traits is the domain wherein neurobiology may be most applicable, although the empirical overlap between A and B suggests its influence is likely a matter of degree. Recalling Kendler's (2008; 2015) argument that biological findings in psychopathology require back-translation to the psychological realm, neurobiological aspects of Criterion B need to be similarly viewed.

An early example of an essentialist approach to PD that links the biological and psychological-subjective realms is Meehl's (1962) conception of *schizotypy*. Meehl (1962) argued for the reality of a taxon (schizotaxia) which manifests in a phenotypic personality organization he called schizotypy which, under certain deleterious conditions, may decompensate to schizophrenia. Schizotypy resembles the contemporary diagnosis of schizotypal PD (SZT), and has been studied extensively (Lenzenweger, 2010; 2015). Some research affirms a taxon structure (Haslam, Holland, & Kuppens, 2012). In the AMPD, SZT PD is defined by elevations in (four of six) trait-facets of cognitive and perceptual dysregulation, unusual beliefs and experiences, eccentricity, restricted affectivity, withdrawal, and/or suspiciousness. An interesting avenue for future investigation is to clarify connections between the putative taxon of schizotypy (including its dimensional characterization) and the dimensional AMPD. Addendum B at the end of this chapter shows an AMPD-profile of schizotypy developed by characterizing Meehl's (1964) clinically rich schizotypic indicators with AMPD Criterion B trait-facets.

Although Meehl (1986) argued for the reality of essentialism (and taxon structure) in psychopathology, he emphasized that this likely applied to only a few areas of psychopathology such as schizophrenia, autism, and bipolar disorder. For PD, Meehl (1986, p. 228) excepted the Cleckley (1955) psychopath and the obsessive-compulsive disorder spectrum and declared that only one rubric was needed: "psychoneurosis, mixed"—analogous to the proverbial "personality disorder, not otherwise specified." He argued personality psychopathology is best viewed quantitatively, in terms of degree and dimension. He said, "In the long run, it may be worth the trouble to teach clinicians to think more dimensionally than categorically and mold their verbal and inferential habits in those directions" (Meehl, 1986, p. 229). In this way, one might say he presaged the AMPD.

Prototypes

The prototype approach to PD seeks to differentiate from a natural-science-based categorical model PD diagnosis but retains certain conveniences of category concepts. Prototype categories are partially dimensionalized (Livesley, 1985; 1991). Individuals are evaluated for degree of resemblance to an ideal type or exemplar diagnosis. Notably, pre-DSM-III (APA, 1980) diagnoses implicitly used a prototype model. The utility of the prototype approach finds support from studies in cognitive psychology that show people naturally "think with categories" (Cantor, Smith, French, & Mezzich, 1980; Medin, 1989). Schwartz, Wiggins, and Norko (1989) suggested the term *ideal type* is conceptually richer than prototypicality, which refers to degree of resemblance. Contemporary argument and evidence for the utility traditional categorical diagnosis often draws on prototypes. Gunderson, Links, and Reich (1991) suggested that severe PDs lend themselves to categorization, and milder PDs may be viewed dimensionally because they are closer to normalcy. Westen (2012) and Westen, Shedler, Bradley, and DeFife, (2012) argued the prototype approach is especially helpful for the identificatory function of making a clinical diagnosis. In this regard, it is important to remember the act of clinical diagnosis is different than scientific validation of psychiatric classifications (Keeley, 2015).

Westen, Shedler, and Bradley (2006) developed a psychometric prototype model for PD diagnosis in the *Shedler–Westen Assessment Procedure* (*SWAP*; Shedler & Westen, 2007; Westen & Shedler, 1999). Spitzer, First, Shedler, Westen, and Skodol (2008) argued prototype approaches possess inherent clinical utility. But, the prototype approach has seen strong critique. Wakefield (2012) observed that cognitive psychology shows people use implicit causal models, not prototypicality, in making diagnoses (e.g., Kim & Ahn, 2002), and false positive diagnoses are likely to increase with prototypes. Many have questioned the conceptual status, reliability, and clinical implementation of a template-matching psychiatric nosology (Jablensky, 2012; Zimmerman, 2011). Verheul (2005) viewed prototypes as hybrid concepts because they profile categories dimensionally. They offer increased utility but fall short of the potential of full dimensionalization. In this regard, Keeley (2015) emphasized that ontological assumptions are implicit in how nosological constructs are measured. Keeley cited Wittgenstein (1975, p. 67): "show me how you are searching and I will tell you what you are looking for." For example, if a structured interview for psychiatric diagnosis queries for presence or absence of a diagnostic indicator (symptom), most basically, a nominal scale of measurement (Stevens, 1946) and categorical model are implied (Keeley, 2015). Cumulating observations permits the application of psychometric analyses, but it also cloaks the categorical aspect of prototype diagnosis and does not change the nature of the underlying construct. Prototype models, despite apparently advantageous metrics, remain basically categorical. Importantly, clinical utility studies have supported prototype models (e.g., Spitzer, First, Shedler, Westen, & Skodol, 2008), and psychometric analyses show that numerous, fine-grained and meaningful factor dimensions of PD pathology can be discerned in prototype assessment (Blagov, Bi, Shedler, & Westen, 2012). Yet, if the object of inquiry is not construed as a taxon, the prototype approach remains a cognitive convenience. Prototypes are approximations which dovetail with cognitive predilection and clinical tradition, but they offer less scientific verisimilitude. Nonetheless, in certain contexts (e.g., clinical practice; see Herpertz et al., 2017), some regard them as sufficient, if imperfect.

There is a potential hidden risk with prototype models. The cognitive ease of prototypes invites causalist and essentialist assumptions, including those of a hard-medical model, and reification. This conceptual slippery slope can introduce (unintended) cognitive biases such as the availability, anchor, and representativeness heuristics (Tversky & Kahneman, 1974). In contrast, the AMPD algorithm requires the metrics of both Criterion A and B to be explicitly articulated. It may not be as "easy" as a categorical diagnosis, in part because it recruits Type II deliberative cognition in addition to fast and generally accurate Type I thinking (Kahneman, 2011) as might be used in exemplar-based prototype diagnosis. In this way, the AMPD might decrease cognitive errors in diagnostic decision making (Croskerry, 2003). This is another line of research awaiting study.

Delineating Paradigm, Construct, and Indicator in Criterion A and B

A nosology strikes a compromise between wide coverage of psychopathology and delineating elements which can be reliably identified in practice (Blashfield & Draguns, 1976). The AMPD likewise must balance comprehensive coverage with the degree of granularity of the PD constructs represented by indicators, and they need to foster practical goals such as efficiency, acceptance, and ease of use. Examining the components of the AMPD, Criterion A and B, with the heuristic scheme offered by McAdams and Pals (2006) illustrates ways these concerns are addressed by the personality indicators, constructs, and paradigms of the model. Different saturations of dispositional traits, characteristic adaptations, and narrative identity personality constructs presumably inhere in Criterion A and B. Jointly, they cover a very broad spectrum of PD constructs, and individually they are informed by partly separable nomological networks and relative influences of certain paradigms of personality assessment (Waugh et al., 2017).

Criterion A (LPFS) delineates four domains of Identity, Self-Direction, Empathy, and Intimacy. Criterion B has five broad trait domains and twenty-five trait-facets. These constituents of the AMPD overlap conceptually and empirically. This overlap is unavoidable for several reasons. First, the subject is the disorder of personality, and personality is a holistic system. Nosological distinctions have practical functions such as clinical diagnosis and documentation in addition to the construct validity goal of (proverbially) carving nature at its joints. This means there is a degree of artifice in such distinctions. In addition, from a factor analytic point of view, personality and PD do not show simple structure (Krueger & Markon, 2014). Going further, Loevinger (1994, p. 6) challenged some assumptions of this approach, saying: "nature is (not) constrained to present us a world in rows and columns…convenient… (for) the statistical programs already installed on our computers." This also reminds us we are dealing with a map, not territory. The phenomena of interest are abstracted and to some degree collapsed, as a guide to that which it refers. How and to what extent these abstractions are collapsed depends on our purposes and presumptions. Insofar as different paradigms are represented in the AMPD, the lens of one paradigm may see similarity, while that of another may see difference within the elements of the AMPD. With these caveats in mind, we consider Criterion A and B.

Criterion A

Criterion A (LPFS) draws on attachment, object relations, and social-cognitive personality and PD theories (Bender et al., 2011). Very generally, this conceptual heritage tilts to characteristic adaptation and narrative identity constructs. In this regard, note that attachment, object relations, and social-cognitive developmental study often utilize performance assessment measures. For example, reflective functioning traditionally is assessed by indicators from the *strange situation paradigm* (Ainsworth, Blehar, Waters, & Wall, 2015). Object relations constructs can be assessed with

Rorschach object representation indices (e.g., Mutuality of Autonomy [MOA]; Urist, 1977), rating narrative descriptions of key figures as in the Object Relations Inventory (ORI; Huprich et al., 2016), and by the Social Cognition and Object Relations Scale-Global Rating Method (SCORS-G; Stein & Slavin-Mulford, 2017), using various types of narrative data, including stories from the Thematic Apperception Test (TAT). Criterion A may be assessed by other methods such as self-report (e.g., Huprich et al., in press, 2018; Morey, 2017), clinical ratings, and with respect to component constructs such as reflective functioning (mentalization) which have neurobiological underpinnings (Frith & Frith, 2003) and methods of assessment. In this regard, note that neuroimaging has shown that Rorschach human movement (M) responses are accompanied by mirror neuron activity (Giromini et al., in press, 2018; Porcelli & Kleiger, 2016). In this respect, multi-method assessment captures an important construct within Criterion A, and the construct overlaps (connects) psychobiological and interpretive or narrative realms (inferring mental states).

Criterion B

Very generally, Criterion B emphasizes personality constructs from the dispositional trait and characteristic adaptation domains. As noted, Criterion B originates from the lexical trait tradition, the Big Five (Goldberg, 1993), and quantitative personality and PD research (Markon, Krueger, & Watson, 2005). The pathological personality traits of Criterion B, like other prominent dimensional personality trait models (e.g., FFM; McCrae & Costa, 2008; Cybernetic Big Five; DeYoung, 2015) may lie closer to the psychobiological end of the conceptual spectrum. Criterion B can be examined from the perspectives of social neuroscience. Notably, Kernberg (2016) argued the seven affective neuroscience domains described by Panksepp (2004) dovetail with the pathological personality traits. Panksepp (2004) delineated key affective systems, conserved across social mammals, in which certain neural regions, neurotransmitters, and behavioral predispositions are coordinated. They are termed SEEKING, RAGE, FEAR, LUST, CARE, GRIEF, and PLAY (Panksepp & Biven, 2012). These basic affective-motivational systems are implicated in a variety of psychiatric conditions. With respect to PD, the GRIEF system, for example, is figural in borderline PD (Kernberg, 2016; Panksepp & Biven, 2012). This is the system that signals social need, drives attachment bonds, generates separation distress, and may underlie the psychic pain of experiences of abandonment. Many psychiatric (and PD) disorders may represent permutations of endophenotypes traceable to affective neuroscience systems such as these (Panksepp & Biven, 2012). Similar points of view are used in other psychobiological dimensional PD models (e.g., Depue & Lenzenweger, 2001; Cloninger, 1987), and they are increasingly supported by results from empirical study of personality traits and neurobiological variables (e.g., DeYoung, Hirsh, Shane, Papademetris, Rajeevan, & Gray, 2010).

Because Criterion B is aligned with the psychometric trait approach, self-report and observer-report methods are well-suited for assessment of its dimensions (e.g., PID-5 self and informant report forms). This facilitates study of Criterion B with trait and neuroscience methods (DeYoung, Carey, Krueger, & Ross, 2016). Like Criterion A, multi-method assessment applies to Criterion B. This includes self- and informant-report, experimental methods, behavior genetic (South et al., 2017; Wright, Pahlen, & Krueger, 2017), and neurobiological approaches (James, Engdahl, Leuthold, Krueger, & Georgopoulos, 2015). Despite the apparent psychobiological emphasis of Criterion B, psychodynamic constructs are also represented. Widiger (2015), for example, demonstrated that several personality features conceptualized in psychodynamic terms could be captured with the pathological personality traits. Similarly, Panksepp and Biven (2012) argued for the advantage of formulating psychodynamics with respect to their seven affective neuroscience systems—as in the mini-paradigm of neuropsychoanalysis.

Overlap and Difference: Separation Insecurity

The pathological trait-facet of *separation insecurity* exemplifies how paradigm, construct, and assessment interweave across Criterion A and B. Note the domain of Intimacy in Criterion A invokes the psychodynamics of separation issues (e.g., "Relationships are based on a strong belief in the absolute need for the intimate other('s) …expectations of abandonment…"; DSM-5 [APA, 2013], p. 777). The construct of abandonment anxiety is figural in psychodynamic approaches to certain PDs, particularly borderline personality organization (Kernberg, 1967; Masterson, 1981) and borderline PD (Gunderson, 2009b). Psychodynamic therapies are often recommended for borderline PD (Clarkin, Levy, Lenzenweger, & Kernberg, 2007; Gunderson, 2009a). In addition, many performance assessment measures, including those within the conceptual heritage of the LPFS such as the ORI and SCORS-G, are used to assess problems in separation and psychological differentiation. Evaluating an individual's performance across levels of structure in assessment (Acklin, 1993; Allison, Blatt, & Zimet, 1968; Singer & Larson, 1981) and in psychotherapy (Clarkin, Cain, & Livesley, 2015; Kernberg, 1967; Masterson, 1981;) is an important strategy to gauge personality vulnerability associated with separation insecurity. In sum, although placed in Criterion B, the pathological personality trait of separation insecurity is closely connected theoretically and technically to the psychodynamic paradigm. Yet, as noted above, separation insecurity also links to psychobiological concepts, empirical referents, and can be assessed as a psychometric trait. Panksepp (2004) established that separation distress and social attachment are tightly coupled in the GRIEF affective neuroscience system. Fonagy et al., (2015) developed a comprehensive, heuristic account of PD integrating attachment theory and social neuroscience (as extended in Fonagy, Luyten, Allison, & Campbell, 2017). In the language of McAdams and Pals (2006), the trait-facet of separation insecurity encompasses psychobiological correlates, behavioral dispositions, and motivational patterns of agentic adaption. It also draws on the domain of narrative identity. This is reflected in the Identity domain within the LPFS as well as the historically important role of identity disturbance in borderline PD (Fuchs, 2007; Kernberg, 1967; Wilkinson-Ryan & Westen, 2000) and in empirical findings. For example, Adler (2013) found that the verbalizations of psychotherapy patients with borderline PD diagnoses reflected changes in narrative identity themes prior to symptom change. Thus, from multiple points of view, the trait of separation insecurity is expected to overlap with Criterion A. This has been found in many empirical studies (e.g., Few and colleagues, 2013). The Zimmermann and colleagues (2015) factor analyses of measures of Criterion A and B speak to this issue. Separation insecurity loaded highly on a dimension dominated by Criterion A variables. Zimmermann and colleagues (2015) discussed distinctions (and lack of distinctions) between Criterion A and B constructs and suggested that Criterion A may *explain* (the how) the *expression* (the what) of Criterion B trait variables. To this, in the language of McAdams and Pals (2006), one might also add the *who* of narrative identity in Criterion A and in the trait of separation insecurity.

Overlap and Difference: Anhedonia, Distractibility, and Impulsivity

Consider the Criterion B trait-facets of *anhedonia, distractibility,* and *impulsivity.* Anhedonia refers to decreased ability to experience pleasure or positive affect. This trait-construct is viewed as neuropsychiatrically mediated (Der-Avakian & Markou, 2012), figures prominently in Meehl's (1962) conception of schizotypy, and it can be linked to Panksepp and Biven's (2012) affective systems of (downregulated) CARE and PLAY. Distractibility refers to disturbance in attention regulation mediated by neuropsychological processes (Posner & Petersen, 1990). Similarly, impulsivity has a strong neuropsychological and neuropsychiatric basis (Cloninger et al., 1993). Note, however, the contrast between these pathological personality traits and the domains of Identity and Intimacy in Criterion A. These include broad psychosocial constructs of interpersonal boundary functioning and the psychodynamics of self-esteem regulation.

Interpersonal boundary dysfunction involves behavior and vulnerability reflected in internalized object representational processes, presumably developed in relation to adverse early experiences (Benjamin, 1996; Luyten, Lowyck, & Blatt, 2017). Regarding impairment in self-esteem regulation, consider narcissistic-spectrum pathology (Kohut, 1977). In such impairment, behavior which does not match the individual's subjective experience may occur (Ronningstam, 2014; 2017). If the sense of self is challenged (wounded), dispositional traits (associated with un-challenged self-regard) may disorganize. Anxiety and shame may flood the (injured) sense of self, fragmenting self-experience and producing explosive rage and distortions in reasoning (e.g., "sliding of meanings," Horowitz, 1975). This occurs in the service of restoring the fragile self, and the conscious self-concept remains inflated (Horowitz, 2009) despite behavior inconsistent with the self-concept.

Comparing the trait-facets of anhedonia, distractibility, and impulsivity with the Criterion A suggests different levels of abstraction underpin the constructs. Interestingly, Zimmermann and colleagues (2015) found that anhedonia and distractibility generally aligned with different factor dimensions than those with Criterion A. In reference to the AMPD, Kernberg (2012) ascribed neurobiological referents to Criterion B traits and viewed Criterion A as a psychostructural dimension of subjective personality processes. Kernberg (2012) furthermore suggested Criterion A may inform general psychotherapeutic strategy (see also Clarkin et al., 2015; Hopwood, 2018). Similarly, tactics of psychotherapy such as developing specific treatment targets might be guided by assessment of Criterion B traits (Bach, Markon, Simonsen, & Krueger, 2015; Hopwood, 2018).

One or Many Personality Disorder Nosologies?

The dimensionalization of diagnosis the AMPD offers the field of PD is a major distinction from traditional (categorical) approaches. Nonetheless, this is not unique to the AMPD. There are several other dimensional approaches to PD with which the AMPD competes for scientific and clinical acceptance. These are briefly noted below.

Livesley (1998) has long advocated for a dimensional model of PD and developed a psychometric instrument for PD, the Dimensional Assessment of Personality Pathology (DAPP; Livesley & Jackson, 2009). The FFM has substantial connections with PD models (Costa & Widiger, 1994; Lynam & Widiger, 2001; Samuel & Widiger, 2010) and has spawned several PD-specific psychometric inventories (e.g., Widiger, Lynam, Miller, & Oltmanns, 2012). Recently, Bagby and Widger (2018) provided an overview of numerous PD scales based on the FFM tradition. Simms and colleagues (2011) developed a dimensional trait PD model accompanied by a psychometric instrument, the Computerized Adaptive Assessment of Personality Disorder (CAT-25) which enjoys increasing use. Crego and Widiger (2016) compared convergent and divergent relationships between FFM-based, PID-5, and CAT-25 dimensional measures of PD. Similarly, Berghuis and colleagues (2017) reported on points of convergence between the AMPD and the DAPP. Oltmanns and Widiger (2018) described a dimensional assessment of PD for the forthcoming World Health Organization International Classification of Diseases. Millon and Strack (2015) conceptualized PDs as spectra of personality dysfunction. Although this scheme employs dimensionalized prototypes, it moves closer to the dimensional paradigm. Suzuki, Griffin, and Samuel (2017) examined the nomological networks associated with the FFM and AMPD Criterion B and concluded they are quite similar. These reports indicate dimensional assessment of PD is receiving strong interest.

What does the advance of the dimensional paradigm mean for categorical diagnosis? A quick answer is that categorical diagnosis has served out its usefulness and will soon become a relic. Yet, there may be a place for the traditional paradigm of DSM-5, Section II (APA, 2013). Recall that Chang (2017), from the perspective of philosophy of science, argued that competing nosological paradigms can operate on parallel tracks. In this way, different paradigms serve the goal of epistemic iteration, a process which occurs in all fields of science. On a practical level, explicitly comparing PD models with respect to external variables of interest to clinicians, for example, should help in transferring knowledge gained from studies of traditional PDs. Maintaining a dual-track analysis of PD paradigms (cross-model comparisons) may help to alleviate concerns expressed over new PD models (e.g., Herpertz et al., 2017; Shedler et al., 2010), including over the pace of nosological revision (Kendler & Solomon, 2016). Studies like those of Bach and Sellbom (2016) and Evans and Simms (2018) mapped cross-model connections between categorical and dimensional diagnosis of PD in borderline PD. Similarly, Morey, Benson, and Skodol (2016) characterized DSM-IV (APA, 1994) PDs with the AMPD using clinician ratings. Their study produced AMPD prototype configurations associated with traditional PD diagnoses, effectively cross-walking the two PD paradigms. Mulay and colleagues (in press) used these Morey and colleagues (2016) AMPD-prototypes as convergent and discriminant validators for newly developed MMPI-2 (Hathaway et al., 1989) PD Spectra Scales. Waugh, Bishop, and Schmidt (this volume) applied the Morey and colleagues (2016) AMPD-prototypes to bootstrap interpretation of the assessment data across diagnostic models in two case studies involving complex differential diagnosis. Strickland and colleagues (in press, 2018) explored empirical connections between the categorical PD model (assessed by interview) and the dimensional AMPD (assessed by the self-report PID-5 [APA, 2013]). They showed the PD models and measures have areas of convergence, but they offer unique contributions as well.

The Psychodynamic Diagnostic Manual-2 (PDM-2; Lingiardi, & McWilliams, 2017) is an alternative psychiatric nosology that integrates psychodynamic concepts with descriptive psychiatry, aspiring to redress perceived limitations of the traditional DSM approach for clinical practice and research (Lingiardi et al., 2015). Diagnosis in the PDM-2 employs a prototype classification model and assesses three axes. PD is assessed on the P axis, covering both style and level of personality organization. In this respect, partitioning style and level of personality organization, the

PDM-2 resembles the AMPD distinctions between Criterion A and B. However, the PDM-2 organizes personality styles via psychodynamic personality constructs which appear partly overlapping and correlated, as opposed to the multivariate dimensional approach of Criterion B. The PDM-2 uses five to six key concerns (e.g., central constitutional maturation pattern, central affects, characteristic pathogenic belief about the self, etc.) to characterize its 12 PDs. These are designed to include the neurobiological end of the explanatory spectrum (e.g., genetics; affective systems) in PD diagnosis, but the emphasis is on subjective experience, internalized interpersonal relations, and adaptive processes of coping and defending. The PDM-2 thus seems to focus on the personality domains of characteristic adaptation and narrative identity (with dispositional traits invoked in central constitutional maturation patterns). In terms of personality assessment paradigms (i.e., Wiggins, 2003), the psychodynamic, personological, and interpersonal paradigms are more strongly represented. Although the PDM-2 seeks to differentiate from the paradigm of descriptive psychiatry found in the DSM-IV (APA, 1994), it retains the syndrome categorical structure for diagnoses. The extent to which traditional DSM-IV categorical PD diagnoses and the AMPD may be cross-walked with the PDM-2 remains to be determined.

Some approaches to PD combine dimensional and categorical models of PD. As noted, prototype models implicitly implement this approach. Multivariate statistical methods also can be used to combine dimensional and categorical conceptions. Lenzenweger, Clarkin, Yeomans, Kernberg, and Levy (2008) combined mixture-modeling techniques and theoretical analysis in the study of variables associated with borderline PD. They found three groupings of borderline PD correlates that cross-validated on external criteria. These corresponded to persons with low levels of aggression and paranoia, a second grouping dominated by paranoid features, and a third with elevated aggressive and antisocial features. Smits and colleagues (2017) found similar results from a cluster analysis of symptom, personality, and life data variables in a sample of borderline PD patients. Hallquist and Pilkonis (2012) combined dimensional and latent class analyses of borderline PD symptoms and found four meaningful groupings (resembling the results of both studies noted above). On this basis, they concluded that a hybrid categorical and dimensional model offers potential. Conceptually, Borsboom and colleagues (2016) argued the distinction between category and dimension itself may lie on a continuum, and people may show individual differences in the degree to which psychological constructs are represented by categorical and continual properties. In other words, psychopathology may require different and nuanced psychometric modeling approaches. In sum, methodologically rigorous studies such as Lenzenweger and colleagues (2008) suggest that combining dimensional and categorical analysis may have a place in PD nosology. In this regard, it is noteworthy that AMPD diagnosis can be expressed in a hybrid categorical-dimensional format.

An important issue in PD nosology is allegiance to paradigms. The tenacity with which adherents of a paradigm hold to views is a major dynamic of the Kuhnian paradigm. Using Terror Management Theory (TMT; Greenberg, Solomon, & Pyszczynski, 1997), Elad-Strenger (2013) called attention to the personal dimensions of allegiance to a paradigm (by both clinician and investigator). Elad-Strenger (2013) pointed out that new paradigms present an emotional challenge to world views of the clinician and the researcher. The challenge is not only to the pride accompanying investment in a paradigm. As formalized in TMT, challenge to one's paradigm elicits epistemological anxiety akin to the existential fear of death (Becker, 1973). Greenwald (1980) described very similar and applicable ideas in the notion of the *totalitarian ego*. He identified the workings of Kuhnian paradigm dynamics in all self-organizing structures. Self-organizing structures include scientific theories, social institutions, business corporations, and individual personalities. As such, each of these organizations seeks self-preservation and they marshal resources against threats to self-identity. In other words, we cling to that which we hold dear. These dynamics also apply to PD nosology.

These issues are clearly alive in debates among clinicians and researchers over preferred models of PD. On this matter, Kendler (2005) declared that the unproductive battle of paradigms must end in the mental health disciplines. This is a worthwhile scientific mantra, but it is likely to be aspirational because scientists and clinicians are human. The pluralism of contemporary philosophy of science (Cartwright, 2004) recommended for psychiatric nosology (Chang, 2017) is one guide to this aspiration. Pluralism is the bottom-line message Wiggins (2003) offered for personality assessment. Jaspers (1913/1997) reminded us our classifications are "provisional fictions." Moreover, Kuhn (1962/2012, p. 12) cautioned, "all past beliefs about nature sooner or later turn out to be false." Our earlier discussion of the case of Ellen West illustrated the limitations of doctrinaire thinking and, importantly, that history reveals our theories have not secured truth.

To the extent dimensional models of PD fulfill the promise of paradigm change, however, it is likely traditional categorical approaches will wane. This is the sociological fate of Kuhnian paradigms. The physicist Max Planck (1950, p. 97) put it this way:

> An important scientific innovation rarely makes its way rapidly winning over and converting its opponents; it rarely happens that Saul becomes Paul. What does happen is that its opponents gradually die out and that the growing generation is familiarized with the idea from the beginning.

Empirically Charting Paradigms and Construct in the AMPD

Mulay and colleagues (in press, 2018) studied clinicians' evaluations of the AMPD for paradigms of personality assessment (Wiggins, 2003) and types of personality constructs (McAdams & Pals, 2006). Noting the LPFS has four domains (Identity, Self-Direction, Empathy, and Intimacy), and within each domain there are three subdomain headings (each rated on a five-point metric), a 60-item scale was fashioned from the LPFS. Zimmermann and colleagues (2015) also formatted the LPFS in this manner to analyze the dimensionality of the AMPD. Then, the 60 items of the LPFS and the 25 Criterion B trait-facets were pooled and randomized, and nine knowledgeable raters evaluated each element for degree of representation of the five personality assessment paradigms, three personality construct types, and level of inference of the item. Rater agreement on paradigm and construct type was strong. The mean Intraclass Correlation Coefficient (ICC; 2, 9) for rating the AMPD with these dimensions was .81 (range of .66 to .91). For Criterion A, the mean ICC was .73 (range .50 to .90), and for B it was .80 (range .73 to .95).

Results showed that Criterion A was viewed as significantly representing the psychodynamic and personological paradigms, the narrative identity construct-type, and a higher level of inference (see Figure 1.2). In contrast, Criterion B showed a predominance of the multivariate and empirical paradigms and the dispositional trait construct. Importantly, Criterion A and B did not differ on the interpersonal paradigm and on the dimension of characteristic adaptation. Thus, although Criterion A and B were viewed as emphasizing different configurations of paradigms and personality constructs, the full AMPD was saturated with the interpersonal paradigm and characteristic adaptation construct. These findings highlight the degree to which PD is understood to be (1) fundamentally

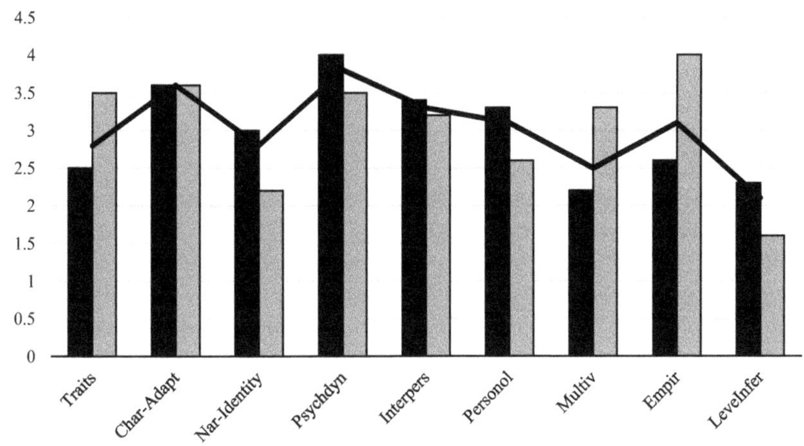

Figure 1.2. Paradigm and construct representation ratings of LPFS, traits, and full AMPD. Dark bar = LPFS; light bar = traits; line = full AMPD. LPFS & traits significantly differed ($p < .002$ or less) except for characteristic adaptation & interpersonal. One-way ANOVA yielded these effect sizes: η^2 = .44, 0, .32, .11, .01, .27, .48, .60, .42). Selected data and figure adapted from Mulay et al. (in press, 2018).

interpersonal in nature (Hopwood, Wright, Ansell, & Pincus, 2013), and (2) reflect processes of maladaptation (characteristic adaptation) to individuals' psychobiological constitution and idiosyncratic social history.

The Big Picture

Viewing the AMPD as a map brings issues of construct validity, types of validators, nomological net, and utility to the fore. As a map, the AMPD minimizes literalism (formative measurement) in PD diagnosis, a risk to which the modern DSMs (Andreasen, 2006; Hyman, 2010) are prone. Instead, the AMPD is composed from diagnostic constructs—with surplus meanings (Morey, 1991) implied by its indicators. These indicators can be multimethod: clinician ratings, self-reports, performance assessment, and neuropsychiatric measurements. Because this map offers several routes to reach the destination of PD diagnosis, the AMPD is more than a diagnostic algorithm. It is an empirically-supported, pluralistic PD model which may be used to chart individual differences both across and within persons and situations (Hopwood, Zimmermann, Pincus, & Krueger, 2015).

The AMPD can also be viewed as a heuristic in the manner of Fonagy and colleagues (2015) and the concept of epistemic petrification in PD. Note that the AMPD organizes broad PD constructs, realizable in multiple types of data and methods (Hopwood & Bornstein, 2014). It also guides treatment planning (Bach et al., 2015; Clarkin, et al., 2015; Hopwood, 2018; Rodriguez-Seijas, Eaton, & Krueger, 2015). The pluralism of the AMPD is congruent with current philosophy of science (Cartwright, 2011). Furthermore, the breadth of personality constructs and paradigms within the AMPD means there is no privileged measurement model or investigative strategy. Given its origins within major paradigms and traditions in the field, many investigators and practitioners will find portions of the model familiar, even if organized in a novel way. Collectively, these features confer conceptual, methodological, and pedagogic advantages. In turn, this ultimately contributes to clinical utility.

The AMPD may be framed within the ideas (and spirit) of the psychotherapy integration movement (Norcross & Goldfried, 2005; Stricker & Gold, 2013). Psychotherapy integration identifies four general modes of bringing together different psychotherapies. These are: (1) analysis of what is common among psychotherapies (*common factors*), (2) strategically combining psychotherapy approaches (*technical eclecticism*), (3) conceptually framing different psychotherapies within a preferred paradigm (*assimilative integration*), and (4) comprehensively synthesizing psychotherapies (*theoretical integration*). The AMPD most resembles the approach of technical eclecticism because no paradigm is privileged. But, the AMPD also incorporates the common factors approach. This is reflected most directly in the primary factor dimension of the AMPD, Criterion A (and its empirical overlap with Criterion B). Conceptually, this is the common core of PD considered by Fonagy and colleagues (2015) to represent maladaptive failures in trust and openness to social learning. The AMPD also can be used in the manner of assimilative integration. This occurs when, for example, a psychodynamic clinician formulates AMPD trait information within psychodynamic ideas. Widiger (2015) provided a converse illustration of assimilative integration, framing psychodynamic constructs within the AMPD trait paradigm. To the extent the AMPD remains ecumenical with respect to both Criterion A and B, it is unlikely to achieve the aspiration of theoretical integration, at least as described in the psychotherapy integration movement. The comprehensive theory of personality and PD developed by Theodore Millon (Millon & Strack, 2015) aspires to such integration. However, the AMPD may approach this status, in a limited way, in the treatment planning heuristic put forth by Clarkin and colleagues (2015). They traced connections between personality constructs in the AMPD and principles underlying diverse psychotherapeutic modalities. From this basis, Clarkin and colleagues (2015) suggested the AMPD can serve as overarching template to guide selection, timing, and implementation of different tactics of psychotherapeutic intervention.

A set of literary metaphors lends a broad view to the AMPD. Discussing world literature and the idea of personal identity, Rorty (1976, p. 302) suggested:

> *Characters* are to be delineated; their traits are sketched; they are not presumed to be strictly unified. They appear in novels by Dickens, not those by Kafka. *Figures* appear in cautionary tales, exemplary novels and hagiography. They present narratives of types of lives to be imitated. *Selves* are possessors of their properties. *Individuals* are centers of integrity; their rights are inalienable. *Presences* are descendants of souls; they are evoked rather than represented, to be found in novels by Dostoyevsky, not those by Jane Austen.

The AMPD is a psychiatric nosology for PD. Its coverage of all that the idea of person conveys is necessarily limited. That which Dostoyevsky has to say about the human condition is not found in any nosology. Yet, the AMPD recalls Theophrastus' *Characters* (Bennet & Hammond, 1902), perhaps in the manner of Charles Dickens and Jane Austen. Along these lines, Hopwood and Waugh (this volume) used the AMPD trait-facets to portray characters from literary fiction. Rorty's (1976) evocations of *Selves* and *Individuals* also find purchase in the AMPD. This is because the model does not shy away from more fuzzy constructs like interpersonal boundary dysfunction and narrative identity—which invoke subjectivity, personhood, and agency. In short, the AMPD is a nosology of disorders of *personality*, reminding us our focus (albeit more limited) on the person shares visons also conveyed in literature.

The AMPD dimensionalizes PD diagnosis consistent with the broad goals of the DSM-5 (APA, 2013; Regier et al., 2009) and embraces the metaphor of a psychological test (Blashfield & Livelsey, 1991). In fact, self-report psychological instruments are intimately associated with the AMPD as in the PID-5 (APA, 2013) for Criterion B, and the LPFS-SR (Morey, 2017) and DLOPF (Huprich et al., in press, 2018) for Criterion A. Being a construct-oriented model, other psychological assessments may be used in AMPD diagnosis, and clinician formulation likely will be the most common way the AMPD is applied. The bridging of diagnosis and psychometrics in the AMPD resembles the DSM-5 diagnoses of intellectual disability, specific learning disorder, and neurocognitive disorder in that these diagnoses reference standardized quantitative assessment procedures. In this regard, Markon (2013) critiqued the authoritative, professional-guild aspect of traditional DSM nosology and argued linking psychometrics and psychiatric nosology would advance its scientific status. The AMPD may contribute to this vision.

The dimensionalization of the AMPD is an important step, but the reach of the AMPD is longer. Its pluralism minimizes risks of paradigmatic myopia. In other words, the AMPD helps us avoid the quixotic "boojum" of Lewis Carroll's (1876/1981) *The hunting of the snark*. The Baedeker of the AMPD is a scientific and clinical heuristic that adds value beyond traditional approaches to PD, as detailed in the chapters to follow.

Highlights of the AMPD

- Psychiatric nosology is provisional
- Psychiatric nosology is affected by historical, social, cultural, political, professional, and scientific trends
- The AMPD is a map of PD
- The AMPD embraces conceptual and methodological pluralism
- The AMPD is construct-oriented, not criteria-constituted
- The AMPD returns personality and its nomological net to PD
- AMPD personality constructs vary in abstraction and may favor certain methods
- The AMPD is amenable to multi-method personality assessment
- Criterion A and B reflect varying paradigms of personality assessment
- The AMPD's inclusiveness and compatibility with clinical and scientific traditions imparts intrinsic clinical utility

Addendum A: Profiling Ellen West with the AMPD

Based on cited historical material and applying a psychobiographical approach, the author rated Ellen West with the AMPD. Figure 1.3 shows her trait-facet profile. Using the LPFS (rated 0–4), she was rated positive for PD with a Global LPFS of 2. Her LPFS domain ratings were: Identity 3, Self-Direction 1, Empathy 1, Intimacy 2. Criterion B trait-facets were

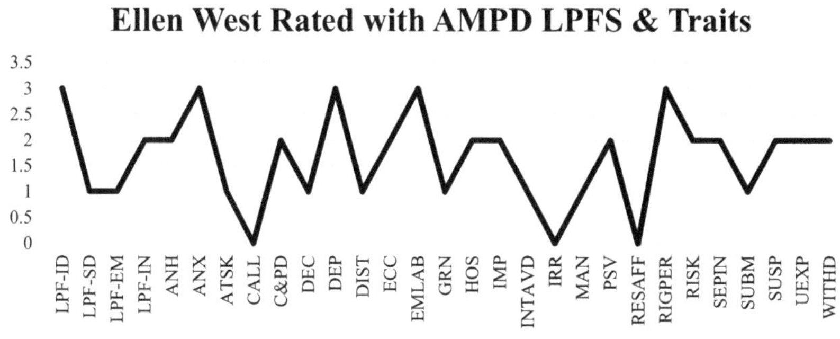

Figure 1.3. Author's rating of Ellen West with the LPFS domains and the 25 trait-facet ratings of the AMPD based on various sources.

rated 0–3. Applying the DSM-5 (APA, 2013), Section III hybrid categorical-dimensional algorithms to these results, she is positive for avoidant PD and borderline PD, and negative for obsessive-compulsive PD. Her AMPD diagnosis also can be stated as PD-TS with anxiousness, depressivity, emotional lability, & rigid perfectionism. Her trait-facet rating profile, when compared with the Morey and colleagues (2016) AMPD profiles associated with DSM-IV (APA, 2000) Criterion Count PD diagnoses, produced the following Pearson correlations: .42 avoidant PD, .08 schizoid PD, .29 borderline PD, -.03 paranoid PD, and .20 obsessive-compulsive PD. Note the modest association with DSM-IV borderline PD. In part, this result may reflect the importance of the trait-facet of rigid perfectionism for Ellen West, a feature not commonly considered prototypical of borderline PD. The relatively stronger correlation with DSM avoidant PD likely reflects the interpersonal sensitivity, withdrawal, and depression seen in her clinical history. The modest association with obsessive-compulsive PD likely derives from her elevated trait-facet of rigid perfectionism, but her emotional lability is not consistent with prototypical obsessive-compulsive PD. As a rough index of rater consistency, Ellen West was evaluated with the PID-5 Informant Report Form (IRF) 3 months after the initial clinical ratings were performed. The Pearson correlation between clinical ratings and the PID-5-IRF trait-facets was .83, suggesting good consistency over time and across two different metrics for the AMPD trait-facets (and yielding a very similar pattern of correlations with the Morey et al. [2016] DSM PD prototypes). These results provide an example of the descriptive utility of the AMPD as well as the advantage of the diagnosis of PD-TS.

Addendum B: Cross-Walking Schizotypy and the AMPD

Meehl's (1964) Checklist of Schizotypic Signs was characterized by the author with the AMPD trait-facets by consulting the detailed clinical

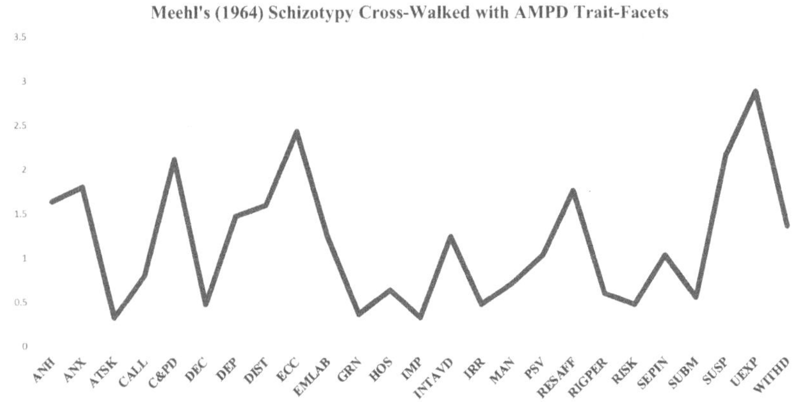

Figure 1.4. Meehl's (1964) Checklist of Schizotypic Signs cross-walked with the pathological personality trait-facets of the AMPD.

Manual (Meehl, 1964). Meehl explicates 25 clinically rich signs which are organized into a checklist rating format. The Checklist Signs can also be weighted with different values reflecting their presumed importance in schizotypy (P. Meehl, personal communication, 1979). Figure 1.4 shows the AMPD trait-profile determined by rating each Meehl (1964) *Sign* for the degree to which the 25 AMPD trait-facets are reflected within the *Sign*. In other words, each Sign was characterized by the suite of AMPD traits. Then, the differential weights for the Signs were applied to the AMPD ratings. Averaging these AMPD-ratings of the (Meehl-weighted) 25 Checklist Signs produced an "AMPD profile" of a generalized Meehl schizotype. Although these ratings were made by a single rater, the rater is very familiar with both the AMPD and the Meehl (1964) Checklist *Manual*, and a reliability estimation was done by repeating the entire procedure 3 months later. This produced a Pearson r of .94 for the ratings of Time 1 and Time 2.

The AMPD profile for schizotypy is positive for the DSM-5 (APA, 2013) Section III hybrid categorical-dimensional diagnosis of schizotypal PD. Applying the Morey and colleagues (2016) DSM PD to AMPD profile algorithms, the following Pearson correlations were found: .84 schizotypal PD; .51 schizoid PD; .39 avoidant PD. These results indicate Meehl's (1964) schizotypy closely corresponds to the AMPD hybrid categorical-dimensional diagnosis of schizotypal PD as well as the DSM-IV schizotypal PD. But, Meehl (1964) schizotypy also resembles the DSM-IV diagnosis of schizoid PD. Thus, Meehl's (1964) schizotypy, cross-walked with the AMPD and quantified with his differential weights (P. Meehl, personal communication, 1979), appears to be a blend of the diagnostic syndromes of schizotypal PD and schizoid PD. It should be noted that Meehl's (1964) *Manual* includes detailed, nuanced clinical observations reflecting his conception of the personality organization associated with schizotaxia which, when decompensated, purportedly results in schizophrenia (Meehl, 1962). This conception incorporates classical ideas from Kraepelin, Bleuler, and Rado and highlights personality traits and clinical signs considered relevant to the (potential but not inevitable) development of schizophrenia. Some Checklist indicators are at a very fine granular level, depicting features, signs, and symptoms narrower than the level of the factor hierarchy of the AMPD trait-facets.

Note

1 The author thanks Christopher J. Hopwood, Ph.D., Jared W. Keeley, Ph.D., Katherine A. Lenger, M.S., and Abby L. Mulay, Ph.D., for helpful comments on earlier versions of this chapter.

2 Paradigms of Personality Assessment and Level of Personality Functioning in Criterion A of the AMPD

Aaron L. Pincus and Michael J. Roche

Waugh and colleagues (2017) argued that the *Diagnostic and Statistical Manual of Mental Disorders, Fifth Edition* Alternative Model for Personality Disorders (DSM-5 AMPD; American Psychiatric Association, 2013) reflects an innovative pantheoretical integration of well-established, evidence-based paradigms of personality assessment (Hopwood & Waugh, in press; Wiggins, 2003). This facilitates professional training, comprehension, and acceptance of the AMPD as it allows clinicians of all backgrounds to recognize familiar clinical concepts and employ familiar measures to assess AMPD features (in addition to existing and emerging AMPD-specific instruments). This chapter furthers the effort to promote clinical use of the AMPD framework in personality assessment by articulating its assessment heritage and its fidelity with contemporary assessment paradigms. Specifically, we describe the interconnections between AMPD Criterion A and interpersonal (Pincus, Sadler, Woody, Roche, Thomas, & Wright, 2014), psychodynamic (Yeomans, Clarkin, & Kernberg, 2015), and personological (McAdams & Manczak, 2015) approaches to personality and its assessment.

AMPD Criterion A assesses the pathological personality features common to all personality disorders, defining general personality pathology in terms of impairments in "self" (identity, self-direction) and "interpersonal" (empathy, intimacy) functioning. Articulated as a set of dynamic regulatory and relational processes that are stratified from "no impairment" to "extreme impairment" in the DSM-5 Level of Personality Functioning Scale (LPFS), these impairments, and thus the core features of personality pathology, involve how individuals think and feel about themselves and others and how they relate to others (Bender, Morey, & Skodol, 2011). Although AMPD Criterion A semantics differentiates self and interpersonal impairments, the two are intertwined in diagnostic criteria such as "Depends excessively on others for identity, self-esteem, and emotion regulation with compromised boundaries"; "Hyper-attuned to others, but only with respect to perceived relevance to self" (APA, 2013), and the LPFS rightly renders a single severity rating. However, this single score reflects an integration of a vast array of clinical concepts that can be organized and fortified by multiple paradigms of personality assessment that focus on self and other.

DSM-5 AMPD Criterion A and Interpersonal Assessment

Interpersonal assessment employs numerous measures and methods to assess interpersonal dispositions and dynamic interpersonal processes (Pincus, 2010; Pincus, Sadler, et al., 2014). A unique strength of this approach is that the organizational metaframework of agency and communion (Wiggins, 1991) provides a common metric for defining and assessing the dispositional and dynamic constructs of interpersonal functioning at multiple levels ranging from broad interpersonal motives and goals to enduring interpersonal dispositions (e.g., traits, problems, efficacies, sensitivities, values) to specific and potentially variable interpersonal behaviors and relational patterns (Dawood, Dowgwillo, Wu, & Pincus, 2018; Pincus & Ansell, 2013). AMPD Criterion A impairments in self (identity, self-direction) and interpersonal (empathy, intimacy) functioning align themselves with agency and communion respectively (Pincus, 2011), the core meta-constructs of interpersonal personality theory (Figure 2.1).

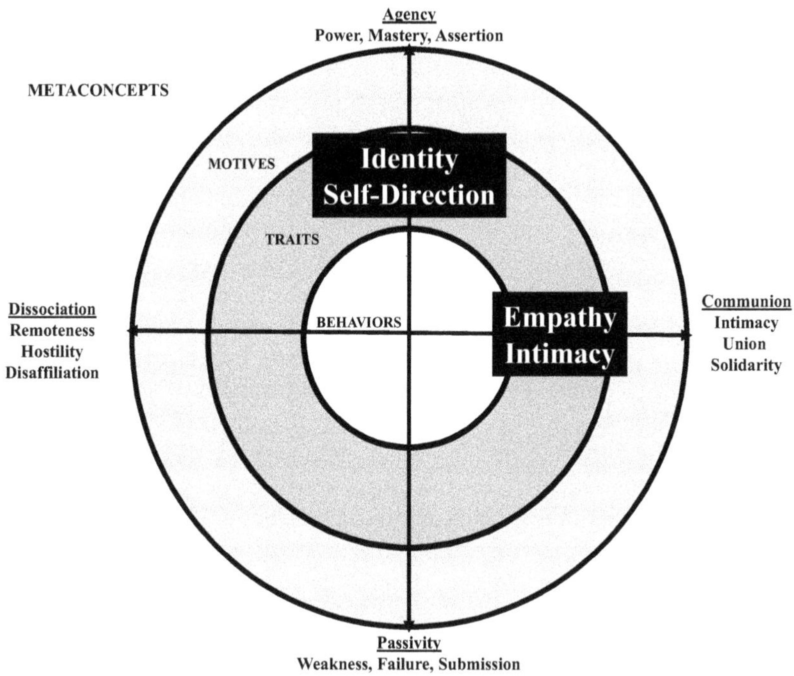

Figure 2.1. Criterion A aligns with Agency and Communion. From Pincus, A.L. (2011, p. 45). Some comments on nomology, diagnostic process, and narcissistic personality disorder in the DSM-5 proposal for personality and personality disorders. *Personality Disorders: Theory, Research, and Treatment, 2,* p. 45. Adapted with permission of the American Psychological Association.

Assessing Interpersonal Dispositions

Many interpersonal dispositions can be assessed using self- and informant-reports that conform to the 2-dimensional interpersonal circumplex model (Locke, 2011). The Interpersonal Adjective Scales (IAS; Wiggins, 1995) use ratings on trait-descriptive adjectives (e.g., *meek, ruthless*) to assesses general interpersonal styles. The Circumplex Scales of Interpersonal Values (CSIV; Locke, 2000) use ratings of the importance of specific interpersonal experiences (e.g., *When I am with others, it is important I do better than them*) to assess prominent interpersonal motives and goals. The Circumplex Scales of Interpersonal Efficacies (CSIE; Locke & Sadler, 2007) use ratings of confidence to enact specific interpersonal behaviors (e.g., *When I am with others, I am confident I can win any arguments or competitions*) to assesses social skills strengths and weaknesses. The Inventory of Interpersonal Problems Circumplex Scales (IIP-C; Alden, Wiggins, & Pincus, 1990) use ratings of distress about interpersonal excesses (e.g., *I argue with other people too much*) and interpersonal inhibitions (e.g., *It's hard for me to show affection to people*) to assess prominent relational difficulties. The Interpersonal Sensitivities Circumplex (ISC: Hopwood, Ansell, et al., 2011) uses ratings of aversiveness of others' behaviors (e.g., *It bothers me when another person says they love me*) to assess prominent social antipathies. The Inventory of Interpersonal Strengths (Hatcher & Rogers, 2009) assesses highly adaptive interpersonal behaviors (e.g., *I am comfortable disagreeing with others*). Finally, the Impact Message Inventory Circumplex Scales (IMI-C; Schmidt, Wagner, & Keisler, 1999) use the actions, emotions, and attributions induced in the respondent by a target other (e.g., *When I am with this person, he makes me feel like I want to stay away from him*) to assess the typical social impressions evoked by the person rated. Agentic (vs. Passive) dispositions inform assessment of potential Criterion A impairments in self-directedness and identity, while Communal (vs. Disaffiliative) dispositions inform assessment of potential Criterion A impairments in empathy and intimacy. We recommend gathering both self- and informant-reports to identify areas of agreement and disagreement that can suggest levels of patient awareness regarding their impact on others, as well as relational blindspots and misperceptions that may maintain and even exacerbate personality impairments (e.g., Pincus & Gurtman, 2003).

Multisurface Interpersonal Assessment

Recently, assessment guidelines were developed to take advantage of the numerous interpersonal disposition measures that conform to the interpersonal circumplex. This multisurface perspective on patients' interpersonal functioning adds to standard interpersonal circumplex profile interpretation for a single measure (Dawood & Pincus, 2016; Hopwood et al., 2016).

Multisurface interpersonal assessment (MSIA), first suggested by Kiesler (Van Denburg, Schmidt, & Kiesler, 1992) and employed by Pincus and Gurtman (2003) in Wiggins's (2003) influential collaborative case study of Madeline G., offers a unique approach to identifying and understanding coherence and conflict within and across different interpersonal levels of a patient's personality (Figure 2.2). This is especially important because conflicts in multiple domains of interpersonal functioning are common in personality disorders and may reflect identity disturbance, as well as underlie impairments in self-direction, empathy, and intimacy (Benjamin, 1996; Leary, 1957). In Figure 2.2, the patient neither values nor feels he is effectively interpersonally cold (DE), yet he views many of his behaviors this way and is distressed by this. Similarly, he views himself as aloof-introverted (FG) and is highly distressed by his avoidant behavior, even though he values this interpersonal behavior more as a core coping strategy. Regarding warm-extraverted behavior (LM/NO), he values these behaviors, but sees himself as only average in warmth and markedly introverted, and neither quality is a recognized strength. Enacting warm behaviors is also highly distressing to him. The additional result of being sensitive to others' cold behavior ties together the picture of a man who desires connection, feels incapable of it and is attuned to others' withdrawal, yet he is often withdrawn and cold himself, contributing to others finding him stand-offish and difficult to get to know, leading to them either pulling away or not engaging him at all. A growing body of case studies show how MSIA batteries can provide a context

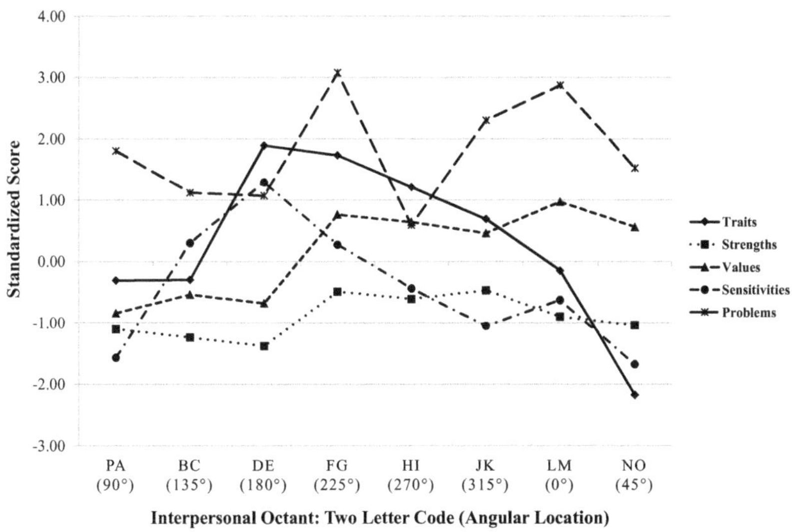

Figure 2.2. A multisurface interpersonal assessment. From Pincus, A.L., Sadler, P., Woody, E., Roche, M.J., Thomas, K.M., & Wright, A.G.C. (2014, p. 60). Reprinted with permission from Guilford Press.

to better understand a patient's symptoms (e.g., depression, anxiety, suicidal ideation) and personality impairments beyond their diagnosis, and demonstrate how the results of an MSIA can inform and enhance case conceptualization and treatment planning (Dawood & Pincus, 2016, Hopwood et al., 2016; Hopwood, Pincus, & Wright, 2019; Pincus & Gurtman, 2003; Pincus, Sadler, et al., 2014).

Assessing Interpersonal Dynamics

Assessment of interpersonal dynamics commonly employs intensive repeated measurement of interpersonal perception and behavior at different timescales (Pincus, Sadler, et al., 2014). For example, experiencing sampling studies using event contingent recording (ECR) assess interpersonal functioning in social interactions in daily life (Moskowitz, 2009; Moskowitz & Sadikaj, 2012). ECR assessment asks patients to record their perceptions of their own and the other's agency (dominance-submission) and communion (warmth-distance), as well as affects, symptoms, functioning, and contextual factors, for each face-to-face social interaction over the course of days or weeks using either paper-and-pencil or electronic surveys accessed via mobile devices (Roche & Pincus, 2016). Such assessments generate data to examine various impairments in the regulatory and relational processes described in Criterion A. For example, one patient reported on his social interactions for 21 days, including many interactions with his wife (Roche, Pincus, Rebar, Conroy, & Ram, 2014). Personality impairments, particularly in empathy, intimacy, and identity were apparent. His descriptions of self and other indicated he had difficulty cooperating with others. His self-esteem was unstable, varying from high when he saw himself as dominant and the other submissive to low when he perceived himself as submissive and the other dominant. He resisted and avoided the latter pattern of relating to others. This was exacerbated in the marital relationship where he uniquely perceived his wife's dominance to be concurrently hostile. These findings can be used to formulate a treatment goal—he needs to learn how to be submissive and cooperative when appropriate, and to maintain his self-esteem while doing so. Beyond the consulting room, empirical support for ECR assessment of interpersonal functioning is growing (for reviews, see Pincus, 2018; Pincus, Hopwood, & Wright, in press).

ECR studies focus on cross-situational behavior. However, important interpersonal dynamics are also revealed in the moment-to-moment unfolding of a specific interpersonal interaction. As an interaction unfolds, an observer can perceive and reliably code various entrainments and temporal patterns, which crucially link the two interactants. Computer-based Continuous Assessment of Interpersonal Dynamics (CAID; Girard & Wright, 2018; Lizdek, Sadler, Woody, Ethier, & Malet, 2012) allows observers, clinicians, supervisors, and even patients to follow and rate a videorecorded interpersonal interaction in the same way that they experience it and to record their moment-to-moment impressions of each person's agentic and communal stance within the context of the unfolding interaction. The CAID method uses the interpersonal circumplex as a parsimonious framework in which dynamic changes in interpersonal behavior are represented as time series for both interactants, coordinated in time such that various patterns of entrainment that link the interpersonal behavior of the interactants can be modeled (e.g., Dermody, Thomas, Hopwood, Durbin, & Wright, 2017). Thus, the data produced from the CAID method are inherently dyadic with the interpersonal behavior of each person in the interaction providing an inseparable context for the interpersonal behavior of the other. For example, CAID was used to code the well-known video of a psychotherapy session between Dr. Donald Meichenbaum and a personality disordered client, Richard (Sadler, Woody, McDonald, Lizdek, & Little, 2015). The assessment (Figure 2.3) captured

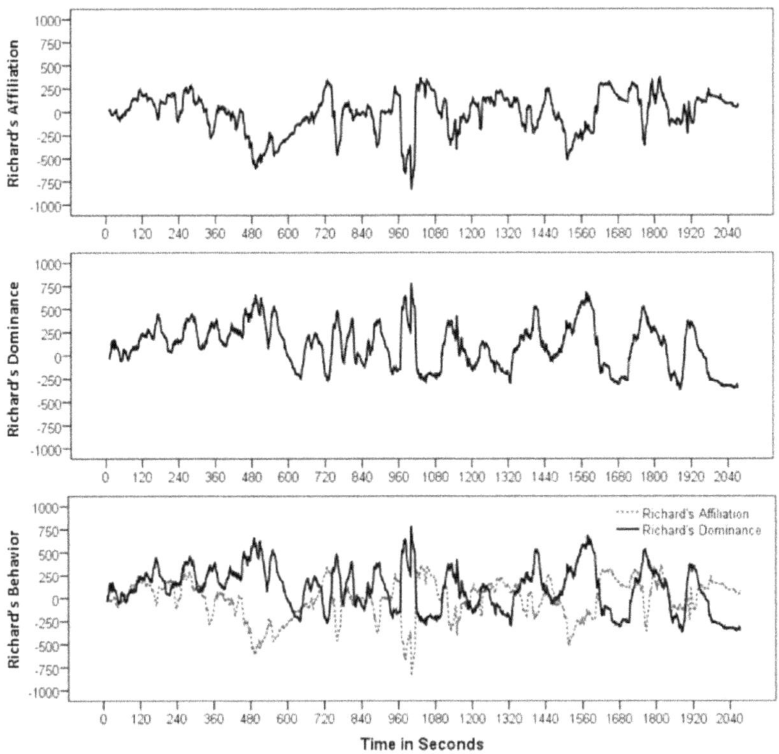

Figure 2.3. Affiliation behavior (top graph), dominance behavior (middle graph), and both affiliation and dominance behavior (bottom graph) over time for Richard. From Sadler, Woody, McDonald, Lizdek, & Little (2015, p. 534). Reprinted with permission from P. Sadler and Guilford Press.

Richard's extreme oscillations from arrogant (hostile-dominant) behavior to more conciliatory (friendly-submissive) behavior which is reasonably consistent with the conceptualization of narcissistic personality disorder that includes both grandiosity reflecting the motive to self-enhance and vulnerability due to self-esteem dysregulation (Pincus, Roche, & Good, 2015). Although there are currently no CAID studies specifically focusing on personality disorders, several studies demonstrate the promising nature of the CAID method for the assessment of personality impairments as they unfold in interpersonal interactions (for reviews, see Pincus, 2018; Pincus et al., in press).

DSM-5 AMPD Criterion A and Object-Relations Assessment

The dominant psychodynamic approach to understanding and treating personality disorders is based in object-relations theory (Caligor & Clarkin, 2010; Kernberg & Caligor, 2005) and Transference-focused psychotherapy (Yeomans et al., 2015). This approach defines the impairments common to all personality disorders in terms of the level of personality organization (Figure 2.4), a dimension reflecting the severity of personality impairment (ranging from normal to neurotic to borderline) based on identity coherence (integrated to diffused), use of defenses (mature to primitive), and reality

PERSONALITY ORGANIZATION

	Identity	Defenses	Reality Testing
NORMAL	Integrated sense of self and others. Investments in work, relations, leisure.	Use of more mature defenses. Flexibility.	Accurate perception of self vs. nonself, internal vs. external. Empathy with social criteria of reality.
NEUROTIC	Coherent sense of self and others but one element of psychic life not fully integrated. Investments in work, relations, leisure.	Use of more mature defenses. Rigidity.	Accurate perception of self vs. nonself, internal vs. external. Empathy with social criteria of reality.
BORDERLINE	Incoherent sense of self and others. Poor investments in work, relations, leisure.	Use of more primitive defenses. Splitting.	Distortion of self vs. nonself; internal vs. external. Variable empathy with social criteria of reality.

Figure 2.4. Aspects of levels of personality organization

testing (intact to tenuous and variable). This dimension of personality organization aligns well with AMPD Criterion A and the LPFS. Also consistent with Criterion A, object-relations asserts that the fundamental unit of personality is a dyadic mental representation of self and other linked with affective coloring. Severity of personality pathology is based in part on the contents and structure of these mental representations, and how they are layered to serve defensive functions and portray intrapsychic conflict (Figure 2.5).

Practitioners familiar with object-relations theory can use several self-reports, interviews, and rating scales to assess level of personality organization and the quality and content of patients' mental representations of self and other (Izdebska, 2015). The instruments most directly assessing level of personality organization as conceptualized by Kernberg and colleagues are the Inventory of Personality Organization (IPO; Lenzenweger, Clarkin, Kernberg, & Foelsch, 2001) and the Structured Interview of Personality Organization (STIPO; Stern et al., 2010). The goal of constructing the IPO was to develop a self-report measure corresponding to aspects of personality organization (Figure 2.4): Identity, Defenses, and Reality Testing. Psychometric evaluations of the IPO suggested this was not the optimal structure of the measure. A revised approach (Ellison & Levy, 2012) suggested that the IPO assesses four dimensions: Instability of Sense of Self and Other (e.g., *I see myself in totally different ways at different times*), Instability of Goals (e.g., *My goals keep changing*), Instability of Behavior (e.g., *I act in ways that appear to others as unpredictable and erratic*), and Psychosis (e.g., *I feel that my wishes or thoughts will come true as if by magic*). These scales are clearly associated with Kernberg's conceptualization of personality organization, as well as

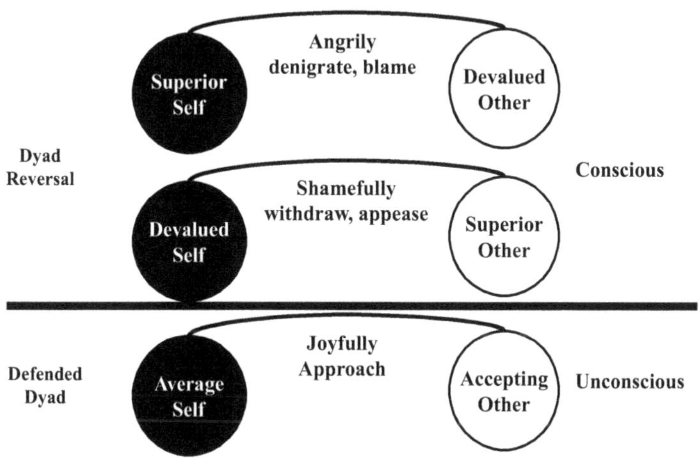

Figure 2.5. Object-relations dyad, dyad reversal, and defended dyad.

LPFS impairments in identity, self-directedness, empathy, and intimacy. Recent research in clinical (e.g., Preti et al., 2015; Zimmermann et al., 2016) and community (e.g., Ensink, Rousseau, Biberdzic, Bégin, & Normandin, 2017; Prunas & Bernorio, 2016) samples supports the reliability and validity of scores on the IPO.

The STIPO is a 100-item interview, taking between 1.5 and 3 hours to complete (Doering et al., 2013), that provides an overall score for level of personality organization and scores for seven domains of personality functioning; Identity (capacity to invest in work, school, and leisure; coherence and continuity of sense of self, stability of self-esteem, coherence and continuity of sense of others), Quality of Object Relations (interpersonal relationships, intimate relationships and sexuality, internal working model of relationships), Defenses, Reality Testing, Coping/Rigidity, Aggression (self-directed, other-directed), and Moral Values. A thorough assessment of these domains would certainly allow a clinician to confidently use the DSM-5 LPFS to evaluate impairments in identity, self-directedness, empathy, and intimacy. Given its depth and focus, it is not surprising that most research supporting the reliability and validity of scores derived from the STIPO involves clinical samples (Doering et al., 2013; Preti et al., 2015; Rentrop, Zilker, Lederle, Birkhofer, & Hörz, 2014).

Many additional instruments assess aspects of personality organization and representations of self and other that are familiar to psychodynamically oriented clinicians. Mentalization and reflective function can be assessed by two recently developed self-report measures, the Mentalization Scale (Dimitrijević, Hanak, Dimitrijević & Marjanović, 2018) and the Mentalization Questionnaire (Hausberg et al., 2012), and by the clinician rated Reflective Functioning Scale (Fonagy, Target, Steele, & Steele, 1998; Taubner et al., 2013). Numerous self-report measures of dimensions of attachment are readily available (Farnfield & Holmes, 2014), and the most widely used interview to assess attachment representations in personality disorders is the Adult Attachment Interview (AAI; George, Kaplan, & Main, 1984). The widely used Structural Analysis of Social Behavior Intrex Questionnaires (Benjamin, 2000) assess representations of self in relation to specific others (e.g., Critchfield & Benjamin, 2010).

Performance-based measures also assess aspects of personality organization and perceptions of self and other. The well-researched Social Cognition and Object Relations Scale (SCORS-G; Stein, Hilsenroth, Slavin-Mulford, & Pinsker, 2011), derived from Thematic Apperception Test (TAT; Murray, 1943) narratives, assesses eight dimensions of the quality of object relations: Complexity of Representations of People; Affective Quality of Representations; Emotional Investment in Relationships; Emotional Investment in Values and Moral Standards; Understanding of Social Causality; Experience and Management of Aggressive Impulses; Self-Esteem; and Identity and Coherence of Self. The Assessment of Self Descriptions (ASD; Blatt, Bers, & Schaffer, 1993) and the Assessment of Qualitative and Structural

Dimensions of Object Representations (AOR: Blatt, Chevron, Quinlan, Schaffer, and Wein, 1992) assess the content and structural aspects of self and object representations derived from narrative descriptions of self and parents. Heck and Pincus (2001) factor analyzed maternal and paternal ratings and identified a three-factor solution that represented the two meta-concepts of agency and communion found in interpersonal functioning, and a third factor that represented the structural components of the representations. Finally, the Rorschach Performance Assessment System (R-PAS; Meyer, Viglione, Mihura, Erard, & Erdberg, 2011; Mihura & Meyer, 2017) assesses numerous variables relevant to impairment of the regulatory and relational processes making up the LPFS.

DSM-5 AMPD Criterion A and Personological Assessment

The personological paradigm recognizes that humans are story tellers (Tomkins, 1987; McAdams, 1993), and that identity is built from the autobiographical stories a person tells themselves and others to integrate one's remembered past, experienced present, and anticipated future (McAdams, 2013). McAdams suggested a developmental model where the purpose of story-telling expands over time to reflect emerging cognitive and emotional capacities during the transition from childhood to adulthood (McAdams, 2013). An individual first tells stories with the primary goal of impressing others (e.g., self as an actor motivated to please his/her audience). Over time, the function of storytelling grows to also include the use of autobiographical stories that articulate one's *own* unique goals and invest in future "potential selves" (self as agent). At the most mature level, autobiographical stories reconcile experiences and bring coherence and stability to an individual's identity (self as a singular author rather than a collection of potential selves). This developmental model accords with AMPD descriptions of impairments to self-direction. For instance, AMPD healthy self-direction is described as goals that are integrated with a realistic assessment of capacities (e.g., self as author), while impairment is noted if one is excessively goal oriented (e.g., self as agent), or views goals as a means of gaining external approval rather than being self-generated (e.g., self as actor).

Recurrent narrative "scripts" for self and other are reminiscent of object relational dyads found in psychodynamic theory, and similarly these scripts can follow AMPD themes of self-impairment (e.g., incompetence scripts) and relational impairment (e.g., abandonment scripts). Life stories can also take on a common sequence, such as a redemptive sequence (e.g., the narrative moves from suffering to enhancement) or a contamination sequence (e.g., the narrative moves from promising to irrevocably spoiled). Research suggests contamination sequences are associated with lower general well-being, along with self-esteem and self-coherence difficulties indicative of AMPD self impairments (McAdams, Reynolds, Lewis,

Patten, & Bowman, 2001). In short, the AMPD model recognizes self and interpersonal impairment as the core of personality dysfunction, and the personological paradigm considers how the content and organization of autobiographical stories can reflect these impairments.

Assessment Approaches in the Personological Paradigm

In this approach, life story data is elicited and then analyzed to distill themes identified by the person providing the life story data and by particular coding schemes. Early approaches within this paradigm include Murray's TAT to evoke implicit life stories, and the psychobiographical approach that analyzes life story data such as works of art or letters to distill psychological themes (e.g., Freud's Leonardo Da Vinci, Erikson's Mahatma Ghandi, see Wiggins, 2003 for a larger summary). While the psychobiographical approach is still employed today (e.g., McAdams, 2010), it is more common to employ a semi-structured interview format within a clinical setting.

The Life Story Interview (LSI; McAdams, 2008) asks participants to divide their life into its main chapters and provide a plot summary for each. Then, participants describe eight key life episodes (high point, low point, turning point, earliest memory, important episode in childhood, important episode in adolescence, important adult episode, and one other important episode). Participants then report on life challenges, main characters (both positive and negative), their personal ideology, a prediction of where their life is going, and then they identify a single integrative theme of their life story. A content analysis of these autobiographical episodes (McAdams, Hoffman, Day, & Mansfield, 1996) revealed eight common themes that align with AMPD aspects of personality functioning: identity (self-mastery, empowerment), self-direction (status/victory, achievement), empathy (dialogue, caring), and intimacy (love/friendship, unity/togetherness). The LSI was also used to examine redemptive themes among highly generative adults (McAdams, Diamond, de St. Aubin, & Mansfield, 1997). These themes again align well with the AMPD model reflecting identity (having an early advantage that promotes positive self-concept), self-direction (establishing a moral steadfastness, overcoming adversity through a redemptive sequence of events that promotes future perseverance), empathy (widening concern for the misfortune of others), and intimacy (perceiving a positive future where the protagonist will benefit society). Thus, the LSI appears to contain information pertinent to determining AMPD personality functioning and impairment. To examine this directly, a sample of 71 undergraduate students completed an abbreviated version of the LSI, along with several other self-report measures of personality dysfunction. Undergraduate coders could reliably rate the LSI life stories for AMPD impairment, and the total score was positively correlated with personality dysfunction (Phillips, et al., 2017).

Several coding schemes exist to evaluate life story data for agentic and communal themes (McAdams, 2002), redemption sequences (McAdams, 1999), and contamination sequences (McAdams, 1998). Beyond these formal coding methods, Alexander (1990) suggested several criteria to determine the "significance" of material found in life stories. These include primacy (what is told first), frequency (what is told often), emphasis (what is given a surprising level of attention), uniqueness (what is unusual), isolation (what does not fit with the overall narrative), omission (what appears missing from the narrative), errors (what is incorrect), incompletion (what is without resolution), and negation (what is denied). Self-report questionnaires are not ideal to capture the richness of life story data. Nevertheless, several studies employ self-report questionnaires to identify individuals who may have particularly adaptive or maladaptive life story themes (McAdams et al., 1997; McAdams et al., 2001). Measures of generativity are commonly used for this purpose (Loyola Generativity Scale; McAdams & de St. Aubin, 1992; Generative Behavior Checklist; McAdams, Hart, & Maruna, 1998). Future research should consider developing a coding framework for developmental level to identify the content of stories as motivated by an actor, agent, or author.

Conclusion

The DSM-5 AMPD is an important advance, in part because it distinguishes general severity of personality pathology (Criterion A; LPFS) from individual differences in expression (Criterion B). The many elements of Criterion A are consistent with the multiple paradigms of personality assessment emphasizing self and self-in-relation-to-others. Linking Criterion A with the interpersonal, psychodynamic (object-relations), and personological paradigms provides theoretically coherent, empirically supported frameworks to define general personality pathology, operationalize self and relational impairments of personality pathology, and inform multimethod clinical assessment (and treatment) while also providing continuity with familiar clinical instruments and practices (Hopwood & Waugh, in press; Pincus, 2018; Waugh et al., 2017).

3 Criterion B of the AMPD and the Interpersonal, Multivariate, and Empirical Paradigms of Personality Assessment

Robert F. Krueger

The purpose of this chapter is to provide the reader with a brief introduction to Criterion B of the Alternative Model of Personality Disorders (AMPD) in the DSM-5. Criterion B refers to a specific set of pathological personality traits that are jointly intended to delineate the variety of presentations of pathological personality that tend to be seen in clinical settings. Pathological personality traits have a rich history in clinical work and research on personality disorders (PDs), and as such, another purpose of this chapter is to provide some historical and conceptual context for the DSM-5 maladaptive personality trait model. Other chapters in this volume focus more specifically on recent research on the AMPD, and instruments that can be used to assess AMPD constructs. Hence, in an effort to provide complementary background for the reader, this chapter will focus more on how Criterion B of the AMPD came about, and the sorts of strategic considerations in play in that process. Nevertheless, the chapter will also touch on how specific literature on the AMPD Trait Model (AMPD-TM) has developed rapidly since the time of the publication of the DSM-5 in 2013. These developments are pertinent in this chapter specifically because they illustrate how strategic considerations that influenced the development of the AMPD-TM are playing out in the literature.

The chapter begins by outlining and discussing the limitations and lack of empirical support for the model of PDs in DSM-IV. This forms the backdrop for the creation of the AMPD, and the AMPD-TM more specifically. After describing the AMPD-TM and its creation, the chapter also addresses the close link between assessment and conceptualization within the AMPD-TM. Specifically, the AMPD-TM (a model of PD features) derived directly from the creation of the Personality Inventory for DSM-5 (PID-5; an assessment instrument). That is, the creation of the PID-5 (an assessment instrument) followed a hypothetico-deductive process (cf. Cattell, 1978), in which the DSM-5 PD committee members nominated clinical concepts that they deemed relevant to understanding clinical PD presentations (i.e., elements of a clinical model of PD features). These concepts were then operationalized in early iterations of the PID-5 assessment instrument, and data on these concepts influenced their ultimate form and structure in the current version of the PID-5, which corresponds with the AMPD-TM as articulated in the DSM-5.

The chapter then turns to discuss connections between the AMPD-TM and three specific paradigms of personality assessment, as articulated by Wiggins (2003) in his seminal book titled *Paradigms of Personality Assessment*. Wiggins' (2003) book has achieved great notoriety because it clearly articulated historically separable approaches to the assessment of personality, along with the nature, strengths, and limitations of these distinguishable approaches. Perhaps most notably, rather than identifying one or another approach as "more correct," Wiggins placed these traditions on relatively equal footing. He also illustrated how personality assessment in the different paradigms can be complementary rather than competing.

Three of Wiggins' paradigms are particularly relevant to placing the AMPD-TM in historical and intellectual context: (1) the *interpersonal* paradigm, which focuses on patterns characterizing how people relate to each other; (2) the *multivariate* paradigm, which focuses on understanding the nature and number of dimensions needed to characterize personality in the broadest sense; and (3) the *empirical* paradigm, which focuses on the ways in which personality items relate to classically defined categories of psychiatric illness. Hence, this chapter briefly describes these three paradigms and how they interweave with the AMPD-TM (cf. Mulay et al., in press, 2018).

Finally, the chapter describes developments in field that post-date Wiggins' (2003) articulation of the personality assessment paradigms. In brief, the hegemony of classical psychiatric category labels as the primary organizing rubrics for clinical and research work in psychology and psychiatry is waning. Various approaches have arisen to frame contemporary efforts, often closely linked with modern technologies that allow for various types of empirical approaches. From this vantage point, the chapter reviews three specific areas of contemporary inquiry: (1) genetic research (e.g., the PID-5 assessment instrument has been used in some recent genetically informative studies); (2) neurobiologically oriented research, particularly the sorts of approaches being promoted by the US National Institute of Mental Health (NIMH; e.g., the recent enthusiasm for computational approaches to modeling psychiatric phenomena); and (3) statistically oriented research, particularly the recently formed Hierarchical Taxonomy of Psychopathology (HiTOP) consortium. The chapter concludes by describing how the approach epitomized by the AMPD-TM is likely to resonate going forward.

The DSM-IV Personality Disorder Model: Structural Limitations and Lack of Empirical Support

The story of the AMPD-TM begins, in many ways, with the DSM-III (APA, 1980). This is because the DSM-III was the first edition of the DSM to clearly distinguish between PDs and other mental disorders, and to place PDs on a separate axis from other mental disorders. The DSM-III articulated a clear set of categorically defined PDs, describing these in their own specialized chapter. As a result, a literature began to develop surrounding these diagnoses and the issues that arise with their application and use in clinical and research contexts. In brief, the intentions inherent in delineating categorical PDs in the DSM-III were clear and well-intentioned. PDs are debilitating psychiatric conditions, and delineating these conditions provided a much-needed boost to research and clinical thinking about PDs.

Nevertheless, the literature that emerged around DSM-III PDs (and their subsequent description in DSMs III-R and IV) illustrates specific conceptual problems that emerge when trying to work with these concepts. These problems are numerous, and they make it essentially impossible to work with the categorical DSM PD concepts, in research and in the clinic, in a conceptually coherent manner. The conceptual and practical incoherence of the DSM PD categories is the essence of what led to the creation of the AMPD.

Comorbidity

One key problem with the DSM PD categories is that they do not tend to apply singly to patients. That is, people who meet criteria for one DSM PD are much more likely to meet criteria for other PDs, compared with the base rates of these conditions (Oldham, Skodol, & Bender, 2014). The logic of categorical diagnosis is to assign the most optimal label to the patient, but if these labels do not apply singly, the ability to study PD categories in research and to apply them meaningfully in the clinic is obviously compromised.

Arbitrary Thresholds

The author of this chapter was a member of the DSM-5 PD Work Group, which provided a unique opportunity to try to understand where the thresholds in DSM-IV originated. For example, why does DSM-IV borderline PD (BPD) consist of nine criteria, with a requirement of five of these criteria as the threshold for assigning a categorical diagnosis? In short, I was never able to get a good answer to this question. Consistent with what others have written about these thresholds (Widiger, 2001) they have a negligible empirical basis and are essentially arbitrary. This is obviously a problematic situation when these labels are used for important clinical and research purposes (e.g., for reimbursement by third party payers).

Within Category Heterogeneity

The flip side of the "comorbidity problem" is the problem of within-category heterogeneity. People who meet criteria for a specific PD are not a homogenous group, with regard to the psychopathology they experience. BPD provides a good example of this problem. This diagnosis is often conceptualized as being associated with interpersonal problems, and Wright, Hallquist, et al. (2013) showed that these problems were highly diverse, within a sample of persons who all met criteria for BPD. Indeed, Wright and colleagues identified six separable classes of interpersonal problems within BPD patients that differed in clinically consequential ways (e.g., in terms of suicide attempts and self-harm propensities). In sum, a "BPD group" is not a homogenous construct, making group comparisons between "BPD" and "other groups" (e.g., control participants) difficult at best to interpret.

PD Not Otherwise Specified (or Elsewhere Classified)

Given all the problems applying PD labels to patients meaningfully, the PD not otherwise specified label (PD-NOS, referred to as "not elsewhere classified" in the DSM-5) is often applied in clinical practice (Verheul & Widiger, 2004). This might often be "the correct" label in the sense that patients tend not to fit into specific PD categories. Nevertheless, the intent of categorical PDs is to provide some sense of how to approach the patient based on the PD label. PD NOS conveys little information in this regard, other than flagging that the patient "has personality problems," a situation that is not particularly helpful in case conceptualization.

The DSM-5 Alternative Model of Personality Disorders (AMPD)

The AMPD arose as a way of dealing with problems with the DSM categorical PD model, such as those described above. In essence, the problems described above occur when dimensional phenomena are artificially segmented. Human personality is too rich of a phenomenon to be readily segmented into categories, and empirical efforts to identify PD categories tend to meet with little success (e.g., Eaton et al., 2011). Although categories seem appealing to some (e.g., they provide convenient labels for encounter forms that facilitate payment by third party payers), the thorny problem with PDs is that there is no compelling scientific evidence for categorical variation. Nevertheless, from a scientific perspective, the fortunate reality is that these category problems largely resolve when PDs are conceptualized dimensionally.

For example, comorbidity results from the way in which underlying (and multiple) dimensions of personality pathology are positively correlated. Elevation on one dimension tends to predict elevation on other dimensions, and arbitrary segmentation of these dimensions produces complex patterns of multi-category membership. This situation resolves once it is understood that complete characterization of clinical PD presentations involves description across multiple dimensions simultaneously. For example, the question is not one of differential diagnosis between borderline and schizotypal PD, in cases where patients show both emotional dysregulation and impairments in reality testing. Rather, cases like this are well-conceptualized as having problems in both areas at the same time.

Indeed, it is generally pointless to try to identify "the right diagnosis" when people have problems in multiple areas. Rather, it works better to describe the extent of problems in multiple areas simultaneously, akin to a panel of dimensional indicators of physical functioning (e.g., providing both blood pressure and weight in a medical chart). Problems of within-category heterogeneity resolve similarly because the relevant heterogeneity is specified via multiple dimensions. For example, there is no need to posit "subtypes" of BPD with better and lesser reality testing. Rather, the dimensions of emotional dysregulation (the essence of what is typically meant by "BPD") and psychoticism (poor reality testing, the essence of what is typically meant by "schizotypal PD") can be considered simultaneously.

Arbitrary threshold problems resolve once it is understood that dimensions can always be characterized by clinically meaningful zones on dimensional constructs. Analogies to physical medicine are readily generated to illustrate the clinical utility of this approach. For example, blood pressure is a continuous variable, and certain zones on this variable are associated with greater and lesser risk of deleterious events (e.g., stroke). These thresholds are understood to be arbitrary in their precise location, yet clinically meaningful (e.g., near the threshold is understood to be a "borderline risk situation;" relatively more extreme elevation is associated with greater need for more immediate intervention, and so on). Generation of such thresholds for psychiatric constructs can be pursued in a principled and empirical manner, by studying relations between psychopathology and its correlates (Markon, 2010). Finally, "NOS" problems resolve because a comprehensive set of dimensions constitutes a practical goal that has been largely realized in personality research (cf. Wiggins' 2003 multivariate paradigm). All patients can be described reasonably well if the phenotypic dimensions characterizing personality differences are generally well-known and well-characterized.

The challenge, however, is how to construct a dimensional alternative to the traditional categorical PD model, and how to bring it into the pages of the DSM. The need to traverse this path is readily apparent; the challenges along this path have pertained to numerous navigational obstacles inherent in efforts to change classification paradigms. The AMPD arose from a specific set of historical circumstances linked to walking this path as part of the DSM-5 construction process.

Briefly, the AMPD approach to PDs involves considering two major criteria in evaluating a patient: Criteria A and B. Criterion A describes overall personality functioning, from relatively normative levels of functioning to severely impaired. It describes functioning in terms of impairment in self-functioning (in areas of identity and self-direction) and impairment in conceptualization of others (interpersonal functioning, including capacities for empathy and intimacy). The chapter by Pincus and Roche in the current volume describes Criterion A in detail.

Criterion B describes the content of personality, in the context of the level of functioning provided by Criterion A. It does this via a set of *facets* and *domains* that jointly constitute the AMPD-TM. Facets are more narrow and specific aspects of maladaptive personality description. Examples in the DSM-5 include *hostility* (being a mean and nasty person) and *anxiousness* (diffuse and relatively free-floating worry). Domains summarize the information in groups of facets. Examples in the DSM-5 include *negative affectivity* (summarizing a variety of negative emotional tendencies, such as the aforementioned *anxiousness* facet) and *antagonism* (behavioral tendencies that put the person at odds with others, such as the aforementioned *hostility* facet). We turn now to describe how the AMPD-TM was constructed, via its operationalization in the Personality Inventory for DSM-5 (PID-5). The reader should feel free to consult the DSM-5 per se for additional details; the entire AMPD is described there (APA, 2013, pp. 761–781).

Criterion B of the AMPD and the Personality Inventory for DSM-5 (PID-5)

Although other parts of this volume focus specifically on AMPD assessment instruments, I describe the PID-5 here also from the perspective of its construction. This is relevant in understanding Criterion B of the AMPD (i.e., the AMPD-TM) because the model derived from the construction of a corresponding assessment instrument (the PID-5). Briefly, the idea was to move away from diagnosis via authority and political processes, and toward diagnosis and case conceptualization via evidence. Traditionally, the DSM has been constructed by having experts delineate criteria for diagnoses based on their clinical experiences and reviews of the literature (much of which is framed by existing DSM rubrics). Those diagnoses might be studied in various ways (e.g., in field trials designed to evaluate the reliability with which the diagnoses are applied; Regier et al. 2013), but their construction is based primarily on work group members listing criteria. Moreover, as described earlier, such criteria lists are then associated with an arbitrary threshold on the criterion count in order to specify the number of criteria required for a diagnosis.

The idea in constructing the AMPD-TM was to move away from this approach by beginning with clinical expertise, but not ending there. Clinical expertise is a logical starting point for delineating constructs relevant to understanding mental health. However, data can be brought to bear on understanding how constructs initially delineated based on expertise are organized in nature. This is an important step in making mental health diagnosis a credible endeavor. It also represents an important change in how a classification, such as the DSM, comes about. Specifically, the idea in constructing the AMPD-TM was to collect data on concepts delineated initially via clinical expertise, and to use those data to refine the resulting model of personality.

Initially, members of the DSM-5 Personality and Personality Disorders Work Group submitted suggestions about constructs they found to be clinically salient in their work with PD patients. This process resulted in a list of 37 specific *facets*. Brief definitions were written for these facets by the group of PD Work Group members and consultants tasked with pursuing the PID-5 endeavor (Krueger, Derringer, Markon, Watson, & Skodol, 2012). With these definitions in place, the next step was to compose personality assessment items intended to capture the essential features of the facet definitions. With multiple items written for each facet, the next step was then to gather data on those items. This was accomplished by working with a survey research firm, which allowed us to collect data on the items from persons who constituted a community-dwelling sample of treatment-seeking participants. That is, participants in the PID-5 construction endeavor were persons who responded previously that they had sought treatment for mental health issues, drawn from an overall US population representative panel of research participants.

In sum, data were gathered on a large pool of items delineating the 37 facets initially suggested by work group members as clinically salient features of PD. These data were then used to refine this list of PD features empirically. Specifically, it was possible to determine if some facets were so highly correlated that it made sense to collapse them into single facets. Similarly, it was possible to refine the items that were used to index the facets, eliminating items that failed to function well, and replacing them with new items. This process was pursued over the course of three rounds of data collection, where the idea was that the third round of data would provide information on the psychometric behavior of the instrument that ultimately was released as the PID-5.

Through the course of this iterative process, we found that the initial list of 37 facets could be reduced to 25, by combining facets that were highly redundant. In addition, in the final round of the project, we found that the 25 facets could be arranged empirically into 5 broad groups, or domains of personality variation. These domains were termed *negative affectivity* (a tendency to experience diverse forms of distressing and unpleasant emotion), *detachment* (preferring to avoid vs. engage in diverse social experiences), *antagonism* (varied ways of being at odds with other people, e.g., through being callous, manipulative, and deceitful), *disinhibition* (pursuing immediate gratification as opposed to being more planful), and *psychoticism* (being odd and eccentric, and having correspondingly unusual perceptual experiences). This entire process of interweaving instrument construction with model development to arrive at the AMPD-TM and corresponding PID-5 instrument is detailed in Krueger et al. (2012). We turn now to describe how this endeavor connects with three major paradigms of personality assessment delineated by Wiggins (2003), specifically, the interpersonal, multivariate, and empirical paradigms.

Connections with the Interpersonal Paradigm

Jerry Wiggins was himself a major contributor to the literature he described in 2003 as linked to the interpersonal paradigm of personality assessment. By "paradigm," Wiggins was referring essentially to the works associated with specific communities of scholars who take a specific type of approach to conceptualizing and assessing personality. By "the interpersonal paradigm," Wiggins meant approaches to personality assessment that focus on the person in interpersonal context. Space limitations preclude doing this rich literature justice in this chapter but, briefly, Wiggins locates the origins of the interpersonal paradigm in the theoretical writings of Harry Stack Sullivan. Sullivan conceptualized personality as taking on its meaning with reference to interpersonal encounters, be those consensually "real" or "imagined." In other words, personality to Sullivan referred to regularities in the way a person relates to "other persons," where "other persons" are not just separate contemporary human beings, but also historical relationships and associated mental models of how interpersonal situations unfold.

Along these lines, one might ask, are any situations truly lacking in interpersonal content? That is, one continually intriguing and provocative aspect of this paradigm is its focus on a kind of "radical inter-personalism." Even when we are physically alone, we are often playing out interpersonal scenarios mentally, and it is difficult to imagine that much of waking mental life is truly without interpersonal content. The interpersonal paradigm focuses on this key aspect of what it means to be human, and the interpersonal aspects of human mental and social life.

Beginning with these key theoretical writings, psychologists working in the late 40s and early 50s began to translate these theoretical concepts into assessment instruments. This literature flourished in the following decades, and it is the literature to which Wiggins became a major contributor (see e.g., Wiggins, 1996, for a review of some of the relevant history). Briefly, this literature converges on the centrality of two domains to organize much of human interpersonal experience, and dispositional tendencies within these experiences. A first domain can be termed *dominance vs. submissiveness*, and, as these terms imply, describes individual differences in tendencies to take the lead in interpersonal situations, vs. backing down and letting others take charge. A second (and independently varying) domain can be termed *warmth vs. coldness* and refers to individual differences in getting along well with others, vs. being actively antagonistic in interpersonal situations.

Interestingly, these domains show a structure known as a circumplex. That is, individual differences can be delineated throughout the two-dimensional space anchored by the dominance and warmth axes. For example, extraverted and outgoing tendencies (as opposed to introverted tendencies) tend to fall between dominance and warmth because they tend to combine both qualities. Being an extraverted, friendly, outgoing person involves both the dominance necessary to take charge in interpersonal situations, as well as the ability to make authentic and warm connections with others while taking charge.

Scholars working in the interpersonal tradition took a relatively early interest in the AMPD-TM and worked to understand how constructs and instruments from the interpersonal tradition intersect with constructs measured by the PID-5 (Wright, Pincus, et al., 2012). Specifically, Wright, Pincus, et al. (2012) studied a large sample (over 2,000 persons) who provided data on the PID-5 and also on the Inventory of Interpersonal Problems—Short Circumplex (IIP-SC; Soldz et al., 1995). The IIP-SC covers problems that correspond with the interpersonal circumplex model described earlier, using eight scales that correspond with eight "octants" (eight scales designed to mark eight segments of a circumplex structure), anchored by dominance and warmth (affiliation) dimensions. The basic idea in relating a structure such as that delineated by the PID-5 (with its 25 facets and 5 domains) to an interpersonal circumplex measure involves working to understand how the PID-5 variables map onto the interpersonal circumplex structure. In the case of the PID-5 and the IIP-SC, PID-5 traits map onto the interpersonal circumplex in relatively predictable ways. For example, the more generally interpersonal domains of the AMPD-TM (*detachment* and *antagonism*) had clear and differentiated associations with the IIP-SC. The most notable interpersonal problems associated with detachment related to being cold-hearted and avoidant, and, by contrast, the notable interpersonal problems associated with antagonism related to being domineering. Interestingly, this analysis also revealed how qualities associated with maladaptive warmth were not heavily represented in the PID-5, suggesting this as an area for future expansion of the AMPD-TM (see also Gore & Widiger, 2015). More generally, however, this analysis showed how the AMPD-TM covers much of the territory also covered by the IIP-SC, showing clear empirical connections between the AMPD-TM and the interpersonal paradigm, in spite of these approaches having distinguishable historical origins.

Connections with the Multivariate (Five Factor Model; FFM) Paradigm

Wiggins' (2003) multivariate paradigm referred to the extensive literature on the multivariate structure of normative personality. A key element in the history of personality psychology in the 20th century is the path toward realization that, given a broad and balanced set of indicator variables, personality variation can be understood as being organized into five broad domains, often termed Extraversion, Neuroticism, Agreeableness, Conscientiousness, and Openness. This perspective is typically termed the "Five Factor Model" or FFM perspective, and this is the approach Wiggins identified as "the multivariate paradigm". In the normative personality literature, this paradigm is closely associated with Costa and McCrae, who worked to instantiate the FFM in the widely-used NEO Personality Inventory (Costa & McCrae, 1992). In the PD literature, Tom Widiger has been a major contributor in demonstrating how maladaptive variants of FFM scales are capable of capturing traditional PDs (Widiger, in press, 2018).

Perhaps owing to the clear conceptual resemblance between the AMPD-TM domains and the FFM domains, a substantial literature has emerged on empirical connections between the PID-5 and various FFM instruments (e.g., DeFruyt et al., 2013; Gore & Widiger, 2013; Suzuki, Griffin, & Samuel, 2017; Thomas et al., 2013). These studies generally show good resemblance between four of the five domains, the exception being lesser direct correspondence between the openness domain of the FFM and the psychoticism domain of the AMPD-TM. Suzuki et al. (2015) probed these connections in a more detailed way through the use of Item Response Theory (IRT) techniques. They found that coverage of the full range the four broad overlapping domains was similar between the International Personality Item Pool (IPIP) version of the NEO and the PID-5, with some slight advantage of the IPIP-NEO at lower, and the PID-5 at higher, trait levels. Regarding openness-psychoticism overlap, the likely explanation for more limited overlap lies in the complexity of this domain. Specifically, openness has two aspects, one more related to openness to sensory and perceptual experiences, and one more related to intellectual and logical analysis of abstractions. Psychoticism content from the PID-5 is related to the more sensory and perceptual aspect, but not to the intellectual aspect (DeYoung et al., 2016).

Connections with the Empirical (Minnesota Multiphasic Personality Inventory; MMPI) Paradigm

By the "empirical paradigm," Wiggins was referring specifically to work associated with the Minnesota Multiphasic Personality Inventory (MMPI; Hathaway & McKinley, 1942). Wiggins conceptualized the MMPI as associated with an "empirical" approach to personality assessment because of the origins of the instrument. Specifically, the original MMPI clinical scales were created through an empirical process, where items were selected for scales because they were correlated with membership in traditional mental disorder diagnostic categories.

What may be interesting to observe here is the extent to which the MMPI literature has moved toward a more contemporary approach to conceptualizing personality and psychopathology, relative to the approach taken to the construction of the original MMPI clinical scales. This change is reflective of the relatively weak empirical basis for DSM-style categories. Although MMPI clinical scales (as instantiated in more recent versions of the MMPI instruments) continue to be used in applied personality assessment, the Restructured Form of the MMPI (the MMPI-2-RF) both structures these scales differently, and organizes them into a more contemporary and empirically derived model (Ben-Porath & Tellegen, 2008; 2011). First, the MMPI-2-RF derived from efforts to construct the clinical scales net of what Tellegen has termed "demoralization." In Tellegen's conceptualization, demoralization is the variance in common among all the clinical scales, inducing positive correlations among those scales. By extracting demoralization content from the scales, the residuals of demoralization then reflect more purely defined constructs, yielding greater utility in case conceptualization. Moreover, factor analyses of the MMPI-2-RF restructured clinical scales show that they group into three larger spectra, termed Emotional/Internalizing Dysfunction, Thought Dysfunction, and Behavioral/Externalizing Dysfunction (Ben-Porath & Tellegen, 2011). These constructs closely resemble constructs in contemporary empirical models of the structure of psychopathology, such as the working model of the Hierarchical Taxonomy of Psychopathology (HiTOP) consortium (Kotov et al. 2017; described in more detail in the section 'Statistical Technologies and the Hierarchical Taxonomy of Psychopathology Consortium (HiTOP)' below).

Scholars working with the MMPI-2-RF instruments took an early interest in the AMPD-TM and the PID-5. One of the first papers in this area examined the overlap between the Personality-Psychopathology-5 (PSY-5) MMPI-2-RF scales and the PID-5 facet and domain scales. The PSY-5 scales represent a seminal effort to delineate the five major domains of personality psychopathology and are in many ways constructs that antedate recent efforts to establish the empirical organization of PDs (Harkness, Reynolds, & Lilienfeld, 2014). Anderson et al. (2013) showed correspondence between the PSY-5 and AMPD-TM empirically by studying the MMPI-2-RF PSY-5 scales and the PID-5 in the same sample. In a joint factor analysis, the PSY-5 scales emerged as markers of the five AMPD-TM domains, with the PID-5 facets "folding into" this space in predictable ways. This illustrates that the PSY-5 constructs, as instantiated by MMPI-2-RF scales, anchor the same domains that tend to emerge empirically from the structure of the PID-5 facets. Moreover, at a higher level of the overall trait hierarchy, Anderson et al. (2015) showed how MMPI-2-RF scales and PID-5 scales jointly converged on the three broad domains that organize the MMPI-2-RF (Emotional/Internalizing Dysfunction, Thought Dysfunction, and Behavioral/Externalizing Dysfunction). In sum, modern approaches to the MMPI demonstrate how the MMPI item pool, particularly organized as per the MMPI-2-RF, clearly covers much of the same individual differences territory mapped out in the AMPD-TM.

Connections with Contemporary Directions in Psychopathology Classification and Research

Wiggins' volume antedates recent ferment in the scholarly literature on the classification of psychopathology. The problems that gave rise to the development of the AMPD-TM are not unique to the PD literature. Issues such as comorbidity and within-category heterogeneity arise not only with PDs, but also with the entire variety of psychopathology categories described within the DSM system. As a direct result, the field is experiencing a period of ferment and change as various forces seek to articulate approaches that might ultimately supersede the categorical DSM-based approach to conceptualizing mental disorders. Here, I consider three specific literatures that have arisen recently, after the publication of the DSM-5 (and therefore, more than a decade after the publication of Wiggins' classic 2003 book). First, I describe genetically informative research connected with the AMPD-TM. Second, I describe recent intellectual trends connected with the US National Institute of Mental Health (NIMH), and NIMH's stated funding priorities. Third, I describe the emergence of the Hierarchical Taxonomy of Psychopathology (HiTOP) consortium, a group of investigators pursuing an approach similar to the approach taken to construct the AMPD-TM, but focused on psychopathology in general, and not just on PD features. In all three cases, an essential driving force is the promise of technology (genomic, neuroscience-related, and statistical) to galvanize real and lasting improvements in our understanding of mental illness. Hence, we will consider how technology may (or may not) connect with conceptual developments tied to the AMPD-TM.

Genetic Research and the AMPD-TM

The AMPD-TM has been a recent focus of genetically informative research, via the inclusion of the PID-5 in recent twin studies in Norway and Minnesota. These studies have shown that the facets and domains of the AMPD-TM are substantially heritable, indicating that substantial proportions of the variance in those constructs traces back to genetic differences among people (South et al., 2017; Wright, Pahlen, & Krueger, 2017). Also of note is evidence from the Norwegian studies showing that essentially all the genetic variation in DSM-IV-defined paranoid, schizotypal, antisocial, borderline, and avoidant PDs could be captured by a considerably abbreviated version of the PID-5 instrument (Reichborn-Kjennerud et al., 2017). This indicates that these classical PD concepts can be entirely captured by the AMPD-TM concepts, at least for these specific PD concepts and at the level of underlying genetic variation.

The AMPD-TM per se has not been the explicit focus of recent efforts to identify genomic variants relevant to personality and psychopathology (e.g., Genome-Wide Association Studies; GWAS). The PID-5 is a newer instrument, and gene hunting requires truly enormous sample sizes and resources. These very large samples are de rigueur because the effect size of any specific genomic variant on complex human traits is small, albeit the aggregate effect of multiple variants is not small. This aggregate effect is the genetic signal picked up on in twin studies.

There are reasons to think the phenotypes of the AMPD-TM are appealing targets for gene hunting, however. Successful gene hunting requires the ability to characterize very large samples on phenotypes that help to differentiate those samples. The clear health relevance of the broad domains of the AMPD-TM and their instantiation in shorter versions of the PID-5 instrument (e.g., Maples et al., 2015) make for a compelling combination for genetic and genomic research.

Neural Technologies, NIMH, the Research Domain Criteria (RDoC), and Computational Psychiatry

The US National Institute of Mental Health (NIMH) has played a key role historically in influencing the psychopathology literature because NIMH controls the purse strings for a fair amount of the total global resources available for mental health research. Thus, it is interesting to consider potential connections between the AMPD-TM and contemporary NIMH priorities. In brief, the overlap here is relatively minimal because the investment strategy (at least in terms of what NIMH leadership is currently promoting) relates to what might be termed "speculative computational neuroscience," as opposed to traditional psychological assessment. A key recent reference in this area is Friston, Redish, and Gordon (2017); of note the senior author here (Dr. Gordon) is currently the director of NIMH. Gordon is invested in promoting these types of approaches because he feels they have promise in better understanding mental illness.

The idea in Friston et al. (2017) is that it might be possible at some time in the future to model underlying neural systems that give rise to manifest psychopathology. To achieve this would require the ability to monitor variables related to underlying mechanistic neural systems in intact living human patients, and then to formalize the behavior of those systems mathematically, with the idea of using those formalisms to predict manifest psychopathological signs and symptoms. The "meta-message" of Friston et al., taken as an indicator of NIMH priorities, is that speculative neuroscience is a priority, and that working from the level of underlying mechanisms toward the level of manifest behavior is a valued strategy. Understanding the observed, phenotypic structure of the manifest symptoms is not highly prioritized because the symptoms can be conceptualized using any convenient list of labels (e.g., traditional DSM labels or labels taken from the NIMH's Research Domain Criteria or "RDoC" project, which bear some resemblance to constructs in the AMPD-TM). The investment strategy of NIMH involves speculation about neural technologies that largely do not exist currently (ambulatory neuroimaging, essentially), as opposed to investment in already available technologies that might be leveraged to help patients who currently suffer from mental illness.

Statistical Technologies and the Hierarchical Taxonomy of Psychopathology Consortium (HiTOP)

One notable issue with the idea of building toward behavioral problems from underlying neural systems relates to the question of how to conceptualize manifest behavioral problems. This was arguably a thorny issue during the RDoC era at NIMH. The RDoC initiative can be thought of from various angles, but one clear aspect of it was to reformulate the organization of constructs relevant to mental health. Rather than referring to traditional DSM labels, the RDoC referred to "domains" such as "negative valence systems." Pains were taken to claim that the intent was not to replace nor supersede traditional DSM labels, but it remained the case that to be "RDoC compliant," investigators needed to somehow refer to "RDoC constructs," which led to a fair amount of confusion about what people were actually supposed to be studying. If part of the intent was to move away from DSM categories and their attendant conceptual problems, yet somehow not "supersede" those constructs, then what is the focus of mental health research? What public health problems are supposed to be tackled, and how are these problems conceptualized?

As of this writing, RDoC remains a unit within NIMH, but the influence of this approach may be waning. This is signaled potentially by the ways in which recent papers promoting computational neuroscience tend to be agnostic about nosological issues and their attendant political implications. Nevertheless, the NIMH program's tendency to promote mechanistic neuroscience is clear. In this general intellectual context, another initiative has arisen in a more grass-roots manner, organized by researchers on the front lines. Specifically, Roman Kotov (a research psychologist at Stony Brook University) approached the author of this chapter and David Watson (a research psychologist at the University of Notre Dame) about organizing an effort focused around using data to arrive at an empirical model of phenotypic psychopathological variation, based on using contemporary statistical technologies to build models from traditional assessment data. Kotov, Krueger, and Watson, along with many others, had all contributed to a literature on the quantitative empirical structure of psychopathology, and Kotov felt that this literature was sufficiently developed that it could form the basis for a consortium. Kotov's idea was basically that a critical mass of front-line researchers was pursuing this type of approach in various ways, and that these efforts could be usefully united by a consortium effort. The result of this conversation was the formation of the HiTOP consortium (https://medicine.stonybrookmedicine.edu/HITOP). The objective of the HiTOP is to organize diverse investigators to develop a more empirically based approach to psychopathology classification, compared with the DSM approach (Kotov et al., 2017).

How do the AMPD-TM, HiTOP, and NIMH priorities relate to each other? Basically, the AMPD-TM is an example of a specific research endeavor that generally fits with HiTOP principles. The AMPD-TM was developed empirically, as opposed to being developed using more political types of processes, free from constraints that are assumed rather than tested (e.g., the traditional DSM constraint that the only legitimate diagnostic concepts are dichotomies derived from arbitrary cutpoints on criterion counts). In this way, it is similar to other instruments developed without these constraints (e.g., the CAT-PD; Simms et al, 2011). The distinction is that the AMPD-TM was developed in the context of the DSM-5 effort per se, and the project was supported by funds provided by the American Psychiatric Association; it thereby has a direct connection to the DSM. However, its coverage of psychopathology is limited to personality psychopathology. In that sense, the AMPD-TM is considerably less comprehensive than what HiTOP aims to cover. For example, HiTOP covers diverse behavioral problems such as eating and sexual functioning problems, whereas these are outside of the scope of traditional PD conceptualizations per se, and therefore outside the scope of coverage that framed the AMPD-TM generation endeavor. The AMPD-TM might therefore be conceptualized as related to the psychological infrastructure underlying nomothetic phenotypic psychopathology. Its coverage tends to focus on more core psychological individual differences, and not on more focal behavioral manifestations of psychopathology (e.g., specific species typical functions such as eating, sleep, and sexuality).

Regarding the AMPD-TM and NIMH priorities, various challenges emerge. For example, RDoC grew out of a situation characterized by animosity between NIMH and the American Psychiatric Association. NIMH's then current director Dr. Insel welcomed the publication of DSM-5 by noting that "patients with mental disorders deserve better." In this same blog post, he touted the potential of RDoC to provide relatively greater progress. Nevertheless, as noted above, the phenotype definition problem remains salient in contemplating not just the RDoC approach, but also other approaches now seen as NIMH priorities such as the computational approach. Neuroscientific technologies are distal from human behavior per se, and the qualia that constitute human experience are conceptually distinguishable from neural activity per se, even if these domains are obviously correlated and a map will ultimately develop. There is a certain sense in which it is obvious that human behavior derives from neural activity, and ultimately, these domains are essentially fungible (in the absence of a ghost in the machine, i.e., a metaphysical influence on behavior inaccessible to scientific inquiry). The challenge is how to build this map in a credible manner, and how to help persons suffering from mental illness as a result of this endeavor. Knowing that specific symptoms are associated with circuit A as opposed to circuit B is important scientifically, but it is an additional step to translate this knowledge into an impact on mental health.

Solutions likely lie in interweaving phenotypic and technologically more recent developments. The ability of technology to drive and transform scientific understanding is undeniable. However, in recognizing the utility of technology in scientific progress, it is useful not to discard the primacy of human experience in understanding psychopathology. To cite an example from the genomics literature, phenotypes such as cognitive ability and educational attainment may seem distant from the human genome, but these phenotypes have yielded novel scientific discoveries about the genetic architecture of these quintessentially human and behavioral phenotypes (e.g., www.nature.com/articles/s41467-018-04362-x). Perhaps surprisingly, educational attainment has been one of the more compelling phenotypes in GWAS research. More generally, both genomic and neuroscientific technologies are likely to bear more scientific fruit when tethered to empirically based phenotypic models such as the AMPD-TM.

Conclusions

A remarkable amount of research on the AMPD-TM has emerged in a relatively short period of time (as of this writing, it has been only 5 years since the publication of the DSM-5). More specifically, according to Google Scholar, as of this writing, the article introducing the PID-5 (Krueger et al., 2012) has been cited 694 times. In this brief chapter, the vast majority of this literature was not considered explicitly. Rather, this chapter aimed to review the origins and strategic considerations inherent in the AMPD-TM and the corresponding PID-5 assessment instrument and link those considerations with Wiggins' (2003) Interpersonal, Multivariate, and Empirical paradigms of personality assessment. Consideration was also given to the ways in which the AMPD-TM intersects with more recent developments, focused around genetic, neuroscience, and statistical technologies. In general, the AMPD-TM provides a set of psychological phenotypes (observable characteristics of humans) that are likely to have utility in tying together a diverse set of approaches, including the approaches reviewed here.

In closing, it is also important to emphasize that the AMPD-TM model and PID-5 instrument are only one instantiation of phenomena that do seem to be reliably observed from a variety of angles. This is clear from considering the ways in which the AMPD-TM intersects with concepts from Wiggins' (2003) paradigms. For example, the five domains of the AMPD-TM are remarkably similar to the domains of the FFM and key organizational constructs delineated thus far in the HiTOP endeavor.

Importantly, the connections between the AMPD-TM and other approaches represent empirical observations and not foregone conclusions.

The facets of the AMPD-TM were generated via work group processes, yet generally organize empirically into five familiar broad domains (at a basic level of the overall construct hierarchy). This emphasizes the empirical reality of these domains, inasmuch as they are observed organizational rubrics in numerous lines of inquiry and are not unique to the AMPD-TM. Finding this kind of regularity is no mean feat in the study of human individual differences. It is this broader regularity and the five major themes that recur in the study of human personality that are likely to be the lasting legacy of this phase in the development of empirical approaches to classifying personality and psychopathology. Hopefully the AMPD-TM can continue to play a role in cementing this legacy, by virtue of having forged a connection between an authoritative nosology (DSM-5) and the empirical literature on the organization of personality and pathology.

4 Research and Assessment with the AMPD

Christopher J. Hopwood

DSM-5 Alternative Model of Personality Disorders (AMPD) Criterion A Levels of Personality Functioning (LPFS) serves to define PD and functions as the diagnostic threshold for determining a patient's PD status. Criterion B Maladaptive Traits can be used to describe the way PD manifests in a given patient. This model is supported both by a long history of research on personality functioning and maladaptive traits in general, and more recent research on the AMPD in particular. During and following the publication of the DSM-5, specific instruments were developed to measure AMPD constructs, leading to an emerging literature on this specific system. In this chapter, I will focus primarily on AMPD-specific research and assessment methods, but will also provide an overview on some of the research and methods that led up to the AMPD. Interested readers may also wish to consult other reviews of the AMPD (Morey et al., 2015; Skodol, 2012) as well as papers describing how to formulate cases using the AMPD (Bach et al., 2015; Garcia et al., in press 2018; Hopwood, 2018; Morey & Stagner, 2012; Mulay et al., in press, 2018; Pincus, Dowgwillo, & Greenberg, 2016; Simonsen & Simonsen, 2014; Skodol, Morey, Bender, and Oldham, 2015; Waugh et al., 2017).

Criterion A Personality Dysfunction

In previous DSM models, PDs were distinguished from normal personality by their associated distress and dysfunction, and distinguished from other disorders by their stability and pervasiveness. However, research does not support clear discontinuities between normal and abnormal personality (Suzuki et al., 2015) or stability differences between PDs and other forms of psychopathology (Hopwood & Bleidorn, 2018). Pre-AMPD DSM definitions were also not particularly clinically useful, in that they did not provide a conceptually meaningful definition of the essence of PD, and communicated a kind of pessimism about the likelihood of treating PD features that was inconsistent with the empirical literature on treatment (Bateman, Gunderson, & Mulder, 2015). Thus, there was a need for a more clinically useful and evidence-based definition of PD in the AMPD.

DSM-5 AMPD Criterion A is an effort to fulfill that need. Bender, Morey, and Skodol (2011) laid out the DSM-5 Personality and Personality Disorder Work Group's rationale for the contents of Criterion A. They cited research showing that the overall level of personality dysfunction, rather than the specific manifestation of disordered traits, tends to be the strongest predictor of symptomatology and dysfunction (Bornstein, 1998; Hopwood, Malone, et al., 2011; Tyrer, 2005). They noted that authors from a variety of theoretical traditions had attempted to articulate the features of personality dysfunction (e.g., Kernberg, 1984; Livesley, 1998; Parker et al., 2004). They then reviewed assessment tools available for the measurement of core features of personality, in an attempt to synthesize the core constructs of personality dysfunction.

This led to the Criterion A model in the AMPD composed of four interpenetrating features. Personality dysfunction is composed of two domains consistently emphasized in the clinical literature: self and interpersonal difficulties. Self dysfunction is comprised of two components: identity and self-direction. Bender et al. (2011) defined identity in terms of appropriate boundaries between self and others, a coherent personal narrative, accurate self-appraisal, stable self-esteem, and the capacity for emotion regulation. Self-direction captured the pursuit of coherent and meaningful goals, the ability to self-reflect, and the existence of internal prosocial standards for behavior. The two components within the interpersonal domain were intimacy and empathy. Intimacy involves having deep and enduring connections with others, desiring relational closeness, and mutuality of regard in behavior with others. Empathy was defined in terms of the ability to comprehend and appreciate others' experiences and motivations, tolerating different points of view, and understanding social causality. These components are interpenetrating in the sense that each of them are expected to impact one another as they manifest in actual situations, in contrast to personality traits that are often understood as relatively independent factors.

Assessing Personality Dysfunction

A variety of tools are available for the assessment of personality dysfunction (Table 4.1). The most straightforward approach to assessing personality dysfunction is to simply add up all of the PD symptoms present in a given patient (Hopwood, Malone, et al., 2011) or sum the number of PD diagnoses the patient meets (Tyrer, 2005). However, this approach is not particularly satisfying conceptually, and it assumes that the contents of whatever PD model being used is valid. Given research showing that borderline personality is nearly synonymous with general personality pathology severity in a psychometric sense (Sharp et al.,

Table 4.1. Measures of DSM-5 Alternative Model of Personality Disorders Criterion A Personality Dysfunction.

Instrument	*Method*	*Scales*	*Administration Time (Minutes)*
General Personality Dysfunction Measures			
Add all symptoms or disorders	Questionnaire or interview	1	<1 (given a previous assessment)
Personality Pathology Ratings Scale (1–100)	Clinician rating	1	<1 (given a previous assessment)
Overall LPFS rating (1–5)	Clinician rating	1	<1 (given a previous assessment)
Psychodynamic Manual M Scale	Clinician rating	1	<1 (given a previous assessment)
Inventory of Personality Organization	Questionnaire	3	15
Structured Interview of Personality Organization	Structured interview	3	60
Object Relations Inventory	Narrative	3	60
Operationalized Psychodynamic Manual Level of Structural Integration Axis	Interview	4/8/24	90
Quality of Object Relations Scale	Interview	5	120
Personality Organization Diagnostic Form	Interview	5	60
Social Cognition and Object Relations Scale	Narrative	2/8	60
General Assessment of Personality Dysfunction	Questionnaire	2/19	45
Severity Indices of Personality Pathology	Questionnaire	5/16	45
Severity Indices of Personality Pathology Short Form	Questionnaire	5	15
DSM-5 LPFS Measures			
Morey et al. (2011) LPFS Questionnaire	Questionnaire	1	10
Levels of Personality Functioning Brief Form	Questionnaire	2	15
DSM-5 LPFS	Clinician rating	1/2/4	10
LPFS-Self-Report	Questionnaire	1/2/4	30

(Continued)

Table 4.1 (Cont.)

Instrument	*Method*	*Scales*	*Administration Time (Minutes)*
DSM-5 Levels of Personality Functioning Questionnaire	Questionnaire	1/2/4	30
AMPD Criterion A Scale	Questionnaire	1/2/4	5
LPFS Self Report Assessment	Questionnaire	1/2/4	5
LFPS Other Report	Rating form	1/2/4	5
Structured clinical interview	Interview	1/2/4	60

2015) and theoretical connections between these concepts (Kernberg, 1984), measures of borderline personality could also be used to represent AMPD Criterion A. However, this approach may conflate what is common to all PDs with one particularly salient manifestation.

A number of more theoretically embedded approaches have been taken to operationalizing personality dysfunction. These approaches can be distinguished in three ways. First, they have been informed by different clinical perspectives. As emphasized in Chapter 3 and described in Bender et al. (2011), the AMPD can be seen as an integration of these various perspectives (Mulay et al., in press, 2018). Second, different methods have been used to assess personality dysfunction, including questionnaires, clinical rating forms, and narrative approaches. Third, assessments of personality dysfunction range in complexity, with some focusing on the core dimension, others on two broad domains, and others focusing on multiple components. In what follows, I will briefly review pre-AMPD assessments of personality dysfunction, followed by a description of instruments designed to specifically assess AMPD Criterion A.

Psychodynamic Approaches

There has been a longstanding interest among psychodynamic theorists in measuring personality dysfunction. Questionnaire (Lenzenweger et al., 2001) and interview (Clarkin et al., 2007) approaches are available to assess Kernberg's (1984) model, which consists of three domains: identity diffusion, maturity of defenses, and capacity for reality testing. Blatt's two polarities model focusing on self-definition and relatedness (Luyten & Blatt, 2011) can be assessed using the Object Relations Inventory (Blatt & Lerner, 1983), which rates a patient's levels of personality organization based on open-ended descriptions of self and important others. The Psychodynamic Diagnostic Manual (PDM Task

Force, 2006) M Scale includes a number of constructs related to personality functioning, including capacity for relatedness to others and for reflection on self. The Operationalized Diagnostic Manual (OPD Task Force, 2008) offers a hierarchical model of personality organization that can be rated based on clinical interview that is similar to the DSM-5 AMPD Criterion A model (Zimmermann et al., 2012). The Quality of Object Relations Scale (Azim et al., 1991) and Personality Organization Diagnostic Form (Diguer et al., 2004) also allow clinicians to rate patients' level of personality organization based on open-ended responses, for example via clinical interview, whereas the Social Cognition and Object Relations Scales (SCORS) can be used to rate narratives in response to the Thematic Apperception Test (Haggerty et al. 2015; Stein et al., 2018).

Factor Analytic Approaches

Two measures have taken a factor analytic approach to developing scales that represent personality dysfunction as distinct from personality traits. Livesley (2006) developed the General Assessment of Personality Dysfunction (GAPD) to operationalize the forms of dysfunction associated with PD, as distinct from the traits that describe how PD is expressed. The GAPD is a 144-item instrument with 19 component scales that fall into self and interpersonal domains. A number of studies have demonstrated its clinical utility (e.g., Berghuis et al., 2013). Roughly concurrent with the GAPD was the development of the Severity Indices of Personality Pathology (SIPP; Verheul et al., 2008), a 118-item scale with 16 components and five higher-order domains. Rossi, Debast, and van Alphen (2017) later made a 60-item short form of the SIPP that recovered this domain structure and was systematically correlated with maladaptive traits in older adults. Together these questionnaires provide a powerful, if complex, approach to assessing the various ways that personality can be dysfunctional. However, concerns have been expressed about the distinctiveness between these multi-dimensional measures of personality dysfunction and instruments designed to measure individual differences in maladaptive traits (Oltmanns & Widiger, 2016). Regardless of the underlying conceptual differences between traits and dysfunction, it has proven to be difficult to develop questionnaires that can distinguish individual differences in personality style from adaptive personality-related failures via factor analytic methods.

Other Approaches

Other approaches, including using a battery of interpersonal circumplex measures (Hopwood, Thomas, et al., 2016), a unidimensional rating scale similar to the Global Assessment of Functioning Scale with content specific to personality dysfunction (Bornstein, 1998), and an interview to assess personality severity for the ICD (Olajide et al., 2018) are also available for the assessment of personality dysfunction.

DSM-5 Levels of Personality Functioning Scale

Since the publication of the DSM-5, there have been several efforts to measure personality dysfunction as instantiated specifically in the Criterion A Levels of Personality Functioning Scale (LPFS). Morey et al. (2011) used item response theory to identify items from the SIPP and GAPD that provided a unidimensional indicator of the LPFS and articulated the core features of that model. Thylstrup et al. (2016) developed the Clinician Administered Levels of Functioning technique, which uses a clinical interview to make inferences about the underlying processes indicated by the LPFS. Hutsebaut and colleagues created brief interview (2017) and self-report (2016) measures to assess the higher order aspects of the LPFS. Morey (2017; in press, 2018; Hopwood, Good, and Morey, in press, 2018) developed the more extended LPFS-SR, a questionnaire whose items correspond directly to the content of the LPFS-SR. Huprich et al. (in press, 2018) developed the DSM-5 Levels of Personality Functioning Questionnaire (DLOPFQ), which has scales for each of the four LPFS domains rated in terms of both occupational and relationship dysfunction. Roche et al. (2016) developed the briefer AMPD Criterion A Scale, which has three items per domain. Roche, Jacobson, and Phillips (in press, 2018) developed brief self- and observer-report methods for scoring the LPFS domains based on interview or narrative data. Finally, First and colleagues (2017) developed a structured interview to assess the AMPD, including both A and B Criteria features. In the next section, we review research on the DSM-5 personality dysfunction model as measured by these Criterion A-specific instruments.

Research on DSM-5 AMPD Criterion A Personality Dysfunction

The variety of scales described above contributed to a relatively large and diverse body of research on personality functioning. Research has also slowly emerged on the specific DSM-5 AMPD Levels of Personality Functioning Scale, which is reviewed presently.

Reliability

Initial validation studies of various LPFS questionnaires support the internal consistencies of their scales. Several studies also support the reliability of LPFS domains when used as an interview or quasi-interview to rate cases. Zimmermann, Benecke, et al. (2014) and Preti et al. (in press, 2018) found that the LPFS could be reliably assessed across raters with very limited clinical training in a small sample of inpatients, and Garcia et al. (in press, 2018) showed similar results with graduate students. Thylstrup et al. (2016) reported ICCs among clinicians who interviewed 30 patients/watched tapes of the interview ranged from .30 to .60 for the LPFS components and .54 for the total score. Although the developers emphasized the need to improve diagnostic reliability, these values compare favorably to diagnostic interviews for syndromes, even though these constructs and the technique requires a relatively greater level of inference. LPFS-SR scales have internal consistencies in the range of .80–.90 when used by individuals with limited training to rate clinical vignettes (Morey, in press, 2018). Buer Christensen et al. (in press, 2018) reported acceptable inter-rater reliability across five raters who evaluated videotapes of 33 patients with the SCID-AMPD interview for the LPFS domains.

Structure

Although the LPFS is a hierarchical model with different components and domains, Bender et al. (2011) emphasized the inter-connectedness of these domains: from the perspective of the AMPD, the self always exists in relation to the other (see also DSM-5 text on this issue). This makes the Criterion A model different from factor analytic models that underlie Criterion B, in that the interpenetration of Criterion A features was assumed whereas Criterion B traits could be thought of as somewhat conceptually discrete from one another, albeit correlated empirically. This raises questions about the degree to which factor analysis can be applied as a fair test of the structure of Criterion A features as well as the overlap between A and B Criteria. On the other hand, the model does imply that individuals could vary more or less on its different components, and it is not clear what alternative there is to factor analysis for evaluating the structure of the model, or what a clinician should do if a patient has severe dysfunction on one component but is doing fine on another.

At any rate, research makes it clear that the Criterion A components are highly inter-correlated with one another and with Criterion B traits (Anderson & Sellbom, 2018; Dereboy et al., in press, 2018; Hopwood, Good, & Morey, in press, 2018; Leising, Scherbaum, Packmohr, & Zimmermann, in press, 2018; Sleep et al., in press, 2018; Williams, Scalco, & Simms, 2018; Zimermann et al., 2015). Based on this empirical literature and the theoretical models of interpenetrating dysfunction upon which Criterion A was conceived (APA, 2013; Bender et al., 2011), the different domains and components of the LPFS should be understood as providing the breadth of content necessary for capturing personality dysfunction as articulated by the AMPD, but as coalescing in a single indicator of general personality dysfunction at the global level, even if they may separate in clinically useful ways at the level of individual patients.

Validity

As discussed above, a number of studies have suggested that a general severity rating is the strongest single indicator of clinical dysfunction, PD symptoms, and other outcomes (Conway, Hammen, & Brennan, 2016; Hopwood, Malone, et al., 2011; Lowyck et al., 2013; Wright, Hopwood, et al., 2016), and a few studies have correlated the LPFS specifically with other indicators of personality problems. For example, Morey, Bender, and Skodol (2013) showed that a single 5-point rating scheme for the LPFS was a significant correlate of other personality pathology indicators and PDs. Morey (in press, 2018) showed sizeable correlations between the LPFS-SR and the GAPD and the SIPP. Hopwood, Good, and Morey (in press, 2018) and Sleep et al. (in press, 2018) found that the LPFS-SR was a strong correlate of maladaptive traits and other forms of dysfunction. Dowgwillo, Roche, and Pincus (in press, 2018) found that all four domains of the AMPD-CAS were related to cold interpersonal problems. There was more differentiation with respect to interpersonal sensitivities: identity was related to sensitivity to dominance, intimacy problems to sensitivity to warmth, and empathy problems to sensitivity to dependency. Roche, Jacobson, & Phillips (in press, 2018) found that scores from their self- and observer-report approaches to the LPFS were related to measures of personality organization, defensive functioning, attachment, and interpersonal values. Dereboy, Dereboy, and Eskin (in press, 2018) found that the LPFS ratings were strongly related to the overall number of PD symptoms in a patient sample. Some studies suggest that personality dysfunction provides incremental validity over and above maladaptive traits for predicting PD symptoms and other clinical outcomes (e.g., Anderson & Sellbom, 2018; Bach & Hutsebaut, 2018; Bastiaansen et al., 2016; Hopwood et al., 2012; Roche, in press, 2018; Williams et al., 2018), whereas others are more equivocal on this issue (e.g., Few et al., 2013; Sleep et al., in press, 2018).

Summary

In summary, there are a variety of tools available for the assessment of Criterion A features from different theoretical traditions, as well as several instruments designed to assess the DSM-5 LPFS specifically. Research supporting the concept of personality dysfunction is rich, and the publication of the DSM-5 has also promoted studies on this topic. It is clear that most personality problems are highly correlated and that there is value in capturing this fact with some approximation of overall personality dysfunction. This approximation can be informative about global issues such as level of care and prognosis. Ongoing challenges involve how to articulate what, exactly, personality dysfunction is (Widiger et al., in press, 2018), both in terms of its own internal structural complexity and vis-à-vis maladaptive traits, to which I now turn.

Criterion B Maladaptive Traits

The purpose of Criterion B is to delineate the traits that account for individual differences in the expression of PD. The notion underlying the transition from ten categorical PDs to a trait system is that PD categories constitute amalgams of basic traits. The fact that different PDs share the same traits explains problematic rates of comorbidity. For instance, a patient with a tendency towards risky, impulsive behavior will be more likely to meet criteria for both antisocial and borderline PD. At the same time, the fact that different traits are diagnostic for the same disorder accounts for the problem of diagnostic heterogeneity, because two patients could achieve the same diagnosis despite having a different pattern of underlying traits. A trait-based system solves these two issues, while also connecting PD diagnosis to basic research on personality, which is predominantly trait-based. Because of the correspondence between the DSM-5 AMPD Maladaptive Traits and other basic models of individual differences in personality, there are a wide variety of approaches to measuring traits along the lines of the AMPD. In what follows, I review pre-AMPD approaches to maladaptive trait assessment as well as the family of instruments designed to specifically assess Criterion B, followed by a summary of research on DSM-5 AMPD Maladaptive Traits.

Assessing Criterion B Maladaptive Traits

There is a wide variety of approaches to measuring personality traits (see Table 4.2), which share their roots in the use of questionnaires and the application of factor analytic techniques to exploring personality structure. Although these measures are often pitted as competitors in the clinical marketplace, an important empirical finding has to do with their essential convergence in a general personality hierarchy (e.g., Markon et al., 2005). While there are specific reasons to prefer certain approaches over others, this general finding suggests that all measures are converging on a general truth regarding the structure of traits, at least as identified via factor analytic research with questionnaires. In what follows, I review some contemporary approaches to measuring

Table 4.2. Measures of DSM-5 Alternative Model of Personality Disorders Criterion B Maladaptive Traits.

Instrument	*Domains*	*Facets*
Normal Range Trait Questionnaires		
NEO Personality Inventory-3	5	30
Multidimensional Personality Questionnaire	4	11
HEXACO	6	25
Big Five Inventory-2	5	15
Big Five Aspects Scales	5	10
Maladaptive Trait Questionnaires		
Personality Inventory for DSM-5	5	25
Dimensional Assessment of Personality Pathology	4	18
Schedule of Nonadaptive and Adaptive Personality	3	15
Computerized Adaptive Test of Personality Disorder	5	33
Common Multiscale Clinical Questionnaires		
Minnesota Multiphasic Personality Inventory-2-RF	3	Multiple
Personality Assessment Inventory	3	Multiple
Interviews		
Structured Interview for the Five Factor Model	5	30
Structured Interview for the DSM-5 Alternative Model of PD	5	25

individual differences in personality in terms of associations with AMPD Criterion B constructs.

Trait Measures

Given that empirical evidence suggests that maladaptive traits represent the extreme tails of normal traits (Samuel et al., 2010; Suzuki et al., 2015), and that most normal range personality instruments have a relatively similar structure that can be more or less summarized with the Five Factor Model (FFM: neuroticism, extraversion, openness, agreeableness, conscientiousness) domains (Markon, Krueger, & Watson, 2005; Widiger & Simonsen, 2005; Wright & Simms, 2014), clinicians and researchers could use one of the many normal range personality instruments, such as the NEO Personality Inventory (McCrae, Costa, & Martin, 2005), the Big Five Inventory (Soto & John, 2017), the Multidimensional Personality Questionnaire (Tellegen & Waller, 2008), The Big Five Aspects Scales (DeYoung, Quilty, & Peterson, 2007), the HEXACO (Ashton & Lee, 2007), the Structured Interview for the Five Factor Model (Helle et al.,

2017), or their public domain analogues (Goldberg et al., 2006) to articulate maladaptive traits underlying PD. The issue with using normal range trait measures is that they are unlikely to capture the clinical range of personality that will often be present in a patient with a PD diagnosis. Several maladaptive trait measures are available for the assessment of individual differences in personality traits in the abnormal range, including the Dimensional Assessment of Personality Pathology (Livesley, 2006), the Schedule for Nonadaptive and Adaptive Personality (Clark, 1993), and the Computerized Adaptive Test of Personality Disorder (Simms et al., 2011). Research reviewed below shows that each of these measures bears a close conceptual and empirical correspondence to the AMPD.

Common Multidimensional Clinical Instruments

Many clinicians have established preferred assessment instruments, and may wish to make inferences about the AMPD based on assessment tools with which they are already familiar. Because AMPD maladaptive traits correlate systematically with the scales of the two multidimensional questionnaires used most commonly in clinical psychology, the MMPI-2-RF (Sellbom, Anderson, & Bagby, 2013) and the Personality Assessment Inventory (PAI: Hopwood, Wright, Krueger, et al., 2013), these instruments can be used to make inferences about maladaptive traits for a particular patient. Moreover, each instrument has scales that correspond directly to AMPD dimensions. Specifically, the MMPI-2-RF PSY-5 scales offer five domains that are very similar to the domains of Criterion B (Anderson et al., 2015), and direct indicators of Criterion B traits have been developed for both the MMPI (Sellbom, Waugh, & Hopwood, 2018) and PAI (Busch, Morey, & Hopwood, 2017; Ruiz et al., in press, 2018).

Personality Inventory for DSM-5

The most direct approach to assessing Criterion B traits would be to use the Personality Inventory for DSM-5 (PID-5), which was developed by the DSM-5 Personality and Personality Work Group for that purpose (Krueger et al., 2012). The work group began with the PD symptoms to develop the trait model. A review of the criteria for the ten categorical PDs in the DSM suggested 37 independent traits (out of 99 symptoms—a fact which itself explains the problematic co-occurrence patterns of categorical PDs). A questionnaire was developed to assess these traits, which led to the reduction of the 37 traits to 25 facet scales. Factor analyses of these scales yielded to a five factor structure which was highly similar to the well-known Five Factor Model in basic personality research. Thus the recovery of this well-established model was an empirical result of using modern psychometric techniques to reorganize the categorical PD symptoms. In addition to the 220-item full version of the PID-5, there is also a 100-item brief version that captures the facets and domains (Maples et al., 2015; see Bach, Maples-Keller, et al., 2016 and Thimm, Jordan, and Bach, 2016), an informant version (Markon et al., 2013; see Jopp & South, 2015), and a 25-item version that allows for the quick assessment of the domains (Krueger et al., 2013; see Fosatti, Somma, Borroni, et al., 2017). Researchers have also developed validity scales to assess over-reporting (Sellbom, Dhillon, & Bagby, 2018) and inattentive responding (Bagby & Sellbom, 2018; Somma, Borroni, et al., 2018). Finally, First et al. (2017) developed the Structured Interview for DSM-5 Alternative Model of Personality Disorders, which assesses both A and B Criteria.

Research on Criterion B Maladaptive Traits

A relatively large body of validity research has quickly emerged on the DSM-5 Maladaptive Traits since the publication of the PID-5 (Krueger et al., 2012; see Chapter 2 of this volume). Indeed, several reviews of this literature are already available. Krueger and Markon (2014) and Krueger et al. (2014) reviewed the maladaptive trait model vis-à-vis psychiatric diagnosis in general. Al-Dajani, Gralnick, and Bagby (2016) provided a general review of research on the PID-5 specifically. Hopwood and Sellbom (2013) described the use of maladaptive personality measures in forensic settings. Krueger and DeYoung (2016) discussed how a maladaptive trait model could inform research on the neurobiology of psychopathology. Dilchert, Ones, and Krueger (2014) reviewed the use of maladaptive personality measures in organizational settings.

Reliability

In the initial validation study, Krueger et al. (2012) reported scale internal consistencies for the PID-5 ranging from .72 to .96. Quilty et al. (2013) also showed acceptable levels of reliability in the DSM field trial, and overall internal consistencies of PID-5 facets have been above or near the common threshold of .70 across different populations (Al-Daljani et al., 2016). Wright, Calabrese, et al. (2015) found relatively high rank order and mean level stability over time, and Few et al. (2013) showed fair clinician inter-rater reliability. Garcia et al. (in press, 2018) found acceptable levels of inter-rater reliability when Criterion B traits were applied to case vignettes. Bach, Sellbom, and Simonsen (2018) found measurement invariance for the PID-5 across clinical and non-clinical samples. However, Debast, Rossi, and van Alphen (2018) found some evidence of differential item functioning between adult and geriatric populations, suggesting potential concerns about the use of the PID-BF for clinical assessment among older adults.

Structure

The general organization of the PID-5 assumes that 25 unidimensional scales can be organized into five correlated domains that roughly reflect the FFM, and that these domains can be summarized at increasingly broad levels of abstraction (Wright, Thomas, et al., 2012). In other words, the model assumes a hierarchy that unfolds from a single score representing what is common to all maladaptive traits, down to 25 reliable and unidimensional facets (Figure 4.1). Several studies have supported this structure in questionnaire (Somma, Krueger, et al., in press, 2018; Wright, Thomas, et al., 2012) and clinician ratings (Morey, Krueger, & Skodol, 2013).

Consistent with the thesis of this book that the AMPD integrates multiple theoretical perspectives on individual differences, there has been significant interest in the conjoint structure of the PID-5 with other models of personality. Crego and Widiger (2016), De Fruyt et al. (2013), DeYoung et al. (2016), Gore and Widiger (2013), Griffin and Samuel (2014), Helle et al. (2017), Thomas et al. (2013), Watson et al. (2013), and Wright and Simms (2014) all tested conjoint models of FFM measures with the PID-5. Suzuki, Griffin, and Samuel (2017) furthermore showed that the PID-5 domains have a similar pattern of external correlates as normal range five factor traits. This body of work generally supports the interpretation that the five domains are close proxies for the FFM factors, such that negative affectivity (NA) is like neuroticism, detachment (DET)

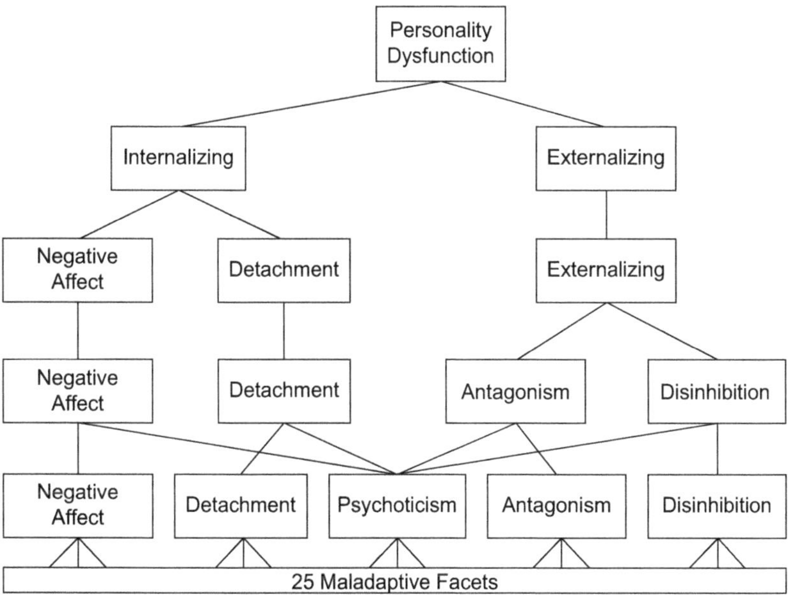

Figure 4.1. DSM-5 AMPD Criterion B Hierarchical Trait Model.

is like low extraversion, antagonism (ANT) is like low agreeableness, disinhibition (DIS) is like low conscientiousness, and psychoticism (PSY) is like openness (openness-psychoticism is admittedly the most tenuous connection among the five factors; see Chmielewski et al., 2014 and DeYoung, Grazioplene, & Peterson, 2012).

This is an important finding, particularly given that this was not an intentional property of the instrument (Krueger et al., 2012). In other words, the PID-5 demonstrates that a psychometrically sound measure whose content is based on DSM categorical PD symptoms ultimately takes the structure of the well-established FFM. This provides a strong rationale for integrating research on normal and maladaptive personality (Krueger & Markon, 2014; Suzuki et al., 2015). Wright and Simms (2015) showed that this structure also applied when maladaptive traits and psychiatric syndromes were included, suggesting that the FFM provides a coherent theoretical model for reconceptualizing psychopathology in general (Krueger et al., 2014). Several other studies have shown structural convergence between the PID-5 and other trait models of personality, including the "Big Three" (Watson et al., 2013), the MMPI-2-RF PSY-5 (Anderson et al., 2013), the HEXACO (Ashton et al., 2012), and the DAPP (Van den Broeck et al., [2014]), indicating that the PID-5 can be flexibly integrated with a number of different approaches to capturing individual differences in maladaptive traits.

Validity: Personality Disorders

Given that the purpose of the AMPD was to replace categorical PDs, it was important for early research with the AMPD to show that it was related to PD constructs. Most of this work focused on the PID-5. Anderson et al. (2014), Bach, Anderson, & Simonsen (2017); Bastiaens, Smits, et al. (2016), Few et al. (2013), Fossati et al. (2013), Hopwood et al. (2012), Morey, Benson, and Skodol (2016), Somma, Krueger, et al. (in press, 2018) and Yam and Simms (2014) found that PID-5 traits could recover most of the reliable variance in PD constructs. Some studies suggest that Criterion B traits are superior to traditional PD constructs for predicting associated impairment (Boland, Damnjanovic, & Anderson, in press, 2018; Fossati et al., 2016b).

A number of studies also focused on the pattern of PID-5 traits associated with specific PD constructs. Strickland et al. (2013) found that the PID-5 adequately captures psychopathy traits. In general, DIS was related to psychopathic disinhibition, meanness was linked to ANT, and boldness was associated with the risk-taking facet and low NA. This pattern was confirmed in research by Anderson et al. (2014), Crego and Widiger, (2014), Decuyper et al., (2014) Sellbom, Wygant, and Drislane (2015) with a variety of instruments in different populations. Of particular interest was a study by Wygant et al. (2016), who found that PID-5 traits outperformed DSM antisocial PD for predicting Psychopathy Checklist scores in inmates. Fossati, Somma, Borroni, Pincus et al. (2016), Miller et al. (2014), and Wright, Pincus, Thomas, et al. (2013) showed that PID-5 scores, mostly involving high ANT, were related to multiple measures of narcissistic PD. Anderson and Sellbom (2015), Bach, Selbom, et al. (2016), Bach and Sellbom (2016), Evans and Simms (2018), and Sellbom et al. (2013) each found strong convergence of PID-5 traits, often involving high NA and DIS, with borderline personality, and Fossati et al. (2016a) found that PID-5 traits could discriminate borderline and narcissistic PDs. Sellbom, Carmichael, and Liggett (2017) found that PID-5 traits involving NA and DET were related to avoidant PD. Gore and Widiger (2015) found strong and relatively specific associations between PID-5 NA traits and dependency. Finally, several studies found reliable associations between PID-5 NA and the rigid perfectionism facet with measures of obsessive-compulsive PD (De Caluwé, Rettew, & De Clercq, 2014; Liggett, Sellbom, & Carmichael, 2017) and perfectionism (Stoeber, 2014).

Overall, this body of work shows that PID-5 traits can adequately recover DSM PD categorical constructs. This should be reassuring in the sense that it is unlikely that important information will be lost in the transition from the DSM categories to the AMPD. This is particularly the case given that much of the work reviewed in this section did not take Criterion A into account. However, a few issues need to be kept in mind when interpreting this research. First, a consistent finding was that more facets were generally needed to optimize predictions of PD constructs than what was proposed by the AMPD. Moreover, Samuel, Hopwood, et al. (2013) found that you need about half of the traits to reproduce prevalence estimates from categories. This suggests that the DSM-5 algorithms for assessing categorical PD constructs may need to be refined, to the degree that there is continued interest in assessing categorical PDs. In particular, the thresholds may not be optimal, and there are more traits related to specific PDs than proposed by the work group. At the same time, if the work group had proposed more traits for any given disorder, they would have increased the overlap between disorders because the same traits would be allocated to different diagnoses. This problem owes entirely to the fact that PD constructs do, indeed, share features. There is no good empirical solution to the "comorbidity" problem that this creates. The best clinical situation is probably to simply abandon the PD categories and move on to an evidence-based model that integrates personality traits and dysfunction, such as the AMPD (Hopwood et al., 2017).

The second issue has to do with the fact that the AMPD was designed to replace the categorical PDs because of well-established empirical and clinical problems with the categorical model. There is accordingly some irony in using the PD categories to validate the AMPD. Although this kind of work was important in the early stages of the AMPD for demonstrating that much of the same information in categorical PDs is retained in the AMPD (albeit organized more effectively), this point has been proven and there is probably not much of a need for further exploration of how categorical PDs relate to the AMPD.

Validity: Other Clinical Phenomena

A very large literature documents the validity of normal and maladaptive personality traits in general. A series of studies published in the last few years has examined the associations between Criterion B traits as assessed with the PID-5 and other important aspects of clinical functioning related to traits, such as beliefs/schema and interpersonal behaviors. Hopwood, Schade, et al. (2013) showed systematic associations with maladaptive beliefs emphasized in cognitive models of PD. Wright, Pincus, et al. (2012) found that while all maladaptive traits relate to general interpersonal distress, they also tend to have specific interpersonal styles. Southard et al. (2015) showed that DET, ANT, DIS, and PSY are generally cold with respect to interpersonal circumplex traits, whereas NA projects towards submissiveness. Bach, Sellbom, et al. (2017) found systematic similarities between PID-5 traits and the traits proposed for the ICD-11.

Relevant to the use of the AMPD and the PID-5 for general clinical assessment, a number of studies have focused on associations between the PID-5 and clinical syndromes or other aspects of distress and dysfunction. Wright, Calabrese, et al. (2015) found that changes in PID-5 traits track with changes in psychosocial functioning and predict future functioning. Simms and Calabrese (2016) found that PID-5 traits provided incremental validity over mental health syndromes, normal range traits, and PDs for predicting psychosocial impairment. Pollock et al. (2016) showed that people with elevated NA, ANT, and DET had more difficulties regulating emotions in response to negative experiences in daily life. De Caluwé, Decuyper, and De Clercq (2013) showed that children at elevated risk on a measure of psychopathology had higher PID-5 scores four years later. Creswell et al. (2016) found that ANT and DIS were related to problematic alcohol use. Dowgwillo et al. (2016) showed that ANT is related to relationship violence for women, whereas DIS was related for men. Russell and King (2016) also found that PID-5 traits were related to relationship violence. James, Anders, et al. (2015) showed that people with PTSD had higher PID-5 traits, especially on DET and PSY. Beanland, Sellbom, and Johnson (2014) found that negative affect predicted poor driving in general, DIS predicted lapses in attention, and ANT predicted aggression on the road. Carlotta et al. (2015) found that ANT and DET were related to pathological gambling. Noser et al. (2015) found links between PID-5 traits and different types of moral concern. Zeigler-Hill, McCabe, and Vrabel, (2016) found associations with different humor styles. Fossatti, Somma, Krueger, et al. (2017) reported associations between PID-5 traits assessed via self-report and behavioral measures of social cognition. Swami et al. (2016) found that psychoticism traits are related to believing in conspiracy theories.

Translations

The popularity of the AMPD has extended beyond the borders of the United States and the English language in the form of translations to a variety of other languages, including Danish (Bo et al., 2016), Dutch (Bastiaens, Claes, et al., 2016; De Clerq et al., 2014), French (Roskam et al., 2015), German (Zimmermann, Altenstein, et al., 2014), Italian (Fossati et al., 2013), Portuguese (Pires, Sousa Ferreira, & Guedes, 2017), and Spanish (Gutiérrez et al., 2017). This work generally shows that translations have scales with acceptable levels of internal consistency, the factor structure indicated by initial research with the English version holds, and the measure correlates with a variety of validated clinical instruments. Research also suggests that the instrument functions effectively in young people (Van den Broeck et al., 2013).

Summary

The validity of trait models for capturing individual differences in personality is well-established, and the development of a hierarchical trait structure that integrates normal and abnormal personality across theoretical perspectives is perhaps one of psychology's most important contributions during the last half-century. AMPD Criterion B leverages this advance in the form of a model that has attracted significant research attention and has substantial clinical utility. Multiple methods are available to the clinician interested in assessing maladaptive traits in order to formulate cases, which should encourage clinicians to adopt the AMPD for PD diagnosis.

Conclusions

The DSM-5 AMPD was built upon a rich body of transtheoretical research on personality dysfunction and traits, and its publication has contributed to a spike of interest in these topics. Overall, this work makes the empirical and clinical superiority of the AMPD relative to the categorical PD model clear. The AMPD addresses problems such as comorbidity and heterogeneity, points to specific treatment targets and reflects the way clinicians actually think about personality problems, and connects PD diagnosis to basic research in personality psychology. Furthermore, many existing and recently developed instruments are available to assess AMPD constructs.

But there is more work to do. I conclude by focusing on two areas in need of further research. First, the integration of personality dysfunction and maladaptive trait models has come at the cost of efficiency. These models reflect different perspectives on personality, with personality dysfunction coming from a more psychodynamic/clinical perspective and traits coming from a more psychometric/empirical perspective (Mulay et al., in press, 2018). Naturally, both of these perspectives cover much of the same territory, so there will be some redundancy when they are placed side by side, even though personality dysfunction and traits can be meaningfully distinguished conceptually. In practice, AMPD A and B criteria are too redundant (Bastiaansen et al., 2016; Few et al., 2013; Zimmermann et al., 2015). Figuring out how to measure personality dysfunction and traits separately, efficiently, and in a way that maximizes discriminant validity is a major challenge for the AMPD moving forward.

There are essentially three approaches. The first is to keep the model the way it is and tolerate redundancy. The second is to eliminate one set of criteria in favor of the other. The disadvantage of this approach is that it favors certain intellectual traditions without any empirical basis and risks losing the important distinction between what a person is like (traits) and what problems s/he is having (dysfunctions). The third solution, which I favor personally (Hopwood, 2011), is to make Criterion B traits normal range. Such a model would better connect Criterion B to basic models of personality, in which traits have two tails and depict more general patterns of individual differences in human behavior. This would have the added advantage of capturing extremes at both sides, in contrast to Criterion B traits which focus on maladaptivity at the tail of each domain where problems are most common, and may be more useful for capturing personality strengths. In such a model, Criterion A would be responsible for capturing dysfunction, which would be understood as separate from the person.

Second, although practice reviews generally find preferences for dimensional models like the AMPD over the categorical PD model, it is also somewhat unfamiliar to practicing clinicians. There are a few ways to address this problem. First, clinicians would be more likely to adopt the AMPD to the degree that it was straightforward, which puts a fine point on the redundancy and complexity issue described immediately above. Second, emerging research showing that AMPD constructs can be inferred from the scores of instruments that many clinicians already use means that adopting the AMPD does not necessarily mean using entirely new and unfamiliar measures. Third, practical guides, like this book, are needed to help clinicians become accustomed to thinking in AMPD terms. Fourth, treatment researchers need to begin orienting their techniques and studies to the basic dimensions that underlie personality problems, rather than PD categories. Finally, it takes time for people to get used to big changes. Given the large body of research supporting the AMPD and the availability of many validated assessment tools for operationalizing AMPD constructs, we are confident that the acceptability of the AMPD will continue to increase as it becomes more familiar.

5 Clinical Utility and Application of the AMPD[1]

Mark H. Waugh

We now examine the practical side of the Alternative Model for Personality Disorders (AMPD; APA, 2013). This may be particularly helpful to those new to the AMPD, both the experienced clinician who is assimilating the model into their knowledge base, and the trainee mastering personality disorder (PD) diagnosis. We frame this discussion with the concept of *clinical utility*. Clinical utility emphasizes practical aspects of a diagnostic system, such as the extent to which it is easy to use, facilitates communication, and enhances treatment (Mullins-Sweat, Lengel, & DeShong, 2016; Mullins-Sweatt & Widiger, 2009).

Pragmatics and theory are not separate. Kurt Lewin's (1943/1999) epigram captures this idea: "There is nothing so practical as a good theory" (p. 336). A diagnostic nosology cannot be atheoretical. The AMPD is pantheoretical (Pincus, 2011) and transdiagnostic (Krueger & Eaton, 2015). To this extent, the model enjoys a degree of inherent clinical utility (Krueger, Hopwood, Wright, & Markon, 2014; Waugh, Hopwood, Krueger, Morey, Pincus, & Wright, 2017). In part, this comes from the multiple theoretical paradigms that lie within the AMPD. This pluralism permits clinicians of different backgrounds and orientations to find resonances with the AMPD. This also facilitates learning and application of the model because clinicians already "know" some of its elements. Moreover, the integrative aspect of the AMPD places it within the contemporary transdiagnostic and trans-therapeutic movement in the mental health sciences and professions.

The concept of clinical utility is widely used in medicine and laboratory clinical testing. Lesko, Zineh, and Huang (2010) noted the multidimensionality of clinical utility, and its important economic, clinical, and humanistic implications to various stakeholders. They emphasized that clinical utility must be considered from the perspectives of different stakeholders (e.g., health care professionals providing care, the person receiving care, insurance administrators, patient advocacy groups). Thus, the type, quality, and extent of evidence for clinical utility must be flexible and relative—depending on the needs of the stakeholder. Lesko et al. (2010) argued that what matters most is the value and meaning of a clinical concept or technique to the person receiving care. This underscores the practical and personal side of clinical utility.

Kendell and Jablensky (2003) distinguished between validity, utility, and disease in psychiatry. They argued that little evidence supports categorical diagnoses and few psychiatric disorders are valid disease entities. They further reasoned that psychiatric diagnoses reflect clinical utility to the extent they speak to etiology, treatment response, and outcome. First, Pincus, Levine, Williams, Ustun, and Peele (2004) broadened the scope of clinical utility. The authors delineated five broad ways in which a diagnostic system assists clinicians. These are: (1) conceptualizing diagnoses; (2) communication of clinical information; (3) using diagnostic categories and criteria in practice; (4) guiding intervention; and (5) prognostic implications. Recent discussions of clinical utility have concentrated attention on the dimensions of ease of use, communication functions, and treatment implications (Mullins-Sweatt & Widiger, 2009). For Mullins-Sweatt and Widiger (2009), clinical utility is a practical and humanitarian matter, with its most essential aspects being reducing suffering and helping clinicians care for patients.

The concerns of the clinician and the scientist, while similar, are not identical. Mullins-Sweatt and Widiger (2009) argued that diagnostic conceptualization and prognosis are often viewed as matters of construct validity (Cronbach & Meehl, 1955). Validity and utility overlap in that classification with no validity is not useful (Mullins-Sweatt & Widiger, 2009). But, the clinician is most interested in specific, practical components of utility such as ease of application, communication value, and relevance to treatment. Recently, Mullins-Sweatt et al. (2016) elaborated these points with respect to the desiderata of a diagnostic manual (e.g., a DSM), and the World Health Organization (WHO) has stated that clinical utility will be central in revisions of its classification system (Reed, 2010).

Clinical Utility of Transdiagnostic Perspectives

The AMPD represents a *transdiagnostic* approach to PD nosology. The term transdiagnostic describes an approach to a content domain (personality, psychopathology, or intervention) not organized by traditional diagnostic categories. Cross-cutting and universal constructs or principles characterize the domain of interest. Contemporary scholarship increasingly employs this perspective. Sauer-Zavala, Gutner, Farchione, Boettcher, Bullis, and Barlow (2017) categorized transdiagnostic approaches to treatment in three ways: (1) *universally applied treatments*, (2) *modular approaches*, and (3) *shared mechanisms treatments*. They noted that universal psychotherapeutic approaches were common prior to the diagnostic expansion promulgated in the DSM-III (APA, 1980). For example, Wolpe's (1958) systematic desensitization was universal because it was based on general learning theory (Barlow, Allen, & Choate, 2004). Similarly, general principles of the psychodynamic, behavioral, and humanistic schools of therapy are extended across specific disorders. Examples of recent universal, cross-cutting approaches are found in the *Psychodiagnostic Manual-2* (PDM-2; Lingiardi & McWilliams, 2017), which organizes PD nosology by core psychodynamic concepts, and the cognitive behavioral therapy (CBT) formulation of PD represented by Beck, Freeman, and Davis (2015). However, over time, CBT generally has become tailored to specific disorders, sometimes with manualized protocols for particular DSM-based diagnoses.

Sauer-Zavala, Gutner, et al. (2017) contrasted the universal focus of schools of psychotherapy to a modular transdiagnostic approach. The modular approach is often empirically guided and problem-focused. Clarkin, Cain, and Livesley (2015) applied this modular perspective to the AMPD. The presence of Criterion A (i.e., PD impairment) implies that in the early phases of psychotherapy, techniques (modules) that address patient safety (e.g., hospitalization, medication, suicide contracting) and establish the treatment frame are important. Later, other techniques (modules), such as clarifying and interpreting maladaptive interpersonal schemas informed by Criterion B, are more relevant. Bach, Markon, Simonsen, and Krueger (2015) provided case history examples of this approach with the AMPD, and Hopwood (2018) formulated the AMPD as a general, step-wise strategy to treatment planning.

According to Sauer-Zavala, Gutner, et al. (2017), the third type of transdiagnostic approach (shared mechanisms) organizes disorders by common mechanisms. They suggested the Research Domain Criteria (RDoC; Insel et al., 2010) illustrates this model. For example, in the RDoC, the class of Negative Valence Systems groups together constructs such as anxiety, fear, loss, and reward frustration. These are analyzed across explanatory levels (e.g., molecular, physiological, behavioral, etc.). Together these dimensions form a matrix, the nosology of disorders based on mechanisms (e.g., molecular, physiological, behavioral, etc.).

Transdiagnostic concepts apply to many personality and psychopathology variables. These range from modelling psychopathology (Caspi et al., 2014; Krueger, 2005; Krueger & Eaton, 2015), personality assessment (Rodriguez-Seijas, Eaton, & Krueger, 2015), to the genetics of mental disorders (Cannon & Keller, 2006). The DSM-5 (APA, 2013) sought increased dimensionalization of diagnosis (Regier, Narrow, Kuhl, & Kupfer, 2009), and in Section III offers cross-cutting symptom measures. The DSM-5 applies the analogy of the review of systems (ROS) of general medicine. Using a ROS perspective, Harkness, Reynolds, and Lilienfeld (2014) described an adaptive systems model of personality based on the psychopathology five dimensions (PSY-5; Harkness, McNulty, & Ben-Porath, 1995). In general, contemporary psychopathology increasingly assumes an overarching transdiagnostic dimension or general factor of psychopathology (e.g., the "p" factor; Caspi et al., 2014; see also the Hierarchical Taxonomy of Psychopathology [HiTOP]; Kotov et al., 2017). Similarly, Dimaggio, Semerari, Carcione, Procacci, and Nicolò (2006) described a shared mechanisms model of PD based on cross-cutting dimensions of (1) problematic thoughts and emotions (subjective and narratively experienced), (2) problems in self and other reflection (metacognition), (3) maladaptive interpersonal schemas, and (4) problematic decision-making. Our interest is the cross-cutting approach to PD found in DSM-5, Section III, the AMPD.

From the study of CBT of anxiety disorders, Barlow and colleagues (2017) evolved the Unified Protocol for the Transdiagnostic Treatment of Emotional Disorders (Unified PrOtOCO), an empirically validated transdiagnostic treatment protocol for anxiety, depression, and related conditions. Recently, this was extended to borderline PD (Sauer-Zavala, Bentley, & Wilner, 2016), as well as treatment of broad personality dimensions (e.g., neuroticism; Sauer-Zavala, Wilner, & Barlow, 2017). Relatedly, Conway, Hammen, and Brennan (2016) assessed a large community sample of high-risk adults by semi-structured interview for PD symptoms and psychosocial functioning. Analyzing these data with bi-factor methods revealed a large transdiagnostic dimension within PDs that was strongly predictive of important clinical outcome variables. Interestingly, this dimension resembles Criterion A of the AMPD. Other well-known clinical variables, such as perfectionism (Egan, Wade, & Shafran, 2011), repetitive negative thinking (Ehring & Watkins, 2012), anxiety sensitivity (Carleton, Sharpe, & Asmundson, 2007), emotion regulation (Stanton, Rozek, Stasik-O'Brien, Ellickson-Larew, & Watson, 2016), and rejection sensitivity (Cohen, Feinstein, Rodriguez-Seijas, Taylor, & Newman, 2016) also can be construed transdiagnostically. Recent work in computational psychiatry employs this transdiagnostic point of view. For example, Friston, Stephan, Montague, and Dolan (2014) argued the common denominator of psychopathology is the production of false beliefs and the inability to update internal models from experience. Their approach, which seeks to explain errors in perception and interpretation (e.g., psychopathology) within the brain's functional architecture, resembles Fonagy, Luyten, and Allison's (2015) formulation of PD as a disorder of premature epistemological hardening. This refers to a closing down of openness to normal processes of social exchange and interpersonal learning arising from interactions between constitutional liabilities, adverse events and environments, and efforts to make sense of life experience.

As Sauer-Zavala, Gutner, et al. (2017) observed, there are precedents to the contemporary transdiagnostic perspective. Achenbach and Edelbrock (1978) pioneered (cross-cutting) multivariate classification of child psychopathology. Pre-DSM-III (APA, 1980) nosologies generally were transdiagnostic insofar as superordinate constructs (e.g., neurosis, psychosis, character disorder, organic mental disorder) organized classification. Relatedly, recent study of the meta-structure of diagnoses suggests similar empirical groupings (Andrews, Goldberg, Krueger, Carpenter, Hyman,

Sachdev, & Pine, 2009). Research on clinicians' natural categorization of mental disorders has also shown a similar meta-structure (Flanagan, Keeley, & Blashfield, 2008). Flanagan and Blashfield (2010) argued that aligning nosology with clinicians' ways of thinking would impart improved clinical utility to psychiatric diagnoses.

An early, basic transdiagnostic perspective is Lewin's (1936) equation for the interrelation of person and environment (B = *f* [P, E]). Lewin (1936) emphasized the practical value of theory, and his formulation applies to the AMPD when viewed with the lens of clinical utility. Most basically, for a theory, model or construct to be useful, it must facilitate the clinical transaction. Furthermore, clinical transactions occur between at least two parties, and they occur in a specific situation. Interpersonal, situational, and contextual factors are inescapable. The Cambridge Model for Symptom Formation (CMSF; Berrios & Marková, 2015) is an example of a transdiagnostic model that bridges clinical constructs from the planes of neuropsychiatry to narrative identity. The CMSF formulates these constructs in terms of how they are expressed and how they are known within a clinical situation. The CMSF, a contemporary elaboration of Lewin's (1936) famous equation, aligns well with the clinician's informed use of the AMPD.

In the CMSF, symptoms, the "objects" of psychiatry, are always hybrid (Berrios & Marková, 2015). This means that they are multi-factorial and formed from a "brain signal" *configured* within situational, personal, social, and cultural contingences. Of these, we focus on *personality configurators* and how they influence PD symptoms in different ways. Widiger (2011) described three forms of interrelation: (1) non-causally affecting the presentation or expression of one another (pathoplasticity); (2) sharing a common etiology represented as a spectrum; and (3) exhibiting bidirectional causal influences. As an example, Widiger (2011) noted that neuroticism and dependent personality traits are bidirectionally causal with depression. Schizotypal PD and the schizophrenic disorders represent a spectrum relationship. Pathoplasticity is seen in the relationship between excessive conscientiousness and anorexia. That is, perfectionism does not cause anorexia, but it alters expression of the condition. One of the ways the AMPD achieves clinical utility is through subsuming clinically useful personality constructs such as found in attachment and interpersonal theory. These connections are discussed later, but now we simply note pathoplastic, spectrum, and/or bidirectional relationships may occur with major personality constructs and the AMPD.

The CMSF posits a symptom can be known only through a dialogical encounter. A symptom is a communication, a process, not an entity, that is transmitted within a clinical transaction. It is embedded in relationship and in context. This is the case whether variously known (assessed) by clinician observation and mental status examination, self-report, informant ratings, laboratory tests, or neuroimaging. As noted, the neuropsychiatric "brain signal" from which a psychiatric symptom originates is configured by cultural, social and personal semantic systems (within a relationship context). Focusing on the level of personality configurator in the CMSF, the model may be expanded with another personality schematic. McAdams and Pals (2006) described three cross-cutting types and levels of personality constructs. These are dispositional traits, characteristic adaptations, and narrative identity. These supra-personality constructs, viewed as *personality configurators*, refer to different patterns of expressing behavior and meaning-making within the person. The McAdams and Pals (2006) constructs evoke metaphors of *actor, agent*, and *author* (McAdams, 2015). The metaphors suggest the relevance of description (actor), observation of clinical process and performance assessment (agent), and narrative methods (author). Major personality constructs such as those found in attachment and interpersonal theory may be viewed through the McAdams and Pals (2006) schematic and then placed within the CMSF. For example, attachment style and dynamics can affect expression of dispositional traits, modes of characteristic adaptation, and aspects of narrative identity. These three angles on personality constructs (personality configurators within the CMSF) may be applied to the AMPD. For example, Mulay and colleagues (in press, 2018) described how the AMPD draws on each of the McAdams and Pals (2006) three types of personality constructs, and that they are reflected in different proportions across Criterion A and Criterion B. There are advantages to coordinating the AMPD with a personality schematic, such as that of McAdams and Pals (2006), and within the more comprehensive CMSF. Doing so reminds us of the diversity of data, developmental pathways, putative etiological mechanisms, forms of expression, and methods of approach needed to understand personality and PD. This reduces theoretical tunnel vision and keeps us humble—reasserting the pragmatic value of theory.

The AMPD includes universal, modular, and shared mechanism aspects. Universal principles are imported to the AMPD by its inherent paradigmatic pluralism (Waugh et al., 2017). Modularity is reflected in the domains of Criterion A and Criterion B, each of which confer specific treatment implications (Clarkin et al., 2015; Hopwood, 2018). An example of a shared mechanism feature is the construct of reflective functioning (RF). RF was part of the conceptual heritage of the Level of Personality Functioning Scale (LPFS; Bender, Morey, & Skodol, 2011). Furthermore, RF and the kindred construct of mentalization are figural in formulations of and treatment of PDs (Bateman & Fonagy, 2004; Choi-Kain & Gunderson, 2008).

As a PD nosology, multiple personality variables are relevant to the AMPD. A non-exhaustive listing of personality constructs presumed to interleave with either or both Criterion A and B include the following: attachment style, anxiety sensitivity, cognitive and affective empathy, dependency and self-criticism aspects of depression, emotional dysregulation, interoceptive sensitivity, interpersonal boundary disturbance, interpersonal style, maladaptive cognitive schemas, neuroticism, psychosis-proneness/psychoticism, rejection sensitivity, and sensation-seeking. These personality constructs are clinically relevant, include various nomological nets, and they bring modular and shared mechanism transdiagnostic aspects to the AMPD. To illustrate these points, this chapter focuses on attachment style, interpersonal style (e.g., Interpersonal Circumplex [IPC; Leary, 1957]), and Blatt's (1974) "Two Polarities" personality dimensions.

Returning to the CMSF, note that the term *dialogical encounter* refers to communication between patient and other (e.g., a mental health professional) and encompasses all that affects communication between the parties. This includes intent, capacity, clarity of message, openness, receptiveness, comprehension, commitment to the encounter, and context. Stated otherwise, the complexity of PD means that if a nosology is to be useful, it must help the clinician and patient communicate and understand as well as address the nature and structure of PD, regarded broadly (such as with the CMSF). To do so, PD nosology must integrate agentic and subjective concerns with the descriptive and objective realms. When this is done, clinical utility follows because the enterprise is inherently interpersonal, humanitarian, and practical.

Ease of Use

For Mullins-Sweatt and Widiger (2009), ease of use speaks to the feasibility and practicality of diagnoses in routine clinical practice. This contrasts with desiderata of the research setting in which structured interviews, inclusion and exclusion criteria, and design considerations are central. Empirical comparisons of these two approaches show they are very different. Samuel's (2015) meta-analysis of studies of naturalistic and research-based PD diagnoses concluded diagnoses made in routine practice were of moderate interrater reliability (e.g., kappa .46 and .40, dimensional vs. categorical). In general, the more systematic (structured) the method of diagnosis, the higher the rater reliability. However, it should be noted that structured, research-based methods are not typical in routine practice. Thus, studies of rater reliability with structured approaches only obliquely relate to gauging clinical utility of a nosology.

How clinicians apply PD diagnostic criteria provides an index of ease of use. Research finds clinicians do not adhere to DSM criteria and algorithms when making diagnoses; rather, they diagnose impressionistically (Davis, Blashfield, & McElroy, 1993; Morey & Ochoa, 1989). Morey and Benson (2016) noted impressionistic PD diagnosis persists even though DSM PD criteria have changed little since DSM-III (APA, 1980). Given it has now been almost 40 years, this cannot be due to lack of familiarity with the criteria-count approach. Kim and Ahn (2002) studied the cognitive psychology clinicians' application of diagnostic criteria. They found clinicians weight diagnostic criteria by perception of their causal importance. Other studies show diagnostic criteria are not "additive" or "commutative" (Keeley, DeLao, & Kirk, 2013), properties implied by the criterion-set model of the DSM. In the mind of the clinician, diagnostic criteria interact with each other and color impressions of other diagnostic data (Keeley, Chmielewski, & Bagby, 2015). As Mullins-Sweatt et al. (2016) noted, one way to enhance clinical utility is to shorten or reduce diagnostic criteria. Yet, with the impressionistic style of diagnosis, abbreviated criteria sets are unlikely to promote strict adherence to criteria, not to mention the psychometric decrease in reliability.

Another approach to enhancing the clinical utility of diagnosis suggests prototype models. This employs a narrative description of an idealized syndrome of correlated features. The logic draws on cognitive science, which finds that clinical diagnoses resemble natural category cognition (Cantor, Smith, French, & Mezzich, 1980; Medin, 1989). The idea is that clinicians, like people in general, think in categories, and that diagnoses based on category cognition may confer clinical utility (e.g., First & Westen, 2007; Westen, Shedler, Bradley, & DeFife, 2012). Indeed, some research finds clinicians prefer prototype models (e.g., Spitzer, First, Shedler, Westen, & Skodol, 2008). The DSM-5 (APA, 2013) Personality and Personality Disorders Work Group initially considered a prototype scheme as one part of PD diagnosis, but ultimately rejected the strategy (Zachar, Krueger, & Kendler, 2016). The proposed prototype approach was strongly criticized on bases of presumed poor reliability and validity (e.g., Pincus, 2011; Zimmerman, 2011) and risk of perpetuating artefactual comorbidity within diagnoses. Further, it was feared prototype diagnosis would constitute return to the pre-DSM-III (APA, 1980) narrative models for PD (Frances, 2012; Jablensky, 2012). Regardless, the ostensible attractiveness of a diagnostic nosology modeled on natural processes of cognitive categorization is open to question (see also Chapter 1 for discussion of these issues). For example, it is known that clinicians do not use unabridged prototypes in naturalistic diagnosis. As noted by Kim and Ahn (2002), clinicians weight information with presumed causal or theoretical significance. In other words, prototype diagnoses are not based on strict judgments of similarity; other (often tacit) assumptions are used.

Several studies show that the AMPD can be learned and used with respectable levels of rater agreement. Few and colleagues (2013) found that trained graduate students could apply the LPFS of Criterion A and pathological personality traits of Criterion B with acceptable levels of agreement (e.g., Intraclass correlations .47 for the LPFS domains; median trait-facet of .55). Moreover, Zimmermann, Benecke, et al. (2014) found that untrained undergraduates demonstrated similar levels of rater agreement. Studies with semi-structured interview formats of the LPFS also revealed moderate to strong rater agreement (e.g., Hutsebaut, Feenstra, & Kamphuis, 2016; Thylstrup et al., 2016). Recently, Garcia, Skadberg,

Schmidt, Bierma, Shorter, and Waugh (in press, 2018) examined the effects of classroom training on the LPFS rater reliability and agreement with expert ratings. They found that the LPFS, assumed by some to be more difficult to learn (e.g., Few et al., 2013), showed high levels of agreement and correspondence with expert ratings. In short, a growing body of research shows the AMPD can be learned and used reliably, although applied use of the AMPD requires further evaluation. Importantly, clinicians generally evaluate the ease of use and clinical utility of the AMPD quite favorably (Garcia et al. in press, 2018; Morey, Skodol, & Oldham, 2014).

The AMPD asks clinicians to use terms and think in ways that may seem new. Change always requires effort, but transition to the AMPD may not be that difficult. First, the paradigmatic pluralism of the AMPD facilitates this. This means clinicians of many orientations are familiar with some features of the AMPD (Waugh et al., 2017). Results of rater reliability studies show the AMPD can be learned and applied to clinical material. Furthermore, traditional PD syndromes cross-connect with the AMPD. There are substantial empirical connections between traditional categorical diagnoses and AMPD dimensions (e.g., Bach & Sellbom, 2016; Evans & Simms, 2017; Hopwood, Malone, et al., 2011; Morey, Benson, & Skodol, 2016). Cross-walking these connections is a way to transfer knowledge gained from studies with traditional PD to the dimensional paradigm. Continued studies like those of Bach and Sellbom (2016) and Evans and Simms (2018) should further this effort and alleviate concerns some have expressed about a potential loss of existing PD knowledge (e.g., Shedler et al., 2010).

Communication (What's in a Name?)

The communication value of a nosology must be assessed from multiple angles. This includes the needs and practices of various stakeholders. The threshold for clinical decisions (e.g., cutting scores) must be established. For forensic application, diagnosis must also connect to psycho-legal constructs. Matters of psychiatric stigmatization are very relevant. This invokes the custom of classifying people (e.g., "borderlines") rather than disorders. This misguided emphasis can perpetuate stigmatization (Flanagan & Davidson, 2007). As well, a nosology may play a supportive (or not) role in providing feedback to patients. A diagnostic system cannot serve all masters equally. Maximizing properties of reliability or coverage, for example, may be contrary to its communicative value (Blashfield & Draguns, 1976). In addition, professional-to-professional and clinician-to-patient communication are not isomorphic. This is particularly important for diagnoses fraught with pejorative associations, such as narcissistic or borderline PD. Clinicians are affected by pejorative implications of diagnoses (Sheehan, Nieweglowski, & Corrigan, 2016) in addition to the obvious impact on patients (Corrigan, 2005).

Vaillant's (1992) article, "The beginning of wisdom is never calling a patient a borderline...," highlights how stigma in PD diagnosis affects clinicians and patients alike. Vaillant (1992) compassionately described life dilemmas of patients with PD, and he related these to the intersubjective experiences clinicians and patients encounter. Vaillant (1992) suggested that evaluation of a patient's level of ego defense mechanism functioning, such as with the DSM-IV Defensive Functioning Scale (DFS; APA, 1994), carries direct therapeutic implications. In detailing therapeutic postures associated with level of defensive functioning, Vaillant (1992) implemented a transdiagnostic modular approach. Furthermore, we may compare the DFS and the LPFS. They are both metrics for impairment in personality functioning. This analogy suggests Vaillant's (1992) tailored treatments (aka modules) and compassionate wisdom may coordinate with the AMPD. Interestingly, Vaillant (1992) tells of asking a group of psychiatric residents to describe countertransference reactions to borderline PD patients. The reactions the residents described essentially mirrored the criteria of borderline PD within the DSM-III (APA, 1980). In short, the residents felt highly stirred up, confused, and oscillated between strong emotions and impulses to react. Clinical communication from such a posture is unlikely to be helpful.

When it comes to psychiatric diagnoses, Shakespeare's famous line "What's in a name? that which we call a rose / By any other name would smell as sweet..." (Shakespeare, 1599/1986/2005, Rom. 2. 2. 47–48), misses the mark. To name something is a powerful act. In this regard, we suggest the naming function of the AMPD may be relatively benign. It may foster communication and help reduce stigma associated with some diagnoses. Bach et al. (2015) pointed out the structure of the AMPD permits readily comprehensible feedback on diagnosis to be given to the patient. Criterion A (i.e., the severity of problems or disorder) conveys impact, pervasiveness, and impairment. Criterion B provides a way to describe an individual's suite of maladaptive traits and sidesteps legacy terms such as "borderline" which carry unwanted connotations. Describing personality diagnosis with understandable language enhances communicability. This advantage derives from the lexical Big Five and Five Factor Model (FFM) traditions associated with Criterion B. As McAdams (1995) and McAdams and Pals (2006) pointed out, the FFM describes personality from the point of view of an observer. In giving patient feedback, we speak from the perspective of an observer. And, the patient observes his/herself with the diagnostic terms used in feedback. Therefore, expressing maladaptive PD features in observer-friendly language (such as that of the FFM trait tradition) improves understandability and acceptance. Borderline PD (BPD), for example, is described in experience-near, less jargonized language. Consider the terms for the hybrid categorical-dimensional diagnosis of BPD: emotional changeability, depressivity, impulsivity, separation insecurity, anxiousness, hostility, and risk taking. The wordings for these maladaptive trait-facet dimensions is quite comprehensible. Furthermore, they can be characterized by severity (Criterion A) and they may serve as targets for treatment intervention. Communication in this language goes far, perhaps promoting the therapeutic working alliance from the start. Harkening to Vaillant (1992), this experience-near and non-pejorative language of Criterion B may also promote clinician empathy, as well as patient acceptance in feedback.

Research tells us clinicians often make generally accurate judgments about persons within seconds to a few minutes (Oltmanns, Friedman, Fiedler, & Turkheimer, 2004). Cognitive psychology and decision theory explain this with a dual-processing model: *Type I* thinking is automatic, fast, generally accurate, global, intuitive, and impressionistic; *Type II* cognition is slower, deliberate, effortful, and more analytic (Evans, 2008; Kahneman, 2011). Dual-processing theory research has shown that medical diagnoses are subject to Type I cognition (Croskerry, 2003; 2009) which, even if generally accurate, introduces higher error rates. By analogy, clinicians' impressionistic PD diagnoses (e.g., Morey & Ochoa, 1989) probably occur through Type I cognition and prototype categorization. We may wonder where the AMPD falls with respect to Type I and Type II thinking, noting that the communication function of diagnosis relies on consistency and accuracy.

As with clinical diagnoses in general, AMPD diagnosis may begin with impressions from clinical signs. But, the AMPD requires these to be translated into severity (Criterion A) and style (Criterion B). This recruits Type II thinking, perhaps to a greater degree than traditional, impressionistic PD diagnosis (where full criterion-checks may not occur; e.g., Morey & Ochoa, 1989). Because Criteria A and B must be conjointly applied, even if the diagnostic act starts with impressions, applying the metric of the LPFS implies a more deliberate focus. Then, even from impressions, dimensions of personality style must be reckoned. Given limitations of human cognition (Meehl, 1960; Tversky & Kahneman, 1974), diagnosis with a nosology that incorporates corrections for cognitive heuristics should improve clinical communication. In routine practice, diagnosis must be navigated without excessive burden and time. There is an inescapable tradeoff between ease of use and the cognitive complexity of the diagnostic scheme. This is a topic for further study of the applied use of the AMPD, but the findings of Morey et al. (2014) suggest mental health professionals seem to feel favorably toward the use and communicability of the AMPD.

Treatment Implications

Mullins-Sweatt and Widiger's (2009) third component of clinical utility concerns treatment implications. This is a very broad domain. Rather than listing and describing ways the AMPD can support treatment, this aspect of clinical utility (treatment implications) is the theme that underlies subsequent discussion of the clinical use of the AMPD. Thus, this theme shows, rather than tells, the story. In so doing, the AMPD answers the call of Mullins-Sweatt and Widiger (2009):

> The function of the DSM is not simply a matter of addressing a scientific interest in understanding and explaining psychopathology; its ultimate purpose is to help reduce pain and suffering within the general population— more specifically, to facilitate the practice of clinicians administering clinical care.
>
> (p. 310)

Our examination is cast with an experience-near focus. To this project, we offer a patient's perspective. The founder of dialectical behavior therapy (DBT), Marsha Linehan (1993; 2015), made the reality of the subjectivity of the patient vivid when, in June 2011, she traveled to The Institute of Living psychiatric hospital in Hartford, Connecticut. There, she announced that in 1961, as a 17-year-old adolescent, she was hospitalized for two years for treatment of what we now call borderline PD. She described her unrelenting suffering and self-destructive behavior (e.g., cutting and burning herself), and recounted:

> My whole experience of these episodes was that someone else was doing it; it was like "I know this is coming, I'm out of control, somebody help me; where are you, God?"…I felt totally empty, like the Tin Man; I had no way to communicate what was going on, no way to understand it.
>
> (Linehan, as told to Carey, 2011; paragraph 15)

Linehan reported she received intensive psychotherapy, anti-psychotic medication, electroconvulsive therapy (ECT), and frequent stays in seclusion. Reportedly, she was regarded as one of the most disturbed patients in the hospital. Linehan said she eventually realized "I was in hell, and I made a vow: when I get out, I'm going to come back and get others out of here." Her life after leaving the hospital was not easy, but she began college study and over time slowly pulled her life together. She held to the conviction that effective treatment for problems like hers required facts, must target emotion, and include *radical acceptance*—what she regarded as the keystone of her recovery. These are the basic standards the AMPD must meet if it is to demonstrate clinical utility. That is, the AMPD must accord with results of empirical study, it must not shy away from emotion and subjectivity, and the AMPD must directly speak to realities of the clinical encounter. The AMPD must support the patient-focused, determined humanism Linehan advocated.

Personality Disorder—Eye of the Beholder?

What is personality disorder? This query gives rise to multiple replies. The clinician and the patient likely differ in responses. The clinician's view also varies by role and purpose: diagnosis, psychotherapy, psychopharmacology, clinical administration, clinical investigation, and (non-mental health) medical practice. Allegiance, explicit or implicit, to a paradigm of treatment also may color response.

Clinicians and patients do not see things the same way. Results of empirical studies illustrate this and provide context. Gritti, Samuel, and Lang (2016) found that clinicians' ratings of their patients, using the Shedler-Westen Assessment Procedure (SWAP-200; Shedler & Westen, 2007), and their patients' self-descriptions with the Millon Clinical Multi-axial Inventory-III (MCMI-III; Millon, Davis, & Millon, 1997), showed a moderate degree of convergence (r = 0.35 for DSM PDs). Similarly, Davidson, Obonsawin, Seils, and Patience (2003) studied clinician and patient agreement for patients' problems, also with structured interview and modified SWAP-200 (Shedler & Westen, 2007) methods. They found that patient and clinician perceptions of PD characteristics corresponded weakly. When examined at the level of PD prototypes, for example, the mean Intraclass Correlation Coefficient (ICC) was .27.

Benchmarks are needed to provide context for these results. Studying cross-informant agreement, Achenbach, Krukowski, Dumenci, and Ivanova's (2005) meta-analysis found that the mean correlations of agreement were about 0.4 when using the same method and target construct. If different methods were used, the correlation dropped to 0.3. Several factors affect cross-informant agreement. These include the observability and nature of the construct, method of assessment, familiarity of the raters, and other personality or situational variables that may be relevant in cases. Some personality characteristics are overt and readily observed, while others are more internal or subjective and less amenable to observation. Also, some individuals are less able to introspect (or are unwilling to report their perceptions).

The relevance of these caveats is also evident from results of studies using ecological momentary assessment (EMA) of personality processes, patient experiences, and informant observations. For example, Roche, Pincus, Rebar, Conroy, and Ram (2014) found from longitudinal EMA study of personality and interpersonal variables that self-perception and observer ratings were person-specific and context-dependent. In other words, global rating, single time point, and nomothetic assessment provide limited views on the clinical encounter. Idiographic and temporally evolving understandings are part of the ongoing clinical work with patients. The AMPD may offer a useful approach to some of this complexity with respect to PD variables. The AMPD can be used to study persons normatively, but it can also offer rich within-person, dynamic interaction data over time within contemporary EMA approaches (e.g.,Roche, Jacobson, & Pincus, 2016; Wright, Hopwood, & Simms, 2015). In this regard, Roche (in press, 2018) recently showed both Criterion A and B of the AMPD provide incremental information when studied over time via EMA, but such results are less evident in cross-sectional studies. The proverbial "the devil is in the details" applies. Clinicians know that subjective experience and interpersonal dynamics unfold within and between the patient and clinician, affecting their perceptions and understandings. Given this truism, the AMPD offers a pragmatic template for coding, tracking, and organizing PD and psychotherapeutic variables and fluctuations.

These caveats are highly relevant in PD. For example, borderline PD, from a mentalization perspective (Fonagy & Bateman, 2008), is characterized by deficits in subjective self-awareness (hypomentalizing) and accentuated awareness of others' mental states (hypermentalizing). This suggests borderline PD informants may perform differently on introspection (or self-report) when compared to observation of others (see also Morey, 2014). Indeed, empirical studies support this idea (Fertuck, Jekal, Song, Wyman, Morris, Wilson, Brodsky, & Stanley 2009; Sharp, Ha, Carbone, Kim, Perry, Williams, & Fonagy, 2013). Utilizing the AMPD, Fossati, Somma, Krueger, Markon, and Borroni (2017) studied social cognition (mentalizing) and the Personality Inventory for DSM-5 (PID-5; APA, 2013). They found that specific AMPD traits were associated with over-interpretive reasoning (e.g., suspiciousness, withdrawal, intimacy avoidance, callousness, deceitfulness, and unusual experiences). Thus, Criterion B trait-facets affected the type and accuracy of social-personal perceptions. A patient who notices the therapist glancing at the clock (to gauge when to reduce the intensity of emotional processing with respect to the end of the session) may conclude something very different than what is in the mind of the clinician. Knowledge of the patient's LPFS rating informs the likelihood of such miscommunications.

The literature on psychotherapy of PD addresses this issue. Studies of the working alliance in psychotherapy show therapists and patients view different features of their relationship as helpful (Horvath, 2001). Irving Yalom's *Every day gets a little closer: A twice-told therapy* depicted a psychotherapy by pairing patient and therapist's accounts as they unfolded (Yalom & Elkins, 1974). The narrative illustrated the importance of common factors (Wampold, 2010) and the therapeutic alliance (Bordin, 1979) in psychotherapy, as well as the process of meaning-making in relationships. Therapist and patient understandings may differ, but the collaborative task of psychotherapy promotes hope (Frank & Frank, 1961/1993) and, with respect to PD, may promote radical self-acceptance (see Linehan, 1993; 2015) and opportunities for restorative social trust (Fonagy et al., 2015). Adler (2012; 2013) empirically studied patient and therapist descriptions of psychotherapy events over time. Specifically, Adler (2012; 2013) examined post-session narratives told by patients with borderline PD in relation to both symptom change and narratives given by their therapists. Overall, increases in themes of agency in patients' narratives *preceded* symptom change. In other words, change began from the inside, so to speak. Interestingly, therapists' narratives did not match those of the patients. This finding harkens to Spence's (1984) hermeneutic point that in psychotherapy, narrative truth (i.e., interpretive accounts) and historical truth (objective events) differ, and that a vital currency of psychotherapy is narrative.

PD and Psychotherapy

Approaches to the psychotherapy of PD may be grouped into four main types. These are briefly characterized.

DBT (Linehan, 1993; 2015) and other forms of CBT (Beck, Freeman, & Davis, 2015) are problem- and action-focused psychotherapies of PD. DBT views borderline PD as originating from invalidating childhood experiences and psychobiological emotional dysregulation. These factors contribute to the maladaptive behavior, thoughts, and relationships of PD. The therapeutic posture is active and behavioristic. The therapist balances patient acceptance with pushing for change, and focuses on emotional hypersensitivity. Several varieties of CBT are available for the treatment of PD. One version, schema therapy (Young, 1994), addresses core pathological beliefs and associated patterns of behavior. Similarly, functional analytic psychotherapy (FAP; Kohlenberg & Tsai, 2007) targets maladaptive beliefs and behaviors that are observed within the therapy session.

Mentalization-based therapy (MBT; Bateman & Fonagy, 2006) uses the construct of RF (and mentalizing) to understand PD and inform therapeutic approach. The concept of mentalizing derives from *theory of mind* (Baron-Cohen, Leslie, & Frith, 1985), an approach to understanding mental states taken from the seminal work of Premack and Woodruff (1978). MBT finds support from the expanding work on the social neuroscience of empathy (e.g., Singer & Lamm, 2009). MBT posits that the subjective task of making sense of self and other's mental states is central to interpersonal interaction and dysfunction (Fonagy, Gergely, Jurist, & Target, 2005). More recently, MBT has emphasized *epistemic petrification* (Fonagy et al., 2015). This is assumed to be a transdiagnostic PD process and refers to ossification of interpersonal receptivity and social mistrust. This constitutes a failure of natural social-personal resilience (Fonagy, Luyten, Allison, & Campbell, 2017). MBT focuses on ongoing monitoring of the patient's subjective states, intervening on non-mentalizing behavior, and promoting RF.

Transference-focused psychotherapy (TFP; Clarkin, Yeomans, & Kernberg, 2006) derives from object relations psychodynamic approaches to PD (e.g., Kernberg, 1967; 1993). From this perspective, PD is the result of ineffective or incomplete internal representations of self and others; these representations also are subject to disruption by strong emotion. Relationships are experienced through fragile and maladaptive templates. The therapeutic approach is to provide structure and to build understanding of these mental templates. The therapeutic focus is on day-to-day experiences and relationships, including enactment within the psychotherapy process.

Good psychiatric management (GPM; Gunderson, 2009a) is broadly pragmatic and emphasizes psychoeducation, support, structure, and the patient's life outside of the therapy. A variety of interventions are used including psychiatric medication, short-term hospitalization (if appropriate), discussion of genetics, therapist responsivity and realness, and the role of patient responsibility and self-care is emphasized (Gunderson & Links, 2008).

Effectiveness and efficacy have been demonstrated for each of these psychotherapies for PD (Budge, Moore, Del Re, Wampold, Baardseth, & Nienhuis, 2013; Cristea, Gentili, Cotet, Palomba, Barbui, & Cuijpers, 2017). Psychotherapy is regarded as the treatment of choice for PD (Zanarini, 2009). This is supported by clinical experience and empirical evidence (e.g., Bateman & Fonagy, 2000; Gabbard, 2000; Lynch, Trost, Salsman, & Linehan, 2007; Perry, Banon, & Ianni, 1999). In addition, other therapies for PD are effective (e.g., interpersonal reconstructive therapy [IRT]; Benjamin, 2003). However, the approaches listed above are the most common, and other models are combinations of elements of DBT, MBT, TFT, and GPM (e.g., IRT combines elements of CBT and TFT within interpersonal theory).

Despite variations in models of mind and specifics of technique, these approaches have much in common. In this regard, Paris (2015) argued distinctions between types of psychotherapy for PD are artificial and even unhelpful. All treatments for PD agree on the importance of the treatment frame, therapeutic alliance, coherent treatment process, motivation for change, increasing self-reflection in the service of patient safety, symptom reduction, affect and impulse control, altering maladaptive patterns, and improving adaptability (Paris, 2015).

The *common factors* (Wampold, 2010) of psychotherapy deserve comment. In *Persuasion and Healing*, Jerome Frank described that which is present in all forms of "healing," from faith healing, cults, medical treatment, to psychotherapy (Frank & Frank, 1961/1993). A basic commonality in healing is the amelioration of *demoralization*, a distressed individual's sense of inability to change their self or environment. Psychotherapy integration takes several forms (Messer & Wampold, 2002), but incorporates common factors and combines tactics and strategies across therapeutic modes (see also Wachtel, 1997). Although psychotherapy integration is often viewed as a relatively modern development, a precursor is found in Rosenzweig (1936), who first used the term "common factors" while critiquing the doctrinaire aspect of different schools of therapy. Over 80 years ago, he emphasized common principles of therapeutic change, exemplifying a transdiagnostic point of view.

The AMPD and Psychotherapy

Theoretical pluralism is a strength of the AMPD. Wiggins (2003) described five paradigms of personality assessment (i.e., psychodynamic, interpersonal, personological, multivariate, and empirical; see Chapter 1). To the extent these paradigms inhere in the AMPD, universal transdiagnostic elements are present. Moreover, each paradigm suggests clinical constructs and methods. For example, the psychodynamic paradigm offers constructs of attachment (Bowlby, 1969), mentalization (Fonagy & Bateman, 2008), and psychostructural level of functioning (Kernberg, 1993). The interpersonal paradigm (Hopwood, Wright, Ansell, & Pincus, 2013; Wiggins, 2003) likewise informs psychotherapy of PD in many ways. A particularly practical contribution comes from the principles of symmetry and complementary interaction (Carson, 1969). This refers to the idea that affiliative behavior promotes similar responses from others, and domineering behavior elicits submissive behaviors. Later, this will be illustrated in discussion of transference, countertransference, and the AMPD. The personological paradigm emphasizes a narrative point of view as seen in Adler's (2012) studies of narrative themes and symptom change in PD. The multivariate paradigm is found in Criterion B which traces from the psychometric trait tradition (Krueger & Markon, 2014). Factor analytic studies show that Criterion A resembles a primary cross-cutting dimension of PD symptoms, that of severity of personality impairment (Sharp, Wright, Fowler, Frueh, Allen, Oldham, & Clark, 2015). The Wiggins (2003) empirical paradigm is organized around concepts and methods applied to traditional diagnostic categories such as borderline PD or major depressive disorder. More generally, this paradigm incorporates the concept of diagnostic syndrome. The empirical paradigm is reflected in the AMPD by the hybrid categorical-dimensional diagnostic algorithms and, for example, the assessment exemplar of Criterion B, the multivariate PID-5.

Clarkin et al. (2015) described an integrated modular model for the psychotherapy of PD which integrates strategy and technique across evidence-based psychotherapies for PD (see also Livesley, 2005). This approach aligns with transdiagnostic models such as the AMPD and trans-therapeutic approaches of psychotherapy integration (e.g., Norcross & Goldfried, 2005). Briefly, Clarkin et al. (2015) delineated psychotherapy strategies and tactics in terms of severity of dysfunction (Criterion A) and specific areas of dysfunction (Criterion B). They showed that general principles of psychotherapy for PD are implied in Criterion A, and specific modular interventions are deducible from Criterion B. This thesis is also used in Bach et al.'s (2015) case illustrations of treatment planning with the AMPD and was recently elaborated by Hopwood (2018).

Criterion A

Criterion A, the presence of PD, implies a major task of psychotherapy is to foster the treatment alliance. Crisis intervention, hospitalization, medication, structure and support, and similar interventions contribute to *patient safety*, a precondition for treatment. This assumption is shared by

DBT, TFT, MBT, and GPM. Over time, focus on structure, support, and monitoring of the treatment frame confers psychological *containment* (Clarkin, Yeomans, & Kernberg, 2006; Linehan, 1993), which furthers the working alliance and increases the patient's hope. As therapy unfolds, the phase of *control and modulation* is entered. This involves many tactics such as labeling emotions, fostering mentalization, self-soothing, and linking thought, affect, and behavior. This then fosters patient confidence and increased capacity for *exploration and change* wherein interpersonal schemas and object relationship patterns are identified and addressed. Finally, self-processes stabilize in the *integration and synthesis* phase. Self-narrative solidifies, becomes nuanced, and interpersonal relationships improve. Collectively, these changes bring not only symptom reduction but also more successful, self-reinforcing personal and interpersonal functioning. In this modular model, Criterion A is crucial. Criterion A posits a basic need for treatment structure, the relevance of in-session modeling of mentalizing, and the need to be alert to threats to the therapeutic alliance. Over time as the patient's level of personality functioning improves (i.e., the individual is less fragile, distrusting, and externalizing), therapeutic attention can constructively address entrenched patterns of cognitive-affective interpersonal schemas which are more directly informed by Criterion B.

Horowitz (2013) outlined a similar strategy for psychotherapy of PD informed by a scale for levels of self-other schematization which resembles the LPFS of Criterion A. Horowitz (2013) suggested interventions such as clarification (as opposed to interpretation) provide structure for patients functioning at lower levels of self-other schematization. Intervening in this manner builds the patient's sense of narrative coherence over fluctuating self-states. Empathic, non-threatening linking of cognition, affect, and behavior also promotes self-coherence. Relatedly, DBT uses the idea of *radical acceptance* (Linehan, 1993; 2015). Starting with the assumption of self-acceptance, the therapist fosters self-soothing and structuring functions and, to the extent the patient embraces self-acceptance, these functions are more readily internalized. Adler's (2012) finding that improved narrative agency precedes symptom change is relevant. Stated in Horowitz's (2013) terms, as level of self-other schematization trends upward, the sense of agency and personal efficacy increases. These improvements contribute to the therapeutic working alliance.

For patients at lower levels of personality functioning, therapist comments can be experienced as criticism or attack. For persons with fragile self-states (e.g., Kohut, 1977), therapeutic communication should convey implicit affirmation. Clarifying comments should be made in language that suggests possibilities and invites collaborative examination, also with the message the therapist is not an all-powerful or infallible authority. Amongst other things, this minimizes risk that a comment is perceived as a declaration of personal failings. Ronningstam (2017, p. 5) illustrated how a therapist's ostensibly benign comments may be experienced by individuals with fragile self-esteem and disturbed emotional regulation. For example, in the following vignette, the therapist summarizes a patient's status, but inadvertently precipitated a rupture in the relationship.

T: With your substance use history you are obviously at high risk for relapse.

PT: No I am not! How dare you say that to me? Your comment really puts me at risk for relapse! I don't want to see you ever again!

Elaborating on this idea, Ronningstam (2017, p. 6) emphasized that a seemingly innocuous and "well-founded" observation about relapse risk, for a patient with a long-term history of substance abuse and PD, may not be a helpful, factual statement. Rather, it is experienced as an attack on the self. In contrast, the following interchange covers the material, but with a subtle, important change in delivery:

T: What do you think could make you want to resume substance use?

PT: I don't intend to pick up substance use again!

T: I understand that, but it may be useful for us here to be aware of what made you resume drugs in the past so we together know what can affect you now in that direction.

Silence.

PT: I see your point … well I know that losing boyfriends and failing at tests have been very devastating for me. But drugs also made me feel very good and in control, especially of my feelings, and I clearly miss that, but I can also see that it would be a failure for me if I resume substance usage, and this time it also will have serious negative consequences for me. Before, it really did not matter.

In sum, models such as Horowitz's (2013) self-other schematization, Vaillant's (1992) application of level of ego defense functioning to PD treatment, and the modular approach of Clarkin et al. (2015) are readily brought to the AMPD. These models use Criterion A (or analogous constructs) as a primary guide for therapeutic tactics. It is a therapeutic "truism" that an individual's capacity to adopt a reflective stance in psychotherapy is vital to interpretative work (i.e., observing ego, Sterba, 1934). To engage content involving maladaptive schemas and behavior patterns, the patient must be able and willing to talk about behavior as an object of abstract focus. If this capacity is absent, or has momentarily faltered, therapeutic discussion may be experienced as criticism. The concept of working alliance involves components of task, goal, and bond (Bordin, 1979). This refers to the extent to which patient and therapist concur on what is to be done in psychotherapy and the aims of treatment, and share a sense of partnership. A patient's position on the LPFS alerts the therapist to the stability of the working alliance and potentially to points of weakness in the alliance.

A clinical vignette further illustrates how knowledge of Criterion A can inform specific therapeutic tactics that otherwise might be overlooked if level of functioning is not made explicit.[2] This involved a patient treated with eye movement desensitization and reprocessing (EMDR; Shapiro & Solomon, 1995) for traumatic anxiety. The patient was a 42-year-old woman who had lived in a remote region of a third world country while working for an international service agency. She had witnessed much suffering including the ravages of armed conflicts. While working in the country, she became pregnant and later developed complications requiring an emergency dilation and curettage (D & C) procedure. Surgery was performed in a make-shift rural site, with inadequate anesthesia, and she was aware of much of what happened to her and around her. Language barrier (and custom) contributed to what she described as indifference to her state on the part of the medical workers. After this event, a suite of anxiety symptoms emerged. Later upon returning to the United States, she was treated for anxiety, and an EMDR protocol was one intervention. Several targets (situations associated with anxiety) were to be addressed due to the multiple stressful experiences she had encountered, but the D & C was primary. The therapist elicited a core negative cognition of "I am powerless" from the patient which was to be the focus of the EMDR protocol. As this was implemented, the therapist felt something was off. Desensitization was not going as expected. Deviating from EMDR protocol, the therapist invoked the concept of developmental level of personality functioning. The therapist changed the negative cognition from "I am powerless" to "I am powerless, and it is my fault." The patient was a ruminative, perfectionistic, guilt-prone woman. The clinician realized the subjectivity of powerlessness did not correspond to the patient's LPFS (or personality traits of Criterion B rigid perfectionism). Although the patient had described her traumatic feeling as "powerlessness," the therapist altered the negative cognition to reflect subjectivity of a higher developmental level (e.g., "it is my fault"). Upon this shift, the patient demonstrated marked success in desensitizing affect from the target traumatic experience.

Criterion B

Criterion B of the AMPD may be particularly helpful in guiding therapeutic focus when a sufficient working alliance is in place. In this vein, Horowitz (2013) suggested that specific attention to maladaptive patterns of behavior generally should be deferred until the therapeutic alliance is secure and level of self-other schematization (i.e., level of personality functioning) is improved. Psychotherapies that target maladaptive cognitive and interpersonal schemas attempt to specify these patterns and elucidate connections with stressors, affects, and events. A patient's ability to receive and accept a therapist's observations on these matters depends on trust and reflective capacity (working alliance). Examples of empirically supported treatments (EST) with this focus, as cited by Horowitz (2013), include configurational analysis (CA; Horowitz, 1994), structural analysis of social behavior (SASB; Benjamin, 1993; 1996), and the core conflictual relationship theme (CCRT; Luborsky & Crits-Christoph, 1990) method. It should be noted, consistent with Paris' (2015) caution about the branding of techniques and the importance of an integrative stance in PD treatment, the methodologies Horowitz (2013) cited are congenial with other ESTs for PD. That is, DBT (and similar CBTs of PD), MBT, TFT, and GPM, with minor changes in terminology and emphasis, accommodate interventions formulated with CA, SASB, and CCRT approaches. The various psychotherapies of PD show more overlap than difference—in both formulation and technique (de Groot, Verheul, & Trijsburg, 2008). As but one example, studies of DBT have used SASB methods to evaluate patient characteristics and measure treatment progress (e.g., Shearin & Linehan, 1992). The methodologies cited by Horowitz (2013) specify maladaptive patterns in greater detail than AMPD diagnosis, but elements of Criterion B provide beginning steps to these approaches.

Consider a patient with high levels of separation insecurity, suspiciousness, rigid perfectionism, and intimacy avoidance. In the process language of the CCRT (i.e., wish and fear of other, response of other, response of self), these characteristics suggest the patient may ambivalently wish for acceptance and closeness, harbor vigilant fears of disapproval and of being "seen" as inherently flawed—to which the person reacts by interpersonal distancing and emotionally closing-down. Thus, these Criterion B traits provide a basis for inferring process relationships associated with maladaptive interpersonal schemas. This conclusion is supported by research that shows correspondence between Criterion B traits and the maladaptive cognitive schemas of Young's (1994) schema therapy (Bach, Lee, Mortensen, & Simonsen, 2016; Hopwood, Schade, Krueger, Wright, & Markon, 2013). For example, Bach, Lee, et al. (2016) found that 15 of the 25 AMPD traits were strongly correlated with schema constructs. Relatedly, Drapeau and Perry (2009) showed specific CCRT variables differentiated borderline PD from other PDs. For example, patients with borderline PD expressed wishes to be both distant and like the other, wishes to be hurt and to hurt others, and viewed others as controlling and bad. Notably, Criterion B trait facets of the hybrid categorical-dimensional diagnosis of borderline PD include separation insecurity, emotional lability, anxiousness, and hostility. These traits connect to the angry, negative, and fluctuating perceptions of oneself and others found with the CCRT method of Drapeau and Perry (2009).

The maladaptive patterns formulated within the SASB or CCRT models draw on both Criterion A and B constructs. Criterion B components are summary descriptors of maladaptive personality patterns that include personality temperament, style, and traits; and, they are not fully separable from level of personality impairment. Thus, even as Criterion B reflects pathological traits, it overlaps with personality dynamics and processes that may seem more immediately referenced in Criterion A. In this respect, note that Kernberg (2016) formulates personality and PD in a rather similar manner. He integrates temperament and basic affective neuroscience systems (e.g., Panksepp & Biven, 2012), putatively closer to Criterion B, with the psychometric trait perspective. This is then conjoined with the dimension of psychotructural level (like Criterion A of the AMPD). In this formulation, narrative data and intentionality apply within both planes of personality. Nonetheless, it is important to remember that despite the relative comprehensiveness of the AMPD scheme, Criterion A and B are part of a diagnostic nosology. A psychiatric nosology is generalized and cannot elaborate dynamical patterns in the detail available with more differentiated methods like the CA, SASB, or CCRT. Yet, as noted earlier, the use of the AMPD framework with EMA approaches may permit some nuanced and contingent interactions in PD to be elucidated (e.g., Roche et al., 2014; 2016). In this spirit, Skadberg, Fox, and Waugh (2018) presented an individual psychotherapy case in which the AMPD Criterion A and Criterion B dimensions were used over time to track changes in level of functioning, emerging symptom patterns, and interpersonal implications for the therapeutic relationship.

AMPD Constructs Guide Treatment

Lorna Benjamin (1993), the developer of the SASB, in an essay aptly entitled "Every psychopathology is a gift of love," cautioned that understanding PD will not come from chasing correlations of myriad personality measurements. For Benjamin (1993, p. 4), that path is a "hall of mirrors." Rather, theory must guide analysis. Benjamin (1993) argued that the fundamental assumption of PD is that it is *adaptive.* PD represents "a gift of love" insofar as an individual's personality style develops over time through efforts to seek order, reduce distress, and maintain connection to others. The specific cognitive and interpersonal pattern the individual internalizes represents the warp and woof of the life circumstances of a person's social, cultural, and biological givens. This assumption is found in many developmental psychopathology models of PD. These generally emphasize complex transactions between biological vulnerabilities and psychosocial risk factors (e.g., Crowell, Beauchaine, & Linehan, 2009). Importantly, keeping this point of view close at hand promotes empathy on the part of the clinician.

Benjamin (1993) noted viewing PD as an adaptive resolution dovetails with object relations psychodynamic theory. For Fairbairn (1949; 1952), psychopathology arises from developmental efforts to resolve distress through incorporating aspects of relationships. Internalizing the relationship pattern preserves connection with the caregiver even if the relationship is experienced as inadequate or of poor attunement. In Benjamin's (1993;

1996) SASB model, these are called *copy processes* and they describe ways in which the individual models, assimilates, and turns on oneself the imprint of important interpersonal relationships.

Similarly, the extended work of Fonagy and colleagues emphasizes this adaptive point of view. Drawing on attachment theory and social neuroscience, Fonagy et al. (2015) theorized that the entrenched problematic behavior patterns of PD are maladaptive only in the sense that they carry over previously successful modes of behaving to new situations, but they are inflexible and may not match the reality of present social context. The natural set point for people is social relatedness, trust, and resilience (Fonagy, Luyten, Allison, & Campbell, 2017). However, if an individual's life circumstances interfere with this *salutagenesis* (Fonagy et al., 2015), developmental challenges are resolved by repeating what worked in the past. Emotional survival strategies become hardened (they term this *epistemic petrification*), reflecting a global breakdown in natural social trust and relatedness which is manifested in inflexible personality patterns.

Building on the axiom that "every psychopathology is a gift of love" (Benjamin, 1993), the goal of clinical relevance is likely to be best served by personality constructs that address processes of adaptation and social relatedness. Attachment theory provides candidate personality constructs, and addresses patterns of adaptation to developmental challenges of need and relatedness. Characteristic patterns of attachment ("style") evidence important associations with adult personality and social functioning. These range from romantic relationships (Bartholomew & Horowitz, 1991), psychotherapy (Wallin, 2007), to personality disorder (Levy, 2005). Moreover, to the extent PD involves adaptation to developmental interpersonal challenges, principles of interpersonal theory are fundamental to the AMPD. Similarly, Blatt's (1974) model of personality and psychopathology, sometimes referred to as the "Two Polarities," describes two central dimensions rooted in developmental theory. One dimension involves hyper-valancing of connections to others (i.e., the anaclitic or dependency dimension), and the other form of adaptation is focused on self-definition (i.e., introjective or self-criticism dimension). Attachment styles, interpersonal functioning, and the Two Polarities model have been extensively studied in relation to psychotherapy. Articulating their connections with the AMPD further illustrates the clinical utility of the AMPD.

Attachment Styles and the AMPD

Attachment theory and research is an enormous area of study. Attachment theory derives from the work of Bowlby (1973), who used the term *internal working models* to describe the cognitive-interpersonal template(s) of relationships an individual develops out of efforts to deal with developmental challenges to security. Attachment has been studied extensively in child development through the original methodology of the experimental "strange situation" procedure in which the child is observed reacting to the caregiver's separation and return (Ainsworth & Bell, 1970; Anisworth, Blehar, Waters, & Wall, 1978/2014). Adult attachment style can be assessed through the multiple methods of interview, projective tests, and self-report measures, and has been studied in relation to many personality, psychopathology, and psychotherapy variables, including PD (e.g., Levy, 2005; Meyer & Pilkonis, 2005; Westen, Nakash, Thomas, & Bradley, 2006). As noted previously, the construct of RF, originating from work within the attachment theory paradigm, is central to mentalization-based theory and treatment of PD (Fonagy & Bateman, 2008).

To link attachment style with PD, it is useful to know the normative prevalence of adult attachment styles. Bakermans-Kranenburg and van IJzendoorn (2009) analyzed distributions of adult attachment styles from over 200 studies representing more than 10,000 persons from clinical and non-clinical groups, different cultures, and genders. They found attachment styles occurred in the following proportions: secure 58%; preoccupied 19%; dismissing 23%; and unresolved 18%. Moreover, attachment style was largely unrelated to language or country of origin. Insecure attachment was over-represented in clinical groups, preoccupied styles were more associated with internalizing disorders, and dismissing styles with externalizing disorders.

Adult attachment patterns are often characterized by two individual difference dimensions of insecure attachment. These are attachment anxiety and attachment avoidance. If these dimensions are plotted in the circular conceptual space of the interpersonal circumplex (ICP), they demarcate regions of secure and insecure attachment. Insecure attachment can be partitioned into anxious-preoccupied, dismissive-avoidant, and fearful avoidant styles (note: some studies add a category of unresolved, disorganized, or mixed attachment status; e.g., Gallo, Smith, & Ruiz, 2003). Numerous psychological and personality correlates of these attachment dimensions have been documented (see Mikulincer & Shaver, 2012). Briefly, an individual with an anxious-preoccupied attachment style tends to deal with threats to security via a "hyperactivating" strategy: seeking proximity and support from others, but expecting succor to be unreliable. Avoidant styles include dismissing and fearful attachment strategies. Dismissing-avoidant attachment style is referred to as "de-activating." The individual paradigmatically distances from others and denies the importance of attachment needs. The fearful-avoidant style, in contrast, blends the avoidant distrusting and distancing posture with the desire for comfort. But, in the fearful-avoidant style, this hope is infused with a sense of unavailability. It is important to note that attachment styles may change, an individual may use more than one style, and attachment style may vary based on the type of relationship (Mikulincer & Shaver, 2012).

Levy et al. (2015) reviewed attachment theory in relation to PD. They noted that, in general, attachment insecurity is associated with PD and has been extensively studied in borderline PD. Results pertaining to specific PDs vary, but associations have been found between attachment anxiety and dependent, borderline, and avoidant PDs. Attachment avoidance has been linked with avoidant and paranoid PDs. Dismissing-avoidant attachment has been linked with paranoid, narcissistic, antisocial, and schizoid PDs. Gallo et al. (2003) examined relationships between attachment styles, interpersonal models, the FFM dimensions, and self-representations. They found that secure versus insecure (fearful) attachment was highly related to interpersonal variables. Specifically, dimensions of attachment anxiety and avoidance were related to a hostile-submissive interpersonal style. Attachment avoidance, relative to attachment anxiety, showed greater interpersonal saturation. This finding is not surprising, given that intimacy avoidance implies an inner working model with direct interpersonal reference. Attachment anxiety, in contrast, involves both an interpersonal referent and involvement of the affect-motivational system of anxiety.

Behavioral genetic study of attachment styles using the Dimensional Assessment of Personality Problems (DAPP; Livesley & Jackson, 2000) found that attachment anxiety showed strong heritability (40%), as well as a high level of heritable association with PD dimensions (63%; Crawford, Livesley, Jang, Shaver, Cohen, & Ganiban, 2007). This cross-cutting, heritable dimension linked to attachment anxiety they termed emotional dysregulation (Crawford et al., 2007). In contrast, they found that avoidant attachment style was almost entirely attributable to environmental variance and was associated with dimensions of restricted expression and intimacy problems. These results underscore the complex interaction between attachment style and heritable PD vulnerabilities (e.g., emotional dysregulation). Furthermore, this also suggests avoidant attachment style relationships with PD are more interpersonal and of psychosocial origin.

Given these and other findings, it is reasonable to expect important connections between attachment styles and the AMPD. This was the subject of recent investigation by Fossati, Krueger, Markon, Borroni, Maffei, and Somma (2015). They examined associations between the Personality Inventory for DSM-5 (PID-5; APA, 2013) and the Attachment Style Questionnaire (ASQ; Feeney, Noller, & Hanrahan, 1994), along with a measure of the Big Five dimensions. They found that attachment style explained significantly more variance in the PID-5 than did the Big Five measures. Removing trait variance, the independent contribution of attachment style to Criterion B (PID-5) was strong, underscoring the interpersonal underpinnings of PD. These results are also consistent with McAdams and Pals' (2006) distinction between the construct levels of traits, characteristic adaptations, and narrative identity. Attachment styles are related to personality traits, but they also incorporate personality variables at other construct levels.

The ASQ (Feeny et al., 1994) has scales for confidence in self (Co; "secure" attachment); discomfort with closeness (DC); relationships secondary to achievement (RS); need for approval (NA); and preoccupation with relationships (PR). Fossati et al. (2015) found that the dismissing/avoidant styles of DC and RS predicted PID-5 facets such as withdrawal, restricted affectivity, rigid perfectionism, grandiosity, and callousness. In comparison, the anxious attachment styles of NA and PR were associated with submissiveness, depressivity, distractibility, separation insecurity, emotional lability, and suspiciousness. The styles of NA and PR were strongly associated with the PID-5 domain of negative affectivity. PID-5 detachment was predicted by the attachment dimensions NA, RS, and DC.

This brief survey of attachment theory and the AMPD establishes their common ground. Knowledge of attachment style informs the clinician of likely Criterion B PD traits (e.g., Fossati et al., 2015), and Criterion B traits suggest attachment styles. Thus, the nomological net of attachment theory is available (Levy et al., 2015). Consider elevated attachment anxiety. This predicts treatment seeking behavior, but at higher levels is associated with worse clinical outcomes (Levy et al., 2015). By analogy, elevated Negative Affectivity may show similar relationships with treatment outcome. Avoidant styles are associated with reluctance to seek care and weaker therapeutic alliance (Levy et al., 2015). Therefore, with a patient with an avoidant style, the clinician may expect elevated Criterion B withdrawal, restricted affectivity, and grandiosity. This may signal the need for extra attention to the therapeutic alliance. Research on the therapeutic alliance shows that attention to problems or ruptures in the alliance is critical to both the alliance and symptom reduction, that the alliance is not a byproduct of symptom reduction, and that therapists working with PD patients seem particularly alert to these issues (Falkenström, Granström, & Holmqvist, 2013).

Relationships between attachment style and PD constructs are not one-to-one. Widiger's (2011) distinctions between pathoplastic, spectrum, and causal relationships are apropos. An attachment style may not be causal in a PD configuration but may affect expression of PD behavior. An attachment style may show a spectrum or etiological relationship as well. In this regard, Crawford et al.'s (2007) finding that avoidant attachment styles are more environmentally determined (relative to the heritability of anxious attachment styles) is relevant. A clinician working with a patient manifesting an avoidant attachment style might hypothesize early adverse life experiences were formative in developing PD impairment and traits. Furthermore, this hypothesis suggests being alert to the dynamics of self-esteem regulation (Ronningstam, 2014; 2017). Most basically, in the language of the AMPD, the level of personality functioning should not be overestimated. Such overestimation could occur if a patient's minimization of distress and presentation of self-sufficiency were taken at face value. The patient may exhibit strong confidence, orientation to perfectionist work (as opposed to relationships), investment in protecting the self, and subtle depreciation of relationships—including the therapy. This may play out in a tenuous working alliance, emphasizing the need to foster and protect the alliance, and address ruptures rapidly.

We now present a clinical vignette that illustrates how diagnosis with the AMPD could have contributed valuable information for treatment planning. This case vignette (identifying details are disguised) is drawn from a previous psychotherapy conducted prior to publication of the AMPD. The vignette describes a commonly used intervention: recording of emotions and events in a daily journal (e.g., Graf, Gaudiano, & Geller, 2008). However, when this intervention was instituted, the patient experienced significantly increased distress and symptoms. The patient's response to the intervention thus became diagnostic information and suggested a change in therapeutic strategy. Retrospective application of the AMPD to these case details shows how journaling as an intervention was inadvisable.

Case Vignette

Ms Q. was a 51-year-old, married homemaker referred by her physician for help with "depression." She was over-weight and secretly abused laxatives. On occasion, she engaged in episodes of near-starvation in unsuccessful efforts to control her weight. She reported no "problems" in her marital relationship, but admitted she kept many of her personal feelings private, and she often painfully missed her spouse when he worked long hours as a business executive. She presented as tentative and anxious, but very earnest and disclosing. She readily agreed to cease laxative abuse and to verbalize about emotional experiences and life events or stresses in psychotherapy. Her physician prescribed antidepressant therapy to which she showed a partial response. Ms. Q. was articulate, non-defensive, and seemed to welcome the opportunity to talk about her experiences, including childhood adversities. She described a domineering, harsh, and critical father; her mother was viewed as meek and submissive to her father's anger and the "high standards," which were expected of all family members. Moreover, she recounted adolescent experiences of humiliation and ostracism from same-sex peers, and feelings of degradation associated with complying with boys' frequent requests for sexual favors. Ms. Q. seemed to make good use of therapeutic clarifications and interpretation, and her eating disorder symptoms stabilized. Thus, supportive-expressive, insight-oriented psychotherapy was continued. Her ability to make use of in-session therapist observations linking behavior, emotion, and interpersonal events gave rise to the idea that she should continue emotional processing using a daily journal. This intervention was explained to Ms. Q., and she readily agreed. Rapidly, however, Ms. Q. became more depressed and her eating disorder symptoms worsened. She continued dutifully journaling over the next handful of weeks, but her condition deteriorated. The therapist explored her experience of journaling. Ms. Q. reported that she rapidly became dysphoric when journaling, sometimes almost paralyzed with emotional pain, resulting in anergia, withdrawal, and self-starvation. She was advised to cease journaling and to use only the therapy sessions for discussion of difficult experiences and events. She immediately responded with improved spirits, symptoms, and functioning.

This vignette illustrates how a common clinical intervention, journaling, can backfire if the patient's PD characteristics are not sufficiently appreciated. Ms. Q's clinical deterioration upon journaling may be understood in terms of level of personality functioning, PD traits of negative affectivity, submissiveness, and separation insecurity, and a fearful-avoidant attachment style. Her initial very positive response to psychotherapy, including productive in-session cognitive-emotional processing, belied her vulnerable level of self-other schematization (Horowitz, 2013) and, very importantly, her need for relationship support to permit exploration of difficult emotional experiences. When she journaled alone at home, she was unable to maintain adequate observing ego in the rush of painful emotions. In the presence of the therapist, however, relationship support provided safety, acceptance, and structure, which enabled such emotional processing.

Tasca, Ritchie, and Balfour (2011) reviewed the literature on attachment styles and eating disorders. They noted that research shows symptom-focused psychotherapy is less successful for eating disorder patients with insecure attachment styles. This is an example of a pathoplastic interaction between clinical condition (eating disorder) and personality construct (attachment style). Furthermore, as Tasca et al. (2011) pointed out, knowledge of attachment style can guide treatment strategy. For example, a patient with attachment anxiety may benefit from consistent therapeutic attention to relationship events and patterns (as opposed to focus on self-system issues) correlated with strong affect and eating disorder symptoms. This type of intervention transacts through the relationship and focuses on relationship content. For an individual with an anxious attachment style, the relationship focus may structure and facilitate cognitive-affective processing.

With Ms. Q., her need for in-the-moment relationship support is deducible from assessment of attachment style (i.e., fearful-avoidant, which combines anxious and avoidant dimensions) as well as AMPD diagnosis that recognizes implications of both Criterion A impairment and Criterion B traits. Ms. Q. was seen in psychotherapy over a three-and-a-half-year period; treatment was then terminated, as a change in her spouse's employment status required her to relocate. Throughout her treatment, the therapeutic relationship and relationship themes remained figural. Over time, eating disorder symptoms largely remitted, relationships with her spouse and others became more reciprocal and rewarding, and her ability to modulate shame-based emotion and anxiety improved. She was helped to find a new psychotherapist on moving, though she experienced strong and contradictory feelings about ending her psychotherapy. Yet, she expressed gratitude for the help that she received.

Interpersonal Theory and the AMPD

There is a vast literature on interpersonal theory, and we focus on basic elements of interpersonal theory to note selective links with the AMPD. The case of Ms. Q. will also be used to this goal. The interpersonal paradigm traces from Sullivan (1953/2013) and has seen extensive use in the interpersonal circumplex (IPC) methods of Leary (1957) and colleagues (Wiggins, 1996). Major interpersonally based contributions to PD were made by Wiggins and Pincus (1989), Pincus and Wiggins (1990), and Benjamin (1996). Gurtman (2009) reviewed circumplex methods and interpersonal theory and offered a useful overview. Hopwood, Wright, Ansel, and Pincus (2013) presented an up-to-date review of interpersonal theory with theoretical and empirical linkages to the AMPD—illustrated with a case example.

Briefly, Hopwood, Wright, Ansell, et al. (2013) argued PD is intrinsically interpersonal in origin and expression. They stated the interpersonal paradigm in the AMPD combines PD nosology with personality theory and in the process spans psychoanalysis, the Big Five, and attachment styles. Hopwood, Wright, Ansell, et al. (2013) furthermore compared the meta-constructs of agency and communion (Wiggins, 2003) to the AMPD Criterion A domains of self (agency) and interpersonal (communion) dysfunction. These domains, broadly speaking, address interpersonal aspects of self-esteem and security operations, respectively. If sufficient problems are encountered, personality dysregulation within self, affect, and interpersonal spheres may result. This is reflected in maladaptive cognitive-interpersonal patterns (e.g., Benjamin, 1993; 1996; Horowitz, 2004) of PD and connect to elements of the AMPD Criterion A (see Hopwood, Wright, Ansell, et al., 2013, Table 1). Of course, the pathological personality trait facets of Criterion B also reflect substantial interpersonal connections.

Wright, Pincus, Hopwood, Thomas, Markon, and Krueger (2012) examined empirical connections between Criterion B traits, indexed by the PID-5 (APA, 2013), and the IPC tradition. Using the *Inventory of Interpersonal Problems–Short Circumplex* (IIP-SC; Soldz, Budman, Demby, & Merry, 1995), they found PID-5 hostility was highly correlated with ICP octant "PA" (managerial-autocratic). Submissiveness was associated with octant "JK" (docile-dependent), and suspiciousness with octant "BC" (competitive-narcissistic). The Wright, Pincus, et al. (2012) results confirmed the interpersonal substrate of the AMPD. Importantly, these results extended the nomological network of the IPC tradition to Criterion B of the AMPD. In addition, Wright, Pincus, et al. (2012) documented different interpersonal profiles associated with the hybrid categorical-dimensional PD diagnoses.

Interpersonal theory posits the principle of *complementarity* (Carson, 1969). This refers to the interactional dynamic between two persons along the dimensions of affiliation/withdrawal and dominance/submission. On the affiliation dimension, the principle of *correspondence* means that a positive, affiliating posture begets a similar response from the other. In contrast, an individual relating to the other from a position of power, control, or dominance elicits *reciprocity*, a dynamic retreat to submission or yielding behavior. These are general, expectable reactions to interpersonal demands. To the extent an individual does not respond in terms of complementariness, questions of a psychopathological adjustment may be raised (Hopwood, Wright, Ansell, et al., 2013).

Cain, Ansell, Simpson, and Pinto (2015) examined interpersonal variables in relation to patients with obsessive-compulsive PD, patients with obsessive-compulsive PD and comorbid obsessive-compulsive disorder, and controls. Cain et al. (2015) found that obsessive-compulsive PD patients showed less empathy in general and responded to affiliative-dominant behavior with hostile-dominance, an atypical interpersonal reaction. Patients with obsessive-compulsive PD and obsessive-compulsive disorder, in contrast, showed submissive responses to warm-submissive behavior of others. These results highlight the fundamental interpersonal nature of PD and its interactional consequences. As well, their results suggest pathoplastic implications of personality variables. Cain, Pincus, and Holtforth (2010) found similar pathoplastic relationships between interpersonal subtypes and social phobia. Cross-cutting dimensions of the AMPD, such as detachment, may partly explain the empirical overlap between symptoms of severe social phobia and avoidant PD (see Rettew, 2000). Many accounts of social phobia and avoidant PD emphasize the role of anxiety, and they recommend anxiety be addressed psychotherapeutically (Hofmann & Otto, 2008) and with psychopharmacological treatment (Blanco, Bragdon, Schneier, & Liebowitz, 2013). However, we note the connections between the AMPD and attachment styles (Fossati et al., 2015) and the relative lack of heritable variance in avoidant attachment style, indicating a strong interpersonal component (Crawford et al., 2007). In other words, despite the significant role of the trait-facet of anxiousness in avoidant PD patterns (and internalizing PDs), the interpersonal aspect is central, as seen in AMPD detachment and avoidant attachment style.

The interpersonal principle of complementarity provides a way to understand countertransference (CT) experiences. Consider the AMPD hybrid categorical-dimensional algorithm for borderline PD. This diagnosis is made if the LPFS shows moderate or greater personality dysfunction along with combinations of emotional lability, hostility, anxiousness, depressivity, separation insecurity, and impulsivity. Examination of these trait dimensions from an interpersonal perspective (with the principle of complementarity) reveals contradictory interpersonal pressures are exerted on the clinician. For example, patient hostility, via interpersonal reciprocity, may induce therapist reserve or withdrawal. But, the patient's separation insecurity, anxiety, and depressivity may elicit approach and reassurance from the therapist (a corresponding pull for affiliation in response to helplessness). Yet, the emotional lability and impulsivity of borderline PD means that the interpersonal field is subject to rapid shifts—with expectable impacts on CT feelings.

In this regard, Betan, Heim, Zittel Conklin, and Westen (2005) found that therapists working with patients with borderline PD report CT experiences of feeling overwhelmed and disorganized (perhaps from the shifting interpersonal field of the patient's lability and impulsivity), criticized (via patient hostility), and variously sexualized, special, and/or over-involved (which may reflect the pull from the patient's "call for help" via separation insecurity, anxiety, and depressivity). Similarly, Colli, Tanzilli, Dimaggio, and Lingiardi (2014) found that therapists reported feelings of helplessness, inadequacy, being overwhelmed, and specialness when working with borderline PD patients. These findings further underscore the relevance of interpersonal complementarity in CT reactions when working with PD patients.

The interpersonal model of Benjamin (1993; 1996), the SASB, provides a theory, methodology, and implications for psychotherapy of PD. This includes a PD-specific psychotherapy called interpersonal reconstructive therapy (IRT; Benjamin, 2003). A novel feature of Benjamin's (1996) approach is that an individual's functioning is assessed with respect to behavior towards others, expected reactions of others, and manner of relating to the self. These relational modes are termed *copy processes* and assumed to have developmental origins. They reflect *identification* (relating like an important other), *recapitulation* (relating as if the other is present), and *introjection* (acting to oneself as the other did). These copy processes show differential relationships with personality, psychopathology, and psychotherapy variables. Critchfield and Benjamin (2008) found that adult interpersonal patterns and those represented in early relationships corresponded to SASB predictions. Psychiatric patients showed maladaptive patterns, and non-patients generally demonstrated copy processes with secure attachment (with affiliation and low hostility; see also Critchfield & Benjamin, 2010). The SASB model can be reliably used in case formulation to predict transference patterns and inform therapeutic focus and technique (Benjamin & Critchfield, 2010; Critchfield & Benjamin, 2010; Critchfield, Benjamin, & Levenick, 2015). Gallo, Smith, and Ruiz (2003) showed that attachment styles could be characterized by SASB copy process variables. Benjamin, Rothweiler, and Critchfield (2006) provided an extended review of the contributions of the SASB model to the assessment, treatment, and study of PDs.

Let us return to the case vignette of Ms. Q. Retrospectively applying Criterion A ratings reveals a LPFS score of 2 (moderate impairment). She showed specific liabilities in identity (e.g., weak emotional boundaries and ability to tolerate and regulate affects; fragile self-esteem). Despite her surface-level ability to relate well with others, circumscribed deficits existed in empathy (e.g., hyper-attunement to others for self-needs and compliance to avoid disharmony) and intimacy (e.g., relationships were organized to avoid rejection or abandonment). Regarding Criterion B trait-facets, she showed elevated anxiousness, depressivity, separation insecurity, submissiveness, and rigid perfectionism. Linking these Criterion B ratings with the data from Wright, Pincus, et al. (2012) reveals connections with the "JK" and "HI" IPC octants. These octants are associated with submissive, self-effacing, deferential, timid, compliant interpersonal styles. Her self-attitudes may also be described in the language of Benjamin's (1996) SASB model. Ms. Q. related to herself with aggression and control (e.g., self-criticism, self-denial, self-starvation). That is, the copy process (SASB introject) of her relationship with her critical and domineering father figure became a template for her attitudes towards herself. Indeed, in psychotherapy sessions, the therapist often felt the interpersonal pressure of being carefully watched (Ms. Q.'s hypervigilance), an indicator of PD (e.g., Fonagy et al., 2015), and Ms. Q. was often self-effacing and self-shaming in comments, while idealizing the therapist. Psychotherapy walked a careful line recognizing that her self-organization was fragile and staying mindful of the interpersonal "pull" to interpretively intervene, perhaps prematurely or overly assertively, which could dovetail with these copy processes. These concerns also needed to be balanced with potentially therapeutic and stabilizing benefits of appropriate interpretation.

The "Two Polarities" Model and the AMPD

Sidney Blatt and colleagues have engaged in extended study of two meta-constructs in a model called "Two Polarities" (Blatt, 1974; 1995; Blatt & Felsen, 1993; Blatt & Ford, 1994; Lowyck, Luyten, Vermote, Verhaest, & Vansteelandt, 2017; Luyten, Lowyck, & Blatt, 2017). These two broad dimensions, termed introjective and anaclitic, address matters of self-definition and dependency, respectively. Notably, they also resemble Wiggins' (2003) meta-constructs of agency and communion. The dimensions of the Two Polarities model differentially relate to psychotherapy process and outcome variables as well as optimal therapeutic strategies (e.g., Werbart, Aldén, & Diedrichs, 2017). For example, patients with anaclitic-dependency issues generally respond better to interpersonally oriented and supportive-expressive psychotherapy. Patients with introjective/self-definition issues tend to fare better in more cognitive, insight-oriented approaches, and they benefit from titration of therapist-patient intimacy and may require a longer treatment duration (see above references). It is important to note that the constructs of the Two Polarities correspond to Beck's CBT dimensions of *autonomy* and *sociotropy*

(Beck, Epstein, Harrison, & Emery, 1983). These dimensions are often measured with the Personal Style Inventory (PSI; Robins, Ladd, Welkowitz, Blaney, Diaz, & Kutcher, 1994).

The nature of these two constructs is illustrated in the below items from the Depressive Experiences Questionnaire (DEQ; Blatt, D'Afflitti, & Quinlan, 1976; Zuroff, Moskowitz, Wielgus, Powers, & Franko, 1983; slightly paraphrased in the interests of test security). These items were chosen because of high factor loadings (in parentheses) on their respective dimensions of dependency and self-criticism. For our purposes, they are labeled in terms of their conceptual link to AMPD Criterion B traits.

Separation insecurity:

Item 45: "I worry about offending or hurting someone to whom I am very close" (.67)

Item 20: "If I lost a very close friend, I would feel like I lost an important part of myself." (.62)

Rigid perfectionism:

Item 13: "There is a major difference between how I am and how I would like to be." (.70)

Item 62 (negatively keyed): "I am highly satisfied with myself and the accomplishments of my life." (.70)

The Two Polarities model has been applied extensively to the study and treatment of depression. The model may be measured with the DEQ (Blatt et al., 1976; Zuroff et al., 1983), a 66-item depression measure assessing constructs of self-criticism, dependency, and efficacy. Some research questions the psychometric status of the original DEQ, and several revisions with improved properties are available (e.g., Bagby, Parker, Joffe, & Buis, 1994; see also Falgares, De Santis, Kopala-Sibley, Scrima, & Livi, 2017). Zuroff and Fitzpatrick (1995) examined DEQ dimensions of self-criticism and dependency, their analogues of autonomy and sociotropy, and attachment styles. They found that self-criticism and autonomy were related to a fearful-avoidant attachment style, and dependency and sociotropy with anxious attachment. There was a substantial interpersonal component to both DEQ dimensions.

Empirical relationships between the Two Polarities and attachment styles have been replicated in several studies (e.g., Alden & Bieling, 1996; Dinger et al., 2015; van Geel, Houtmans, Verboon, & Laumen, 2016). These relationships have also been demonstrated using alternative methods, such as clinician (SWAP-based; Shedler & Westen, 2007) ratings of introjective and anaclitic PD dimensions. For example, Miller and Hilsenroth (2016) developed SWAP-based scales for self-criticism and dependency. These showed theoretically consistent relationships with a measure of interpersonal problems. Similarly, Rost, Luyten, and Fonagy (2018) found SWAP-based ratings of the dimensions provided nuanced information in portraying depressive symptoms and experiences in patients with treatment-resistant depression. Relatedly, Dinger et al. (2015) likewise found that dependency was associated with low dominance, high affiliation interpersonal problems; self-criticism was associated with low affiliation interpersonal problems and the cognitive symptoms of depression. Furthermore, these associations were not related to severity of depression.

To our knowledge, the DEQ has not been used in a study with the AMPD. However, with the existing nomological net of the Two Polarities model and the AMPD, meaningful connections may be anticipated. While all dimensions of the DEQ would be associated with the trait domain of negative affectivity, anaclitic/dependency/sociotropy should relate to affiliation-based PD traits involving ways of managing insecurity. These would prominently include separation insecurity and submissiveness. The introjective/self-criticism/autonomy dimension would be expected to correlate with the detachment trait domain and with the trait-facet of rigid perfectionism. To the extent these likely relationships are confirmed empirically, cross-model connections between the lines of research from the Two Polarities model, as well as from CBT-based studies of autonomy and sociotropy (Beck et al., 1983), may be extended to AMPD diagnosis.

A brief comment on such cross-model relationships is relevant. Recalling Widiger' s (2011) position that personality constructs and PD interrelate in different ways, we note both pathoplastic and spectrum relationships may occur with the Two Polarity dimensions and depression. The dimension of self-criticism, for example, modifies the expression of depression and it also reflects a form of depression. A study by Lieberman, Gorka, Huggins, Katz, Sarapas, and Shankman (2016), comparing self- versus other-ratings of personality traits with depressed patients, illustrates this nuance. For patients with major depression, self- and other-ratings agreed. But, for non-patients, ratings for negative affectivity did not show agreement. Thus, clinical status (level of depression) interacts with evaluations of personality traits.

Returning to our case vignette of Ms. Q., the results of Lieberman et al. (2016) support our ability to make (observer) judgments about her probable self-report of elevations on the DEQ. Ms. Q. suffered from major depression. Research on the DEQ shows major depression is associated with elevations on all three subscales (self-criticism, dependency, and self-efficacy; Blatt et al., 1976; Zuroff et al., 1983). Thus, we expect she would demonstrate elevations across the DEQ. However, given her interpersonal style (self-effacing, submissive, compliant) and attachment style (fearful-avoidant), coupled with an estimated elevation on the LPFS and the Criterion B trait-facets of submissiveness and separation insecurity, we expect high endorsement of anaclitic-dependency items. Such a DEQ profile would inform treatment planning. Higher levels of dependency needs (sociotropy) are associated with positive response from supportive-expressive, relationship-oriented approaches (e.g., Blatt & Felsen, 1993). Yet, Ms. Q. would also likely show substantial self-criticism (autonomy) issues. This would suggest treatment may need to occur over a long period and address issues of self-definition such as perfectionism. Relatedly, Shahar, Blatt, and Ford (2003) found patients with mixed anaclitic and introjective psychopathology, although showing more symptom impairment and personality vulnerability, exhibited greater improvement than patients with more uniform personality styles while receiving long-term treatment. Ms. Q's history and course of psychotherapy as described in the vignette was consistent with the above observations.

The Clinician's Experience Treating PD

This discussion begins with two clinical examples.

Hamburger

Several years ago, the author spoke to an audience of primary care physicians and mental health professionals on the topic of "dealing with difficult patients" (Waugh, 1997). The main message was how to manage interactions with difficult patients (likely unrecognized PD), including physicians' personal reactions, in the medical practice setting. A caricatured, metaphorical example was offered. The audience was asked to imagine working with a patient who reported being hungry. As a helping professional, one might imagine offering something to eat, perhaps a hamburger (falafel or grilled cheese sandwich; your choice). This is eagerly accepted. Yet, your patient remained unsatisfied. Over several visits, similar requests are made and reciprocated with a sandwich. Soon, however, the request contains vague insinuations. They eventually become complaints. One day, while taking a walk behind your office building, you come across a pile of (decomposing) hamburgers. Suddenly, you realize your "gifts" were regularly tossed out the window.

Ms. X

Many years ago as a trainee in a hospital that provided long-term psychodynamically oriented treatment, the author was assigned a therapy patient. But, this was for short-term psychotherapy because the training year was about to end; a few weeks later the patient would transfer to a new trainee-therapist.

The patient, Ms. X., had an extensive history of psychiatric treatment and hospitalizations. About nine months prior to the current hospitalization, she sought help at a local hospital emergency room (ER), complaining of depression and suicidal thoughts (she had a history of non-suicidal self-injury, as well as overdose suicide attempts). She was evaluated, given support, and she seemed to stabilize. Hence, arrangements were made for outpatient treatment, to which she consented. Reportedly in improved spirits, Ms. X. left the ER. However, she then drove to a commuter rail terminal and jumped onto the tracks in front of an oncoming train. She survived because upon hitting the moving train, she was knocked back away from its path. But, she sustained serious orthopedic injuries. After receiving treatment, she could ambulate, but required leg braces and crutches.

In this psychiatric hospital, patients were seen three times weekly for individual psychotherapy. Before each appointment, the trainee met Ms. X. at her hospital room and accompanied her down the hall to the therapist's office for the session. In a staffing case conference, the trainee learned the hospital administration was planning to file a legal petition to declare Ms. X. incompetent. The hospital intended to obtain guardianship and then fund extended inpatient psychiatric treatment with the ample money she had been awarded from her successful lawsuit against the hospital ER. The trainee was informed this legal maneuver would occur simultaneously with the transfer to a new therapist.

This was the scenario. Three times a week, the trainee walked slowly alongside Ms. X, keeping pace with her awkward and very public struggle with crutches, her metal braces clanging on the tile floor. Staff and patients could not escape the loud but tacit communication she had "been wronged." And, the trainee knew that this psychiatrically fragile woman would soon face a concerted legal challenge from the hospital to remove her rights—and her funds.

These examples evoke a sense of complicated emotional reactions that may occur when working with individuals with PD. The first example shows that appearances may be deceptive. This can be the case when working with "difficult" patients in medical settings. Yet, the message delivered in the presentation also could be viewed as pejorative. The case of Ms. X illustrates how strong emotional reactions (e.g., trainee-therapist; staff and patients witnessing her walk; hospital administration) may be experienced by those working with persons suffering with severe PD.

Countertransference

Treating PD patients undoubtedly will induce occasional experiences of frustration, confusion, and "un-therapeutic" feelings at some point. One might oscillate between feelings of resentment and of having failed as a helper. This is the realm of countertransference (CT). CT is defined in several ways (Gabbard, 1995). Broad conceptions of CT emphasize the totality of the therapist's reactions to a patient. Narrower conceptions focus on a therapist's specific transference reactions, based on personal dynamics, activated in relation to a patient. Winnicott (1949) introduced the idea that certain kinds of patients induce similar reactions across therapists, termed "objective" CT. In contrast, a CT reaction based on the therapist's personal issues was called "subjective" CT. Racker (1968/2002) differentiated "concordant" CT, involving the therapist empathically identifying with the patient's experience, and "complementary" CT, in which the therapist feels disavowed aspects of the patient's experience (e.g., the therapist feels "I am worthless," reflecting disavowed feelings of the patient). Sandler (1976) emphasized that a *role responsiveness* occurs in the therapist through CT reactions. Relational aspects are particularly emphasized in contemporary psychodynamic conceptions of CT. This also includes the view that mutual enactments of disavowed material (i.e., both patient and therapist enacting aspects of their own "issues") may occur within the therapeutic relationship (Maroda, 1998; 2013).

It should be noted that the subject of CT originated in the psychoanalytic and psychodynamic traditions, but the literature of CBT also discusses the strategic use of the therapist's emotional reactions and the importance of attention to the therapeutic relationship (Gilbert & Leahy, 2007; Leahy, 2008; 2017; Leahy, Beck, & Beck, 2005; Safran, 1984). The literature within the CBT tradition continues to assimilate and apply CT ideas (Cartwright, 2011; Ivey, 2013; Najavits, 2000). For example, Prasko et al. (2010) discussed how multiple maladaptive cognitive-interpersonal schemas may be enacted in patient transference and therapist CT reactions in CBT-based treatments.

A selective review of CT highlights the importance of this topic. Bourke and Grenyer (2013) compared therapist reactions to patients with borderline PD and those with major depression. They found that therapists reported much more stress, a greater need for supervision or consultation, and experienced borderline PD patients as more hostile, anxious, difficult, narcissistic, and sexualized. Black et al. (2011) surveyed 706 clinicians about their work with PD patients. They found that nearly 50% of the therapists actively avoided working with borderline PD patients. Importantly, however, they noted that caring attitudes, optimism, and empathy were greater for those clinicians who reported more frequent work with these patients. Chartonas, Kyratsous, Dracass, Lee and Bhiu (2017), similarly found that therapists were more negative and nihilistic about working with borderline PD, relative to affective disorders. Gabbard (1995), writing on the psychotherapy of borderline PD, outlined common CT experiences therapists may encounter. These include guilt, rescue fantasies, boundary transgressions, anger, helplessness and worthlessness, and anxiety. As noted above, Vaillant (1992) unpacked the many levels of meaning within the plea to "never call a patient borderline."

Building on Winnicott's (1949) thesis that certain types of disorders induce similar reactions in others, PD has been studied in terms of clinician CT reactions. Betan et al. (2005) developed a psychometric questionnaire to assess CT reactions. They found eight meaningful dimensions of therapist reactions which also were independent of clinician theoretical orientation. These were labeled overwhelmed/disorganized, helpless/inadequate, positive, special/overinvolved,sexualized, disengaged, parental/protective, and criticized/mistreated.

Betan et al. (2005) found that Cluster A PDs were associated with therapists feeling criticized/mistreated. Cluster B PDs evoked strong CT reactions including feeling overwhelmed/disorganized, criticized/mistreated, disengaged, sexualized, and less positive. Quite different reactions were reported in relation to Cluster C PDs. These were associated with the therapist feeling parental/protective. Borderline PD was associated also with therapist feelings of being special/overinvolved, and narcissistic PD generated therapist feelings of disengagement. Based on these findings, Betan et al. (2005) concluded clinicians can make systematic use of their emotional reactions in understanding PD patients.

Bender (2005) suggested CT reactions may offer heuristic guides for working with PD patients. With borderline PD, emotional lability, demandingness, and acting out suggest how to support and engage the individual. The patient's longing for relationship and responsivity to warmth may be recruited in the service of the therapeutic alliance.

Colli et al. (2014) investigated CT feelings with mental health therapists using an adapted form of the Betan et al. (2005) questionnaire. Their results were even stronger in magnitude than those found by Betan et al. (2005). CT feelings of being criticized/mistreated, for example, were associated with paranoid and antisocial PDs. Borderline PD tended to induce feelings of helplessness/inadequacy, overwhelmed, and specialness. Schizotypal and narcissistic PD were correlated with therapist disengagement. Similar results were found by Gazzillo, Lingiardi, Del Corno, Genova, Bornstein, Gordon, & McWilliams (2015) who incorporated assessment of psychostructural level. They found severity of PD was associated with the therapists feeling overwhelmed and helpless.

This brief survey of CT and PD offers important points. First, CT is a common experience regardless of therapist theoretical orientation and may be pronounced when working with patients with PD. Second, although each patient and therapist is unique, certain PDs tend to induce similar reactions. The empirical and clinical literature on the psychotherapy of borderline PD indicates that therapists are prone to feel variously overwhelmed, inadequate, helpless, special, and at times in ways they regard as untherapeutic. Gabbard (1995) noted the CT pitfalls of guilt, rescue fantasy, boundary transgression, anger, helplessness, worthlessness, and anxiety. Thirdly, level of PD functioning is a key variable (Gazzillo et al., 2015). Thus, Criterion A of the AMPD is predictive of likely CT, including feelings of being overwhelmed and helpless, when working with patients with severe personality impairment. Relatedly, in discussing these implications, a colleague recently observed that sometimes CBT-oriented clinicians may steer clear of working with patients with significant PD impairment. The colleague opined that the transdiagnostic implications of the AMPD, combined with knowledge that certain therapist reactions are predictable from the LPFS, might help CBT clinicians to be more inclined to take up the task because the terrain would seem more comprehensible. The point of view, moreover, is transtheoretical. As Vaillant (1992) noted, therapists of all stripes often feel intimidated by severe PD. Whenever one ventures into unknown or difficult territory, a map is useful, and the AMPD is one such map.

AMPD and CT

The following vignette depicts how CT reactions, translated into the language of the AMPD, may suggest clinical hypotheses and strategies. To use the AMPD scheme in this way permits use of the intersubjective aspect of CT as a source of initial, preliminary clinical hypotheses derived from a clinical encounter. To these impressions, the template of the AMPD is applied to organize subjective and objective data through deliberative, Type II cognition (Croskerry, 2009).

Dr. S. was a 52-year-old- surgeon whose career had been impacted by substance dependence. He retained a limited license to practice (under direct supervision) but engaged in little direct patient care presently. He had been terminated from two medical practices because of substance abuse. His main employment was as an adjunct clinical professor teaching anatomy in a physician's assistant (PA) program. He was referred for treatment by the State Medical Board. He had abused multiple substances, but his drugs of choice were dissociative agents (e.g., Ketamine, Stadol [Butorphanol Tartrate]). He was being treated by a psychiatrist with Effexor (venlafaxine; antidepressant) and low-dose Resperdal (risperidone; atypical antipsychotic) for sleep. Within the first few sessions of psychotherapy, the therapist experienced the following vivid image, as Dr. S. talked about an ostensibly neutral topic, with no overt evidence of emotion. The image was stark: a scene of a cold, wind-swept, desolate, and frozen land, like the Siberian tundra, with not a person or living thing present. The image was multi-sensory and unfolded as if a cold wind was blowing through the room, bone-chilling, and imparting a sense of isolation and emptiness.

The therapist's CT reaction captured the patient's unverbalized (likely currently unavailable to conscious awareness or discussion) experience of profound isolation. If this CT experience is regarded as a communication within an interpersonal field, the unspoken message (and pull) was for the therapist to withdraw (i.e., cold distance begets cold distance interpersonally) in futility and hopelessness. In terms of the psychodynamic thesis of Bollas (1989), it could be said that Dr. S.'s experience of the *unthought known* was being communicated. That is, an inaccessible but embodied sense of unredeemable loneliness was expressed intersubjectively, giving rise to the therapist's vivid CT reaction. Let us now frame this CT communication within the language of the AMPD and translate it into a heuristic for initial clinical hypotheses. Note that the logic for this heuristic derives from the general literature on CT (e.g., Gabbard, 1995), the inherent intersubjective aspect of CT (e.g., Maroda, 1998), and empirical findings linking therapist CT reactions to patient personality features (e.g., Bender, 2005; Colli et al., 2014).

Regarding Criterion A, PD impairment is suggested both by the content and intensity of the CT reaction (Gazzillo et al., 2015). For example, the LPFS Identity domain at the level of severe impairment (3) includes the benchmark of "emotions may be rapidly shifting or a chronic, unwavering feeling of despair" (DSM-5; APA, 2013; p.777), and in the Intimacy domain (extreme impairment [4]) a descriptor is "desire for affiliation is limited because of profound disinterest or expectation of harm. Engagement with others is detached, disorganized, or consistently negative" (DSM-5, p. 778). Similarly, turning to Criterion B traits, the intersubjective CT image experienced with Dr. S. resonates with trait-facets of withdrawal, intimacy avoidance, anhedonia, restricted affectivity, depressivity, and possibly cognitive and perceptual dysregulation.

This CT image, translated into AMPD terms, should be regarded as tentative information requiring corroboration by other diagnostic evidence. In this regard, his history was quite consistent with the implications of the CT image. Dr. S was married with two children, but reported feeling estranged within his family. His moods were generally stable on the current psychiatric medications. His problematic work history and repeated substance abuse were consistent with PD impairment. He reported a history of childhood sexual abuse from an uncle, but in an emotionless manner stated he did not feel inclined to discuss the subject. He described his parents as work-oriented, demanding, and emotionally unexpressive. Although he did not miss therapy sessions, he had arrived a few minutes late for two of the five sessions. The content of sessions focused on work, particularly on how, despite his good intentions, he frequently fell behind on academic obligations. He tended to attribute this to feeling "depressed," at which times he felt unable to "perform." He commented that the PA students were impressed with his encyclopedic knowledge of anatomy. Outwardly, he presented a demeanor of quiet coolness with an aspect of pre-emptive (but not hostile) assertive confidence—as well as studied nonchalance. He described intermittent depressive states accompanied by guilt, shame, self-recrimination, hopelessness, and feeling alienated from others. He recalled these feelings starting in his adolescence when he was an academically high-performing student. He spoke with irritation about his wife's inability to understand his "stress" when she complained of his distance, irritability, and moodiness. He generally minimized the seriousness of his substance abuse, despite its consequences on his career, and he said it was only when he was under the influence of dissociative drugs (or alcohol, as a poor second choice) that he felt like himself.

Dr. S's history and presentation fit with the communicative thrust of the CT image. That is, he showed significant PD impairment (particularly in domains of identity and intimacy) and elevated detachment with elements of negative affectivity and antagonism. His history of childhood abuse and proclivity for dissociative drugs suggested underlying posttraumatic stress disorder (PTSD) as well. His PTSD may have contributed to the apparent low-level traits of psychoticism. That is, dissociative dynamics may have been reflected in his idiosyncratic experience and behavior. Given this clinical picture, a psychotherapeutic strategy of carefully titrated closeness (i.e., not pushing for rapid disclosure and intimacy) and a gentle, inquisitive focus on self-esteem issues was adopted. He accepted occasional observations (of no more than moderate depth) that linked current interpersonal events and emotional experiences with a sketch of relationship patterns associated with performance and achievement (identified over time). Dr. S. attended psychotherapy with only a few missed appointments, but he suddenly discontinued after about eight months and he did not respond to efforts to contact him. While the AMPD per se would not predict premature ending of therapy, the level of PD impairment and his profile of personality traits, including the detached attachment style (e.g., Fossati et al., 2015), were consistent with this outcome. However, three years later he indirectly communicated to the therapist something of the value he must have taken from psychotherapy. He phoned and asked to bring his young adolescent son for a psychological evaluation. This was done, and the young man was subsequently seen in short-term psychotherapy for anxiety and academic underachievement problems. Notably, Dr. S brought his son to each session. He seemed eager for parent management advice, but he was disinclined to talk about himself. Regarding his own treatment, he indicated the medical board had "relaxed" some of his practice restrictions, thus he felt he no longer needed psychotherapy.

The Experience of PD

Heretofore the AMPD has been examined primarily from the clinician's point of view. The model was framed in terms of clinical utility, connected to clinically relevant personality variables, and illustrated with patient material (e.g., Ms. Q, Ms. X, and Dr. S). The clinician's experience of patients with PD is a common theme across this survey. We observed that the clinician and the patient with PD frequently do not see things the same way (e.g., Adler, 2012; Gritti et al., 2016; Yalom & Elkins, 1974).

A few empirical studies have examined the experience of PD from the patient's point of view. This often relies on narrative methods. For example, Briand-Malenfant, Lecours, and Deschenaux (2012) explored the subjectivity of sadness in borderline PD. They concluded that these states represent non-mentalized, multi-themed experience more complex than sad mood. Likewise, Zanarini and Franenburg (2007), Silk (2010), and

Fertuck, Karan, and Stanley (2016) emphasize differences between depression and the mental pain in borderline PD (see also Persius, Ekdahl, Asberg, & Samuelsson, 2005). The nature of the mental pain these investigators have observed reminds us of the self-experience narratively described by Linehan in her courageous interview of 2011. Of course, windows to such subjectivity are also found in the narratives of literature, for example in the penetrating, soul-splitting poetry of Sylvia Plath. But let us contrast this subjectivity with that associated with the hedonic deficit (anhedonia) in the schizoid and schizotypal PD spectrum (e.g., Lenzenweger, 2015). Parnas and colleagues have charted elemental, qualitative differences in the subjectivity of schizophrenic-spectrum disorders, including schizotypal PD (e.g., Raballo & Parnas, 2010). Early writers on the psychotherapy of schizoid conditions likewise made use of the phenomenology of aberrant self-experience and derived implications for treatment therefrom (e.g., Fromm-Reichman, 1959; Guntrip, 1968). Taking again a clue from literature, the short story "Silent Snow, Secret Snow" (Aiken, 1932), vividly portrays the experience of an individual opening him/herself to a welcoming, protective cocoon of schizoid alienation by detaching from others. Like the mental pain to which Linehan referred, but cloaked in interpersonal retreat and diffidence, the character of Laura Wingfield in Williams' (1944/2012) play, *The Glass Menagerie*, similarly offers glimpses of the subjectivity of the avoidant personality spectrum. From Shakespeare to Faulkner to Joyce Carol Oates, literature has long been a way someone's inner world may become known to the other, illustrating what we have in common, trafficking in empathy (e.g., Kidd & Castano, 2013). We similarly seek to understand PD from the inside.

Regarding this first-person point of view, note that the constructs of reflective functioning and mentalizing, important in conceptions of PD, refer to the capacity to glimpse others' mental states. We know empathy is one of the clinician's key tools. It both heals the patient and brings information to the clinician. We may have only glimpses, but this inner, first-person perspective is vital in understanding PD. Therefore, we ask, what is PD for the person we call personality disordered?

PD is everything in the sense it is who one is. Recall that Freud's original meaning of the word *ego* was self (*das Ich* or "the I"; Laplanche & Pontalis, 1988). Scholars speculate the conception of personhood itself emerged in the "axial age" of human history (800–200 BCE; Jaspers, 1953/1976). The sense of self then is basic to being human as we understand the word. Viewed in this light, to characterize PD problems as ego syntonic is a bit of a misnomer. That is, PD symptoms are not syntonic, they *are* the self. When psychiatric nosology pairs disorder with personhood, more than self-esteem is on the line; the person is. It is a truism that interpretation of personality processes creates a sense of exposure and vulnerability (Schafer, 1954). As does a diagnosis of PD. In this regard, the accessible, less pejorative language of the AMPD may help to promote acceptance of information about one's personhood.

With the AMPD, PD is described in a way that connects and communicates with the person. The presence of PD (Criterion A), reflected in problems in self-definition, might be stated as "people are not always perceptive; they may not see that your confident manner does not tell the whole story; alongside your strength, you wear your feelings on your sleeves. You are much more sensitive than folks know." For someone with narcissistic fragility, this may be felt as accurate and empathic, and not too disarming. Directly stating the problem enhances credibility and may help build trust, particularly if delivered with words and tone in sync with the person's style (Searles, 1986). This kind of clinically practical language is immediately available within AMPD diagnosis.

Benjamin's (1993) thesis that every psychopathology is a gift of love cannot be overstated. Personhood develops and expresses interpersonally (Fairbairn, 1949; Sullivan, 1953/2013). Very broadly, the scope of Criterion A is the dance of self and other relationships, the earliest steps of which are one's mode of attachment (Bowlby, 1969), cycling over time between self-definition and connection (Blatt, 1974), seeking security within one's interpersonal field. These steps to personhood are guided variously by genes and epigenetics, ability and temperament, care and valuing, agency and authorship, and social and cultural context (Fonagy & Luyten, 2016; Kernberg, 2016). Switching metaphors, is this a patchwork, stitched neatly or not? Or, is it more like a tessellated mosaic? We see Criterion A in coarse, uneven, or frayed stitching. Criterion B emerges from iterations of tiles so tightly coupled that something seems off. Yet, in both crafts, someone has tried to make it work.

The CMSF (Berrios & Markova, 2015) reminds us PD is a way of being known through a clinical encounter, itself shaped by context and culture. In an individual's life, PD is always *adaptive*. Or, perhaps this is better said as *was* adaptive. Personhood, one's way of being, in part represents the legacy of best efforts (if flawed) to navigate existential situations. This is not a new idea. This idea lies within the mechanisms of defense, for example (A. Freud, 1946/1992; see also Vaillant, 2000). It also underlies transdiagnostic accounts of self-processes that range from Kelly's (1955) personal construct psychology, White's (1959) effectance motivation, Loevinger's (1976) conception of ego development, Bandura's (1989) agentic social-cognitive model, to the philosophical core of contemporary acceptance and commitment therapy (ACT; Hayes, 2016).

The heuristic of epistemic petrification emphasizes that the adaptation of PD protects the self, but at the cost of social trust and flexible personal functioning (Fonagy et al., 2015). In the control-mastery theory approach to psychotherapy, it is assumed the patient enters the clinical encounter with hope (Weiss, 1993). That is, the specific hope that one's (problematic) interpersonal schemas *just might not be true*. The patient unwittingly tests and probes the therapist, hoping to disconfirm the suspicion that people are unsafe in the manner they have internalized. Unfortunately, the individual too often concludes their fears are confirmed. Searles (1986, p. 8) observed that in trying to master that which was problematic in their past, patients do not try to relive earlier experiences. Rather, they seek "to live it for the *first* time—to live it, that is, with full emotional participation."

These ideas are not specific to a psychodynamic point of view. Many CBT approaches to PD are idiographic, relationship oriented, and focus on maladaptive cognition and schemas. This includes schema therapy (Young, 1994), DBT (Linehan, 2015), and FAP (Kohlenberg & Tsai, 2007) (see also Mansell, Harvey, Watkins, & Shafran, 2009). To these emphases, ACT (Hayes, Strosahl, & Wilson, 2011) adds the importance of personal context and the present moment. Like Fonagy et al. (2015) with epistemic petrification, ACT presumes that psychological inflexibility is the central axis of psychopathology. The notion of schema itself largely derives from the pioneering work of Tomkins (1978; 1995) on "script theory." For Tomkins (1995), the script is the affectively laced distillate of figural interpersonal situations. The script organizes how one lives life.

The person suffering from PD lives the *das Ich* that someone regards as flawed. Perhaps oneself, another, or both see it that way. The AMPD is one map for charting the idiom (Bollas, 1989) of the self. Criterion A gauges the extent of psychological entrenchment (Hayes, Strosahl, & Wilson, 2011) and level of epistemic petrification (Fonagy et al., 2015). Criterion B characterizes the regularities of self-expression. This framing recalls Winnicott's (1967/1986) classic statement about the tacit hope that resides within delinquency. This he called the "antisocial tendency." For Winnicott (1967/1986), no matter how self-defeating or off-putting, acting out represents the vestiges of developmentally frustrated hopes of being understood. Acting out, in other words, expresses problematic life scripts that are currently maladaptive, but were not originally so. Using this Winnicottian lens, we may say PD symptoms represent noise, but the basic message, the vital signal within the person, is the hope that things might be different.

This perspective reminds us we have much in common with deeply suffering patients and helps us reclaim empathy despite pushes and pulls of interpersonal pressures to feel otherwise. Yet, empathy does not imply therapeutic softness. Discussing the compassion and firmness required in therapeutic assessment, Finn (2007) described a difficult, acting out patient, Mary, with whom strong limits were needed to help to complete an evaluation. Early assessment sessions were bumpy, and the assessor's customary empathic manner seemed unable to establish a connection. Eventually, Mary arrived for one appointment "with a beer in her hand and a glint in her eye" (Finn, 2007, p.258). Not only did this require a firm limit, but Mary's provocation jarred the assessor into a clearer perception of her needs. Testing feedback was delivered in direct, no-nonsense language.

Mary listened with much more respect and eventually said "you really got me," supported by the relief experienced when her dyscontrol and disrespect were met with firmness. Relatedness sometimes means limits. Criterion A of the AMPD immediately cues the clinician for structure, safety, containment, and non-interpretive reflection and mirroring. Criterion B describes specific ways Winnicottian "antisocial tendencies" are encoded in patterns of behavior, symptoms, narratives, and subjectivity. Although the signal of the person is obscured by the noise of PD symptoms, the AMPD may clarify some of these communications. With this map, we are better able to calibrate our clinical posture with compassion and firmness, a task essential to disconfirming the life scripts of the person with PD.

Notes

1 This chapter benefits from the helpful comments of several clinicians including Lorrie G. Beevers, Ph.D., Leticia Y. Flores, Ph.D., Katherine A. Lenger, M.S., Katie C. Lewis, Ph.D. and Abby L. Mulay, Ph.D.

2 Acknowledgement is given to Lorrie G. Beevers, Ph.D. for this case vignette.

6 The AMPD and Three Well-Known Cases

Christopher J. Hopwood and Mark H. Waugh

A number of approaches may be taken to examine clinical utility. One approach is to examine the empirical properties of the model, on the assumption that empirical validity sets an upper bound for clinical utility (Mullins-Sweatt & Widiger, 2009). As reviewed in Chapter 4, evidence for the validity of the Alternative Model of Personality Disorders (AMPD) has accumulated rapidly and is generally strong, although this body of evidence also shows points where more work is needed. When trainees and practitioners are surveyed regarding their perception of the utility of the model, they generally endorse it as useful, and tend to prefer it to the categorical model of DSM-5 Section II (Garcia et al., in press, 2018; Morey & Hopwood, in press; Nelson et al., 2017). The bottom line for clinical utility, however, is whether a model like the AMPD can be used to adequately describe individuals. A number of studies have used the AMPD framework to describe individual cases (Bach, Markon, Simonsen, & Krueger, 2015; Garcia et al., in press, 2018; Hopwood, 2018; Morey & Stagner, 2012; Pincus, Dowgillo, & Greenberg, 2016; Simonsen & Simonsen, 2014; Waugh et al., 2017). But there is particular value in describing cases that are well-known because readers can determine relatively easily whether the AMPD captures their personalities and can use other sources to help make this determination. This is the approach we take in this chapter.

We distributed brief descriptions of three fairly well-known cases in the clinical assessment literature to 25 practicing clinicians, each of whom were proficient in assessment and/or PD, along with an AMPD rating form, requesting that the clinicians rate each case in terms of AMPD features (for a similar study in which an independent sample of students rated these and other cases, see Garcia et al., in press, 2018). The AMPD form we used was created by Waugh (2014) to allow for a depiction of the entire AMPD on a single page. It corresponds directly to the AMPD as described in the DSM-5 (APA, 2013). Each level of personality functioning variable is given a score of 0 (no impairment) to 4 (extreme impairment), and each trait is rated from 0 (false/absent) to 3 (true/present). A value of 2 or higher is considered "clinically significant" for all of these variables.

The average age of clinicians was 47.72 (SD = 11.90), and they had on average 19 years of clinical experience (SD = 12.09). While all raters had experience in both applied practice and academic work, 13 identified primarily as clinicians and 12 primarily as academics. We computed ICC values as a two way random effects model of absolute agreement, mean rating ($ICC_{(2,25)}$), which indicates agreement across multiple raters on the 4 level of functioning and 15 maladaptive trait AMPD variables. These values ranged from .93 to .97, indicating excellent inter-rater reliability for the scores we present below. These findings build on a growing body of work documenting the reliability of the AMPD as rated by clinicians (see Chapter 4 of this volume).

Our presentation of the cases is focused on interpreting them through the lens of the AMPD. However, each case is extremely interesting and of central importance in the history of personality assessment, and we highly recommend primary sources for any reader who is not already familiar with them. We selected these three cases because personality problems are prominent in all of them, the nature of those problems differ across each of them, and extensive descriptions and—in two instances—psychometric data, are available in the literature. We disguised the names of the cases to the raters because we hoped to avoid any influence of raters' familiarity on their ratings.

Case 1: Madeline

Madeline consented to be part of a project conducted by Wiggins (2003) whose purpose was to demonstrate and compare five paradigms of personality assessment: narrative, psychodynamic, empirical (i.e., MMPI-2), multivariate (i.e., trait), and interpersonal. In many ways, the Wiggins book was an inspiration for the current volume, insofar as we see the AMPD as exemplary of Wiggin's multi-paradigmatic vision (Waugh et al., 2017). In a recent study, Mulay et al. (in press, 2018) found that the AMPD accommodates the content of each of the paradigms described by Wiggins, as covered in more detail in preceding chapters by Pincus and Roche on Criterion A and Krueger on Criterion B. The general conclusion of the Mulay et al. study was that expert raters saw Criterion A as more representative of narrative and psychodynamic constructs whereas Criterion B was seen as more representative of empirical and multivariate constructs; interpersonal constructs were thought to be represented in both sets of criteria.

Madeline's complex history and charismatic presentation made for a rather compelling personality assessment demonstration. This is the description and test data we gave the raters:

> Ms. C is a 35-year-old Native American woman employed as a defense attorney. She reported a "harrowing" childhood with working

class parents who showed little warmth to her and her three siblings. There was extensive parental discord involving frequent violent arguments, physical fighting, and drunkenness of parents. Her mother made several suicide attempts. She, her siblings, and mother were physically abused by her father. Her father was gregarious in public and socially well-known and respected in their community. However, she harbors tremendous resentment and "hatred" for her father. As a child, she reports occasional alcohol abuse on her part in elementary school and she was often in trouble at school. As a teenager, she abused alcohol and marijuana, got into physical fights, hung out "on the streets," and was involved in minor thefts. By age 12 she left home but was vague on where she lived. She was arrested several times as an adolescent and was in and out of jail. As an older adolescent, she was violent to another inmate and received solitary confinement. Later, however, she "discovered books" and began to read widely. She resolved to "turn her life around" and eventually went to community college, did well, and applied and was accepted to an Ivy League school from which she obtained advanced degrees in law and social work. She married briefly, said the relationship was not strong, and that they had "good sex." For 6 years now she has lived with a man, a college professor, but says she will "never marry." She does not have children. She had difficulty obtaining her law license due to her legal record, but eventually did. She now has a solo practice and is regarded as very successful, particularly in defending minority clients. She is viewed as brash, earthy, spirited, opinionated, and audacious. Being invited to one of her infamous parties is regarded as a social coup. She tells interesting stories and tales, but they clearly are embellished and can be fantastical. Psychometric data:

WAIS-III: VIQ 110; PIQ 113; FSIQ 112

MMPI-2: L 38; F 82; K 52; S 43; Hs 35; D 30; Hy 35; Pd 66; Mf 69; Pa 49; Pt 37; Sc 60; Ma 88; Si 30; ANX 43; FRS 31; OBS 37; DEP 42; HEA 40; BIZ 61; ANG 76; CYN 58; ASP 85; PTA 60; LSE 35; SOD 35; FAM 62; WRK 43; TRT 46; A 38; R 31; Es 64; Do 56 Re 30; Mt 42; PK 48; MDS 50; Ho 61; O-H 48; MAC-R 72; AAS 67; APS 55; GM 69; GF 30

Rorschach: R = 26; W=6; Total F=14; Total F+=9; F Quality=64%; Extended FQ=79%; P=8; Experience Balance 4.5:4.0; M=3 (good form); 6 Confab; 1 Fabcom; 1 Agg [Rappaport Scores]

Rorschach free association from two cards is presented to give a qualitative flavor, the "sign in" and "sign out" responses (first and last).

Card I: (1) Oh, the Rorschach! Never saw! Looks like a woman holding her hands up. Great big wings. Like she's professing. Very powerful. I like that! [W+ Mo H, P, Incom] [Exner Scores]

Card X: (1) Look at this. Looks like a party in a psychedelic aquarium. Star Wars meets Disney on acid. A party—they're having fun. Everybody's smiling. They live in an ecosystem, all in some way attached. Fine, no one's trying to get away. All enjoying themselves at the party. All so very, very, very different, but all work well together. Having a great time (*examiner note*: patient starts to tear up). [W+M. CFo Party, Fabcom, Cop]

(2) This blue crab. Guy's forlorn, defeated. There is the eye. Big ole nose. Not so much sad as hopeless. This (other side) is not a mirror image. Otherwise, an underwater circus! A great thing going on. [Do Fo A, P, CP, Incom, DR (2)]

Thematic Apperception Test (selected cards)

Card 3GF. (woman, downcast head, face covered with hand): Oh no! Just had a fight with her boyfriend. He came over and yelled at her. She's in despair. She didn't tell him because she's pregnant. In doing that, she sealed her fate. He said some pretty nasty shit. (Q) Accused her of sleeping around. Little trollop! (Q) Single mother, poor, guilt-ridden, resentful, very lonely. Sad story.

Card 13MF. (young man with downcast head; figure of woman in bed behind): Oh, he's going home to his wife. "Thank you very much, mistress. That was great." He's happy and she's happy. She's smart, too. She loves the good sex—not the trappings of a relationship. And he likes sex with her. If his wife ever found out, his ass would be killed. Not a major age difference, there. They're about the same age. Age-old story. Nothing too complex there.

Card 5. (woman standing on threshold of a half-open door): She's his wife! She suspects something! She wasn't supposed to be home! She hears him! He's got that look on his face—"I've been caught!" She wants to know, but doesn't. If he did it, out he goes! The only one who has nothing to lose is the beautiful mistress. He should have had a shower before he went home! She's gonna be able to smell that!

Madeline's AMPD profile is presented in Figure 6.1. She is above threshold (i.e., ≥ 2) for intimacy problems and has an elevated albeit subthreshold score on empathy problems, indicating prominent personality problems. Her score on identity problems is somewhat lower but there is a clinically meaningful score on identity. Her self-direction is within normal limits. This combination of scores indicates general personality problems with particular difficulties in the interpersonal domain, but also hints at some conflicts or contradictions in her functioning. For instance, Madeline clearly has a long history of difficulties with intimacy, but at the time of the assessment she was involved in what she perceived as a satisfying relationship. Sadly, it turned out that her boyfriend was quite unhappy and would leave her shortly after the data were gathered (as reported in Wiggins' [2003] follow up on Madeline). In other words, the raters were correct to

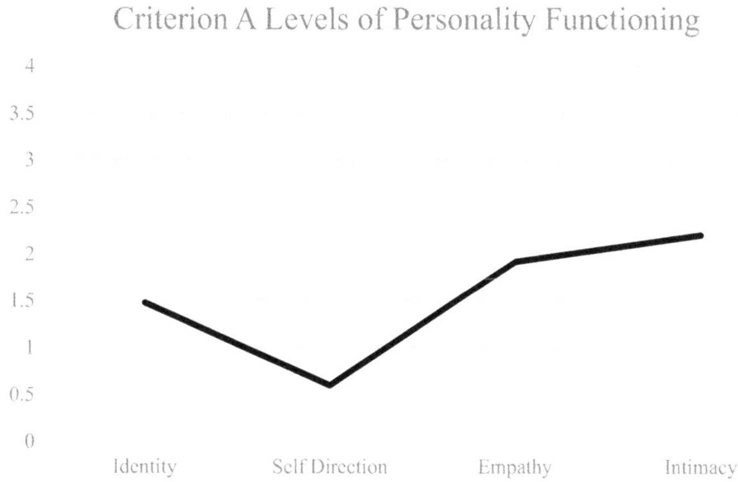

Figure 6.1a. Madeline's Level of Personality Functioning profile

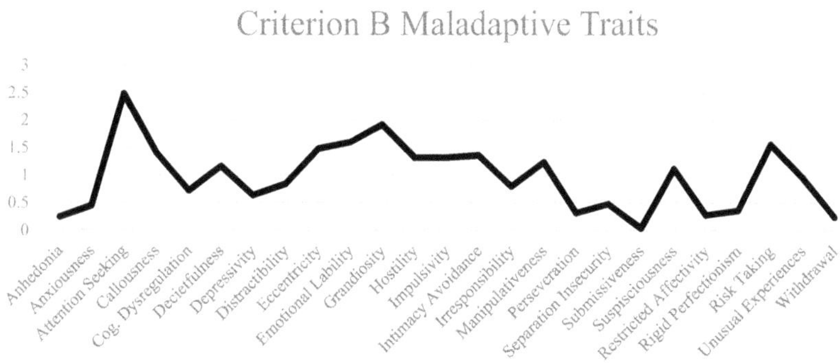

Figure 6.1b. Madeline's Maladaptive Traits profile

identify intimacy as a core deficit, although at the time of the assessment Madeline might not have been aware just how core it was.

There is even greater contradiction for empathy. On the one hand Madeline was brash, uncompromising, self-centered, and seemed willing to trample others to get what she wanted; on the other hand, this was often in the service of helping the unfortunate and underprivileged, an ambition to which she devoted her career. It was as if her lack of warmth in personal relationships served the purpose of a deeper sort of empathy to a community with a diminished voice.

The third example of two extremes summing to a moderate dysfunction score was that her identity seemed to be much more firmly established in the domain of work than love. Each of these scores, in juxtaposition with

Madeline's story, exemplify how the dynamics of an individual's life and context are needed to provide flesh for the bones of a relatively abstract assessment such as can be provided by the AMPD.

Madeline's trait profile seems to provide a generally accurate portrait of her characteristic way of relating to others as detailed in Wiggins (2003). Her only clinical elevation (i.e., ≥ 2) was attention-seeking, but grandiosity was not far behind. From an AMPD perspective, then, she would meet criteria for narcissistic PD. She also had sub-threshold scores for risk taking and eccentricity. This paints a relatively accurate portrait based on the rich description in the Wiggins book and the psychological test responses (e.g., MMPI-2, TAT, Rorschach) sampled in the text we provided raters. Madeline was the life of the party, passionately disinterested in conventional norms, who brusquely flew by the seat of her pants in a way that was compelling but also ultimately self-focused, and potentially distasteful to some. Her responses to the first and last Rorschach cards exemplify this personality style. She begins with a theme of power and agency and ends with a peculiarly imaginative and highly communal party.

There is also a level of superficiality in her responses that seems characteristic of her general presentation. But at the same time this feature of her personality stands in stark contrast, or perhaps provides cover for, something rather deep (as indicated by her complex history, courageous struggle to overcome numerous obstacles early in life, and devotion to the underprivileged). In the second response to the last card, negative affect briefly peeks through in the form of a sad crab. Her attention immediately turns back to the underwater circus, conveying the impression that Madeline's behavior is an ardent effort to keep pain, hopelessness, and defeat out of her awareness. In fact, these observations were also emphasized by the different experts who evaluated Madeline in Wiggins (2003).

Madeline never expressed interest in treatment and, so far as we know, has never been diagnosed with a mental health disorder. Without presuming she should seek treatment, we can speculate about how that might go based on her AMPD profile. Initially, we might expect her to use therapy as an opportunity to seek attention through flamboyant and provocative behavior. This presentation could be expected to test the clinician, whose challenge would be to find a way to access the inner pain that seems to drive at least some of her behavior. This would require a type of reflection her character seems organized to keep at bay. Her highly successful sublimation of many childhood disadvantages seems to have depended on avoiding this kind of reflection, leaving unresolved extremes between her many positive virtues and some of her underlying vulnerabilities. In the Wiggin's (2003) book, Madeline is presented as a person who simply denies any vulnerabilities, and instead emphasizes all she has had to overcome and can do. But her behavior and the perspective of her common-law husband, who also provided data for the initial assessment, indicate a more complex picture. Helping Madeline synthesize these extremes would seem to require some recognition of her vulnerabilities, which would likely take a fair amount of time and therapeutic care because she would experience vulnerability as dangerous. Madeline's historical challenges with intimacy and empathy were understandable given her attachment history and life trauma but they also represent significant obstacles to successful treatment. Her impulsivity and risk-taking tendencies suggest an increased likelihood of premature termination. Maintaining the therapeutic alliance would thus be crucial. Given her rather dominant and competitive interpersonal style, any attempt by the therapist to take an authoritative position would likely be counter-productive. The more relational clinician would be advised to be cautious with open-ended, overly expressive techniques in favor of a more supportive, structuring position, whereas the more behavioral clinician would be advised to emphasize collaboration and motivational techniques, as opposed to moving forward too quickly with change-oriented strategies. This being said, Madeline's remarkable resilience, intelligence, and interpersonal strengths should engender optimism that a successful therapy could substantially enhance the meaning Madeline could find in life, particularly with respect to the development of a trusting, mutually satisfying, and sustained relationship.

Case 2: Mr. Z

Mr. Z was a patient with narcissistic personality features described by Heinz Kohut (1979), whose AMPD was presented briefly in Waugh et al., (2017). Kohut documented two analyses with Mr. Z in order to contrast psychoanalytic technique based on classical drive theory from psychoanalytic technique based on Kohut's newer "self psychology" (Kohut, 1979). In the first treatment, the analyst would interpret Mr. Z's occasional narcissistic behavior as a defense against an unfulfilled wish that was related to his experiences with an over-gratifying mother. This approach, which was consistent with orthodox psychoanalytic technique at the time, contributed to dysregulated behavior and ultimately to a failed treatment. In the second treatment, Mr. Z's narcissistic behavior was conceptualized as part of a normal developmental process and responded to more empathically by the psychoanalyst. As the story goes, Mr. Z got better. Kohut (1979) framed the difference between the two treatments as a matter of the analyst's need to overcome his own counter-transference, that he saw as central in effective analysis from a self psychology perspective. In contrast, Kohut (1979) wanted to convince the reader that classical analysis could provide the context for the analyst's countertransference to contribute to a critical and judgmental approach which was counter-therapeutic. In other words, Kohut used these two analyses as a rhetorical devise to subtly demonstrate the advantages of his approach to psychoanalysis relative to the more traditional approach. An interesting backdrop of the description of the treatment of Mr. Z is subsequent scholarship indicating that Mr. Z was an autobiographical statement. That is, reportedly Heinz Kohut described his own experiences in two psychoanalyses (Strozier, 2001).

Whatever the reader's feelings about psychoanalysis in general or Kohut's views in particular, this rich case provides significant details about Mr. Z's personality that might be unpacked with the AMPD. It is for this reason that the case was selected. We summarized the case for our raters with the following text:

> A 28-year-old European-American male presents for psychotherapy. He is soft-spoken with halting speech. He has an athletic build but a pale, sensitive face. He reports mild somatic symptoms including sweaty palms, a feeling of fullness in his stomach, constipation alternating with diarrhea, social isolation, loneliness, feelings of shame, and sensitivity to slights. Fragile self-esteem is observed in initial interviews. Interpersonally, he can be arrogant but is also vulnerable to hurt and self-esteem injury. Historically, he is an only child of a well-to-do executive and artistically inclined mother with whom he reports a close relationship growing up and currently. He reports a "happy childhood," reporting he was the "apple of his parents' eye," but says his parents fought a lot and his parents split up in his youth. He did well in school academically and currently is a graduate student. At age 11, he was befriended by a male teacher with whom he maintained a close relationship for several years; this included hugging and other expressions of physical intimacy with two instances of full sexual activity. Currently he resides with his mother; his father passed away four years ago. He has no relationships with women and one close friend, a man, who also is socially isolated. For recreation, he attends movies alone or with his mother and his male friend, and he enjoys reading. In initial psychotherapy sessions, he reacted to therapist interpretations angrily and dismissively. He also reacted to a therapist's absence with fleeting suicidal ideation, hypochondriacal symptoms, and mild depression. He attends sessions as scheduled and fully participates in the therapy.

Figure 6.2 shows Mr. Z's AMPD profile. Identity and intimacy were above 2 for Criterion A, whereas self-direction and empathy were very close to this level. This pattern of scores would qualify Mr. Z for a PD diagnosis and suggest moderate personality impairment and more severe dysfunction in the domain of intimacy. It suggests that the core deficits for Mr. Z involve the impact of his underdeveloped identity on the generation and maintenance of mutually satisfying adult relationships.

Mr. Z was rated as having four traits above 2, on average: anxiousness, depressivity, intimacy avoidance, and withdrawal. This is the portrait of a classical internalizing type. He is not a clear match to any of the PD types in the DSM-5 AMPD, and unlike Madeline would certainly not qualify

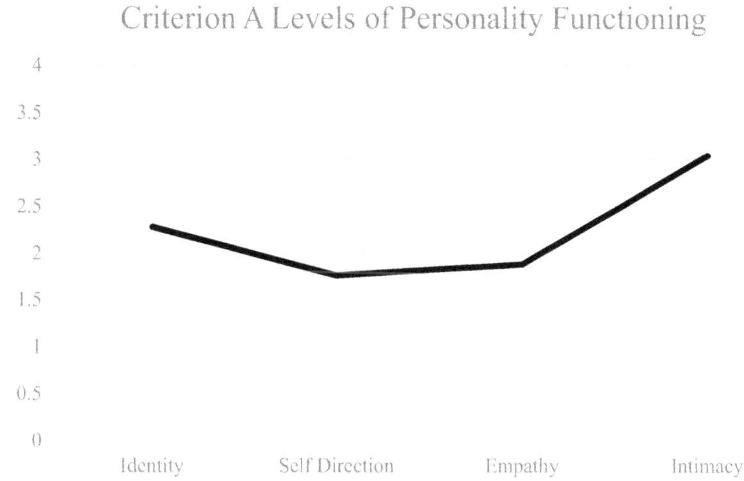

Figure 6.2a. Mr. Z's Level of Personality Functioning profile

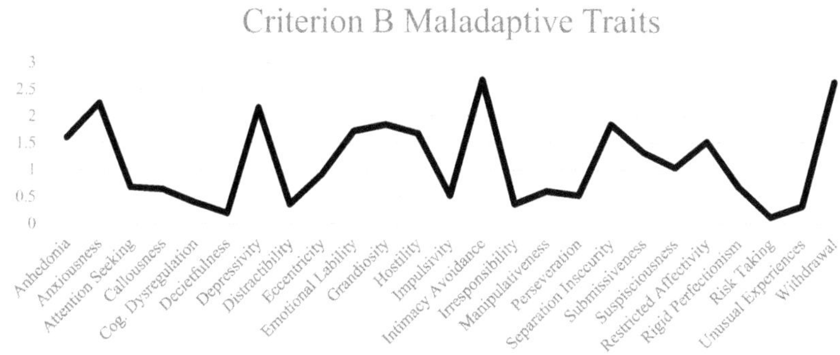

Figure 6.2b. Mr. Z's Maladaptive Traits profile

for the narcissistic type (which is defined by attention-seeking and grandiose traits). His depiction as narcissistic by Kohut reflects the psychoanalytic view of narcissism that emphasizes an inner vulnerability which may be associated with only occasional reactivity, in contrast to the trait and medical model perspectives that tend to understand narcissism in terms of a relatively stable pattern of grandiose behavior (Cain, Pincus, & Ansell, 2008). However, trait levels just below 2, including emotional lability, grandiosity, impulsivity, and separation insecurity provide useful data about the dynamics of his presentation. These scores indicate that, while he is characteristically withdrawn and depressed, within that general tendency he is prone to occasional but dramatic outbursts of narcissistic rage. Thus, this case demonstrates the value of examining the full range of scores in a personality profile, as the clinician is able to do using the AMPD.

The AMPD results allow for the generation of dynamic hypotheses based on these cross-sectional data. The combination of above-threshold internalizing with meaningful but sub-threshold pockets of externalizing problems (e.g., grandiosity) would suggest a dynamic in which a veil of withdrawn negative affect (e.g., restricted affectivity) is punctured intermittently with affective flares (e.g., emotional lability). This leads to questions about what might provoke such flares. In the case of Mr. Z, the LPFS scores might suggest that issues related to identity and intimacy would be a good place to look, including issues of separation and loss as seen in separation insecurity (Kohut, 1979). The clinician might hypothesize that highlighting his fragile identity or interpersonal failures would provoke undermentalized, impulsive coping. If that hypothesis, which could be tested in the therapeutic encounter or using other kinds of dynamic assessment tools, proved true, a specific treatment target would have been established: one clinical task would be to help Mr. Z mentalize questions about who he is and his closeness to others. Indeed, both classical and self-approaches in Kohut's (1979) paper identified this as the therapeutic target, although they differed in terms of how to go about ameliorating the personality deficit.

Although Mr. Z was a psychoanalytic case study, the more behaviorally inclined therapist would obviously have some ideas about how treatment might be approached given the AMPD profile as well. The most prominent problems involve negative affect and detachment, areas of concern for which a number of treatments from this tradition have proven effective (e.g., behavioral activation, skills training, cognitive restructuring). Modifications to standard cognitive and behavioral techniques could be applied to address Mr. Z's personological deficits, such as a dialectical attitude in which change is balanced with acceptance. Successfully addressing these two clusters of Criterion B traits would be anticipated by the behaviorally oriented clinician to reduce Criterion A deficits, such that Mr. Z would have a clearer sense of who he is and would be more successful in relation to others.

Case 3: Jeffrey Dahmer

Jeffrey Dahmer killed 17 young men, most of whom he had had sexual relations with, and some of whom he had also cannibalized. He was taken into custody in 1991, after which he cooperated fully with the investigation. He would eventually be killed by a fellow inmate. He took the MMPI and Wechsler Adult Intelligence Scale in 1992, and these data and other primary sources formed the basis of Nichol's (2006) award-winning report, which was the primary basis for the description we provided raters, as follows:

A 31-year old Caucasian man was interviewed and tested with the WAIS and MMPI while in jail subsequent to arrest for a violent felony charge. Psychometric data are presented below. History: eldest child of a PhD chemist and homemaker mother. His father was described as reticent, non-demonstrative, and rather absent due to his work. His mother was described as insecure, high-strung, and prone to depression. He reported a close relationship with a grandmother. He reported his parents chronically argued. As a young child, he suffered several medical issues including a hernia operation at age 4 which was experienced as traumatic. He reportedly changed from being "happy" to being serious and withdrawn after this event. He reported being sexually abused at age 8 by an older neighbor boy. He had few friends in his youth and was bullied in school. He reported fascination with animals in early adolescence; this included collecting and dissecting road-kill. He reported using fantasy to escape as a youth and adolescent. He abused alcohol and marijuana as an adolescent. He was a "class clown" in school, was suspended at least once, and made mediocre grades despite seeming bright. He attended the State University, but dropped out after the first quarter of classes due to missing classes, poor grades, and heavy drinking. He enrolled in the army, but was medically discharged for alcohol abuse after nine months. Others described him as quiet and reserved, but when intoxicated he became talkative and defiant. Early adulthood saw a series of jobs (fast food, laborer, stock clerk) with some absenteeism, continued heavy drinking, and occasional fighting. He has five previous arrests involving Disorderly Conduct, Open Container, and/or Indecent Exposure. Interpersonally, he was a loner. He occasionally attended gay nightclubs and bars. He reported fascination with movies such as *The Exorcist* and *A Nightmare on Elm Street.*

WAIS FSIQ: 121
MMPI T Scores: L 47; F 75; K 63; Hs 66; D 90; Hy 75; Pd 110; Mf 70; Pa 90; Pt 88; Sc 100; Ma 58; Si 53; A 60; R 57; Es 39; HEA 58; DEP 83; ORG 53; FAM 47; AUT 43; FEM 52; REL 58; HOS 52; MOR 59; PHO 55; PSY 62; HYP 47; SOC 49

Dahmer's AMPD scores are given in Figure 6.3. All four of his Criterion A scores were above threshold, indicating that raters perceived his as the most poorly functioning personality of the three cases we asked them to rate. Seven facet scores were above 2, including (from highest to lowest) irresponsibility, callousness, impulsivity, hostility, risk taking, and withdrawal. Manipulativeness and deceitfulness were subthreshold but elevated. Depending on the clinician's willingness to count either of these latter two traits as clinically significant, he would meet AMPD hybrid criteria for antisocial personality disorder. The fact that this diagnosis would depend on this relatively subjective decision documents one of the critical

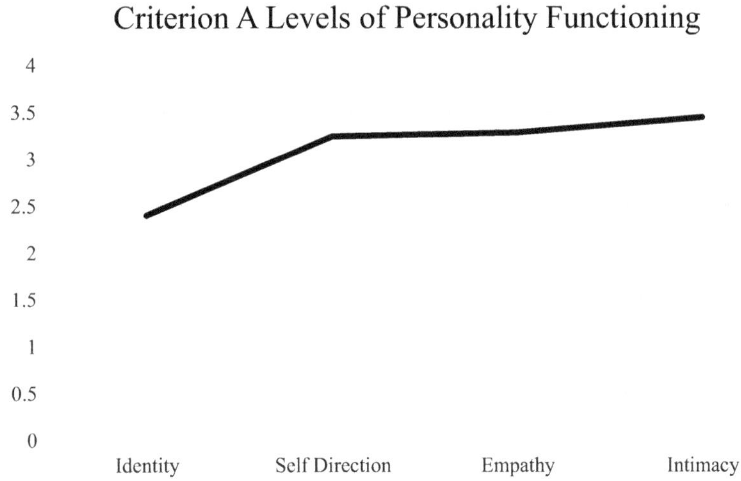

Figure 6.3a. Jeffery Dahmer's Level of Personality Functioning profile

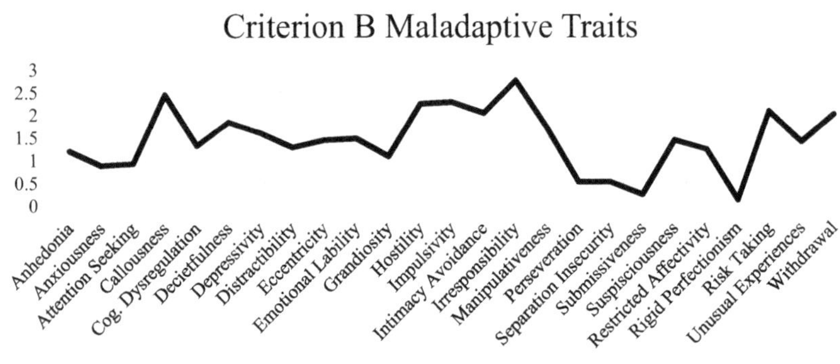

Figure 6.3b. Jeffery Dahmer's Maladaptive Traits profile

problems with categorical diagnosis that have arbitrary diagnostic cutoffs. The clinician who was rigid about using 2 as a cutoff for clinically significant traits would miss the diagnosis by an unreliable hair.

From a more holistic, psychometric perspective, this pattern paints the picture of a classic externalizer, with problems focused in the disinhibition and antagonism domains of personality. He had many of the tell-tale behavioral signs as well, including a history of misbehavior and conduct problems in childhood, difficulties holding down jobs or keeping other responsibilities, substance abuse issues, and extreme criminal behavior.

This portrait is qualified by his high score on withdrawal, a facet of detachment, which reflected the description of Dahmer as a "loner" who tended to be "quiet and reserved" when he was not intoxicated. Indeed, one of the interesting dynamics that comes through in our brief narrative, and substantially more clearly in Nichol's study, is that Dahmer was a sad and lonely figure. It is not difficult to draw upon his childhood for hypotheses about his loneliness; he was neglected by both his workaholic father and his severely depressed mother. In many ways his criminal behavior could be construed in terms of attachment: he wanted to be close to people but had a severely maladaptive way of achieving this goal. In this regard it is interesting to think of his demise and compare his personality to that of his murderer. Whereas his killings happened in the context of a quasi-romantic, albeit manipulative, situation, his killer acted on impulse and in an apparently sadistic manner. Whereas his killer's externalizing personality was unmitigated, Dahmer's was used as a means to satisfy a desire for closeness. This feature of Dahmer's personality, so critical to a clinical conceptualization of the case, peeks through in the AMPD data in a way that would probably be missed based on his criminal profile alone, or a diagnosis of simple antisocial personality disorder.

Dahmer also had scores approaching 1.5 for eccentricity, unusual beliefs and experiences, and suspiciousness, highlighting psychotic features that were somewhat more prominent in the MMPI data (his codetype was 48, or "psychopathic deviate" mixed with "schizophrenia"). The discrepancy between the MMPI results and the AMPD profile very well could have been a result of the way we described Dahmer in our brief narrative. He clearly engaged in a number of odd behaviors and approached life in a way that was unconventional, to say the least. These would have absolutely been relevant data had clinical services been initiated.

Our last observation about this case is that Dahmer's score on irresponsibility, which was highest among Criterion B traits, is perhaps too simplistic. He had indeed acted irresponsibly throughout his life, as depicted in the narrative above. But we already mentioned his compliance with the investigation after he was arrested. He also expressed the wish that he had been caught earlier, acknowledged that it was right that he should be punished, and claimed in a television interview that the only thing that really made him angry was when people blamed his parents for his behavior. He seemed more than ready to claim responsibility for his criminal behavior, which would be an important clinical detail perhaps missed in our description and, thus, the AMPD profile.

Conclusion

These case descriptions and AMPD ratings by 25 experts have shown that the AMPD can be used to provide a clinically useful and relatively comprehensive depiction of a case based on limited information. We observed generally strong agreement among our raters. Moreover, our raters described the AMPD model, with which most were only somewhat familiar, as clinically useful. To assess clinical utility, we used the items from Morey, Skodol, and Oldham (2014), who asked mental professionals to rate the traditional PD categories and AMPD in terms of six facets of clinical utility. As in their study, raters concluded that the AMPD was clinically useful in each of these categories (Table 6.1).

It is instructive, in thinking about clinical utility, to compare the AMPD profiles in Figures 6.1–6.3 with the categorical PD diagnosis (or diagnoses) each might receive with the Section II PD nosology. To facilitate this comparison, Table 6.2 shows profile correlations between each individual trait profile and the trait profiles for different PDs taken from the work of

Table 6.1. Perceived clinical utility of AMPD among 25 clinician raters.

Clinical Utility Question	*Mean*	*SD*
How easy do you feel it was to apply these concepts to these cases?	3.56	0.77
How useful do you feel these concepts would be for communicating information about these cases with other mental health professionals?	4.08	1.04
How useful do you feel these concepts would be for communicating information to the individual patients?	3.72	1.06
How useful are these concepts for comprehensively describing all the important personality problems the individuals have?	3.64	1.04
How useful would these concepts be for helping you to formulate effective interventions for these individuals?	3.76	0.88
How useful were these concepts for describing the individuals' global personalities?	3.84	1.03

Note. All items rated on a scale from 1 (not at all) to 5 (extremely). Based on scale used by Morey, Skodol, and Oldham (2014).

Table 6.2. Correlations between AMPD profiles and Morey, Benson, and Skodol (2016) personality disorder prototypes.

	Madeline	*Mr. Z*	*Jeffery Dahmer*
Avoidant	–.67	**.71**	–.43
Antisocial	.63	–.62	**.64**
Borderline	.45	–.08	.26
Dependent	–.47	.39	–.49
Histrionic	**.73**	–.61	.28
Narcissistic	**.73**	–.51	.44
Obsessive-Compulsive	–.41	.27	–.44
Paranoid	.51	–.36	.47
Schizoid	–.44	.62	.05
Schizotypal	–.17	.16	–.02

Note. Highest value is in bold for each case.

Morey, Benson, and Skodol (2016). Briefly, Morey et al. (2016) provided AMPD trait profiles associated with DSM-IV PD criterion count sums. These were developed from a study by Morey, Skodol, and Oldham (2014) in which 337 clinicians described a patient they knew well using all DSM IV PD criteria and the AMPD. Thus, this methodology provides an AMPD-based profile (like a "prototype") of each of the DSM-IV PDs. With a common metric (the AMPD ratings), we are able to correlate ratings of our three case vignettes with DSM-IV PDs to evaluate similarities. Based on their profiles (Figures 6.1–6.3) and these summary correlations, Madeline would have received a primary PD diagnosis of narcissistic personality disorder, Mr. Z perhaps of avoidant personality disorder or PD not otherwise specified, and Jeffrey Dahmer of antisocial personality disorder. While none of these diagnoses would be inaccurate per se, each would miss important clinical information readily identified in the AMPD. In other words, the AMPD provides substantially more information that categorical diagnoses, with about the same amount of effort in data gathering and only somewhat more effort in data communication. At the same time, as Table 6.1 shows, the AMPD can be used to indicate categorical diagnoses in a manner that appears relatively accurate, which may have value under some circumstances. This exercise also further demonstrates that the two approaches to PD nosology can be "cross-walked," as other investigators have reported (e.g., Evans & Simms, 2018).

We would add that a fuller and more accurate AMPD depiction would have been possible had the profiles been based on a careful assessment using multimethod techniques and in-person interaction. In other words, the context of a more typical, full clinical assessment should only enhance the clinical utility of the AMPD. This is illustrated in Chapter 8 wherein two comprehensive case evaluations use the AMPD to guide case formulation and treatment planning. In the next chapter, a similar study is conducted with three well-known literary characters, and in the chapters that follow, the clinical utility of the AMPD is demonstrated in greater detail in the context of less well-known but more richly described individuals.

7 The AMPD and Three Well-Known Literary Characters

Christopher J. Hopwood and Mark H. Waugh

In the preceding chapter, we illustrated the capacity of the Alternative Model of Personality Disorders (AMPD; APA, 2013), as rated by clinicians, to recapture the personalities of three clinical cases based on brief descriptions and psychometric test data. In this complementary chapter, we test the limits of the AMPD. Rather than evaluating clinical vignettes, we asked a diverse set of raters to apply the AMPD to three complex literary characters. Social neuroscience suggests that reading literary fiction promotes mentalizing (Kidd & Castano, 2013; Pino & Maza, 2016) and simulates the social world for the reader (Mar & Oately, 2008; Oately, 2016). Thus, investigating the extent to which the AMPD can capture elements of "character" paradoxically constitutes a test of its ecological validity (Brunswik, 1955). Essentially, in this chapter we aim to ask whether raters can "get inside the head" of literary characters using the AMPD.

The use of literature for psychological studies of character has a long history. For example, Sigmund Freud regarded Fyodor Dostoevsky as an unparalleled investigator of the mind (Breger, 2009), and Henry Murray felt that Herman Melville's *Moby Dick* provided a master map of the human psyche (Murray, 1951). Several researchers have illustrated the power of various measurement models to depict the personological nuances of literary cases (e.g., Allik et al., 2011; Johnson, Carroll, Gottschall, & Kruger, 2011; McCrae, Gaines, & Wellington, 2012; Pennebaker & Ireland, 2008; Rapp, Gerrig, & Prentice, 2001). An advantage of this technique is that authors of literary fiction elaborate the subtleties and complexities of their characters, giving personality theorists and raters a lot to go on.

There are many elements to literature, but character and character development are most relevant to our purposes. Indeed, the ability of masters like Dostoyevsky, Harper Lee, and William Shakespeare to draw us in so that we feel ourselves within the social worlds of the characters they portray is a defining achievement of literature. In his 1948 lectures on literature, Vladimir Nabokov (1980/2017) asserted that the essence of the craft of writing novels is enchanting the reader. Readers whose imaginations are captured by characters from literary fiction in effect curate interesting cases for psychological study by making them popular.

The personality assessor's challenge, in contrast, is to convey a complex individual personality in a manner that can be efficiently and reliably comprehended and communicated. Unlike the writer who shows but does not tell, we turned the tables and asked how much can be told by the AMPD from what is shown in the characters. In our study, we constrained ourselves to brief narrative summaries, 15 raters, and 29 maladaptive personality features represented on a single page: a significant handicap in comparison to the many pages used to transport us into the minds of Rodion Raskolnikov, Atticus Finch, and Prince Hamlet!

But freedom can be found in constraints. In this case, we emphasize two liberties associated with using the AMPD. First, we can directly compare characters whose descriptions focused on distinctive, individual elements using a model that captures their personalities with a common set of variables. This constraint becomes a common template that allows for a direct comparison of the complex nuances that distinguish each character from the other. Second, we focus on the individuals' maladaptive personality features. Characters' flaws and foibles typically make for a rich story in literature, particularly in the cases we selected. In clinical assessment the focus on maladaptive features is due to the need to justify diagnoses and organize treatment plans. In this study, it allows us to link the life stories of literary characters with personality informed clinical diagnosis.

Although our approach in this chapter and the preceding chapter has obvious roots in narrative psychology (e.g., McAdams, 2001), we took particular inspiration from the work of McCrae, Gaines, and Wellington (2012), whose second and third authors rated characters from Moliere (Alceste) and Voltaire (Candide) with the 30 facets of the NEO-PI-R version of the Five Factor Model (FFM) of personality traits. As in Chapter 6, we developed textured albeit brief synopses of characters drawn from literary fiction and asked raters to read these descriptions and rate each character using the AMPD.

We chose three cases from highly regarded books whose reputations hinge, in part, on the psychological complexity of the characters. Joyce Carol Oates's (2012) novel *Mudwoman* was selected because Oates is an accessible writer who places emphasis on psychological character development, and the protagonist of the book represents a rich tapestry of personality features and dynamics. Two characters from Nabokov's (1955) *Lolita* were chosen for study. Nabokov is a consummate stylist and *Lolita* is regarded a masterwork of world literature—one in which the reader is drawn in empathically to the mind of a pedophile (Humbert Humbert) and his complicated, evolving relationship with the rebellious and flawed Dolores Haze (Lolita)[1].

We asked 15 raters to evaluate our summaries of these literary characters with the AMPD scheme. We also provided them with plot summaries of the books. The primary professional backgrounds of the raters (n = 15) were as follows: practitioners of clinical psychology (6), academic clinical psychologists (2), personality psychologist (1), theater professor (1), literature professor (1), and doctoral students in clinical psychology (4). We again used the AMPD form created by Waugh (2014) for the ratings and two-way random effects absolute agreement Intraclass Correlation Coefficients (ICC) to evaluate inter-rater reliability across the four Level of Personality Functioning Scale (LPFS) domains and 25 maladaptive trait scores. These comparisons varied to some extent across the three rated characters and by LPFS and the trait domains, but when the full AMPD model of LPFS and trait domain was examined, the mean ICCs ranged from .88 to .92, indicating strong overall agreement in applying the AMPD to these three literary characters.

Case 1: Mudwoman

The first case was "Mudwoman" (M.R. Neukirchen), the protagonist of Joyce Carol Oates' (2012) book by the same title. The appellation Mudwoman apparently emerged in a vision by Oates of a woman whose makeup was so thick and dried that it resembled mud. The name works as a reference to an attempted drowning in a mudflat at the hands of Neukirchen's deeply disturbed mother and as an effective metaphor for the layers of depth in her personality, which serve to cover up a long history of trauma that unravels over the course of the novel.

In the book, Dr. Neukirchen is an accomplished, respected professor of philosophy and President of an Ivy League university who is liked by all for her attentive, pleasing manner and supreme dedication to helping and being friendly. Somewhat like James Joyce's *Ulysses* (1922/1986), the book is structured in parallel tracks in which realistic present-tense chapters alternate with bizarre, hallucinatory scenes. Track 1 chronicles Mudwoman's experience and events in the present tense, whereas track 2 describes "Mudgirl's" childhood experiences and events.

The present-tense narrative opens in a scene in which she, as the recently inaugurated first female President of Princeton University, is the keynote speaker at the *Fiftieth Annual National Conference of the American Association of Learned Societies* at Cornell University. While waiting for her hotel room to be readied, she impulsively rents a car and drives out into the countryside, recalling how the names of small towns there had beckoned to her as she was chauffeured to Ithaca from Princeton. She becomes mired on a small, dirt and gravel road; her cell phone fails to work, and she misses the evening dinner and keynote address. She has a hallucinatory-like experience there, but later recalls little and her indiscrete absence is covered up by University staff.

From track 2 we learn that she was born as Jedina Krack in upstate New York. Her early childhood was marked by severe abuse, culminating in her psychotic mother's attempt to "ready" (sacrifice) her to God, by throwing her into the mudflats of a river. She sank into the mud and was left to die. Days later she was rescued by a fur trapper and given to the authorities. She suffered from malnutrition, exposure, and infections. Although she recovered slowly in the hospital, she was mainly mute. When she spoke, she took the name of her older sister, Jewel. She was placed in a harsh group foster home, from which she was adopted by a kindly Quaker couple whose daughter had died at age 4. They renamed Jewel "Merry," after their deceased child, and explicitly raised her as if she was their original daughter. Merry could not look them in the eyes. She recalled how:

> I could not know, it was love in their eyes. Love for the little Mudgirl, shining in their eyes. I could not bear this love! How could Mudgirl bear this love! Merry experienced Momma's anger and outrage. Momma's grip—her fingers like ice…Not every night now did she lie awake in the night waiting for Momma to appear at the foot of her bed.

Mudgirl precociously learned to read, was extremely compliant, worked hard at everything, pleased others at all costs, and never made waves. She excelled in school, respected and complied with elders, and had few friends. An eccentric, outcast, "nerdy" high school math teacher recognized her talent and perceived her as like him on the inside. He took an interest in Mudgirl and eventually made a clumsy pass at her. Her rejection was humiliating. He resigned, left town, and was suspected of suicide. This event propelled Mudgirl to defy her parents, who wanted her to stay close to home and work as a teacher, to secretly apply to Cornell University. She received a scholarship to Cornell, then a fellowship to Harvard, and achieved acclaim in philosophy through her productivity and incisive, original scholarship. As a youth, although a "good girl" to everyone, she was private, distrusting, self-sufficient, and had occasional distracted moments and self-loathing ideation.

Back on track 1, the reader learns that early on as University President, Mudwoman has an encounter with a disturbed, provocative student who faked his own campus assault to publicly advance his antagonistic political agenda. She is unable to win him over with her trademark understanding and likeability. She becomes obsessed with her perceived failure. He subsequently attempts suicide when facts of his faked assault surface, but he is unsuccessful and remains in a comatose state. The event receives national media attention when the students' parents initiate a lawsuit against the University. Mudwoman experiences increasing intrusive memories and nightmarish dream-like mentation at times. Her performance suffers: she is uncharacteristically late for appointments, makes unilateral, impulsive decisions, and asserts provocative, radically liberal opinions to University Trustees and conservative donors. Late at night she cuts her forehead after slipping on the dark stairs in the President's mansion. She keeps this injury a secret by covering her face with layers of haphazardly applied makeup.

Mudwoman becomes erratic, disheveled, anxious, suspicious, loses weight, and develops symptoms including GI problems, insomnia, weight loss, hives, and ear and throat infections, all of which she ignores. She has increasing "lurid dreams," some of which resemble fugue states. Content of these "dreams" become increasingly morbid. One involves an abduction from the campus swimming pool, public humiliation, and forcible rape and impregnation. In another she is pursued and attacked in the President's mansion by a campus foe, a well-known conservative faculty member who serves as advisor to the US Vice President on the Iraq War. This "dream" culminates in her attacker striking his head as he falls on stairs. He dies, and she hides the "crime" by dismembering his body and depositing trash bags of body parts around town during the night. She thinks of her dreams: "…like one mired in mud; her deeper, most inward life had become a concatenation of random and humiliating dreams that left her exhausted and broken. But she would not give in." Eventually, she collapses. She is hospitalized and treated for malnutrition and severe infections, and against her will is assigned three months of medical leave. She is profoundly humiliated by her collapse, need for treatment, and forced leave of absence. She feels she has betrayed everyone and that her lover, a reserved astronomer, will surely abandon her. She wants to die.

She returns to her small home town and lives with her father (her mother has passed away). She ceases professional activities and can sleep regularly. She accompanies her father on charity visits to the state psychiatric and the VA hospitals. A series of pivotal interactions ensue, including her father disclosing that her birth mother has been hospitalized as criminally insane in a state hospital nearby. She confides in him about her long-distance relationship with the aloof astronomer. He says "Your astronomer-friend is very special, I can see. But you, too, are very special, Meredith—don't forget. And don't forget, the future doesn't have to be a repetition of the past." She meets her old high school math teacher at the VA hospital where he escorts a neighbor lady visiting her wounded son. The math teacher is transformed. Mudwoman thanks him for teaching her how to teach.

Through several interactions she feels glimpses of self-acceptance, and for the first time openly states her love for her father. She places a wreath on the side-by-side grave marker for her adoptive mother and their deceased "Merry," communicating her acceptance of her parents' posture of treating her like their original daughter. She has a vivid dream in which she is a bride who marries a horribly disfigured combat-injured veteran in the local VA hospital. She is happy, feeling "*Mudwoman* is loved. At last." As she prepares to leave at the end of the summer, her father says "When you return to your home, remember: you have been placed in this world for a distinct purpose, and at the University, you have found that purpose" and "You must not enslave yourself, as you would not enslave any other person. You must be the custodian of your *self*."

The novel ends as Mudwoman drives back to resume her job. She detours off the highway to a tiny hamlet to search for the ramshackle shed she lived in with her mother and abusive boyfriends as a child. She becomes caught up in the idea that her unknown natural father may still be in the area and asks locals of the whereabouts of "Kracks." She cannot locate the shack or find him. But, she thinks "I am breaking into pieces now. I must save myself. No more. Enough. I have a father." At a highway rest stop, she narrowly escapes an aggravated assault by a stranger, shakes off the experience, and returns to the University prepared to commit fully to her boyfriend and her career responsibilities.

In addition to the preceding plot summary, we also gave this description of Mudwoman to raters:

Biographical Data

Name (adoptive): Meredith Ruth Neukirchen's (nickname "Merry"), goes by "M.R."

Birth Name: Jedina Kraeck; assumed the name of her older sister Jewell when rescued, age 3

Place of Birth: Rapids, New York, population 370 (upstate New York)

Age: 41

Education: Ph.D., Philosophy, Harvard University; B.A. Cornell University

Occupation: President, Princeton University, and Professor of Philosophy

Marital Status: Single; 19-year long-distance relationship with Andre Litovik, an older married Harvard astrophysicist

Developmental History

Jedina is the younger of Marit Kraeck's two daughters. Father is unknown. Her mother was mentally ill and suspicious of all government offices; they moved about in low-rent residences. Mother was neglectful, paranoid, hyper-religious, and alcoholic. Occasional boyfriends were in the home(s). She recalls a boyfriend playing "tickle games" with her at bath time. Her mother, in the throes of religious delusion, "readies" Jedina by shaving her head and throws her, near naked, into mudflats by a river, offering her to God, and leaves her to die. Her sister is locked inside a junked refrigerator and dies. Jedina lay partially submerged in the mud for several days, suffering exposure, before being spotted by a fur trapper.

She is rescued but her health is precarious. She recovers with hospital treatment but remains largely mute. Her mother disappears, and she becomes a ward of the state (New York). In foster care she is quiet, standoffish, and distracted. She claims her name is "Jewell," (her sister's name); this becomes her name because there is no way to verify and the sister is presumed missing. She is 3 years old, but sister

Jewel was 6. After three months in a chaotic group foster home, she is adopted by Konrad and Agatha Neukrichen, kindly Quakers, who pity her and "replace" their daughter, Merry, who died at age 4. Her adoptive parents dote on her. She remains reserved but wholly compliant, never making waves. She suffers repetitive nightmares.

The adoptive parents are bibliophiles. "Merry" precociously and privately learns to read. Later, in school, she is alert and attentive but slightly disconnected, and nonetheless excels, with a tremendous ability for memorizing and reading. She is also a good athlete and a reliable team player. She seeks to please her parents and teachers through her work. She excels and graduates valedictorian but is not asked to the Senior Prom. She attends Cornell University on a scholarship, performs outstandingly, and completes her Ph.D. in philosophy at Harvard University, specializing in ethics and epistemology.

Notable statements by/descriptions of Mudwoman from text

"My dream is to be of service! I want to do good."

"smiling—a reflex she learned as a child."

"keep a cheerful heart, and keep busy."

"prided herself on her lack of pretension, her friendliness."

"She was very good at forgetting, also. To forget is the very principle of forgiveness."

"(Momma) had burrowed into her heart like a mean little worm that could not so easily be extricated. Just when she believed that Momma was faded and left behind that very night a dream would come to her…it was clear to her… that her new mother and her new father were… emissaries of Satan" [Re: her new, adoptive parents]

"No more potent narcotic than work."

"and to write, rewrite, revise, and rewrite through a succession of drafts until her words were finely honed and shimmering—invincible as a shield."

"Open-minded friendliness to all"

"High point of my life—to be admired, loved." (when nominated/elected President)

"there is happiness in alone, if you believe you have chosen it."

Known as "thoroughbred workhorse"

For each essay or paper she cultivates a "voice distinct and appropriate to the subject of the piece, as to the publication, and its (presumed) audience…M.R. had no 'voice' of her own—or so she believed."

Re: public speaking: "scrutiny is abstract, anonymous!"

"lonely—beyond the protective boundaries of her work: her work that was words; walls, barriers, concentric circles of words like the rings of Saturn."

"this is my role: to bring happiness to others. If I am strong enough!"

"no one loves a weak, needy child"

"you are safe inside a book"

"Her Quaker instincts led her to apologize for wrongs not her own, to minimize conflict."

"her life flashed before her eyes…because Andre didn't want me."

"he wouldn't have known how not there she was in his arms"

After an argument with a boyfriend, she fears choking on own her vomit, the specter of dying and decaying flashes in her mind, with the thought "Die why don't you. Mudgirl, garbage girl—die."

A tight schedule is "redeeming." Open time is "unmoored and adrift."

"to be known, to be identified—how disagreeable this was to her, at such a time." (While swimming laps alone early in morning, when she felt "invisible")

Mudwoman's AMPD profile is presented in Figure 7.1. She is above threshold (≥ 2) for identity and intimacy problems, indicating significant impairment in personality functioning and the diagnosis of PD. Identity problems are primary, as also symbolized by the many names she chooses (or endures) and the multiple seemingly incompatible roles she enacts within her own life. The fractured nature of her identity and inner experience are furthermore signified by the novel's use of dual tracks of narrative. Identity problems are Mudwoman's central characteristic, her *basic fault* (Balint, 1968) or metaphorical fault line in her personality organization (Ahktar & Samuel, 1996). In Oates' novel, Dr. Neukirchen finds tentative purchase in her life, achieving a degree of redemption by pulling together her part-identities and committing to a life worth living, seeking to serve a greater cause in the manner described by McAdams (2013).

Intimacy problems are prevalent throughout the book beginning dramatically with her troubled childhood, running through her faux identity as a lesser substitute for a previously deceased daughter in her adoptive home, her ever high-achieving but empty persona, and culminating in her role as the gracious, helpful University President along with her yearning for the ambivalent (and married) astronomer boyfriend. As discussed below, intimacy avoidance is her highest maladaptive trait elevation. However, it is also the intimacy of her adoptive father that plays a pivotal role in helping Mudwoman begin to recover and find balance. Her commitment to risk romantic intimacy is offered as evidence for her potential well-being at the end of the story.

Mudwoman's sub-clinical elevation in self-direction is likely a compromise between her tremendous professional achievement and occasional imprudent behaviors (some of which reflect dissociative symptoms) during key moments of the story. The self-direction score also points to an

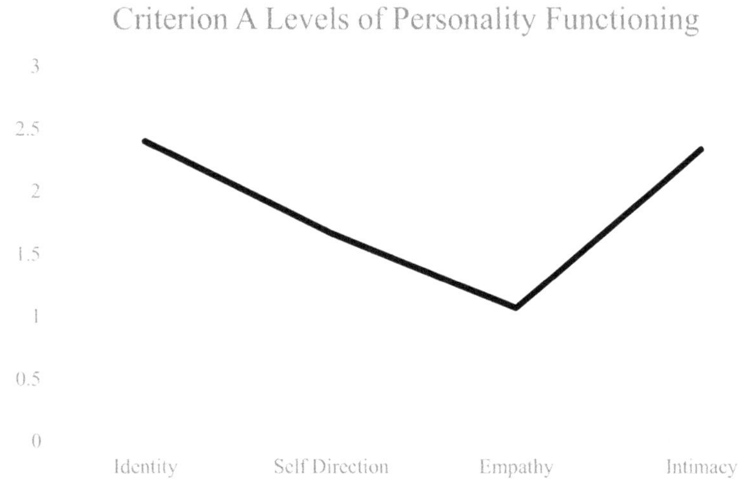

Figure 7.1a. Mudwoman's Level of Personality Functioning profile

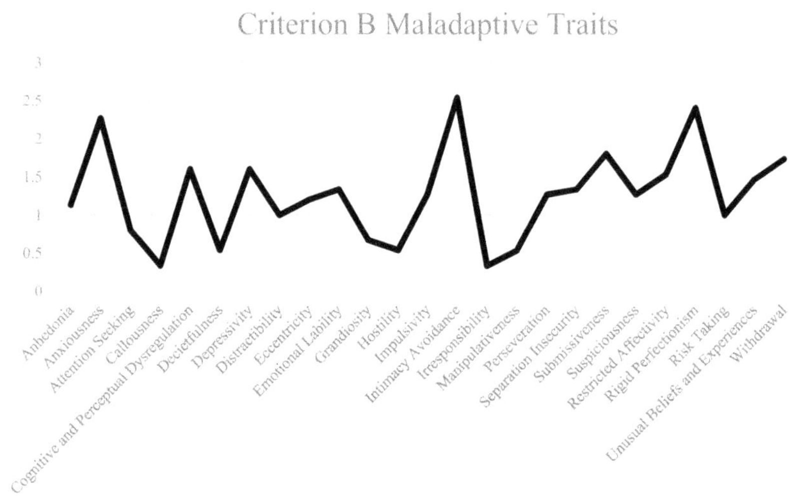

Figure 7.1b. Mudwoman's Maladaptive Traits profile

interesting potential distinction between Criterion A, which is moderately elevated, and Criterion B, which is somewhat suppressed. The raters may have been reacting to the high level of self-directed agency in her general personality structure and functioning. However, this is an element of her personality that fractures during her moments of greatest dysfunction. Thus, Criterion A may represent Mudwoman at her worst, whereas Criterion B may indicate Dr. Neukirchen's general personality more generally.

Mudwoman's score on empathy problems is low; her lack of empathy is primarily self-directed. There was no evidence of incapacity to empathize with others. In fact, her perceived failure to help a student who probably didn't deserve her help was a major stressor for her.

Clinical elevations on Mudwoman's maladaptive trait profile include intimacy avoidance, anxiousness, and rigid perfectionism. These traits would not qualify her for a categorical PD diagnosis in the AMPD, so she would be trait specified. This constellation paints the portrait of a person whose cardinal features are anxious detachment and excessive self-reliance. Her past certainly gave her plenty of justification to distance from others and go her own way. She had little reason to trust attachment figures and she learned through her life experiences that "safety," acceptance, and success were found only by hard work and the pleasing persona within which her fractured, nascent self was protected.

This constellation provides an example of the value of facet-based personality data. Each of these traits is most closely associated with a different domain: anxiousness with negative affectivity, intimacy avoidance with detachment, and rigid perfectionism with (low) disinhibition. But together they weave a coherent story: her anxiousness drives both self-protective distance-keeping (low affiliation with others) and self-driven motivation to excel, expressing the theme of agency and denial of the need for connection (see Modell, 1975). These traits work together in a way that doesn't correspond to nomothetic personality structure but is coherent with respect to this individual life.

Mudwoman's perfectionism and drive can be understood as a defensive reaction to her understandable anxiety about close relationships. In other words, her primary personality constellation could be understood as self-reliance *in the service of* anxious detachment. Mudwoman's academic and career success were an initial source of self-esteem for her that protected her from a hostile and unpredictable social environment (see Modell, 1975). This allowed her to thrive and achieve a level of unexpected success, somewhat comparable to the life story of Madeline from the previous chapter. However, her personality disorganizes, as reflected in her increasing self-neglect, lapses of judgment, and dissociative episodes as University President. Interestingly, the book's resolution involves a merger of her agentic and communal motives, in the form of both going back to work and vowing to commit to an attachment relationship.

Mudwoman had sub-clinical elevations on two constellations of scores that undergird this general dynamic. The first were in the domains of neurotic introversion, including depressivity, withdrawal, submissiveness, and restricted affectivity. These scores fill out the portrait of her dispositional traits and interpersonal adaptations. In addition, she was prone to self-loathing and reflexive detachment. She would retreat in the face of interpersonal challenge, feeling a deep sense of inefficacy, and shut down her emotions, channeling her energies into work and pleasing others.

Literature and the mental health sciences alike afford a prominent role for the "return of the repressed," or the compelling drive to process and master trauma one has experienced (e.g., Caruth, 2016; Chu, 1991; Levy, 2000; Loevinger, 1966; Van der Kolk & Van der Hart, 1991). Mudwoman's curiosity about her past and intrusive experiences in which she includes relived fragments of her past were pathways to finding herself, but they only occurred through the cracked psychic glass of fantasy and memory, attended by severe emotional dysregulation.

The second major dynamic reflected in the AMPD traits is in the domain of psychoticism, and included cognitive and perceptual distortion and unusual beliefs and experiences. These scores indicate the occasional cracks in her self-organization communicated in track 2 of the narrative. These tracks reflected dissociated material from her past and expressed the progressively deteriorated behavior of Mudwoman. Some raters commented that Mudwoman seemed to meet diagnostic criteria for dissociative identity disorder, as well as PD. Oates' depiction of Mudwoman's unraveling in the service of saving herself recalls Winnicott's (1974) paradoxical idea that anxiety associated with disorganized experience may reflect reemergence of a previous "breakdown," a notion that may apply to Mudwoman. The novel shows Mudwoman's development and changes, evoking the possibilities of self-transformation available to us all. Thus, she is not a static character. Raters probably would have regarded her as more "psychotic" at certain points in the story than others, and the obtained AMPD scores for the domain of psychoticism probably reflect a compromise between her healthier and her more deteriorated states, which oscillated and then evolved as the story progressed.

Mudwoman received notably low scores on externalizing traits, including callousness, hostility, irresponsibility, and deceitfulness. She was generally socially skilled and restrained. But these character strengths may also have served defensive purposes, helping her avoid the (threatening and disorganizing) complications of mutual relationships, allowing her to concentrate on her more conflict-free zone of work and individual achievement. Her difficulties with appropriate expressions of behavior on the dimensions of "callousness" (self-assertion) and "irresponsibility" (being relaxed and carefree) caused her much angst at times, such as when she suffered through ruminating about perceived failures that most people would accept as part and parcel of being in a powerful position.

In part, *Mudwoman* is a story about healing, with Mudwoman's father playing a catalyzing role as healer. But to understand the novel in this way is insufficient. *Mudwoman* describes a traumatized child who achieves a shell of mastery through over-functioning but whose past returns, in momentary fragments and then through decompensation. Through expressing her neediness and accepting her father's ministrations, she finds "herself". But even this is too simple. Life is messy. Mudwoman vows to commit to a romantic relationship and to serve her life purpose by returning to her career. But the final scene in which she barely survives an assault at a roadside rest stop and re-organizes herself with cheery optimism for the future portends how the "basic fault" (Balint, 1968) may not be vanquished. Oates leaves the reader feeling relief, a sense of hope for Mudwoman, but not completely so: this may not be the end of the "story."

What would this AMPD profile tell a psychotherapist about how to formulate and treat a person like Mudwoman? Clarkin, Cain, and Livesley (2015) and Hopwood (2018) describe how the AMPD helps the clinician organize psychotherapy and psychiatric intervention. For significant levels of impairment, as in LPFS-defined PD, structure and support are needed. If we consider Mudwoman when she is at her lowest point, which is when people usually present for treatment, an initial goal might be to provide structure, support, and then to shore up her cognitive processing and reduce anxiety. Having stabilized her thinking and developed initial, tentative rapport, the clinician might leverage her professional success and social skills to encourage growth and re-build her self-esteem. Longer-term goals would include titrating the level of intimacy in the therapeutic relationship to develop sufficient trust and a level of attachment that would allow her to work through past trauma and pain. Moreover, her AMPD trait profile suggests psychotherapeutic attention to her driven perfectionism, which may be viewed as a sublimated response to attachment conflicts. A greater balance between agency and communion that could include more mature, close, and trusting relationships and a life in which she can tolerate minor failures at work would be evidence of therapeutic success.

Case 2: Humbert Humbert

The second two characters we examined with the AMPD are from Vladimir Nabokov's (1955) novel, *Lolita*, which has been described as one of the most important works of fiction from the 20th Century. The first of these is Humbert Humbert, the lead character. It is largely through the eyes of Humbert and the narrative of his actions that the reader is provided views of the second character, Lolita (his nickname for Dolores Haze), the prepubescent girl with whom he is obsessed. The novel is structured as the personal account of Humbert delivered to his attorney shortly before Humbert died (of coronary thrombosis while in jail prior to his trial), with the instruction that it be published only after Lolita's death.

Humbert's past marriage in France to a woman named Valeria is described as a "cover" for his pedophilic sexual predilections. She has an affair when he treats her shabbily. They divorce, and he moves to America as per the terms of the inheritance from his uncle, who insisted he work in the perfume business in New York. Humbert is treated in a sanitarium twice for "melancholia and a sense of insufferable oppression" after his arrival. He is then employed as a psychological observer/note taker on a research expedition to the Canadian arctic for 20 months but is later re-hospitalized. He attributes his improved mood to the opportunity to toy with the psychoanalytic therapists through inventing elaborate, "fake primal scene" dream reports. After signing out of the sanitarium, he goes to the small New England town of Ramsdale to rest and recuperate.

Humbert rents a room for the summer from Mrs. Charlotte Haze, a widow and the mother of the 12-year-old 7th grader, Dolores. Charlotte Haze falls in love with Humbert, who feels repulsed by her. However, he is enraptured over Dolores, his "Lolita," a perfect "nymphet." He finds ways to be alone with her, including casually brushing against her. She is coy, plays along, and finds excitement in breaking rules and defying her mother.

Charlotte pleas with Humbert to either marry her or leave. He decides to marry her as another "cover" to be close to Lolita and, as a stepfather, be able to hold and stroke her. Charlotte adores Humbert, so it is easy for him to string her along. He fabricates stories about his past to appease and entertain her, likening them to "soap operas, psychoanalysis and cheap novelettes…upon which I drew for my characters." Humbert fantasizes that if they have a baby together, Charlotte will be in the hospital for a while and he can be alone with Lolita. He also ruminates on ways to murder Charlotte so he could inherit Lolita as sole parent. He obtains sleeping pills from a doctor with plans to drug Charlotte and Lolita so as to be able to have his way with Lolita while she sleeps.

Humbert keeps a secret journal and therein he describes how he detests Charlotte and covets Lolita. Charlotte discovers the journal and, blind with anger, runs out of the house and is struck and killed by a man having a heart attack while behind the wheel of a car. Lolita is away at summer camp when her mother is killed. Humbert picks Lolita up from camp and spirits her off on a road trip alone, telling her that her mother is sick and in the hospital. When he drugs her at a hotel, she passes out but is not fully unconscious. In delight, he lays next to her but does not take advantage of her. In the morning she awakes and rolls over, kisses Humbert, and whispers to him, "let's play a game, let's do it." They have intercourse three times.

Humbert and Lolita then set out on a year-long road trip across America, staying in roadside motels and moving from town to town. He keeps her in check ("terrorized") by threatening to (1) send her to a strict boarding school, or (2) if she tells authorities, with the threat that he will go to jail and she will become an orphan ward of the state and sent to reform school. They travel "27,000" miles before returning to Ramsdale and enrolling Lolita in the Beardsley School for Girls.

Lolita is paid a weekly allowance "under the condition she fulfill her basic obligations," but she learns to "cruelly negotiate" with escalating prices for various sexual favors. Humbert would secretly "burgle her room" when she was at school. He restricts her from associating with boys and most extracurricular activities because his "jealousy would constantly catch its ugly claw in the fine fabrics of nymphet falsity." Lolita becomes very involved in a school play. The director, Clare Quilty, is a writer, playwright, and also a secret child pornographer.

Humbert discovers that Lolita is skipping piano lessons to practice for the play, and in his "incandescent anger" he confronts her, threatening to yank her from school and "lock her up." They yell at each other and she screams "unprintable things" ... "she said she loathed me...made monstrous faces at me...she said she was sure I had murdered her mother." She runs out of the house, and he finds her in a telephone booth. She says: "I want to leave school. I hate the school. I hate the play. Never go back. Leave at once. Go for a long trip again. But this time we'll go wherever I want, won't we?" Lolita prepares the trip route, marking roadmaps with lipstick.

They set off for a second cross-country trip, again staying in roadside motels. Humbert suspects she is contacting some other person when she occasionally slips away from him at service stations. He specifically suspects that "detective Trapp" is following them on the highway but using different vehicles. He tries to "lose the tail," but is unable to do so. At one point, Lolita disappears in a small town in the Mountain West, at a prearranged post office where they pick up mail. Humbert panics. She returns in "28 minutes," at which point Humbert shows her "detective Trapp's" license tag number and says he has taken "precautions." Lolita scrawls over the written number, making it illegible. He then gives a "tremendous backhand" to her face, then breaks down in remorse of "sobbing atonement, groveling love." Increasing incidents of the kind occur in which Humbert is consumed with jealousy and anxiety. He develops GI problems and wonders if he has developed "persecution mania."

In a small town in the Rocky Mountains, Lolita becomes ill with a fever and Humbert takes her to the local hospital where she is admitted and treated for respiratory infection. Humbert can see her only at visiting hours presided over by a rigid nurse. He becomes increasingly apprehensive and desperate, turns to drinking, and cannot sleep. He also falls ill and must stay in bed in their motel for a couple of days. When is able to return to the hospital he discovers that Lolita has checked out with her "uncle Gustave," the hospital bill has been paid, and the nurse reports that they have departed for "Grandpa's ranch, as agreed."

Humbert is blinded by anger and fear. He makes a scene, but apologetically retreats when the police come. He sets out retracing their road trip, checking out the motel registries for signs of Lolita or the suspected abductor, detective Trapp. Humbert furthermore believes that detective Trapp had laid a trail of witty fictitious names, toying with him psychologically, having "affinities with my own." Eventually, he returns to Ramsdale with no productive evidence of their whereabouts in hand.

Three "empty years" follow, one of which Humbert spends in the same Quebec sanitarium as before. He meets Rita, a woman who is down on her luck and hapless in relationships. He sees her as far from bright but a "soothing companion" and an "amiable drunk." Humbert returns to New York to manage his deceased uncle's business. He finds a letter from Lolita addressed to him. The letter states that she is married to a Mr. Richard Schiller, is pregnant and broke, and needs $300 so they can move to Alaska. Humbert leaves Rita while she is passed out from drink to track down Lolita using the postmark on the letter (there is no return address). He brings a pistol and plans to murder Mr. Schiller, believing him to be detective Trapp.

He locates the small industrial town and the rundown home where Lolita and her husband live. Lolita is 8 months pregnant, with "washed-out grey eyes" and "faded" looks. She is now 17 and "hopelessly worn." Humbert demands to see her husband. She points outside where he is working on a neighbor's house. He is a simple, backward, down-on-his-luck blue collar worker, and Humbert instantly realizes he is not his adversary, detective Trapp.

Lolita tells Humbert that her husband knows nothing about their history, and that she has told him Humbert is her upper-class father from whom she ran away. Humbert demands to know the name of detective Trapp. At first, she declines to disclose the name, but Humbert wears her down and she admits he was Clare Quilty, the playwright and director of the school play. She says he was the "only man she had ever been crazy about," and that Humbert had "never counted." She reveals that she had known Quilty even prior to Humbert, that he was a relative of their neighbor, and once when visiting, he had placed her on his lap and she had kissed him.

She tells of her escape from Humbert to go with Quilty, who had been following them on the second cross-country trip that she had pre-planned. Quilty was a heavy drug user and drinker who was into "freaky sex matters," "crazy things, filthy things." He intended to use Lolita in pornographic films, but she refused to participate in group orgies he orchestrated because she "loved only him." In response, he kicked her out. She drifted between waitress jobs in various small towns for two years and eventually met her husband.

Humbert realizes that he "loved her more than anything I had ever seen or imagined on earth" and proposes she leave with him that very moment. She refuses. He nonetheless gives her ten times the money she requested, with no strings attached, and breaks down in tears. Humbert is ashamed and demoralized and begins drinking heavily.

Humbert then resolves to track down and kill Clare Quilty. When he eventually finds his home, the door is unlocked and the house is disheveled and littered with evidence from a party the night before. Quilty is wandering around in a bathrobe, still half-drunk. Humbert confronts him and Quilty tries to smooth talk him out of the situation, although he doesn't seem to take Humbert seriously. When Humbert's threats break through

Qulity's daze, he offers Humbert the house and money and says "it was she who made me remove her to a happier home."

After a heated albeit highly intellectualized argument and parade of word play, Humbert ineffectually fires his pistol. They scuffle, and Humbert eventually shoots him several times. He drives off, dazed, deliberately traveling on the wrong side of the road for several miles before police cars surround him when he drives off the road. As noted earlier, Humbert pens his words in jail prior to the trial.

In addition to a plot summary, we also gave the raters the following description of Humbert Humbert. This was structured somewhat in the fashion of a clinical history with the addition of notable quotes and bits of text from the novel.

Biographical Data
Name: Humbert Humbert
Place of Birth: Paris, France
Age: b. 1910; d. 1952; 42 years
Education: College, London and Paris; English Literature
Occupation: Occasional writer & teacher; part time advertisement copy writer for perfumes
Marital Status: divorced once, widowed once

Developmental History
Father was Swiss citizen, owned luxury hotel on the Riviera. Mother died in lightning strike at a picnic when Humbert was 3, no memories of mother. Raised by maternal Aunt Sybil, her spouse a perfumer with a business in NYC and at whose death, bequeathed an annual stipend to Humbert. As a child growing up in the luxury hotel: "everybody liked me, everybody petted me." Excellent student.

As a teenager fell in love with another young teen, Annabel (13 years), with whom he had a brief fling; as adult, 24 years later, "I broke her spell by incarnating her in another," (p.15). He studied English literature in college; first jobs were teaching English. He was attracted/obsessed with "nymphets," certain girls between ages 9 and 14; initial sexual relations with prostitutes, especially young ones; decided to marry as a "cover."

Notable statements by/descriptions of Humber Humbert from text
Opening line: "Lolita, light of my life, fire of my loins. My sin, my soul. Lo-lee-ta: the tip of the tongue taking a trip of three steps down the palate to tap, at three, on the teeth."

"My habit of being silent when displeased, or, more exactly, the cold and scaly quality of my displeased silence, used to frighten Valeria out of her wits."

"Tried hard to be good. Really and truly…he had the utmost respect for ordinary children, with their purity and vulnerability, and under no circumstances would he have interfered with the innocence of a child…"

"Sometimes I attempt to kill in my dreams…I hold a gun…I aim at a bland, quietly interested enemy. Oh, I press the trigger all right, but one bullet after another feebly drops on the floor from the sheepish muzzle. In those dreams, my only thought is to conceal the fiasco from my foe, who is slowly growing annoyed."

"I was still firmly resolved to pursue my policy of sparing her purity by operating only in the stealth of night, only upon a completely anesthetized little nude."

"alas, that I could obtain at the snap of my fingers any adult female I chose"

"Despite my manly looks, I am horribly timid."

"Mentally I found her to be a disgustingly conventional little girl. Sweet hot jazz, square dancing, gooey fudge sundaes, musicals, movie magazines and so forth…she it was to whom ads were dedicated: the ideal consumer…"

"I was clever enough to realize that I must secure her complete co-operation in keeping our relations secret, that it should become a second nature with her, no matter what grudge she might bear me, no matter what other pleasures she might seek."

"I would park at a strategic point, with my vagrant schoolgirl beside me in the car, to watch the children leave school…and she would insult me and my desire to have her caress me while blue-eyed little brunettes in blue shorts, copperheads in green boleros, and blurred boyish blondes in faded slacks passed by in the sun."

"Lo was a late sleeper, and I liked to bring her a pot of hot coffee in bed…how sweet it was to bring that coffee to her, and then deny it until she had done her morning duty."

"from the thought that around 1950 I would have to get rid somehow of a difficult adolescent whose magic nymphage had evaporated—to the thought that with patience and luck I might have her produce eventually a nymphet with my blood in her exquisite veins, a Lolita the Second."

Returning East from their one-year road trip: "We had really seen nothing. And I catch myself thinking today that our long journey had only defiled with a sinuous trail of slime the lovely, trustful, dreamy, enormous country that by then, in retrospect, was no more to us than a collection of dog-eared maps, ruined tour books, old tires, and her sobs in the night—every night, every night—the moment I feigned sleep."

"What I feared most was not that she might ruin me, but that she might accumulate sufficient cash to run away."

"…I unbuttoned my overcoat and for 65 cents plus permission to participate in the school play, had Dolly put her…hand…I simply had to take advantage…" re: sitting behind her while she studied in a school room and Humbert could view another young school girl.

"…nothing could make my Lolita forget the foul lust I had inflicted upon her. Unless it can be proven to me—as to me I am now, today, with my heart and my beard, and my putrefaction—that in the infinite run it does not matter a jot that a North American girl-child named Dolores Haze had been deprived of her childhood by a maniac…I see nothing for the treatment of my misery but the melancholy and very local palliative of articulate art."

"Thus, neither of us is alive when the reader opens this book. But while the blood still throbs through my writing hand, you are still as much part of blessed matter as I am, and I can still talk to you from here to Alaska….do not pity C.Q. (Quilty). One had to choose between him and Humbert, and one wanted Humbert to exist at least a couple of months longer, so as to have him make you live in the minds of later generations. I am thinking of aurochs and angels, the secret of durable pigments, prophetic sonnets, the refuge of art. And this is the only immortality you and I may share, my Lolita."

Humbert Humbert's AMPD profile is presented in Figure 7.2a. All Criterion A scores are above 2, indicating a serious and pervasive level of personality dysfunction. His scores on empathy and intimacy problems, both in the interpersonal domain, are particularly severe. The raters' responses characterize Humbert as a disturbed person with very little concern for others, such as indicated by his willingness to kidnap,

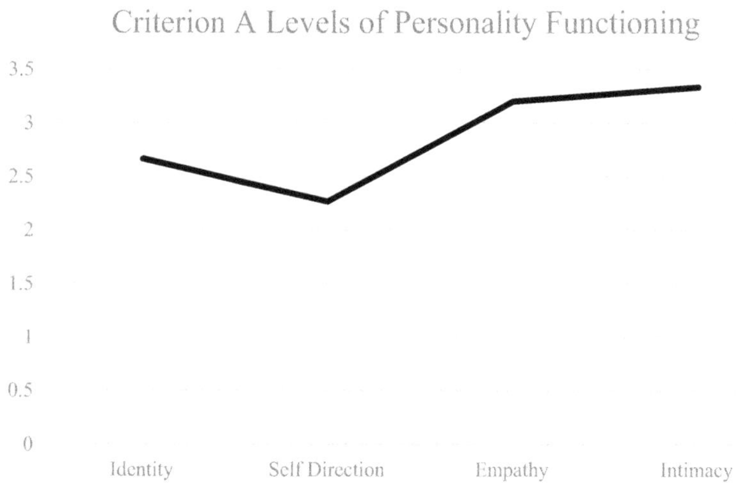

Figure 7.2a. Humbert Humbert's Level of Personality Functioning profile

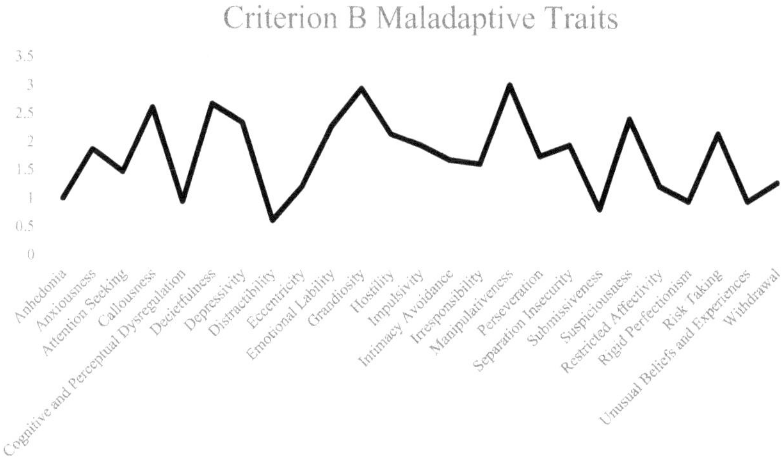

Figure 7.2b. Humbert Humbert's Maladaptive Traits profile

manipulate, and murder others, and in the end to minimize his misdeeds and justify his behavior with his claim that he was driven by love.

Humbert was also rated with many Criterion B maladaptive trait scores above 2 (Figure 7.2b), including callousness, deceitfulness, depressivity, emotional lability, grandiosity, hostility, manipulativeness, suspiciousness, and risk taking, as well as sub-clinical scores on anxiousness, intimacy avoidance, impulsivity, irresponsibility, separation insecurity, and perseveration. All in all, 15 out of 25 scores were above 1.5, and these were spread across all five personality domains except psychoticism. These traits would not qualify Humbert for a categorical PD type diagnosis in the AMPD, so his diagnosis would be trait specified.

The concept of a general factor of psychopathology that has recently gained traction in the psychopathology literature (Caspi et al., 2014) has roots in personality disorder research (Hopwood, Malone, et al., 2011). Psychometrically, the idea is that most personality or psychiatric problems are positively correlated, creating a positive manifold that can be represented as a single number and which accounts, at least to some degree, for diagnostic co-occurrence. Diagnostically, this number provides an indicator of the patient's overall level of severity that can be useful for determinations like level of care and general prognosis. Clinically, it reflects the fact that problems tend to beget other problems, and it portends a very difficult road to recovery.

Humbert had lifelong psychiatric issues that likely fed into one another, and over which he never achieved resolution. Because of the generality of his difficulties, the story of their dynamic interconnections can be told in many ways. We could see his neurotic insecurities manifested in egocentric disregard for others, covered up with occasional impulsive and reckless behavior and defended against through social isolation and intellectualization. Or, we could see his basic antagonism, albeit also situated in a highly intellectualized complex of ideas, as giving rise to justification for flagrantly reckless and risky things which got him into trouble, but also causing him much inner turmoil and leading to a self-protective avoidance of others. We could alternatively formulate his case as one of existential isolation and neurotic dread, coped with through intellectualization and intermittent recklessness and breakthroughs of antisocial acts. In the end, all of Humbert's problems agglomerated, leaving a trail of suffering and damage in his own and others' lives. We get the sense that by the time he is introduced to us, it is too late to help him all that much, and a more appropriate focus might have been to protect society (and particularly Lolita) from him.

There were some potential signs of hope. In his perverse and idealized attachment to Lolita, there nonetheless was a deeply but inadequately modulated communal impulse. His cleverness could have possibly been put to more prosocial goals. Low scores on his trait profile indicate his ability to be focused, lucid, and assertive, and one could even imagine him as an effective leader in certain environments. There is irony in Nabokov's character as conveyed within the novel, for Humbert is reflective, if ruminative, and can be highly perceptive and sensitive interpersonally; but he is an absolute prisoner of his obsession and thereby doomed. Overall, for the raters taking stock of Humbert with the AMPD template, he is a dark caricature of the patient with severe PD, to whom well-being and socialization are elusive.

Our interpretation of Humbert follows the raters' judgments of the character using the AMPD template. The raters were not instructed to read the novel prior to providing ratings. To enter into the novel *Lolita*, however, is to find oneself piqued by paradox and complexity. Nabokov takes the reader into the mind and heart of Humbert, and a common response is to feel conflicted empathy for Humbert, despite his egocentric and despicable behavior. Moreover, Nabokov is not simply describing character (personality) in his portrait of Humbert. Nabokov's ultimate aim as a master stylist is art, and his comments on the human condition, much less of "character," are of secondary importance. The writer and critic Annie Dillard (1982) argued that authors of modernist fiction (like Nabokov) tend to deploy the element of character not in the service of person-description but as a vehicle to convey other aims. The form and content of *Lolita* reveal Nabokov's interest is celebrating art, and character is a means to this higher end. These aims transcend the limits of the pragmatics of psychiatric nosology and scientific personality description.

Case 3: Lolita

Below is the description of Lolita we gave to raters.

Biographical Data
Name: Dolores Haze, aka Lolita; later Mrs. Richard F. Schiller
Place of Birth: Pisky, small town in Midwest. Moves with mother to Ramsdale (New England) with mother after father passes away
Age: b. 1935; d. 1952 in childbirth at age 17
Education: mid-high school
Occupation: waitress; housewife
Marital Status: married

Developmental History
Mother's report: spiteful, starting as a one-year-old; poor grades in school; moody, sullen, evasive; rude and defiant; stabbed school girlfriend in rear with fountain pen. Mother's descriptions of her on a psychological inventory: aggressive, boisterous, critical, distrustful, impatient, irritable, inquisitive, listless, negativistic, obstinate; school testing IQ 121 (but underachiever and no interest in intellectual or academic affairs); first sexual experience at a previous camp with female campmate and with an older boy; description by Headmistress of Beardsley School for Girls Re: 15-year-old Dolores: "attractive, bright though careless," "marks are getting worse," "defiant," "though mind seems to wander," "sighs a good deal in class," "chews gum vehemently," "cannot verbalize her emotions," "impudent," "antagonistic, dissatisfied, cagey".

Notable statements by/descriptions of Lolita from text
A "wayward child with egoistic mother"

Self-statement when picked by Humbert from summer camp: "Bad girl, bad girl, juvenile delickwent, but frank and fetching."

"Wouldn't mother be absolutely mad if she found out we were lovers?"

"…she considered—and kept doing so for a long time—all caresses except kisses on the mouth or the stark act of love either 'romantic slosh' or 'abnormal'."

Later in the day after she initiates intercourse with Humbert: "You chump…revolting creature. I was a daisy-fresh girl, and look what you've done to me. I ought to call the police and tell them you raped me. Oh, you dirty, dirty old man."

"…she stood…and stared at herself contentedly, not unpleasantly surprised at her own appearance, filling with her own rosy sunshine the surprised and pleased closet–door mirror."

"…in the slouching, bored way she cultivated…"

"…when she chose, could be a most exasperating brat…disorganized boredom, intense and vehement griping, …diffused clowning which she thought was tough in a boyish hoodlum way."

"she radiated, despite her very childish appearance, some special languorous glow which threw garage fellows, hotel pages, vacationists, goons in luxurious cars, maroon morons near blued pools, into fits of concupiscence…For little Lo was aware of that glow of hers…(casting) in the direction of some amiable male, some grease-monkey…hardly had I turned my back…"

"Cruel Lo…would mimic my nervous tic"

"…those furious harangues of hers where entreaty and insult, self-assertion and double talk, vicious vulgarity and childish despair… ('swell chance…I'd be a sap if I took your opinion seriously…Stinker… You can't boss me…I despise you')."

"Lo was even more scared of the law than I."

"I could never make her read any other book than the so-called comic books or stories in magazines for American females."

"…this world (is) just one gag after another, if somebody wrote up (my) life nobody would ever believe it."

"She had entered my world, umber and black Humberland, with rash curiosity; she surveyed it with a shrug of amused distaste; and it seemed to me now that she was ready to turn away from it with something akin to plain revulsion. Never did she vibrate under my touch, and a strident 'what d'yu think you are doing?' was all I got for my pains. To the wonderland I had to offer, my fool preferred the corniest movies, the most cloying fudge. To think that between a Hamburger and a Humburger, she would—invariably, with icy precision—plump for the former. There is nothing more atrociously cruel than an adored child."

"Lolita always had an absolutely enchanting smile for strangers… tender, nectered, dimpled brightness plays, it was never directed at the (person) in the room but hung in its own remote flowered void…or wandered…over chance objects…"

Lolita's Criterion A scores were all above 2, suggesting severe personality pathology across all domains of functioning, with little differentiation between domains. Evidence of Lolita's splintered and weakly developed identity was littered throughout the book, and indeed she played many roles in her relatively short life. Despite moments of focused motivation, in general Lolita was aimless, which exposed her at many crucial points to the guidance of adults who did not have her best interests in mind. There was evidence of interest in intimacy, but affiliation was always disturbed in some way and Lolita ultimately failed to achieve a mature, mutually satisfying, adult relationship. Importantly, Lolita's interpersonal behavior was manipulative and unempathic throughout the novel. Even before Humbert entered her life, she was rebellious, underachieving, and oppositional. In addition, the novel depicts a difficult mother–daughter relationship from early on.

Based on these scores, she qualifies for a PD diagnosis, and indeed, she was seen by raters as having a level of personality dysfunction close to

Humbert's. But, is it fair to diagnose Lolita with a PD? After all, she was a youth for much of the storyline of the novel and, very importantly, the reader sees Lolita largely through the eyes and actions of Humbert, her paramour and captor. Although PD in this case is a complex question, the AMPD data are clear; the raters viewed her as warranting a PD diagnosis.

Examining the ratings by the categories of student or early career psychologist (n = 6), experienced clinical psychologist (n = 6), and non-clinical expert (n = 3), mean and standard deviation LPFS sums were: 9.8 (2.4), 12.3 (3.1), and 10.3 (1.5). Each group of raters perceived significant PD dysfunction. However, there was less rater agreement for LPFS ratings for Lolita compared to the other two characters. For the four domains of the LPFS, the mean ICC associated with ratings of Lolita was .38, compared to .89 for Mudwoman and .79 for Humbert. These data suggest that raters had more difficulty and varied in how they perceived Lolita, even though she was viewed as impaired. Also, the more experienced clinicians perceived a little more PD pathology than the younger clinicians. We speculate that raters may have been concerned for Lolita as a victim of molestation while also reacting to her relatively young age. Furthermore, Lolita is known mainly through Humbert's perceptions and actions. To this extent, a degree of indeterminacy to her character is inherent. As to her youth, however, it is known that PD features and diagnoses can emerge in adolescence (Johnson, Cohen, Kasen, Skodol, Hamagami, & Brook, 2000), that traits associated with the development of PD emerge in youth (Shiner, 2005), and these observations may be particularly apt for cases of childhood abuse (Westen, Ludolph, Misle, Ruffins, & Block, 1990). Thus, in sum, the AMPD data indicate PD and this finding is comprehensible from what is known about the development of PD.

However we explain the scores on Lolita's AMPD profile (Figure 7.3), there can be no doubt that her personality had some severe functional deficits. The specific flavor of her personality problems is articulated by the Criterion B maladaptive traits (Figure 7.3b). Her profile features clinical elevations on attention-seeking, callousness, emotional instability, hostility, impulsivity, and manipulativeness, as well as subclinical elevations on distractibility, grandiosity, intimacy avoidance, and irresponsibility. These traits fall primarily in the domain of antagonism and, to a lesser degree, negative affectivity and disinhibition. Only one trait-facet elevation comes from detachment and none are from psychoticism. This trait constellation would not qualify her for any specific PD category type in the AMPD, so her diagnosis would be trait specified.

We can again raise questions about Lolita's antagonism. First, to the degree that this is an accurate description of her behavior, was it maladaptive or adaptive? Callous manipulation might be understood as an adaptive strength for an abuse and kidnap victim. We might hope that all people in her situation could figure out ways to trick their abductor, as Lolita did in escaping the hospital with the help of Quilty. Particularly to

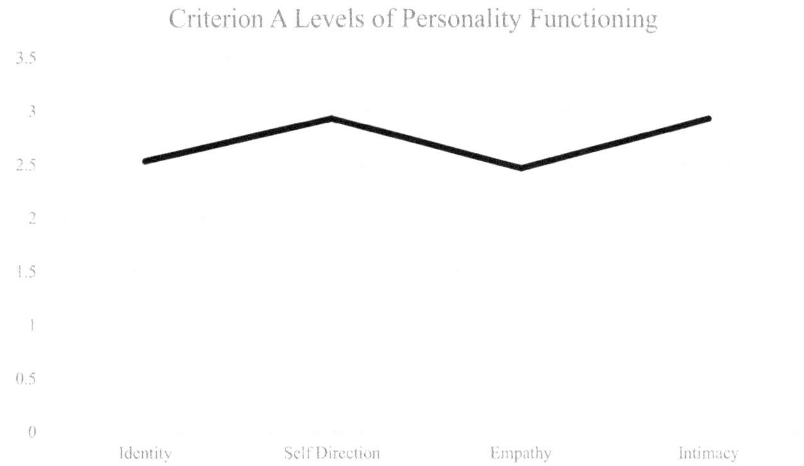

Figure 7.3a. Lolita's Level of Personality Functioning profile

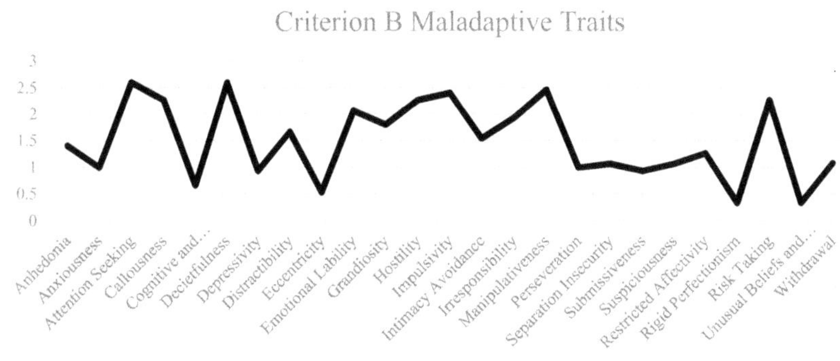

Figure 7.3b. Lolita's Maladaptive Traits profile

the degree that this behavior apparently remitted when she eventually married Mr. Schiller, this trait could be understood more as a temporary adaptation than a stable, maladaptive personality trait. Yet to these caveats we also note that Lolita's antagonism to her mother predated Humbert, and recall the idea that personality psychopathology is often adaptive in relation to the individual's life circumstances (Benjamin, 1993; see also Chapter 5 for extended discussion of this thesis). It is important not to let our sympathy for Lolita's predicament color our discernment in relation to her personality functioning.

A second issue is also relevant. How accurate is the description of Lolita in the book, which our raters used to inform their AMPD assessment? Multimethod assessment is generally regarded as a way to achieve a more holistic picture about a person. Because self-report is so common, it is typically recommended to try to get other data, like informant reports, as well. The general idea is that a person may not have insight about herself or may be motivated to distort certain information, so it is good to gather information from someone who knows her well but may not have the same blind spots and motivations. In the case of Lolita, we have the opposite scenario, and some of Lolita's narrative told from her own perspective would have been helpful.

Humbert's preoccupations and feelings towards Lolita were obviously complex and at least some of them reflected perverse affection. But at the end of the day, he kidnapped and molested her. It was naturally upsetting to him when she would try to get away, and he clearly felt manipulated and underappreciated. She also apparently had complex feelings towards him, which was likely confusing to both parties, and which Humbert might have perceived as vacillating between attention-seeking and hostile. But it remains very difficult to say what picture we might have had of Lolita if it had been painted by someone other than Humbert, whose perspective was highly personalized and not objective.

Yet, even these speculations cannot fully mitigate the picture of Lolita. After all, she became the "master," so to speak, on the second cross-country road trip, flipping her role as victim to victimizer in relation to Humbert. Humbert himself was "slave" to his obsession, and Lolita was able to use this dynamic to manipulate, dominate, and control him during the second road trip. This dynamic calls to mind Karpman's (1968) triangle (i.e., that victim can quickly move to victimizer). Adding to these layers of psychological and literary complexity, we note that Lolita herself was "slave" to her "love" for Quilty, who was less conflicted in his antisocial motives and behavior than the tortured Humbert.

It is likely that Lolita would have benefitted from treatment. Given the murkiness of our picture of her personality, it is not as clear what such a treatment might entail. And, it would depend on when treatment was provided. Early in her youth, which was marked by oppositonality and parent–child conflict, treatment would differ from that designed to address her personality functioning later after the years of her abuse by Humbert. Treatment later on surely would include helping her recover from her trauma, consolidate her identity, and develop the capacities for trusting relationships and self-directed goals without resorting to acting out.

Conclusion

These descriptions of literary cases supplement the clinical cases in the preceding chapter by showing that the AMPD can be used reliably by a diverse set of raters to provide a fairly nuanced depiction of the psychologically complex personalities of literary characters. We found strong inter-rater agreement in this study and meaningful distinctions between our three characters.

As in the preceding chapter, we correlated each character's trait profile with the AMPD profiles of DSM-IV (APA, 2000) PDs from the Morey, Benson, and Skodol (2016) paper. Recall that none of the characters would have met diagnostic criteria for a categorical PD type (data indicated the diagnosis of PD-trait specified for Mudwoman, Humbert, and Lolita). However, these correlations show that when all the profile information is considered, rather than just those few traits that are above a threshold of 2, the characters' personalities approximated some categorical PD types more than others, and for some there was actually a fairly close match (Table 7.1). Mudwoman's profile was distinctly avoidant, which may represent a fair albeit incomplete summary of her interpersonal style. Humbert and Lolita both had moderately high correlations with narcissistic, antisocial, paranoid, histrionic, and borderline profiles. This showcases a striking similarity between the trait profiles for the two characters in *Lolita*: and indeed, the correlation between the profiles for Humbert Humbert and Lolita was .57, whereas both profiles correlated negatively with Mudwoman's. Humbert and Lolita can be regarded as showing significant externalizing PD features (also with some negative affectivity for Humbert) whereas Mudwoman evidences primarily internalizing PD elements.

This resemblance may be surprising, because on the surface it doesn't seem like Humbert Humbert the captor and Lolita the captive have particularly similar personalities. A few things need to be kept in mind here. First, they did indeed share some prominent features, such as deceitfulness, manipulativeness, emotional lability, and attention seeking. These are qualities often associated with narcissistic spectrum disorders and borderline

Table 7.1. Correlations between AMPD profiles and Morey et al. (2016) personality disorder prototypes.

	Mudwoman	*Humbert Humbert*	*Lolita*
Avoidant	**.80**	–.45	–.60
Antisocial	–.81	.52	.66
Borderline	–.38	.47	.51
Dependent	.49	–.28	–.41
Histrionic	–.43	.49	.66
Narcissistic	–.81	**.59**	**.71**
Obsessive-Compulsive	.54	–.24	–.33
Paranoid	–.53	.51	.56
Schizoid	.54	–.34	–.39
Schizotypal	.37	–.37	–.52

Note. Highest value is in bold for each case.

personality organization (Kernberg, 1967). Second, some of the nuance in the actual trait profile is lost when it is summarized using PD types. For instance, Humbert was higher in traits involving negative affect, such as separation insecurity and depressivity, than Lolita. Third, and importantly, the reader, and thus also the raters, mainly perceive Lolita through the eyes of Humbert, as discussed above. It is likely that he projected aspects of his personality onto hers, or they are otherwise blended together, in the telling of her story. Nabokov's artistic aims reflected in the structure of the novel, while not the focus of the AMPD ratings, likely affected the AMPD ratings when deployed for personality description.

Using the AMPD to describe literary characters as we did in this study involves some inherent challenges. First, these were not actual people, but characters originally created by an author with particular authorial intents in mind, whose characteristics were further filtered by us to provide raters with target stimuli. Second, some of our raters were not clinicians with professional experience in assessing other peoples' personalities in this manner. For all three literary characters, the non-clinician experts' mean ratings fell lower than the more experienced clinicians' ratings, and above those of the graduate student and early career psychologist ratings. In fact, these data suggest the variable with the greatest degree of influence amongst the raters was clinical experience. Comparing the young with seasoned clinician ratings for LPFS sums across the characters, we find a moderate correlation between clinical experience and LPFS (point biserial $r = .34$; $p < .04$). Third, as discussed above, Lolita in particular is given much less of her own voice in the book (and in these stimuli); rather, her personality is filtered through Humbert's skewed perceptions. Fourth, both novels trace characters over a very extended period of time, illustrating evolution (and deterioration), whereas personality judgments are typically based on what a person is like at the time of the assessment. Many personality features with these characters changed meaningfully over time, and we did not give raters detailed guidance about how to deal with that when providing their ratings other than to apply ratings with the general DSM definition of PD in mind (e.g., an enduring pattern of experience, pervasive, inflexible, and not better explained by another disorder, etc.). In view of all of these potentially obscuring factors, we conclude the ability of the raters to reliably evaluate each character, and the ability of the AMPD to provide nuanced descriptions of them, is all the more impressive.

Applying the AMPD in this manner can serve an educational purpose for those learning the model. Reading a novel or short story offers an opportunity to practice assessment approaches, recruiting the representative and simulative aspect of reading fiction (Mar & Oately, 2008) to provide nuanced and textured "persons" for study. Thus, the student may consider characters from fiction with the lens of the AMPD, and in so doing increase their skill in applying the model. This harkens to comments made by Sidney Blatt, Ph.D., many years ago in a seminar on personality assessment (personal communication to MHW, 1983). Speaking to a group of post-doctoral fellows in seminar, Dr. Blatt recalled that as a student-clinician, riding the subway in Chicago, he often would try to conjecture the Rorschach and MMPI profiles of the different "characters" riding the train with him based on observations of their demeanor and behavior. We suggest the student may consider this exercise with the AMPD while reading literary fiction.

Note

1 The choice of Nabokov for this project has a touch of irony. It is well-known that Nabokov was an unrelenting and very public critic of the Freudian psychoanalysis of his era. Critics have offered various opinions about Nabokov's distaste for psychoanalysis (which is also alluded to within *Lolita*), and one argument is that Nabokov prized the *particulars* of persons and of experiences, and he felt Freud did violence to persons via the *generalizations* of psychoanalytic theory (De La Durantaye, 2005). Perhaps Nabokov is rolling over in his grave at the psychologizing we invite the raters to do applying the personality generalizations with the AMPD.

8 The AMPD in Assessment, Treatment Planning, and Clinical Supervision

Mark H. Waugh, Jennifer L. Bishop and Megan R. Schmidt

The Alternative Model for Personality Disorders (AMPD) is more than a novel approach to dimensional diagnosis of personality disorder (PD). It is a clinical heuristic. The word *heuristic* derives from the Greek word for discover. Indeed, the AMPD invites the clinician to consider, explore, and perhaps discover additional angles on an individual's personality functioning while rendering a diagnosis of PD. Formally, the AMPD combines assessment of level of personality impairment and styles of problematic personality functioning in making PD diagnoses. Evaluating these dimensions references overlapping but separable planes of personality functioning, Criterion A and Criterion B, along with the diverse clinical and research traditions from which they have been formulated (Waugh, Hopwood, Krueger, Morey, Pincus, & Wright, 2017). Given this conceptual complexity, it is no surprise that the AMPD offers the clinician more than nomenclature for diagnostic coding of PD. The model can inform case analysis, point to likely personality dynamics, become a template for differential diagnosis, and help in treatment planning and communicating recommendations. The AMPD also contributes to clinical training in differential diagnosis and case formulation. In these and other ways, the AMPD is a scaffold from which the clinician may draw on multiple points of view to evaluate problematic personality functioning.

The variety of personality constructs schematized in the AMPD suggests the phrase *field of view* or *angles of vision*. This refers to properties of a lens. A lens focuses the view in a specific direction and depth. But if the lens is flexible, varying the angles of vision illuminates different ranges and depths. McWilliams (N. McWilliams, personal communication, February 2, 2018) uses the phrase *angles of vision* to describe the many domains of contemporary psychodynamic thinking (e.g., clinical symptoms, temperament, personality and attachment style, implicit cognitions, internalized object relations, and level of psychostructural organization). The AMPD is not specifically psychodynamic, although this perspective is available with the model (Bender, Morey, and Skodol, 2011). Rather, the AMPD supports multiple angles of vision on personality and PD functioning (Waugh et al., 2017). Pincus (2011) refers to this as the pan-theoretic aspect of the AMPD. With its multiple angles of vision, the AMPD encourages the clinician to consider PD functioning from different perspectives. This increases the likelihood that insightful and practical clinical implications accompany PD diagnosis.

We illustrate the clinical utility of the AMPD in case presentations of two complex psychological evaluations. Each multi-method assessment was conducted by a doctoral student in clinical psychology under supervision in a training clinic that serves an urban catchment area and university community. Our analysis emphasizes observations and assessment findings most relevant to the role of the AMPD in case formulation, rather than other interesting details of the comprehensive evaluations of "Mr. M." and "Ms. K." (all identifying data are disguised). In addition, after the initial psychological evaluations were completed, assessment data were subjected to further quantitative comparisons. Results from these analyses show how the AMPD bridges with traditional PD diagnosis. They also helped to confirm the original case conceptualizations. A brief review of the literature on the psychotherapy and countertransference issues in PD treatment further illustrates how the AMPD becomes a clinical heuristic. Using the AMPD scheme in these ways in the clinical supervision of students evaluating patients supported an educational mission as well.

The clinician in the trenches may find the AMPD interesting, appreciate its dimensional character, and note its connections to prominent clinical paradigms (Waugh, et al., 2017). But, the AMPD is placed in Section III of the *Diagnostic and Statistical Manual for Mental Disorders-5* (DSM-5; APA, 2013). Some may conclude from this that the model is not ready for "prime time," and it is not permissible to use in routine clinical practice. We suggest another point of view. First, practically speaking, the AMPD can be coded in formal diagnosis and used for purposes such as billing for reimbursement. In this respect, note that the DSM-5, Section II includes the rubric "Other specified personality disorder" (OSPD; 301.89 [F60.89]). This code is used to denote the presence of PD symptoms not adequately covered by the traditional PDs in Section II. In these situations, the clinician may diagnose OSPD and then specify additional descriptors. Proceeding in this way, the clinician may formally code with the diagnosis of OSPD, and then utilize the vocabulary of the AMPD to specify appropriate additional PD descriptors. It is also important to realize that by inclusion in Section III of the DSM-5 (APA, 2013), the AMPD in effect became one of the two officially promulgated PD nosologies (Zachar, Krueger, & Kendler, 2016), even if its formal coding requires translation into the Section II nomenclature as OSPD, for example. Advantages of this approach are shown in the cases of Mr. M. and Ms. K. presented below. As these cases are reviewed, note the parsimony of diagnosis offered with the AMPD. For example, with Mr. M., the traditional categorical PD diagnosis of Section II would have required numerous co-morbid PD diagnoses. Even then, this would have been inadequate to convey important diagnostic nuances that are more apparent when specified with the AMPD.

The Case of Mr. M.

Mr. M was a 21-year-old Caucasian male who requested psychological evaluation at the urging of his mother. Mr. M reported significant symptoms of anxiety, panic, depression, long-term difficulty in social relationships and uncertainty about his future.

Social, Educational, Medical, and Psychiatric History

Mr. M. was raised by his natural parents who had divorced three years prior to the evaluation. Mr. M. indicated he remained very upset by this event, he distanced himself from his mother, and he blamed her lack of steady employment (she worked in insurance sales) and "slovenly" behavior for the divorce. His father, a truck driver, traveled frequently. He denied developmental delays or childhood trauma but reported a history of academic problems. He received special education services in elementary school, but this was discontinued in later grades. Academically, his performance was erratic and school marks ranged from above average to poor. He attended college for 1.5 semesters, majoring in chemistry, but withdrew because of poor grades. He reported having "no friends" or social support and no romantic involvements. He said he had been a "loner" since he was in middle school and also described a period of being bullied. He denied medical problems and/or current prescription medications, however he reported treatment with a stimulant medication (Vyvanse) as a youth and a more recent, very brief use of antidepressant medication. Furthermore, prior to starting college, Mr. M. was psychiatrically hospitalized for a few days. He was unable to describe the problems leading to his hospitalization other than saying he "felt bad." While in college, he participated in individual psychotherapy at the university student counseling center. There, he was prescribed Sertraline (antidepressant), but he discontinued this after about two months because "it did not help." Mr. M. complained that despite his experience with several mental health professionals, his need for counseling or psychiatric medication had never been explained to him. In terms of family history, he reported a first-degree relative with dyslexia and depression. Occupationally, he had occasionally worked summer jobs in food service, and at the time of the evaluation he was employed part-time in retail. He was very vague about his future wishes, intentions, or plans.

Psychological Evaluation

Although Mr. M. minimized his emotional distress, the severity and duration of his emotional, social, and educational problems suggested a full psychological evaluation would be helpful. This consisted of clinical interviews and multi-method assessment. He was prompt and polite in appointments, but he was aloof, seemed disengaged, and made minimal eye contact. He spoke in monotone and often gave vague responses to questions. When queried, he seemed irritated. His affect was generally flat, but occasionally he became briefly tearful in addition to more typically being openly self-critical and/or irritable. Notably, he seemed to have great difficulty responding to the less structured test stimuli of the Thematic Apperception Test (TAT; Murray, 1951) and the Rorschach procedure. He initially rejected four of the twelve TAT cards he was given. These were later re-administered, and he then offered stories to three of the four TAT cards. During the Clarification phase of the Rorschach assessment (when he was queried on his responses), he was often irritated, defensive, and produced highly elaborate justifications. These sometimes emphasized the physical features of the inkblot (e.g., blot symmetry) and suggested he approached the task somewhat literally, rather than imaginatively. Over the course of five assessment sessions, he failed to warm up to the examiner, although he was compliant and showed strong effort on tasks. From history and his presenting behavior, working diagnostic hypotheses were developed. These included social anxiety disorder, depressive disorder, attention deficit hyperactivity disorder (ADHD), autistic spectrum disorder (ASD), and PD (e.g., avoidant, schizoid, schizotypal, and paranoid PD). In addition, assessment of thought quality and possible psychotic functioning were needed.

Psychological tests included the Wechsler Adult Intelligence Scale—Fourth Edition (WAIS-IV; Wechlser, 2008), the Personality Assessment Inventory (PAI; Morey, 2007) the Personality Inventory for DSM-5 (PID-5; APA, 2013), the TAT, and the Rorschach Inkblots using the Rorschach Performance Assessment System (RPAS; Meyer, Viglione, Mihura, Erard, & Erdberg, 2011). Using all the assessment data, clinician ratings with the AMPD Level of Personality Functioning Scale (LPFS) and 25 pathological personality trait-facets were performed. The Clinician Rating Personality Disorder Level and Traits (PDLT-C; Waugh, 2014) template, an unpublished template for AMPD ratings, was used to guide ratings independently made by the examiner and supervisor. Meehl's (1964) Checklist for Schizotypic Signs also was used as an assessment heuristic. This is a clinical guide, with a summary index, to signs of schizotypy. The Meehl (1964) Checklist was formative in the development of many subsequently widely used self-report and structured-interview assessment procedures for this construct.

Assessment Results and Interpretation

To provide a qualitative "feel" for Mr. M.'s testing responses, his story to Card 14 of the TAT (this depicts a dark scene of a person silhouetted by a window), is reproduced. Notably, this story was obtained only after re-administration.

> *(First Presentation)* I don't know, I already screwed up all the other ones. I don't know what this one is. (*Second Presentation)* He's tired of sitting in a dark room, doing nothing with no one, and he decides to look out the window, but not be part of the world outside. Then he'll just go back to sitting in the dark. *Examiner: What led up to the current situation?* He got tired of sitting in a dark room, so he went to the window to look at the rest of the world. And he's too scared or lazy or sad or whatever to be a part of it. *Examiner: How is he feeling?* I don't know, like he needs a fresh breath of air.

Mr. M. showed High Average, nearly Superior-Level, general intellectual functioning on the WAIS-IV. But, a relative weakness in working memory and cognitive (psychomotor) processing affected his overall scores (WAIS-IV Full Scale IQ [FSIQ] 117; Global Ability Index [GAI] 126; Working Memory Index [WMI] 108; Processing Speed Index [PSI] 97). These results were consistent with the reported historical diagnosis of ADHD and other observations. Validity scales of the PAI indicated credible self-report responding. Assessment of personality functioning revealed Mr. M. experienced considerable dysphoria, tension, and anxiety, and he was given to cynical thoughts and pessimistic attitudes (Figure 8.1). Despite his evident distress, he was quite hypervigilant and maintained an interpersonally distant and detached posture. Responding to the less structured performance testing procedures (e.g., TAT, Rorschach), he was apprehensive and defensive. On the TAT, his stories were simplistic, and therein he described relationships fraught with antagonism, disappointment, and negativity. Similarly, on the Rorschach, he was vague and gave

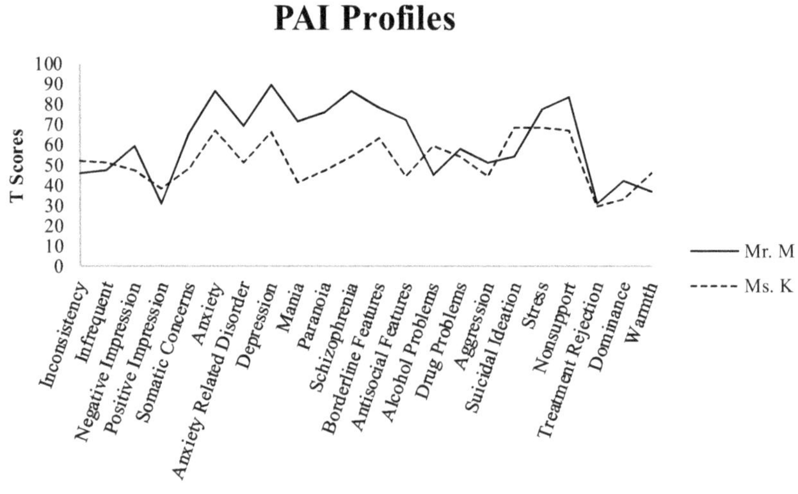

Figure 8.1. PAI profile for Mr. M & Ms. K.

responses less complex than would be expected given his intellectual level. The performance testing data reflected emotional distress, reflexive self-criticism, hypersensitivity to perceived threats, and an underlying but disavowed sense of emotional neediness. His thinking processes were generally organized and accurate, but he occasionally lapsed into idiosyncratic and distorted cognition. However, Mr. M. typically was able to recover to more conventional thinking after giving a poor-quality response. This was usually achieved by intellectualizing and interpersonal distancing. These findings, in addition to the Meehl (1964) Checklist results (Table 8.1), did not support the diagnosis of a psychotic spectrum condition.

Rater agreement on the Checklist was Excellent with Intraclass Correlation Coefficient (ICC 2-way, random, absolute) values of .84 single and .91 mean. Note, we characterize all ICCs with Cicchetti's (1994) qualitative descriptors for ICC ranges: Excellent (1.0–.75), Good (.74–.60), Fair (.59–.40), and Poor (< .40). The Checklist may be examined by differential item-weights that reflect Meehl's (1964) presumption of high-value indicators. Mr. M.'s ratings summed to 25. Although norms are not available for the Checklist, Meehl (personal communication, January 1979) recommended an item-weighted cut score of 13, far lower than found with Mr. M. Also, the assessment data were consistent with high ratings for anhedonia and demandingness but did not support indicators with psychoticism-like content (e.g., micropsychotic episodes, cognitive slippage, body-image aberrations, and magical ideation). Thus, the Meehl (1964) Checklist was consistent with other assessment results and did not

Table 8.1. Meehl (1964) Checklist of Schizotypic Signs: Mr. M (positive rated items: 16 of 25).

Item	*Meehl Weights*	*Item*	*Meehl Weights*
Ambivalence	1	Pan-Anxiety	1
Anhedonia	3	Poor Outcome	1
Countertransference Strain	1	Rage, Disproportionate	2
Deflated Self-Esteem, Severe	1	Distrust, Testing	2
Dependency, Demandingness	3	Social Fear	1
"Different from Others"	2	Special Signs	2
Failure to Achieve	1	-hopelessness	yes
Flat Affect	2	-night owl	yes
Hatred of Mother, Expressed	1	-energy depletion	yes
Narcissism	1	SUM (cut at 12/13)	25

indicate psychoticism (see Acklin, 1992), and Mr. M. did not show signs of schizophrenic spectrum disorder or meet criteria for Attenuated Psychosis Syndrome (DSM-5)—even though the Checklist was positive for shizotypy. It was also noted that his ADHD-related distractibility likely contributed to cognitive irregularities seen in some assessment data. The Meehl (1964) Checklist is described in some detail here because it shows how a conceptual template may contribute to differential diagnostic reasoning beyond the level of the summary score, much like how the AMPD may be used.

In sum, the assessment concluded that Mr. M. viewed himself as unlikeable, expected rejection, and had developed a self-protective interpersonal style of detachment, hypersensitivity, distrust, and avoidance. Although socially maladroit, his social dysfunction did not reach the impairment level of ASD. His protective and pre-emptively antagonistic stance pushed people away, in the process also serving to confirm the expectation that others were unsafe and rejecting. These results yielded diagnoses of persistent depressive disorder, social anxiety disorder (SAD), ADHD-inattentive type, and PD. However, he showed symptoms and personality dynamics reflecting several traditional PDs. These included avoidant, schizoid, paranoid, and schizotypal PD features. Evaluation results were considered sub-threshold for borderline PD (see Acklin, 1992; 1993).

AMPD Organizes Differential Diagnosis and Feedback

Mr. M. showed mixed symptoms of the DSM-5 Section II avoidant, schizoid, paranoid, and schizotypal PDs. Despite elevations on the PAI Schizophrenia-Thought Disorder subscale (87 T) and Rorschach indices associated with cognitive and perceptual dysfunction (e.g., Form Quality Minus [FQ-] 95th percentile and Ego Impairment Index-3 [EII-3] 92nd percentile), Mr. M.'s ability to recover from reality testing lapses argued against schizotypal PD. As noted, ADHD-related distractibility underpinned some scale elevations. His history of trauma from childhood bullying was likely relevant to his social retreat and paranoia. Having ruled out schizotypal PD and psychotic-spectrum conditions, differential diagnosis between avoidant, schizoid, and paranoid PD remained.

Assessment of Criterion B with the self-report form of the PID-5 showed very significant elevations on anhedonia, anxiousness, and withdrawal. The Busch, Morey, and Hopwood (2017) algorithm for predicting PID-5 scores from PAI scale data was not available at the time of Mr. M.'s evaluation. However, it was subsequently applied to his PAI scores. His highest elevations from this procedure were anhedonia, anxiousness, eccentricity, and distractibility.

Mr. M. was evaluated with clinician ratings of the AMPD based on all assessment data (except for the Busch et al. [2017] PID-5 score predictions). A PD was confirmed by a Global LPFS rating of "Severe Impairment" (score of 3; both raters). Figure 8.2a displays the ratings for Global LPFS and the four domains (Identity, Self-Direction, Empathy, Intimacy). In addition, an exploratory, fine-grained analysis of dimensions embedded in the LPFS was conducted. Although this is not standard use of the LPFS, we used it in this manner in clinical training and to generate additional interpretive hypotheses. Notably, in a research context, Zimmermann and colleagues (2015) used the LPFS in a similar way. They developed a multi-item LPFS format by partitioning three "facets" for each domain across all five levels of the scale. Analogously, we abstracted three constructs (called "facets" by Zimmermann et al., 2015) from the text descriptions of each LPFS level across each domain (see DSM-5; APA, 2013, pp. 775–778). This yielded 12 sub-component constructs. For example, the LPFS domain of Identity includes sub-components we termed as impairment in emotional or interpersonal boundaries, self-esteem regulation, and emotional functioning and regulation. Rater agreement (ICC; 2-way random effects) for this fine-grained analysis was Poor to Fair for absolute agreement (.39 single and .54 mean) and Fair to Good for consistency agreement (.48 single and .65 mean). In a similar study of inter-rater reliability,

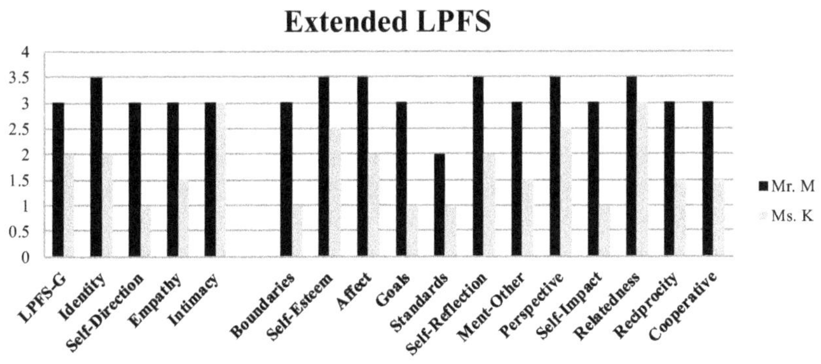

Figure 8.2a. Mr. M & Ms. K combined (mean) ratings on LPFS (extended) constructs

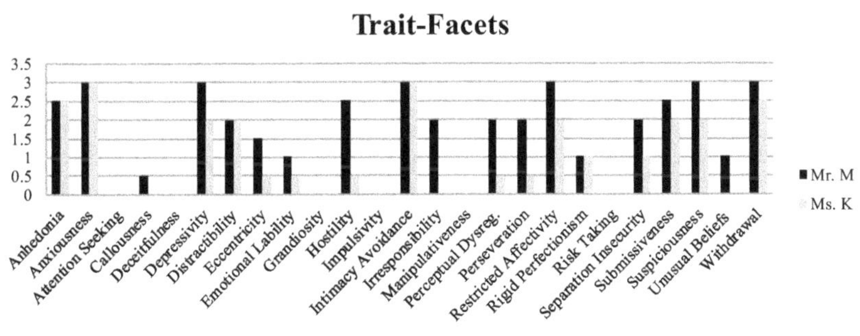

Figure 8.2b. Mr. M & Ms. K combined (mean) ratings on 25 trait-facets

Zimmermann, Benecke, et al. (2014) obtained higher levels of interrater agreement (e.g., ICC .51 single, and 0.96 mean) on their 12-component, multi-item LPFS. However, their application was different and used 22 raters, rather than 2. Furthermore, they used verbatim LPFS text, rather than abstracted constructs. Our adapted, expanded LPFS ratings suggested severe impairment in self-esteem and affect regulation, self-reflectiveness, perspective taking, and social relatedness.

Using all assessment data, the 25-pathological personality trait-facets were rated by both raters. The ICCs for the raters were Excellent at .86 (single) and .92 (mean) for trait-facet ratings. Across the full AMPD (expanded LPFS plus trait-facets), agreement was Excellent (.87 single, .93 mean). A composite score for the trait-facets was formed by the mean of the two raters' scores and used in subsequent analyses (see Figure 8.2b).

The composite ratings showed significant trait-facet elevations (≥ 2.5) on anhedonia, anxiousness, hostility, intimacy avoidance, restricted affectivity, submissiveness, suspiciousness, and withdrawal. It should be noted that elevated clinician-based Criterion B scores were more numerous than those from self-report (PID-5 and PAI-to-PID-5). This is not unsurprising and itself represents useful information. Accurate self-report requires willingness, capacity, and self-reflectiveness. Regarding PD dimensions, self-report and observer assessment generally show moderate correspondence (Oltmanns & Turkheimer, 2006). Furthermore, we know clinicians and patients view patient PD phenomena rather differently (Gritti, Samuel, & Lang, 2016; Samuel, Suzuki, & Griffin, 2016).

Differences between clinician ratings and self-report were found for intimacy avoidance, hostility, restricted affectivity, submissiveness, and suspiciousness. Some of these divergences involved trait-facets with apparent lower social desirability (e.g., hostility, suspiciousness). Convergent trait-facets (self-report, PID-5, and clinician ratings) at a high elevation (≥ 2.5) were: anhedonia, anxiousness, and withdrawal. Many trait-facets at a level of ≥ 2 also converged across methods. Self-report PID-5 and clinician ratings corresponded at a Fair to Good level when indexed with an ICC (.52 single; .69 mean).

In summary, application of AMPD confirmed PD (LPFS) and revealed trait domain elevations in negative affectivity (anxiousness, depressivity, submissiveness, and hostility) and detachment (withdrawal, anhedonia, intimacy avoidance, depressivity, restricted affectivity, and suspiciousness).

Despite Mr. M.'s social difficulties and elevated AMPD-detachment domain, he showed more avoidant PD qualities than paranoid or schizotypal features. This was seen in brief moments of relatedness with the evaluator and in some TAT stories that reflected realistic social interactions, albeit depressive and negative in tone. On the Rorschach, he also produced two adequately perceived Human Movement (M; 45th percentile) responses, and R-PAS indices reflected interpersonal distancing (e.g., Cooperative [COP] 21st percentile), anxiety (e.g., Shading-Achromatic responses

[YTVC'] 99th percentile), and neediness (e.g., Oral Dependent Language [ODL] 95th percentile). Thus, much of his off-putting, antagonistic behavior was viewed as driven by anxiety, rejection sensitivity, and maladroit social skills rather than reflecting core paranoid personality dynamics.

The DSM-5, Section-III hybrid categorical-dimensional algorithms for the composite clinician ratings were positive for avoidant, borderline, and schizotypal PDs. Rather than reporting 3 PD diagnoses, however, we used the AMPD diagnosis of PD-trait specified (with problems in detachment and negative affectivity). Thus, Mr. M.'s final diagnoses were: persistent depressive disorder, SAD, ADHD-inattentive type, and PD-TS (detachment and negative affectivity).

The AMPD also helped in communicating assessment feedback to Mr. M. At this time, he was reserved and mildly apprehensive and listened intently with little emotion. The role of ADHD in academic performance problems was emphasized. This provided one rationale for recommendations that he increase the level of structure in his life, as well as consult a psychiatrist for medication evaluation—which might address ADHD as well as symptoms of anxiety and depression. Moreover, the meanings of detachment and negative affectivity elevations in his life were discussed with him, aided by the congenial vocabulary of the AMPD. In part, this derives from the connections of Criterion B with the Five-Factor Model (FFM) and Big Five lexical trait traditions which utilize comprehensible language (Bach, Markon, Simonsen, & Krueger, 2015).

Mr. M concurred with the assessment feedback. We hoped his agreement with testing feedback would facilitate acceptance of additional recommendations. These included the suggestion to enroll in a community college class, increase physical activity (e.g., working out in a gym where he would be physically proximate with others), and try individual psychotherapy. He was advised that, "being slow-to-warm-up," counseling initially might emphasize social skills and social avoidance concerns, proceed gradually, and that the counselor might maintain a professional, somewhat formal manner of relating (the recommended therapeutic posture). Most importantly, he was encouraged to ask questions at any time in any future treatment. He indicated that he understood the test results and rationales for recommendations. However, he remained reserved, essentially impassive. It was revealing that while discussing results with Mr. M., the examiner experienced feelings previously encountered during testing sessions. She noted it felt like "sitting with an alien, a shell of a person." When asked for his thoughts about the test results, Mr. M. answered flatly, saying "I get it" and "makes sense," and little more.

The Case of Ms. K.

Ms. K. was a 37-year-old Caucasian woman referred for psychological evaluation by her psychotherapist, a doctoral trainee in clinical psychology. Ms. K. reported symptoms of social anxiety and difficulty in social communication. She complained of trouble "processing" verbal information when interacting with others. Ms. K. voiced the concern she might have "Asperger's disorder" (ASD; autism spectrum disorder) because of a family history of this, or possibly ADHD, as she reported an inability to focus and think in interpersonal interactions.

Social, Educational, Medical, and Psychiatric History

Ms. K. denied any developmental delays or childhood abuse or violence. She said her family's devout Catholicism was a major force in her life growing up. For example, she reported she and her two siblings were not permitted to associate with non-religious peers. She attended a private parochial school until fourth grade, at which time her parents withdrew the children from school over a conflict about sex education. They were then homeschooled. Ms. K. said she did well in school, making A's and B's. She participated in limited extracurricular activities (e.g., ballet class) but described herself as feeling "introverted" and "embarrassed" by her family's outspoken promotion of religious values. She stated that romantic or sexual attraction was regarded as immoral and shameful in her family. She was actively discouraged from interacting with opposite-sex peers and described once being punished for holding hands with a male friend. Later, she graduated from community college and was presently working as a bookkeeper in a mid-sized company. At the time of the evaluation, she was single, did not have children, and lived alone. Ms. K. complained of difficulty making friends and interacting with colleagues and felt pessimistic about finding a romantic partner. She had not had a romantic relationship in several years. She reported very occasional consumption of alcoholic beverages, at times to help with social anxiety. Ms. K. denied any significant medical history and no prescription medication. She had been in individual psychotherapy for four months prior to the evaluation. She reported a positive family history of ASD, social anxiety, and auditory processing problems, as well as delays in speech and motor functioning in first-degree relatives.

Psychological Evaluation

Ms. K. was seen over four assessment sessions. She was administered the WAIS-IV, Conners' Adult ADHD Rating Scales (CAARS; Conners, & Erhardt, & Sparrow, 1999), Autism Spectrum Quotient (AQ; Baron-Cohen, Wheelwright, Skinner, Martin, & Clubley, 2001), Reading the Mind in the Eyes Test-Revised, Adult (RMET-R-A; Baron-Cohen, Wheelwright, Hill, Raste, & Plumb, 2001), PAI, R-PAS, and TAT. In addition, she was evaluated with the AMPD using the PDLT-C template. Behaviorally, she was cooperative and gave strong effort, but initially she was apprehensive, stiff, and formal. Over time, she appeared to warm up, but she reported feeling anxious throughout. She had difficulty maintaining appropriate eye contact, and at times made self-critical remarks about herself and her performance.

Assessment Results and Interpretation

Ms. K. demonstrated High Average intellectual functioning with no indication of cognitive processing difficulties (WAIS-IV FSIQ 116; WMI 105; PSI 124). Self-report behavior rating scales for ADHD symptoms were not elevated. The AQ scale and the RMET-R-A, a performance test for social-emotional perception and cognition that can reflect mentalization deficits in ASD (Baron-Cohen, Wheelwright, Hill, Raste, & Plumb, 2001), were insignificant. These results helped to rule out ADHD, ASD, and similar explanations for her communication problems. Thus, her difficulty in "verbal comprehension" when interacting with others was interpreted as social anxiety disrupting her focus and thinking.

Across assessment data, Ms. K. evidenced interest in and desire for social relationships. Yet, pervasive social anxiety, self-doubt, sensitivity to rejection, and the expectation of being judged harshly affected her social functioning. Performance testing with the TAT and Rorschach procedure illuminated these issues and emotional dynamics and confirmed severe social dysfunction.

Ms. K.'s R-PAS verbalizations and indices reflected a capacity for and interest in social relationships. For example, she gave five Cooperative (COP; 99th percentile), five Human Movement (M; 72nd percentile), two Texture (T; 89th percentile), and eight Human Content (H; 74th percentile) responses. Her TAT stories were clear, organized, and reflected awareness of social complexity in relationships—even though themes of social failure, inadequacy, disappointment, and guilt were present. The assessment data suggested that Ms. K.'s reaction to social interactions, especially as the level of intimacy increased, produced intense anxiety (e.g., YTVC'; 89th percentile) that affected her cognitive appraisal and impelled her to withdraw and blame herself.

Interpretation of Ms. K.'s Rorschach responses was aided by sequence analysis. This involves interpretation of consequential and sequential alterations in response process across verbalization, formal scores, and content variables (Peebles-Kleiger, 2002). Her responses revealed social interaction was associated with anxiety, negativity, or danger. This is vividly illustrated in the examples below. In response to three separate cards, Ms. K. produced a response with connotations of cooperative social relatedness, but these responses were immediately followed by a negative, frightening percept (i.e., Aggressive Content [AGC]; bolded below). Note, some wording in the Clarification Phase is omitted (R-PAS coding).

> II. R#4. "2 people touching hands like they're dancing or something" [W H 2 o Ma COP, MAH GH]

R#5. "**a sting ray**"
[D SR A o F AGC]
III. R#6. "2 people cooking"
[D H Sy o P Ma COP, MAH GH]
R#7. "**face of a monster**"
[D (Ad) o F AGC]
VII. R#17. "2 women talking to each other."
[D H 2 o Ma DR1 COP, MAH GH ODL]
R#18. "**an evil pig-face**."
[D Ad o Y FAB1 AGC ODL]

At other points, responses with sexual content were given. Each was associated with poor form quality, suggesting momentary impingements on the quality of her thought processes, as well as Oral Dependent Language (ODL; Bornstein, 1999). These test signs were consistent with her history of family disapprobation and shaming about romantic and sexual matters.

To give a flavor of Ms. K.'s responses on the TAT, her story to Card 2 (girl with books in arms, looking out on a farm scene) is reproduced.

> This girl wants to get a good education, but she has this family on the farm and they think it's a waste of time. She feels guilty for not helping out more. Her sister is pregnant, and she can't do anything, so she feels bad wanting to pursue her dream. She decides to follow her own path, but she never completely feels she's done the right thing. She goes on to live with the guilt of not pleasing her family.

Ms. K.'s TAT stories (Cards 1, 2, 3BM, 4, 13GF) were coded with the Social Cognition and Object Relations Scale: Global (SCORS-G; Hilsenroth, Stein, & Pinsker, 2007) for the dimensions of Complexity of Representation of People (COM), Affective Quality of Representations (AFF), Emotional Investments Relationships (EIR), and Social Causality (SC). These indices provided a quantitative metric and normative information regarding her experience and representation of social-emotional relationships.

Ratings of the SCORS-G scales were averaged across cards and compared with clinical norms (Stein et al., 2014). Referring to Stein et al. (2014, Table 3, p. 342), their clinical normative data and reliability figures permit estimation of a standard of error of measurement (SEM) for the SCORS-G. This calculation provides an approximate SEM of .18 for the constructs of the SCORS-G which aided interpretation of Ms. K.'s TAT stories with this method (but note that we used Card 13GF rather than 13MF which introduced a minor degree of inexactness in the normative comparisons). The results confirmed Ms. K.'s strong social interest, capacity, and satisfactory social reasoning, yet they also pointed to her anticipation that relationships are negative, disappointing, or dangerous. Her scores were as follows (clinical norms in parentheses, calculated from Stein et al., 2014): COM 5.4 (3.4); AFF 2.6 (3.3); EIR 4.6 (3); SC 5 (3.2). Ms. K.'s mean for these rated dimensions across all Cards was 4.4 compared to a lower corresponding mean (3.2) from the normative data of Stein et al. (2014). Ms. K. showed higher Complexity and awareness of Social Causality, but lower Affective quality of her social cognitions relative to a clinical population. Comparing Ms. K.'s results to descriptions of selected scale anchors from the SCORS-G Manual (paraphrased below) helps to see the significance of her scores (1–7 range).

COM: 5; non-problematic or stereotypical representations, able to integrate positive and negative qualities and awareness of others
AFF: 3; largely negative or unpleasant relationships but not abusive
EIR: 5; adequate relationship investment and sentiments such as friendship, caring, love, empathy
SC: 5; straightforward narrative accounts of interpersonal events, actions result from how relationships/events are experienced or interpreted

At this point, SAD was confirmed and ASD, ADHD, and related conditions were ruled out. The question of PD remained. On the one hand, she was living independently and performing satisfactorily in her occupation. However, her distress and functional deficits in social relationships were suggestive of PD. Ms. K. was anxious, formal, and self-critical. She made limited eye contact and seemed hypersensitive to examiner reactions—despite strong efforts to reassure her. Performance on the less structured assessments (TAT and Rorschach) also revealed rejection sensitivity and readiness to feel shame, as well as characterological distancing and avoidant behavior. Given this picture, our task was to differentiate between severe SAD and PD.

AMPD Organizes Differential Diagnosis and Feedback

Differential diagnosis involved distinguishing SAD and PD, as well as differentiating between avoidant PD and schizoid-like symptoms. The AMPD offered a simultaneous conceptual and empirical method to accomplish this, with treatment implications derivable from the formulation.

Using all available information, both raters independently evaluated Ms. K. with the LPFS and 25 pathological personality traits of the AMPD. The ICCs for rater agreement were computed for LPFS domains and the 25 pathological personality trait-facets. Agreement was Excellent for Criterion A and Criterion B variables. For the LPFS domains, ICCs were .83 (single) and .91 (mean); for the 25 trait-facets, ICCs were .89 (single) and .93 (mean). The ratings of each clinician were averaged to a composite score for subsequent quantitative comparisons.

LPFS ratings indicated a "Moderate" (2) level of PD impairment. The LPFS domain rating scores were Identity 2, Self-Direction 1, Empathy 1.5, and Intimacy 3. Pathological personality trait elevations (rated 2 or 3) were found for anhedonia, anxiousness, depressivity, distractibility, intimacy avoidance, restricted affectivity, submissiveness, suspiciousness, and withdrawal. Thus, Ms. K. showed Moderate impairment in personality functioning, which was manifested in personality patterns of negative affectivity (e.g., anxiousness, depressivity, submissiveness) and, most strikingly, detachment (e.g., anhedonia, withdrawal, intimacy avoidance, restricted affectivity, suspiciousness). Applying AMPD hybrid categorical-dimensional diagnostic algorithms yielded the diagnosis of avoidant PD.

Close examination of the dimensions of the LPFS illustrated areas of specific vulnerability and impairment. The Identity domain of the LPFS involves self-esteem instability and preoccupation with approval. Ms. K. showed Moderate PD impairment in these areas. Her impairment, however, was greatest in the domain of Intimacy (Severe). Despite a desire for interpersonal relationships, she both feared and retreated from involvement with others. We understood this as reflecting: (1) entrenched, highly negative, and rigid self-schemas; (2) an overall avoidant attachment pattern (Shaver & Mikulincer, 2002); and (3) anticipatory anxiety that interfered with her social functioning. Her readiness to perceive criticism and feel shame kept her on edge, expecting danger. These vulnerabilities and personality dynamics are indexed in the LPFS Intimacy domain, as are her problems in mutually and cooperatively interacting with others.

Her complaints of "focusing" and "sensory processing" problems when interacting with others are consistent with research findings that avoidant attachment patterns and traits are associated with cognitive processing errors for social stimuli (Fraley & Brumbaugh, 2007; Edelstein, 2006). Meyer and Carver (2000) linked this symptom set with long-term emotional sensitivity and pessimism (greater than seen in depression). In this respect, Ms. K. described life-long feelings of isolation, hypersensitivity, vulnerability to criticism and shame, and pessimism. Ms. K. was given the final diagnoses of SAD and avoidant PD (hybrid categorical-dimensional). In support of this formulation, we briefly review relevant research findings.

There is phenomenological overlap between SAD and avoidant PD, which has led some to question their distinctiveness (e.g., Ralevski et al., 2005). Yet, some research suggests utility in distinguishing the disorders. Eikenaes, Hummelen, Abrahamsen, Andrea, and Wilberg (2013) found that avoidant PD was associated with greater overall personality impairment than SAD alone. Similarly, Cox, Pagura, Stein, and Sareen's (2009) epidemiological study suggested the distinction between the two disorders is pragmatic. Lampe and Sunderland (2015) found greater symptom severity and co-morbidity in patients with combined SAD and avoidant PD, compared to either disorder individually. They argued this may reflect the effect of higher symptom load from a second disorder, as opposed to a more severe variant of SAD (see also Lampe, 2016).

Aligned with this research literature, we concluded diagnoses of both SAD and avoidant PD were supported in Ms. K.'s case. Although she showed areas of adaptive psychosocial functioning and some test results (e.g., PAI) were less suggestive of personality impairment, the AMPD provided a strategic integration of multi-method interview, test, and historical data.

Post-Hoc Analyses of Case Data

After the evaluations of Mr. M. and Ms. K. were completed, additional analyses were performed. These analyses illustrated different aspects of and ways the AMPD may be used, supported the educational mission of clinical training, and corroborated conclusions from the initial evaluations. First, metrics of rater agreement and between different AMPD-related measures were calculated. Second, a cross-model prototype analysis was undertaken to explore relationships between the AMPD and other PD conceptions. This exercise provided a way to examine from other perspectives convergences and divergences within the data, and offered the student multiple perspectives on PD diagnoses and formulations. Precedent for cross-model prototype analysis is seen in Lynam and Widiger (2001) who assessed DSM-IV (APA, 1994) PDs by expert Five Factor Model (FFM) ratings. They developed expert-consensus PD prototypes codified within the FFM (see Miller, 2012).

Two types of cross-model comparisons were done. First, the clinician ratings of AMPD trait-facet data for Mr. M. and Ms. K. were compared to PD prototype profiles that were developed from expert raters' characterizing of prototypal PDs with the AMPD. Second, the Morey, Benson, and Skodol (2016) study of clinicians' descriptions of DSM-IV (APA, 1994) PDs with the AMPD provided another cross-model comparison to be used with our assessment results.

Agreement Between Different AMPD-Related Measures

As noted, the evaluations of Mr. M. and Ms. K. included clinician ratings of the AMPD (PDLT-C) as well as self-report (e.g., PID-5, PAI, etc.) and other relevant assessment measures. Table 8.2 summarizes (1) levels of agreement between raters (student clinician and supervisor), (2) agreement between composite clinician AMPD ratings and other assessment measures, and (3) results of the PD prototype analyses.

Mr. M. was given the self-report PID-5 and PAI. Ms. K. was not given the PID-5, but was rated with the PID-5-Informant Form (Markon, Quilty, Bagby, & Krueger, 2013) and given the PAI. The PAI was also used to calculate PAI to PID-5 predicted scores (Busch et al., 2017). The

Table 8.2. Post-hoc AMPD comparisons of raters, measures, and prototype correlation.

Rater and Measure Agreement

Mr. M.			**Ms. K.**		
Measures	**Single**	**Mean**	**Measures**	**Single**	**Mean**
PDLT-C	0.87	0.93	PDLT-C-LPFS	0.83	0.91
PID-5, PDLT-C	0.52	0.69	PDLT-C-Traits	0.89	0.93
PID-5, PAI to PID-5	0.50	0.68	PID-5-IF ratings	0.78	0.86
PDLT-C, PAI to PID-5	0.28	0.44	PID-5-IF, PDLT-C	0.91	0.95
			PID-5-IF, PAI to PID-5	0.63	0.78
			PDLT-C, PAI to PID-5	0.47	0.64

Prototype Analyses

Rater Reliability			**Prototype Correlations**				
PD	**# Raters**	**ICC**		**Expert**	**Morey**	**Expert**	**Morey**
		mean	**PD**	**Mr. M.**	**Mr. M.**	**Ms. K.**	**Ms. K.**
AVD PD	2	0.93	**AVD PD**	0.72	0.78	0.88	0.86
SZD PD	3	0.81	**SZD PD**	0.65	0.69	0.64	0.70
SZT PD	2	0.93	**SZT PD**	0.70	0.40	0.63	0.25
BOR PD	10	0.90	**BOR PD**	0.04	–0.31	–0.11	–0.38
PAR PD	na	na	**PAR PD**	na	–0.30	na	–0.49
OCPD	na	na	**OCPD**	na	0.32	na	0.38

ICC (2-way, random effects, absolute agreement) comparisons for rater agreement with the AMPD for both Mr. M. and Ms. K. were Excellent (mean ICCs > .9). Agreement between Mr. M.'s self-report PID-5 and clinician ratings were Good (mean ICC .69). Similarly, his self-report measures (PID-5 and PAI to PID-5 estimates) showed Good agreement (mean ICC .68). However, the PAI to PID-5 estimate agreed with clinician ratings only at a Fair level (mean ICC .44). With Ms. K., PID-5-IF showed Excellent agreement (mean ICC .86). The composite PID-5-IF showed Excellent agreement with the more global AMPD clinical ratings from the PDLT-C (mean ICC .95).

Ms. K.'s PID-5-IF also closely corresponded with the PAI to PID-5 estimates (mean ICC .78). The PAI to PID-5 and PDLT-C ratings were Good (mean ICC .64).

Context is important to understand these results. The PID-5 and PAI were self-report assessments, and the PID-5-IF and PDLT-C were clinician ratings. These different methods of assessment generally show moderate agreement (Oltmanns & Turkheimer, 2006). Samuel's (2015) meta-analysis of agreement between sources of PD diagnoses found that clinician-to-clinician dimensional PD diagnosis ratings averaged (Pearson *r*) .46. In comparison, clinician-to-self-report dimensional PD diagnosis averaged .23. With these figures as benchmarks, we see the clinician agreement for both Mr. M. and Ms. K., as well as construct agreement across methods of assessment, was quite respectable. Agreement decreased as the method of measurement (self vs. informant) and complexity of PD algorithm increased (e.g., PAI to PID-5). Interestingly, comparisons between Mr. M.'s self-report PID-5 and the PAI to PID-5 estimates, and likewise for Ms. K.'s PID-5-IF, showed the Busch et al. (2017) algorithm provides useful clinical information for PD (e.g., .68 and .78 mean ICC, respectively). Our levels of rater agreement and correspondence across self-report-to-clinician ratings compare very favorably to those reported by Few and colleagues (2013) in their study in which patients were interviewed and rated with the AMPD as well as administered the self-report PID-5. They presented their data differently, but reported a median ICC value of .55 for two raters across the 25 trait-facets, and an overall convergent correlation of .55 between clinician ratings and the PID-5.

Agreement Between AMPD Ratings and "PD Prototypes"

Two AMPD prototype analyses were carried out. First, Mr. M.'s AMPD trait-facet clinician ratings were compared with AMPD PD "profiles" developed from experts' characterizations of prototypical avoidant PD (N=2), schizoid PD (N=3), schizotypal PD (N=2), and borderline PD (N=10) using the AMPD trait-facets. Clinicians with expertise in these PDs were asked to depict a "prototypical" patient with the disorder using the AMPD (we acknowledge Donna S. Bender, Nicole M. Cain, Ronald J.

Ganellan, Robert M. Gordon, Jan H. Kamphuis, James H. Kleiger, Mark F. Lenzenweger, Jenny Macfie, John Porcerelli, Allan Sugarman, Mark H. Waugh, & Aidan G. C. Wright for providing ratings). Agreement between raters (ICC 2-way, random, absolute, mean) for the prototypes was: avoidant PD .93; schizoid PD .80; schizotypal PD .93; borderline PD .90. Thus, mean rater agreement was Excellent.

Pearson correlations between the expert-generated AMPD prototypes and Mr. M.'s composite clinician ratings were as follows: avoidant .72; schizoid .65; schizotypal .70; borderline .04. These results show Mr. M's clinician ratings on the AMPD strongly resemble avoidant, schizoid, and schizotypal, but show no resemblance to borderline PD prototypes. Note that intercorrelations between the PD prototypes of primary interest were: avoidant and schizotypal .44, avoidant and schizoid .57, and schizoid and schizotypal .76, indicating a range of similarity ("co-morbidity").

A similar procedure was used with Ms. K.'s data. Pearson correlations between expert prototypes and Ms. K.'s clinician ratings on Criterion B trait-facets were: avoidant .88; schizoid .64; schizotypal .63; borderline -.11. These results show Ms. K.'s clinician trait-facet ratings very strongly resemble the avoidant PD prototype, with good correspondence to the schizoid and schizotypal PDs, but essentially no resemblance to borderline PD prototype.

A second prototype analysis compared these clinician ratings on the trait-facets with the Morey et al. (2016) AMPD-profiles associated with categorical DSM-IV PD diagnoses. This analysis further illustrated convergent and divergent relationships in Mr. M. and Ms. K.'s assessment data.

The following Pearson correlations were found for Mr. M.'s AMPD clinician ratings and the Morey et al. (2016) PD profiles: avoidant .78, schizoid .69, schizotypal .40, borderline -.31, paranoid -.30, and obsessive compulsive .32. These results show Mr. M.'s AMPD trait-facets strongly resemble DSM-IV avoidant and schizoid PD, and further differentiates him from borderline and paranoid PD.

Similarly, for Ms. K., Pearson correlations were: avoidant .86, schizoid .70, schizotypal .25, borderline -.38, paranoid -.49, and obsessive compulsive .38. Thus, Ms. K.'s clinician-rated AMPD traits strongly corresponded with DSM-IV avoidant PD, with a slightly lower but sizeable similarity to schizoid PD. Her clinician rated trait-facets differed from the borderline PD prototype, and they were very different from paranoid PD. She showed a moderate correlation with the OCPD prototype.

In sum, cross-walking the ratings of Criterion B dimensions for Mr. M. and Ms. K. with two different AMPD-to-DSM PD prototype approaches provided results very consistent with the original psychological assessments. This included further support for the differential diagnostic conclusions and rule outs (e.g., ruling out paranoid PD with Mr. M.). These analyses suggest cross-model translations between the AMPD and traditional categorical PD prototypes can be done reliably and show convergence with other assessment data. Of note, other investigators have demonstrated cross-model connections between the AMPD and DSM-IV PDs in nomothetic studies (e.g., Bach & Sellbom, 2016; Evans & Simms, 2018).

Treatment Planning with the AMPD

Clarkin, Cain, and Livesley (2015) described a transdiagnostic model for treatment planning with patients with PDs (see also Hopwood, 2018). In this model, the presence of PD specifies the need for approaches (modules) suited to early phases of psychotherapy. This includes emphasis on patient safety (e.g., structure, contracting for safety, medication, hospitalization), containment (e.g., treatment frame), followed by control and modulation approaches such as mindfulness, mentalization, and functional analysis of behavior. This phase of treatment strives to develop awareness and links between thought, emotion, and action. Beyond preliminary treatment modules, as a therapeutic alliance deepens, interpersonal schemas and object relationships are explored, fostering mentalization, improved relationships, and self-care.

Bach, Markon, Simonsen, and Krueger (2015) similarly showed how the AMPD informs psychotherapy planning. Briefly, the Criterion A establishes the presence of PD. In this regard, psychotherapy is considered a first-line, effective intervention for PD (e.g., Perry, Banon, & Ianni, 1999). Bach et al. (2015) also noted that significantly elevated Criterion B maladaptive personality traits direct attention to problem content and treatment targets. Assessment of Criterion B may come from clinical ratings, the PID-5, and other assessment instruments (see Crego & Widiger, 2016; Furnham, Milner, Akhtar, & De Fruyt, 2014).

Mr. M.'s AMPD assessment results may be framed in terms of Clarkin et al. (2015). First, he showed significant PD impairment. This suggested psychotherapy should focus on providing stabilization, structure, and establishing a therapeutic frame. Secondly, elevations on detachment and negative affectivity suggested specific problem areas on which to focus. However, his elevated LPFS, prominent detachment traits, dismissive attachment style (Mikulincer & Shaver, 2012), and avoidant PD-like traits (Lampe, 2016) suggested the pace of treatment would be slow, necessitating careful attention to the alliance and potential ruptures. The therapeutic alliance would need care, time, and would not be guaranteed.

For Ms. K., her LPFS indicated Moderate PD impairment despite areas of intellectual and personal competence. Maladaptive personality trait-facets within the detachment and negative affectivity domains were found (anhedonia, anxiousness, and withdrawal). This suggested the importance of proceeding slowly in psychotherapy, setting and working within the treatment frame, and nurturing areas of trust. Yet, her level of relatedness portended a dependable therapeutic alliance, despite her distancing personality style.

Transdiagnostic Constructs, Therapeutic Alliance, Treatment Strategy

Chapter 5 discussed connections between the AMPD and key personality constructs and models. These included Luyten & Blatt's (2016) hierarchical model of interpersonal relatedness and self-definition (analogous to sociotropy and autonomy; Beck, Epstein, Harrison, & Emery 1983) and attachment theory (Bowlby, 1973; Mikulincer & Shaver, 2012). These are relevant to understanding Mr. M. and Ms. K.

The evaluations of Mr. M. and Ms. K. revealed both individuals showed a primary avoidant (dismissive) attachment pattern in close relationships, as seen in the AMPD detachment trait domain as well as other assessment data. In this attachment style, interpersonal contact triggers deactivating behavior which functions as a security operation (see Gallo, Smith, & Ruiz, 2003; Mikulincer & Shaver, 2012). Mr. M. and Ms. K. also showed significant negative affectivity. Ms. K.'s PD functioning resembled a mixed anxious-avoidant attachment style (sometimes referred to as fearful-avoidant; Mikulincer & Shaver, 2012). This attachment style reflected her desire for relationships but conflicting sense of insecurity—with which she coped by distancing. Fossati, Krueger, Markon, Boronni, Maffei, and Somma (2015) showed that attachment style substantially predicts AMPD PID-5 scores, even when the influence of Big Five trait variance is removed. These empirical results give us greater confidence in drawing on the literature on fearful-avoidant attachment style in formulating diagnosis and treatment planning for Ms. K.

Luyten and Blatt (2016) discussed psychotherapeutic tactics with respect to the relative salience of interpersonal relatedness versus self-definition. Blatt, Zuroff, Hawley, and Auerbach (2010) showed that for patients with self-definition personality impairment (e.g., dismissive/avoidant-attachment style), the therapeutic relationship was surprisingly important despite their primary distancing posture. Thus, Blatt et al. (2010) concluded that even though eventual results of psychotherapy were often largely in the self-definition domain (through decreased perfectionist, self-critical, and harsh self-schemas), the therapeutic relationship nonetheless was the fulcrum for these changes. This is an important point. Patients with self-definition problems likely will show clinical improvement within a dimension less oriented to relationship matters, but relationship factors are key drivers of change.

Mr. M. and Ms. K. were both diagnosed with social anxiety disorder and PD. Relatedly, Kopala-Sibley, Zuroff, Russell, and Moskowitz (2014) found that dependency and self-definition were associated with differential expression of symptoms in SAD. High self-criticism predicted self-consciousness in SAD, and dependency was associated with emotional insecurity in social situations. We noted Ms. K.'s SAD symptoms were associated with marked self-consciousness, consistent with self-definition psychopathology. Daly and Mallinckrodt (2009) surveyed expert clinicians who worked with avoidant PD. They found psychotherapists prioritized focus on issues of avoidant attachment style, but they used a strategy of very gradually increasing the level of closeness in the therapy relationship. Over time, this strategy decreased personality disengagement and minimized avoidant defenses. For both Mr. M. and Ms. K., this line of reasoning suggested treatment should focus on self-definition problems (e.g., Criterion B detachment; self-criticism, feelings of low self-worth), and use a strategy of titrating the level of closeness in the therapeutic relationship. With Mr. M.'s more severe personality impairment and trait-suspiciousness, great care would be needed to prevent ruptures in the therapeutic alliance. Regarding therapeutic alliance and personality style, Lingiardi, Filippucci, and Baiocco (2005) found that clinicians tended to underestimate the strength of the alliance in patients with avoidant PD styles. This observation seemed quite relevant to Ms. K.'s treatment.

In view of Mr. M.'s suspiciousness and Ms. K.'s hypersensitivity and shame-proneness, the extensive clinical literature on treatment of narcissistic hypersensitivity is apropos (Gabbard & Crisp-Han, 2016; Kohut, 1971; Ronningstam, 2012). Narcissistic hypersensitivity may be expressed through quiet or covert grandiosity and traits (Gore & Widiger, 2016; Pincus & Lukowitsky, 2010; Ronningstam, 2014). Avoidant and schizoid personality styles also involve hypersensitivity and vulnerable self-esteem dynamics (Hess, 2016; Guntrip, 1962; Lampe, 2016; Thylstrup & Hesse, 2009), but in avoidant functioning, fears of rejection may be figural. In contrast, in schizoid sensitivities, safety may be sought through balancing social distance with remaining "proximate" to the other (Guntrip, 1962; Orcutt, 2018). These differences may reflect the rejection sensitivity of avoidant traits relative to the ambivalence (Thystrupp & Hesse, 2009) and anhedonia of schizoid experience (Winarick & Bornstein, 2015).

Bender (2005) called attention to the hypersensitivity associated with avoidant PD functioning. With these individuals, the therapeutic alliance is delicate. Even seemingly innocuous comments may be experienced as criticism. Bender (2005) noted with schizoid patients the need for emotional distance is strong yet belies an underlying wish for connection. Mr. M.'s "shutting down" on several TAT cards and Ms. K.'s Rorschach sequence analysis, amongst other data, illustrated these personality dynamics.

Ronningstam (2017) recommended a psychotherapeutic strategy for hypersensitivity that focuses on self-esteem, rather than affect and emotion. In this approach, the therapist empathically validates experiences of self-esteem injury early in therapy, and eventually shifts to fostering curiosity and reflective functioning about events associated with self-esteem injury. For Ms. K., this strategy implied that anxiety reduction techniques should be integrated with focus on self-esteem dynamics. This also applied to Mr. M., but his level of personality impairment and degree of suspiciousness meant the alliance would be fragile, and a cognitive and rather formal therapeutic style would be strategic.

Countertransference and Feedback/Follow-Up

Countertransference (CT) is important in the treatment of PD (e.g., Tansey & Burke, 1989; Gabbard, 2009). CT is a transdiagnostic construct that applies across therapeutic orientations. This includes treatment of PD with dialectical behavior therapy (DBT; Linehan, 1993) and cognitive behavior therapy (CBT; Gilbert & Leahy, 2007), as well as psychodynamic (e.g., transference focused therapy [TFT; Kernberg, Yeomans, Clarkin, & Levy, 2008]) and attachment-oriented approaches (e.g. mentalization-based therapy [MBT; Bateman & Fonagy, 2006]). We briefly note empirical studies of PD and CT (Betan, Heim, Zittel Conklin, & Westen, 2005; Colli, Tanzilli, Dimaggio, & Lingiardi, 2014; Gazzillo et al., 2015).

Research shows various forms of PD are associated with the likelihood of specific therapist experiences. Avoidant PD traits may induce a protective, parental, or disengaged response from the therapist; schizotypal traits may pull for therapist disengagement; and schizoid PD traits can bring feelings of helplessness and inadequacy (Colli et al., 2014; Gazillo et al., 2015). Knowing this, assessment of CT reactions may provide useful information for the psychotherapy of PDs. Instruments for the assessment of CT have been developed. These include the Countertransference Questionnaire (CQ; Betan et al., 2005), which has been refined as the Therapist Response Questionnaire (TRQ; Colli et al., 2014). Subsequently, we report results of TRQ assessment of CT reactions with Ms. K.'s therapist and compare them with predictions made from her original psychological assessment.

Psychological evaluation of Mr. M. and Ms. K. indicated they were prone to distancing behavior and a likelihood that they would perceive anger, criticism, or rejection from the therapist. Mr. M.'s more severely impaired personality functioning and greater dismissive/avoidant attachment style suggested the patient-therapist relationship would be distant, fragile, and reflect issues of power and control. These findings suggested likely CT reactions of disengagement and the therapist feeling a sense of inadequacy. For Ms. K., prominent avoidant PD traits suggested the therapist might be inclined to over-involvement, wishes to protect, and perhaps moments of disengagement (see Colli et al., 2014; Gazillo et al., 2015).

Psychotherapy was recommended for Mr. M., but no information on his follow through is available. The assessor's emotional experiences in providing feedback to Mr. M. are relevant in this regard. The evaluator reported experiencing him as if he were a "shell of a person," likening the session to "sitting with an alien." These CT reactions are consistent with experiences of clinician disengagement and feelings of therapist inadequacy noted by Colli et al. (2014) and Gazillo et al. (2015) in the treatment of individuals exhibiting schizoid and schizotypal PD functioning. Similarly, the sense of being with "an alien" likely reflected Mr. M.'s ambivalence about social relatedness (Thystrupp & Hesse 2009).

When Ms. K. received testing feedback, she expressed relief at not receiving a diagnosis of ASD, feared because she found her sibling (with ASD) very disagreeable. Symptoms of SAD and the disruptive effects of anxiety on cognition were discussed as were hypersensitivity and her fears of rejection. This helped in framing treatment as more than targeting anxiety-reduction, although CBT techniques for social anxiety were recommended. She was recommended to seek psychiatric consultation for medication (e.g., SSRI antidepressant). Of note, although she did not comment about this during feedback, her non-verbal reactions indicated she disliked the idea. It was later learned her therapist had previously suggested psychiatric medication consultation, a recommendation Ms. K. experienced as criticism as well as confirmation of her sense of defectiveness.

Ms. K. participated in psychotherapy for about one year, and then she transferred to a new therapist when the previous therapist left the clinic. The original therapist recently completed the TRQ based on her time with Ms. K. The TRQ was elevated for Positive/Satisfying (99th percentile) and Parental/Protective (53rd percentile). The lowest score was Criticized/ Devalued (25th percentile). These results suggest the therapist clearly felt connected with Ms. K. and found the work pleasant, enjoyable, and satisfying. On the TRQ Parental/Protective scale, the therapist rated these items as most relevant: "I feel like I want to protect him/her" and "I feel nurturant toward him/her." The TRQ results thus were very consistent with prototypical CT reactions associated with treating patients with avoidant PD (Colli et al., 2014; Gazillo et al., 2015).

Summary

The cases of Mr. M. and Ms. K. illustrated the use of AMPD-related assessment measures as well as ways the AMPD may be employed as a clinical heuristic in the interpretation of assessment data. Both Mr. M. and Ms. K. showed internalizing psychopathology. This was seen in their similar PAI profiles (e.g., ICC .47 [absolute]; .72 [consistency]). Nonetheless, their different levels of personality functioning, and specific profile of personality traits and associated dynamics revealed important differences not fully captured in the PAI or any single assessment approach. Several important clinical observations (e.g., Mr. M.'s shutting down on the interpersonally oriented TAT) and patterns in the test results (e.g., Ms. K.'s Rorschach sequence analysis) were interpreted as convergent with the AMPD assessment. This increased confidence in the diagnostic formulation. Post-hoc cross-model comparisons between PD prototypes and AMPD trait-facet ratings supported the original differential diagnostic conclusions. In addition, cross-walking the AMPD with traditional DSM categorical approaches to PD in these prototype comparisons was instructive within the context of clinical teaching. Notably, the trainees cited two main ways they felt the AMPD was helpful to them. These were: (1) its clinical flexibility, helpful in formulating PD diagnoses; and, (2) its easily communicated trait- and behavior-specific language, which supported patient feedback. In sum, these case analyses demonstrate the AMPD's dual role as a PD nosology and a framework for case formulation. The AMPD is a clinical heuristic in addition to a diagnostic scheme.

9 Forensic Applications of the AMPD and Case Illustration[1]

Abby L. Mulay and Mark H. Waugh

Forensic psychiatry (Simon & Gold, 2010) and psychology (Heilbrun & Brooks, 2010) are rapidly expanding areas of investigation and clinical practice. In addition to the more "traditional" nexus between mental health and the law, psychiatric and psychological forensic consultation is needed by numerous stakeholders. This includes arenas of public policy, corrections, hospitals, schools, governmental agencies, and private citizens. Broadly speaking, forensic mental health involves psycho-legal issues within criminal (i.e., concerning statuary matters of crime and punishment) or civic (i.e., focusing on dispute resolution, capacity, and compensation) law. Careful psychiatric or psychological assessment is often at the heart of these matters. A very cursory listing of areas in which forensic assessment is central includes capital sentencing, child custody and parenting fitness, civil commitment, competence for decision-making and managing personal affairs, competency to stand trial, criminal responsibility, disability determination, educational accommodations, fire-arm eligibility (when at issue), fitness for duty, immigration law, mitigation and sentencing factors, police consulting, national security clearance, risk assessments (e.g., dangerousness, recidivism, sexual re-offending, violence, etc.), and workplace discrimination. Furthermore, policy and societal changes leading to the increased presence of psychiatric disorder in the criminal justice system ensures the relevance of forensic psychiatry and psychology will continue to expand (e.g., Konrad, 2002; Sadoff, 2015; Soderstrom, 2007).

To meet the needs of the referring source (e.g., court, attorney, individual client, institution, agency), forensic consultation often must frame evaluation results and conclusions with respect to a codified psychiatric diagnosis. In fact, a psychiatric diagnosis may be a "threshold requirement" (p. 132; Wills & Gold, 2014) in forensic matters. In the case of the insanity defense, for example, the Model Penal Code requires that, as a result of *mental disease or defect of the mind*, the defendant lacks *substantial capacity* to appreciate the quality of the criminal act, the ability to know if the criminal act was wrong, or the ability to control one's conduct (American Law Institute, 1985). This fundamental and historical role of psychiatric diagnostic assessment (and other principles) was emphasized by Gutheil (2005), who cited the words of a Mr. Macer, from the year 180 AD in the time of Emperor Marcus Aurelius:

> If you have clearly ascertained that [the defendant] is in such a state of insanity that he is permanently out of his mind and so entirely incapable of reasoning, and no suspicion is left that he was simulating insanity when he killed his mother, you need not concern yourself with the question how he should be punished…he should be kept on close observations and, if you think it advisable, even kept in restraint….
>
> (p. 316; Spruit, 1998)

Gutheil (2005) pointed out that "ascertainment" is basic to the forensic mental health enterprise, as well as ruling out malingering and a focus on the ultimate issue. Psychiatric diagnosis, psycho-legal constructs, and the ultimate legal issue are complexly inter-related. Some of these issues involving personality disorder (PD) are examined below, with special reference to transdiagnostic models such as the Alternative Model for Personality Disorders (AMPD), outlined in Section III of the *Diagnostic and Statistical Manual, Fifth Edition* (DSM-5; APA, 2013).

The DSM-5 is a major psychiatric nosology, and the authors issue a carefully worded "cautionary statement for forensic use" in the diagnostic manual (APA, 2013; p. 25). The DSM-5 states the primary purposes of the manual are for diagnostic assessment and treatment planning, while also serving clinical, investigatory, and public health needs. It is pointed out that the manual does not directly address specific psycho-legal constructs and ultimate questions of interest to courts, adjudicative entities, and other forensic audiences. Furthermore, clinical assessment differs in many and fundamental ways from forensic psychiatric or psychological assessment, as articulated by Greenberg and Shuman (1997) and many others. Nonetheless, the DSM-5 asserts that careful clinical diagnosis, along with assessment of functioning, impairment, and other variables, plays an important role in some legal proceedings.

Historical Segue

PD and the legal system have a long, complicated, and intimate historical relationship. A historical precis is instructive. Although the term "personality disorder" is modern, it is based upon ancient notions, including those of Theophrastus (371–287 BCE), a colleague of Aristotle, who wrote a treatise describing 25 curiously modern descriptions of problematic personality "types." In terms of nosology, Pinel, working in the asylums of Paris, differentiated a disturbance of personality from other forms of insanity, referred to as *manie sans delire*, or mania without delusions (Berrios, 1993; Crocq, 2013; Zachar, 2015). It is revealing that Pinel noted these individuals were often male, impulsive, had poor frustration tolerance, and were prone to violence—as in "a deficient and ill directed upbringing of the child, or an undisciplined or perverse nature…" (Pinel, 1801; quoted in Crocq, 2013, p. 149).

Irrespective of Foucault's (1977) thesis on the interrelations of power, society, and criminology (*Discipline and Punish: The Birth of the Prison)*, it is undeniable that historically (and presently) some individuals secured in various forms of institutionalized exile (e.g., hospitals, prisons) have suffered from PD. Kraepelin (1904) introduced the term *psychopathic personalities,* referring to PD in general (as opposed to the contemporary idea of psychopathy). In Kraepelin's (1904) seventh edition of his famous textbook, he distinguished four types of "PD:" *criminals*, the *irresolute, liars and swindlers,* and *pseudoquerulants* (i.e., paranoid personality). Kraepelin's contribution was to provide a natural-science-based conception and classification of PD (Berrios, 1993; Zachar, 2015).

In the 19th Century, "degeneration theory," which was based upon a theological metaphor of the Fall and Lamarckian inheritance, was a widely held paradigm for understanding *psychopathic personalities* (Berrios, 1993; Zachar, 2015). Degeneration theory added a form of "evolutionary" explanation to the conception of "PD" as "moral insanity" (Prichard, 1835). Schneider (1923; 1950) rejected degeneration accounts and formulated "PD" as statistical abnormality and used empirical criteria. In the mid-20th Century, psychoanalytic concepts of "character" became influential (e.g., Reich, 1945/1972). Narrower and more modern ideas on psychopathic personalities began to emerge, and the sociological dimensions of psychopathology were actively debated (see Gough, 1948; Karpman, 1948). Cleckley's (1941) well-known *The Mask of Sanity* differentiated a specific *psychopathic* syndrome. Cleckley (1941) was descriptivist, not psychoanalytic, and was an important precedent to Hare's (1980) pioneering measurement of psychopathy. The diagnostic term antisocial PD (ASPD) was codified in the DSM-III (APA, 1980), although precursor terms were listed in earlier DSMs. A continuous theme in the evolution of PD diagnoses involves "moral taint" (Sadler, 2013). As this brief segue into the history of PD illustrates, many of the symptoms of "psychopathic personalities" or PD implicate values of society, and matters of virtue and vice. This is but one small step to the forensic arena.

Regarding the inextricable inter-relationships of PD and society (e.g., the legal system), Wakefield (2006), a prominent theoretician of psychiatric nosology, argued that the DSM cultural deviance criterion for PD provides a conceptually satisfactory definition of PD. Wakefield (2006) conceptualizes psychiatric disorder in terms of *harmful dysfunction*: (1) behavior that is harmful according to cultural values, and (2) caused by dysfunction or failure of an evolved natural function. Wakefield's (2006) argument is that culture is an evolved mechanism for people as social beings. Thus, PD crosses disciplinary boundaries, involving biology, medicine, psychology, and sociology—including criminology and the legal system. Later in the present article a complex forensic case is presented. This will illustrate not only the forensic role of the AMPD, but pivot on cultural context in the interpretation of PD.

Psychopathy and Antisocial PD

Sometimes a diagnosis of a personality disorder (PD) becomes relevant to forensic case issues and psycho-legal constructs, and, as Johnson and Elbogen (2013) highlight, this relationship has historically been "complex" (p. 203). While there has been a dramatic increase in the number of forensic assessment instruments available in recent years (Edens & Boccaccini, 2017), the assessment of antisocial personality disorder (ASPD) remains an important research focus in the forensic domain. This focus is likely because the diagnosis is overrepresented in both forensic and correctional populations, with some research suggesting that prevalence rates are as high as 40–60% (e.g., Moran, 1999). Fazel and Danesh (2002), for example, identified surveys of prisoners from around the world (N = 22,790 prisoners). They found that 81% of surveyed prisoners were male, 65% of these prisoners were diagnosed with a PD, and approximately 46% had a diagnosis of ASPD. Relatedly, Roberts and Coid (2010) studied lifetime offending behaviors in a large sample of prisoners and found that ASPD, as opposed to other PDs, was associated with lifetime offenses. The personality traits associated with ASPD are also predictive of institutional misconduct and violent behavior (e.g., Gardner, Boccaccini, Bitting, & Edens, 2015; Reidy, Sorensen, & Davidson, 2016). Accurate identification of this disorder may therefore have important implications for the safety of the correctional institution, or community into which offenders are released.

Forensic assessors generally rely upon measures of psychopathy to assess for the presence of antisocial traits. Psychopathy, though not a formal DSM-5 (APA, 2013) diagnosis, is a cluster of personality traits that are characterized by interpersonal (e.g., grandiosity, superficial charm, manipulation), affective (e.g., superficial affect, lack of empathy), and behavioral (e.g., sensation seeking, impulsiveness, lack of responsibility) components (e.g., Hare & Neumann, 2015). A commonly utilized measure of psychopathy within forensic settings, the Psychopathy Checklist, Revised (PCL-R; Hare, 2003), offers a method to assess for the presence of the construct. However, there is an emerging body of research that speaks to important issues in the scoring and interpretation of the PCL-R, which negatively impacts the psychometrics of the measure (e.g., Edens, Cox, Smith, DeMatteo, & Sörman, 2015; Jeandarme, Edens, Habets, Bruckers, Oei, & Bogaerts, 2017). It is also important to note that forensic psychological testing may not be accurate, sometimes due to an individual's attempt to portray themselves in a negative way (e.g., "feigning" or "malingering"), as well as non-standardization of test administration

(Heilbrun, 1992). As such, forensic assessment of PDs remains hindered by a number of important concerns. As Gutheil's (2005) above quote from Mr. Macer the "expert witness" from the time of Emperor Aurelius' Rome indicates, malingering and methods of discernment remain figural tasks in the forensic diagnostic task.

Transdiagnostic Approaches to PD

The challenges of accurate forensic assessment may be particularly plagued by the current state of categorical PD diagnosis. In fact, Zachar and Kendler (2017) contend that psychiatric nosology more broadly is undergoing a true Kuhnian paradigm change, and they argue that there are two forces in play. The first is dimensionalization of diagnosis, and the second, from the Research Domain Criteria (RDoC; Insel et al., 2010) initiative, is the rejection of traditional syndrome diagnoses for a natural science taxonomy of presumed cross-cutting causal constructs. The movement away from traditional categorical diagnoses (i.e., Section II of the DSM-5; APA, 2013) and towards a dimensional conceptualization is a major current within the field of PD (see Clark, 2007; Krueger, Eaton, Derringer, Markon, Watson, & Skodol, 2011; Widiger & Trull, 2007). As an example of an issue with the traditional diagnostic paradigm, writing of the nexus of PD and forensic psychiatry and psychology, Johnson and Elbogen (2013) point out that the categorical approach does not take into account "to what extent" (p. 204) an individual may endorse characteristics that are associated with a given PD. As such, the categorical traditional model may not adequately capture severity of pathology, not to mention the often-noted problems of diagnostic co-morbidity. To address these and other concerns, the DSM-5, Section III, the AMPD, offers a strategic alternative to the traditional categorical diagnostic paradigm.

Forensic Application of AMPD

Although research is limited in this domain, Hopwood and Sellbom (2013) lay out a compelling case for the use of the AMPD in the forensic arena. They note that, although the DSM meets the admissibility criterion of Frye v. United States (1923) because it is generally accepted within the scientific community, and indeed certain forensic questions specifically hinge on DSM diagnoses (some disability determinations, academic accommodations, etc.), the scientific basis of traditional diagnostic schemes is increasingly being scrutinized. This may be particularly acute in the realm of PD diagnosis. Thus, as Hopwood and Sellbom (2013) noted, the *Frye* or *Daubert* (Daubert v. Merrell Dow Pharmaceuticals [1993]) status of DSM diagnoses may be ripe for challenge. They recommend the quantitative psychopathology paradigm in general, and the AMPD in particular, as a scientifically sound diagnostic framework for forensic application.

There have also been a number of recent peer-reviewed publications that speak to both the strong psychometric properties and clinical utility of the AMPD (e.g., Waugh, Hopwood, Krueger, Morey, Pincus, & Wright, 2017), which further highlights the model's potential relevance and usefulness in the forensic arena.

We therefore argue that the AMPD may be used in conjunction with other assessment tools in the forensic setting. In a recent judicial decision (State of NY vs. Nicholas T., 2017), for example, state mental health experts utilized the AMPD to support the diagnosis of psychopathy, which itself was a key aspect of the forensic assessment. Nicholas T. pled guilty to a number of charges, including Burglary in the First Degree and Attempted Rape in the First Degree. He had also been convicted of Attempted Rape in the First Degree in adolescence. As he was deemed a threat to reoffend, a petition for sex offender civil management was later filed. The use of the AMPD was challenged by Nicholas T.'s attorney who argued, amongst other things, that the AMPD should be questioned on *Frye* grounds. The Court upheld the use of the AMPD, as per the following:

> There is nothing invalid, in this Court's view, in the reliance by an expert, in part, on the alternative DSM-5 model for personality disorders. Indeed, the DSM-5 itself, as noted supra, indicates that the alternative model is designed to address deficiencies in the existing DSM-5 approach to such disorders. In this Court's view, although the DSM-5's alternative diagnoses can be validly characterized as "emerging" and warranting "further study" (see DSM-5, p. 731), that does not mean psychiatric experts may not rely, in part, on such diagnostic criteria in forming their expert opinions.

The Court's determination vindicated the reasoning and recommendations of Hopwood and Sellbom (2013) and sets a precedent for future use of the AMPD in forensic assessment.

Moreover, those who are hesitant to use the measure in a forensic setting should know that psychometrically sound assessment tools designed to capture personality functioning from the perspective of the AMPD exist. Criterion A (i.e., level of personality functioning) and Criterion B (25 maladaptive trait facets) of the AMPD, for example, have a growing empirical basis, both in self-report and clinician rated formats (Bender, Morey, & Skodol, 2011; Huprich et al., in press, 2018; Hutsebaut, Feenstra, & Kamphuis, 2016; Krueger, Derringer, Markon, Watson, & Skodol, 2012; Morey, 2017; Wright, Calabrese, et al., 2015; Zimmermann et al., 2015). If one takes into consideration components of *Daubert*, the standard used by most jurisdictions in the determination of the admissibility of expert testimony, Criterion A and Criterion B have been subjected to both peer review and publication and have arguably gained acceptance within the psychological/psychiatric community. As the Court stated in the case of Nicholas T., simply because a measure is new or emerging does not mean that an expert cannot utilize the technique when combined with other sources of data. The forensic assessor is warned to always use multiple sources of data in rendering an opinion, regardless of the psychometric robustness of the selected measures, which is also congruent with the multimodal assessment perspective more broadly (Hopwood & Bornstein, 2014).

At this point, the forensic clinical utility of the AMPD is illustrated with a case presentation. In this example, the AMPD was strategic in responding to diagnostic and psycho-legal questions posed in the forensic referral. The case, like many, is complex, involving clinical, social-cultural, situational, and legal layers. The background context is described below.

Background of the Forensic Case

Mr. Smith is a 54-year-old African-American man employed as a safety and security administrator in a large federal defense contractor company in the mid-Atlantic region of the country (identifying features of Mr. Smith have been disguised). As part of his job, he is required to maintain a US government security clearance, which he has successfully held for 23 years. He was arrested for the charge of Domestic Violence in an incident with his spouse, allegedly involving alcohol consumption. His spouse subsequently recanted and withdrew charges. However, the incident triggered a formal investigation of his continued suitability for a security clearance. This process involved information gathering from Mr. Smith, his spouse, employer, and other collateral sources. The personnel security division of the federal agency sought an independent psychological or psychiatric evaluation, and Mr. Smith was referred for psychological evaluation with specific questions as to alcohol disorder, its status or treatment needs, and the presence of "significant defect in judgment or reliability" caused by an "illness or mental condition." These concerns are corollaries of federal statute. Thus, these are the ultimate questions with which the forensic assessment must connect. In these referrals, the psychologist or psychiatrist provides a written report and may offer in-person expert witness testimony.

Psychological evaluation of Mr. Smith included review of extensive background and collateral information, interview data, and psychological assessment of response credibility, alcohol disorder, and personality functioning utilizing psychometric tests. Results of the evaluation were as follows.

Initially guarded and apprehensive, Mr. Smith warmed to the evaluator over time and reported events of the incident and his history consistent with that of collateral sources. Psychometric indices of defensiveness and underreporting were moderately elevated but not invalidating. He was obviously offended over being scrutinized for his psychological status and security clearance. He reported longstanding minimal consumption of alcohol and no previous problems with alcohol. The Alcohol Use Disorders Identification Test (AUDIT; Babor, Higgins-Biddle, Saunders, & Montiero, 2001) was negative (score of 2; ≥ 8 is considered significant), as was the Substance Abuse Subtle Screening Inventory-3 (SASSI-3; Miller & Lazowski, 1999). Results of the Personality Assessment Inventory (PAI; Morey, 2007) were unremarkable, except for personality traits of interpersonal assertiveness, sociability, and self-confidence. There were no indications of impulsivity, aggression, emotional reactivity, or substance problems on the PAI (Morey, 2007).

Importantly, Mr. Smith reported a previous charge for Domestic Assault, also dismissed, 18 years previously. He stated he had struck his spouse during an argument, which occurred in their kitchen while she was cooking. He stated that she attempted to throw boiling water on him, he pushed her away to defend himself, and she called the police on him at that point. Mr. Smith described his spouse as "moody," and said they had been under significant stress around the time of the recent incident, primarily involving disagreement about child-care for their grandchildren (with whom they were highly involved). Furthermore, Mr. Smith reported no employment reprimands, workplace performance problems, or security infractions over 23 years, and this was corroborated by collateral sources. Mr. Smith said he was well-regarded in the workplace, but in recent years, he had felt slighted in not receiving the promotions that he expected. He attributed this to "prejudice." In this regard, it is important to note that his father was a popular and esteemed pastor in their small-town community, but he felt as though the family had suffered from a great degree of "racism." In addition, his grandfather had been a leader in civil rights protests over segregation. Mr. Smith denied physical abuse as a child, as well as any family history of alcohol or psychiatric disorders. Mr. Smith had completed a college degree, was active in a church, enjoyed playing golf, was invested in caring for his grandchildren, and described no problems in social relationships.

The evaluation concluded that there was no evidence of an alcohol disorder, nor any defect in judgment or reliability. Research literature on domestic violence/intimate partner violence (IPV) was cited in support of these conclusions. Mr. Smith's situation was characterized as an example of common couple violence (CCV; Johnson & Ferraro, 2000), as opposed to a more malignant pattern involving pathological control dynamics. CCV is less likely to recur and/or be severe, is the more common form of IPV, and is more likely to involve both partners. The extensive background and collateral data corroborated absence of impulsive, aggressive, or violent behavior—outside of the two IPV incidents, both of which the alleged victim, his spouse, subsequently recanted. Mr. Smith was diagnosed (DSM-IV-TR; APA, 2000) with the following: I. Partner Relational

Problem; II. None; III. Deferred; IV. Problems with Primary Support Group; V. Global Assessment of Functioning (GAF) = 65. The evaluation noted problematic family relationship dynamics, but there was no evidence of general judgment or reliability concerns.

The Role of the AMPD with Mr. Smith

One year later, the federal agency requested a second psychological review of Mr. Smith's case. This was occasioned by their receipt of a forensic psychiatric assessment which offered different conclusions. The human resources (HR) and Occupational Health Services (OHS) departments of his employer (the defense contractor) had requested an independent fitness for duty evaluation of Mr. Smith. A forensic psychiatrist stated (verbatim) Mr. Smith demonstrated I. Narcissistic personality disorder (NPD), obsessive personality traits (no impairment), alcohol-related disorder not otherwise specified (no impairment), and R/O cognitive impairment; II No diagnosis; III. Pain post-carpel tunnel surgery; IV. Moderate; V. GAF = 76. Interestingly, the psychiatric assessment was made within the DSM-IV-TR (APA, 2000) multi-axial format, yet the diagnosis of NPD was listed on Axis I, and Axis II was given as "no diagnosis." These procedural inconsistencies were noted in the response to the referral source. With these diagnoses, the psychiatrist opined there were serious concerns about fitness for duty in a safety and security-sensitive job.

The federal agency then wondered if the psychiatric assessment results would alter the conclusions of the previous psychological evaluation. In responding to this request, the 32-page psychiatric report and updated HR information and other collateral information were reviewed. This resulted in the opinion that the original psychological evaluation conclusions did not require altering.

It was noted that, subsequent to the original psychological evaluation, Mr. Smith received continued scrutiny from various departments of his employer. He apparently became increasingly defensive and attributed ongoing employment review to "racism."

Several lines of evidence supported the conclusions of the original evaluation results. There was no previous or new evidence of alcohol disorder. The contradiction between the psychiatric diagnosis of alcohol-related disorder and "no impairment" also was pointed out in the response to the referring source. Most importantly, systematic analysis of personality disorder (PD) from the DSM-IV-TR/DSM-5 (APA, 2000; 2013), and explicit argument based on the AMPD, failed to support a diagnosis of PD or impairment in judgment or reliability. This reasoning is described below.

1. Criterion A of the general criteria for PD involves an enduring pattern of maladaptive experience or behavior that deviates markedly from the individual's culture. Specifically, PDs "...should not be confused with

problems associated with…expression or habits, customs, or religious or political values professed by the individual's culture of origin" (p. 648; APA, 2013). Mr. Smith was an African-American man who became increasingly defensive and sensitive to racial issues since the domestic assault charge and ongoing security and employer reviews. Mr. Smith reported childhood experiences of racial prejudice and an idealized grandfather who was prominent in regional civil rights demonstrations in the 1960s. Race and prejudice were personal family themes, and having become entangled in allegations, evaluations, and proceedings of external systems of authority (e.g., legal, security clearance, employment HR matters, etc.), Mr. Smith (not unexpectedly) had become sensitized to perceptions of harmful intent by authorities. Furthermore, the psychiatric evaluation made extensive note of Mr. Smith's defensiveness and external attributions. Epidemiological research shows increased prevalence of NPD in African-Americans (Stinson et al., 2008). African-Americans socio-culturally value expressions of "specialness" or "importance" (Komarraju & Cokley, 2008) and generally report higher levels of "self-esteem" (Zeigler-Hill & Wallace, 2011). Iwamasa, Larrabee, and Merritt (2000) demonstrated that PD criteria may be liable to differential attribution based on racial and ethnic factors (e.g., with paranoid and antisocial traits more often attributed to African-Americans). Garb (1997) summarized issues of race and ethnicity in relation to foibles of clinical judgment, and T. N. Brown (2003) noted the relevance of sociological forces in mental health attributions with respect to race and ethnicity. A further caveat with respect to psychological or psychiatric indicators and race is illustrated in the results of Monnot, Quirk, Hoerger, and Brewer (2009). They found that most Minnesota Multiphasic Personality Inventory (second edition [MMPI-2]; Hathaway, McKinley, Butcher, Dahlstrom, Graham, & Tellegen, 1989) scales were higher (in some cases, significantly higher with $T > 5$ points) for African-Americans compared to Caucasians in a clinical sample.

Based on this research base and clinical reasoning, it was concluded that Mr. Smith's personal and family experiences of racial sensitivity and the situational context of increasing scrutiny by external authorities did not constitute sufficient evidence of diagnostic criteria for NPD. Mr. Smith's sensitivity in this domain was noted, but not considered defining of PD.

2. Criterion A and D for PD requires evidence of enduring and inflexible symptoms across a wide range of situations. There was no evidence of significant NPD symptoms outside of the timeframe of recent legal, security, and employment concerns, which were interpreted as producing a sense of self-esteem injury on a situational basis.
3. Criterion C refers to symptoms that cause significant impairment or distress. It was noted that the psychiatric assessment of GAF was 76,

which implies "transient and expectable reactions to psychosocial stressors" (DSM-IV-TR, APA, 2000; p. 34). The previous psychological evaluation had rated a GAF of 65. Neither of these estimates of GAF supports the diagnosis of PD.

4. Finally, the AMPD Criterion A and B were invoked. The LPFS was rated based on the complete history and results of the two independent mental health evaluations. Mr. Smith was rated with "moderate" impairment (2) in the self-domain of Identity, and "some impairment" (1) in the self-domain of Self-Direction and interpersonal domains of Empathy and Intimacy. From these ratings, his LPFS was rated as (1), "some impairment," a score that does not identify the presence of PD. Furthermore, Criterion B was reviewed in the service of comprehensiveness. The Personality Inventory for DSM-5-Informant Form (PID-5-IF; APA, 2013) was reviewed and the trait domain of Antagonism items produced a score of 1.3, also sub-threshold for the diagnosis of a pathological personality trait. It is relevant to note that Dowgwillo, Ménard, Krueger, and Pincus (2016) found that the AMPD trait domain of Disinhibition was uniquely associated with reports of IPV in males. Mr. Smith showed no recent or historical evidence of Disinhibition traits (i.e., irresponsibility, impulsivity, distractibility, risk taking, [lack of] rigid perfectionism).

Summary of the Forensic Use of the AMPD

Heilbrun (1992; 2001) and Lander and Heilbrun (2009) argue that forensic psychological assessment must satisfy the criterion of legal relevancy, which should be further supported through principles drawn from law, ethics, science, and professional practice. Psychological tests and assessment procedures can fulfill these desiderata in two ways, either through development and validation of a technique for a specific legal construct, or through assessment procedures that demonstrate conceptual linkage to a legal standard. Heilbrun (1992) suggests several ways in which this can be accomplished. These include being commercially available with documented psychometric properties (e.g., reliability), relevance can be argued with the support of published validity studies, administration of the assessment occurs in a standardized way, and effects of response style are considered. Similarly, in addressing psycho-legal constructs, Salekin (2015) argues forensic evaluation of juveniles, for example, profitably makes use of personality concepts (e.g., temperament, traits) and personality assessment, which can be integrated with diagnoses conforming to official diagnostic nosologies.

Hopwood and Sellbom (2013) forcefully argue that the AMPD more than satisfies relevancy standards. This flows from numerous points. Its burgeoning conceptual and empirical base in the scientific literature, the consensus that traditional categorical PD diagnosis is problematic, and growing acceptance of the merits of PD dimensionalization (Bernstein, Iscan, & Maser, 2007; Rodriguez-Seijas, Eaton, & Krueger, 2015). Furthermore, the AMPD is enjoying rapidly expanding use and applicability (Krueger, Hopwood, Wright, & Markon, 2014) and clinical utility (Morey, Skodol, & Oldham, 2014; Waugh et al., 2017). Measures of the AMPD, whether clinical ratings or with psychometric procedures, demonstrate acceptable to strong psychometric performance which typically exceeds categorical PD diagnoses (Samuel, 2015), and the AMPD trait dimensions have been demonstrated to be temporally stable in PD individuals (Wright, Calabrese, et al., 2015). The AMPD is an official psychiatric nosology (DSM-5, Section III; APA, 2013) and operationalizes important and reasonably comprehensive psychological dimensions of personality functioning. The reliability and validity of traditional forensic assessment instruments are often called into question, with studies finding that the psychometrics reported in user manuals are not consistent with what is found in field studies (Edens & Boccaccini, 2017). Thus, in forensic applications where personality functioning and sound psychometric properties are issues of concern, the AMPD is poised to offer an empirically supported diagnostic framework. Employing concepts of severity of dysfunction and psychological traits, it is an understandable system. Thus, it is relatively easy to explain in written and oral testimony.

It is also important to highlight that the AMPD should be explored further within forensic research contexts. For example, a starting point could consist of the AMPD's ability to predict future violent behavior, which is a significant aspect of forensic assessment. AMPD "profiles" of defendants who are found not competent to proceed with trial or not guilty by reason of insanity could also be helpful in understanding the offender from a dimensional, rather than categorical, personality perspective. The AMPD could also be explored in relation to measures of effort or feigning, which would benefit both criminal and civil matters. Importantly, the forensic use of the AMPD has been supported in recent case law (State of NY vs. Nicholas, 2017), and the above case example illustrates one of the many potential forensic applications of the AMPD. As Hopwood and Sellbom (2013) state, the AMPD is ready for "prime time."

Note

1 The authors thank Dr. Katherine R. Smith, forensic psychologist, for helpful comments on this chapter.

10 Concluding Comments

The Value of AMPD Diagnosis

Nicole M. Cain

In his forward for this volume, Roger Blashfield notes that diagnosis is simple; yet, any topic that is simple, when analyzed carefully, becomes increasingly complex. Personality disorder (PD) diagnosis is beautifully captured by this dialectic—simple yet incredibly complex. A PD diagnosis conveys meaning often through the use of a simple label yet the implications of the label are far reaching and the information needed is often complex and at times contradictory. As articulated throughout this book, the Alternative Model for Personality Disorders (AMPD) is well suited to adequately capture both the simplicity and intricacy of PD diagnosis through its integration of multiple paradigms and perspectives.

One of the hallmark strengths of the AMPD is that Criterion A and B are derived from different clinical and empirical traditions in personality science. For example, Bender, Morey, and Skodol (2011) drew on concepts and methods from psychodynamic, attachment, and social-cognitive perspectives to formulate the Level of Personality Functioning Scale (LPFS) of Criterion A (e.g., Social Cognitions and Object Relations Scale [SCORS; Hilsenroth, Stein, & Pinsker, 2007]; Reflective Functioning Scale [RFS; Fonagy et al., 1998]; Object Relations Inventory [ORI; Bers, Blatt, Sayward, & Johnston, 1993]), while Criterion B derives from the general lexical trait tradition in personality science (e.g., Allport & Odbert, 1936; Goldberg, 1993; McCrae & Costa, 1987) and organizes the multivariate space of pathological personality traits into a set of five correlated dimensions (Krueger & Markon, 2014). Chapter 2 and Chapter 3 of this book provide excellent overviews of the rich theoretical and empirical underpinnings of Criterion A and B respectively, while Chapter 4 examines the current research and the instruments of the AMPD. Chapter 3 in particular highlights the connection between the trait-facets of Criterion B and some biological models of PD.

Importantly, one of the central arguments of this book is that the value of the full AMPD model is its theoretical pluralism. In Chapter 1, Waugh noted that the AMPD could be illustrated via Wiggins' (2003) five paradigms of personality assessment (psychodynamic, personological, interpersonal, multivariate, and empirical). Wiggins' seminal book on personality assessment articulated that these five paradigms differ in their focus, scope, and preferred assessment instruments (Waugh et al., 2017; see Chapter 1 for a full review of the paradigms). In a recent paper, Waugh and colleagues (2017) argued that the psychodynamic, interpersonal, and personological paradigms of Wiggins (2003) are largely embedded within Criterion A, given the emphasis of these paradigms on self and other boundaries, the dynamics of self-esteem regulation, and interpersonal relatedness. The authors further argued that Criterion B largely reflects Wiggins' (2003) multivariate, empirical, and interpersonal paradigms, given that the trait facets are derived from models of normal and abnormal personality data.

Waugh and colleagues' (2017) assertions about the relationship between the AMPD and the Wiggins (2003) paradigms of personality assessment were recently empirically supported. Mulay and colleagues (in press, 2018) investigated the AMPD for degree of representation of the five paradigms by asking nine knowledgeable raters to evaluate each element of the AMPD (the 60 items of the LPFS and the 25 Criterion B trait-facets). Rater agreement was strong and results showed that Criterion A possesses a greater psychodynamic and personological paradigm representation while Criterion B showed a predominance of the multivariate and empirical paradigms. Interestingly, results demonstrated that the interpersonal paradigm did not differ between Criterion A and B, suggesting that although Criterion A and B emphasize different paradigms, the interpersonal paradigm can be found throughout the AMPD, thus highlighting the degree to which PD is fundamentally interpersonal (Hopwood, Wright, Ansell, et al., 2013). Waugh and colleagues (2017) note that these results suggest that the AMPD is both traditional and innovative, in that it benefits from the extensive knowledge base of each of these generative paradigms while also pushing PD diagnosis beyond traditional categorical models.

In fact, one of the key contributions of the AMPD is that it necessarily re-introduces theory into PD diagnosis. In Chapter 1, Waugh provides a comprehensive examination of how diagnosis has evolved throughout the various DSM iterations, reminding us that the DSM is in fact a medical model, which may have points of friction with the more subjective and complex nature of PDs. Waugh notes that early versions of the DSM reflected the growing influence of the psychodynamic paradigm and focus on neurosis, which meant that most diagnoses contained elements of personality dynamics. However, with the dawn of DSM-III, we saw the rise of organic cause, natural course, and progression of disease as important aspects of diagnosis, along with a minimization of theory in order to improve diagnostic reliability (likely to the detriment of diagnostic validity).

As various proposals emerged for DSM-5, researchers and clinicians emphasized the importance of using empirical evidence from multiple perspectives to shape the future of PD diagnosis. Pincus (2005) noted, "classification of personality disorders in the post DSM-III/IV era will require greater coordination of definitional theories and systems for describing variation in expression of personality pathology" (p. 287). In other words, the diagnostic nosology for PD should not be atheoretical. Through its integration of disparate views from various traditions in personality science, the AMPD offers a pluralistic lens through which to understand the nuance of personality pathology.

When viewed from this perspective, Waugh and colleagues (2017) argued that Criterion A of the AMPD may be regarded as assessing the *genus* of personality pathology (Pincus, 2011), what PD's have in common that distinguishes them from healthy personality and other forms of psychopathology, while Criterion B may be regarded as the *species* of PD (Pincus, 2011) where particular variations of PD are profiled through the assessment of maladaptive trait dimensions. In this way, the AMPD addresses many of the problems that have plagued PD diagnosis in previous editions of the DSM, such as extensive comorbidity, limited convergent validity, heterogeneity within categories, arbitrary diagnostic thresholds, and lack of treatment implications (Waugh et al., 2017; Widiger & Trull, 2007).

By articulating both the genus and species of PD, another key contribution of the AMPD is that it allows for the assessment of personality pathology outside of the existing categories of DSM-IV/DSM-5 Section II. For example, researchers and clinicians have noted that the criteria for narcissistic personality disorder (NPD) in DSM-IV/DSM-5 Section II are overly narrow and do not sufficiently cover the breadth of personality impairments associated with pathological narcissism (Miller, Widiger, & Campbell, 2010; Pincus, 2011; Ronningstam, 2009). These impairments can be summarized as manifesting in two broad phenotypic expressions referred to as narcissistic grandiosity and narcissistic vulnerability (Cain, Pincus, & Ansell, 2008). Narcissistic grandiosity reflects maladaptive and exploitative self-enhancement strategies, a grandiose self-image, entitled expectations, and self-serving beliefs, while narcissistic vulnerability reflects self and emotional dysregulation in response to disappointed expectations and self-enhancement failures. Narcissistic grandiosity is well represented within the criteria for the categorical NPD diagnosis, while narcissistic vulnerability has been relatively neglected by DSM NPD conceptualizations (Cain et al., 2008).

However, the AMPD successfully broadens the construct of NPD in ways that improve its fidelity with the actual clinical presentation of pathological narcissism by emphasizing self and interpersonal impairments. For example, Criterion A in the AMPD allows for an NPD diagnosis when identity impairment includes both inflated and *deflated* self-appraisals and emotion regulation that mirrors fluctuations in self-esteem. Self-direction impairment for NPD includes goal setting based on gaining approval from others as well as personal standards that are either unreasonably too high or *too low* based on a sense of entitlement. Empathy impairment involves deficits in the ability to recognize or identify with the feelings and needs of others while intimacy impairment describes relationships that are largely superficial and exist to serve self-esteem regulation. For Criterion B, the AMPD explicitly specifies that grandiosity may be overt or *covert* along with elevated attention seeking (Kealy & Rasmussen, 2012; Pincus, Cain, & Wright, 2014; Pincus, Dowgwillo, & Greenberg, 2016; Skodol, Morey, Bender, & Oldham, 2015).

It is unsurprising that much of the recent literature illustrating clinical applications of the AMPD typically include at least one NPD case study (Bach, Markon, Simonsen, & Krueger, 2015; Caligor, Levy, & Yeomans, 2015; Morey & Stagner, 2012; Pincus et al., 2016; Schmeck, Schlüter-Müller, Foelsch, & Doering, 2013; Skodol et al., 2015; Waugh et al., 2017). Indeed, Chapter 6 of this book discusses two clinical cases with elevated narcissistic features, Madeline and Mr. Z. The inclusion of Madeline in Chapter 6 makes perfect sense given the central thesis of this book is to show that multiple paradigms exist within the AMPD. Madeline is a fairly well-known case for those familiar with the Wiggins (2003) book. Experts representing each of the five personality assessment paradigms assessed her for the Wiggins book. Hopwood and Waugh subsequently provided Madeline's history and snippets of her testing data to 25 independent raters who evaluated her AMPD profile for this book (see Chapter 6 for the information provided to raters as well as Madeline's AMPD profile).

Interestingly, Madeline's AMPD profile exhibits both function and dysfunction, especially with regard to Criterion A. For example, she was rated as clinically elevated for intimacy problems indicating her eligibility for a PD diagnosis. When she was initially assessed for the Wiggins book, Madeline reported that she was in a satisfying romantic relationship; however, her partner would leave her soon after the assessments ended. Thus, the AMPD raters were correct in noting the presence of intimacy impairment even though this core deficit was seemingly out of Madeline's conscious awareness at the time of her assessment. Madeline was also rated as subthreshold for problems with empathy with a lower but still clinically meaningful score for identity impairment. Her score on empathy reflects her often contradictory presentation—Madeline was described as brash, self-centered, and willing to do anything to get ahead, yet she also reported a deep devotion to advocating for the underprivileged in her community. It may be that her lack of empathy in her personal relationships was perhaps balanced by her concern for her community at large. Madeline's self-direction score was within normal limits, suggesting an area of relative strength for her and is in line with her reported success at work. Madeline's pattern of results for Criterion A demonstrates the importance of considering the dynamics of an individual's life and context when interpreting an AMPD profile. Taking into consideration important contextual information as part of the diagnostic process is a significant strength of the AMPD. Criterion A in particular allows for a fuller evaluation of self and interpersonal functioning, embraces the often contradictory information provided by patients with personality pathology, and captures the complexity of human life.

With regard to Criterion B, Madeline's only clinical elevation was attention seeking, though she was also elevated on grandiosity. She was subthreshold for risk taking and eccentricity. These traits are very consistent with her presentation in the Wiggins book and the testing data provided to raters. Madeline was described as the life of the party, someone who disavowed conventional norms and who liked to be the center of attention, but who could also be abrasive and difficult to be around. Again, we can see how the AMPD allows for complexity in diagnosis. While Madeline would likely meet criteria for NPD (using a categorical diagnosis and the AMPD), it is her full AMPD profile that would provide possible targets for treatment. Specifically, a clinician would likely approach their work with Madeline focused on her deficits in intimacy coupled with her high levels of attention seeking, while also appreciating her relative strength in self-direction.

As a contrast to Madeline's overt grandiosity and attention seeking, Hopwood and Waugh next report on the case of Mr. Z, a patient with more covert narcissistic personality features described by Heinz Kohut (1979). Hopwood and Waugh used the same 25 independent raters to evaluate Mr. Z's AMPD profile, providing them with a brief case vignette comprised of details from Kohut's depiction of Mr. Z's history, presentation, and behavior from the early phase of his psychoanalysis. In the vignette, Mr. Z is described as being soft-spoken with fragile self-esteem, feelings of shame, and social isolation. At the same time, he also exhibits anger and is dismissive of his therapist's interpretations (see Chapter 6 for the information provided to raters and Mr. Z's AMPD profile).

Results showed that Mr. Z was clinically elevated for identity and intimacy problems on Criterion A. His ratings for self-direction and empathy were subthreshold, though very close to clinical impairment, suggesting that overall Mr. Z had moderate to severe personality dysfunction. Mr. Z's Criterion B ratings were elevated for anxiousness, depressivity, intimacy avoidance, and withdrawal. Hopwood and Waugh note that Mr. Z's trait-facet elevations resemble a typical internalizing, withdrawn, depressed character. However, it is important to also consider his subthreshold ratings on the trait-facets of emotional lability, grandiosity, impulsivity, and separation insecurity, which complicate his clinical picture. Mr. Z's case exemplifies how the AMPD can capture both the overt clinical presentation (e.g., his internalizing pathology) as well as his more covert symptoms (e.g., his grandiosity, lability, and impulsivity). In fact, Mr. Z's AMPD profile is consistent with narcissistic vulnerability (Pincus, Cain, et al., 2014). Importantly, if we were to consider Mr. Z using the lens of DSM-IV/DSM-5 Section II only, his diagnosis may have been PD not otherwise specified or perhaps avoidant personality disorder, which would miss the important clinical information that was readily identified with the AMPD. While Madeline would meet criteria for DSM NPD, Mr. Z's narcissistic vulnerability would have been largely ignored without an assessment of the full range of his personality pathology using the AMPD.

Both of these case examples demonstrate how the AMPD provides substantially more information than categorical diagnoses alone, with essentially the same amount of effort in data gathering. In fact, the numerous clinical and literary cases sprinkled throughout this book highlight another key contribution of the AMPD—its clinical utility (see Chapter 5 for a discussion of the clinical utility of the AMPD). Clinical utility emphasizes the practical aspects of a diagnostic system, such as the extent to which it is easy to use, facilitates communication, and enhances treatment (Mullins-Sweatt, Lengel, & DeShong, 2016; Mullins-Sweatt & Widiger, 2009). The 25 independent raters who evaluated Madeline and Mr. Z (as well as the case of Jeffrey Dahmer—see Chapter 6) provide excellent evidence for how easy the AMPD is to use and implement. The raters included 12 clinicians and 13 academic clinical psychologists (theoretical orientations included psychodynamic, interpersonal, cognitive-behavioral, and integrative), with a median of 20 years of clinical experience. Raters were not formally trained, they were simply asked to provide an AMPD diagnosis for the case and to refer to DSM-5 Section III as needed. They varied from very little to extensive familiarity with the AMPD, yet inter-rater reliability was excellent in applying the AMPD to the cases in Chapter 6. This high level of inter-rater reliability, despite varying backgrounds, shows that the AMPD can be easily learned and applied to clinical material. This suggests that the transition to the AMPD may not be all that difficult for most clinicians due to its pantheoretical nature. While some terms may seem new within the AMPD, the underlying constructs are familiar to most clinicians of diverse theoretical backgrounds thus enhancing its clinical utility. Importantly, research has shown that clinicians generally evaluate the ease of use and clinical utility of the AMPD quite favorably (Garcia et al., in press, 2018; Morey, Skodol, & Oldham, 2014).

One final area where the AMPD has the potential to have a significant contribution is treatment planning. The DSM has struggled to provide a clear link between diagnosis and treatment recommendations, limiting its clinical utility as a diagnostic manual (Mullins-Sweatt et al., 2016). The pantheoretical and transdiagnostic nature of the AMPD may facilitate treatment planning across different theoretical models and disorders. We can clearly see the treatment implications of the AMPD through the many case examples woven throughout this book, and specifically in Chapter 5, which discusses clinical utility, Chapter 8, which focuses explicitly on treatment planning with two cases at a training clinic, and Chapter 9, which provides one of the first forensic context discussions of the model.

Returning briefly to the case of Mr. Z in Chapter 6, Hopwood and Waugh offer their thoughts on how his AMPD profile generates clinical hypotheses and treatment goals from both a psychodynamic and behavioral perspective. For example, when thinking more psychodynamically, they note that Mr. Z's internalizing pathology (e.g., anxiousness, depressivity, withdrawal) combined with his intermittent externalizing pathology (e.g., lability, impulsivity, grandiosity) might suggest a dynamic in which his withdrawn negative affect may be punctuated by angry affective outbursts especially when faced with threats to identity and/or intimacy. The goal of a psychodynamic treatment with Mr. Z would likely involve helping him to better mentalize the therapeutic relationship, as well as tolerate questions about his identity. This parallels Kohut's (1979) self-psychology approach to the treatment of Mr. Z. In contrast, from a behavioral point of view, Hopwood and Waugh note that the most prominent areas of Mr. Z's treatment would likely be his negative affect and detachment. They argue that a behavioral therapist might consider behavior activation, skills training, and cognitive restructuring with Mr. Z and that it is likely that a dialectical stance would be most appropriate, in which acceptance and change are balanced.

While it is helpful to consider how clinicians from different theoretical orientations may approach the same case using the information from an AMPD profile, the AMPD is also consistent with many of the tenets of psychotherapy integration as well. For example, Clarkin, Cain, and Livesley (2015) described an integrated modular approach to the treatment of personality pathology that emphasizes: (1) the individuality of the patient, not the category of the disorder; (2) the domains of dysfunction in the individual patient; (3) the therapeutic use of modules of intervention from existing clinical approaches, especially those that have been empirically investigated; and (4) the construction of a smooth fabric of intervention in the context of a developing alliance between therapist and patient. The AMPD lends itself nicely to thinking about treatment from an integrated modular perspective. For example, as we saw in Madeline's case, her AMPD profile provided us with her relative strengths and her relative impairments in self and other functioning, thus highlighting her individuality as a patient. With Mr. Z, we saw his complex domains of dysfunction—anxiety, depressivity, and detachment coupled with grandiosity, impulsivity, and lability—which may not have been fully captured if we had conceptualized his case using only a categorical model of personality pathology. Moving from diagnosis to treatment, Clarkin and colleagues delineate specific strategies and tactics to address the severity of dysfunction, or Criterion A, and the specific areas of dysfunction, or Criterion B. As clinicians from diverse theoretical backgrounds begin to use the AMPD for treatment planning, more research will be needed to understand how the AMPD can be used to identify the specific targets for treatment. Specifically, research should focus on the clinical implications of understanding the genus and species (Criterion A and B, respectively) of personality pathology and how an integrated modular approach can be used to target both severity of impairment and the specific domains of dysfunction.

In conclusion, Roger Blashfield opened this book by offering us two important lessons—that understanding psychopathology requires the blending of multiple paradigms *and* knowledge from many domains. This book has shown that the AMPD has embraced these two lessons through its integration of multiple theories and traditions within personality science. The innovation of the AMPD is that it pushes clinicians beyond a simple categorical label and allows us to understand, diagnose, and treat the complexity and nuance of personality pathology. The AMPD adequately addresses many of the limitations inherent in categorical PD diagnosis. The theory and research reviewed as well as the illuminating clinical and literary examples that brought the AMPD to life in this book suggest that the Fourth Era of our diagnostic nomenclature is alive and well, and in fact, thriving. While the Fourth Era will not be the last word in PD diagnosis, it has moved us many steps forward.

References

Achenbach, T. M. (1966). The classification of children's psychiatric symptoms: A factor-analytic study. *Psychological Monographs: General and Applied*, 80, 1–37.

Achenbach, T. M., & Edelbrock, C. S. (1978). The classification of child psychopathology: A review and analysis of empirical efforts. *Psychological Bulletin*, 85, 1275–1301. doi:10.1037/0033-2909.85.6

Achenbach, T. M., Krukowski, R. A., Dumenci, L., & Ivanova, M. Y. (2005). Assessment of adult psychopathology: Meta-analyses and implications of cross-informant correlations. *Psychological Bulletin*, 131, 361–382.

Acklin, M. W. (1992). Psychodiagnosis of personality structure: Psychotic personality organization. *Journal of Personality Assessment*, 58, 454–463.

Acklin, M. W. (1993). Psychodiagnosis of personality structure II: Borderline personality organization. *Journal of Personality Assessment*, 61, 329–341.

Adler, J. M. (2012). Living into the story: Agency and coherence in a longitudinal study of narrative identity development and mental health over the course of psychotherapy. *Journal of Personality and Social Psychology*, 102, 367–389. doi:10.1037/a0025289

Adler, J. M. (2013) Clients' and therapists' stories about psychotherapy. *Journal of Personality*, 81, 595–605.

Ahn, W. K., Flanagan, E. H., Marsh, J. K., & Sanislow, C. A. (2006). Beliefs about essences and the reality of mental disorders. *Psychological Science*, 17, 759–766.

Aiken, C. (1932). Silent snow, secret snow. *The Virginia Quarterly Review*, 8, 568.

Ainsworth, M. D., & Bell, S. M. (1970). Attachment, exploration, and separation: Illustrated by the behavior of one-year-olds in a strange situation. *Child Development*, 41, 49–67. doi:10.2307/1127388

Ainsworth, M. D. S., Blehar, M. C., Waters, E., & Wall, S. (1978/2014). *Patterns of attachment: A psychological study of the strange situation*. Abingdon, UK: Psychology Press.

Ainsworth, M. D. S., Blehar, M. C., Waters, E., & Wall, S. (2015). *Patterns of attachment: A psychological study of the strange situation*. Abingdon, UK: Psychology Press.

Akhtar, S., & Samuel, S. (1996). The concept of identity: Developmental origins, phenomenology, clinical relevance, and measurement. *Harvard Review of Psychiatry*, 3, 254–267.

Al-Dajani, N., Gralnick, T. M., & Bagby, R. M. (2016). A psychometric review of the Personality Inventory for DSM–5 (PID–5): Current status and future directions. *Journal of Personality Assessment*, 98, 62–81.

Alden, L. E., & Bieling, P. J. (1996). Interpersonal convergence of personality constructs in dynamic and cognitive models of depression. *Journal of Research in Personality*, 30, 60–75. doi:10.1006/jrpe.1996.0004

Alden, L. E., Wiggins, J. S., & Pincus, A. L. (1990). Construction of circumplex scales for the Inventory of Interpersonal Problems. *Journal of Personality Assessment*, 55, 521–536.

Alexander, I. E. (1990). *Personology: Method and content in personality assessment and psychobiography.* Durham, NC: Duke University Press.

Allik, J., Realo, A., Mottus, R., Pullmann, H., Trifonova, A., McCrae, R. R., Yurina, A. A., Shebanets, E. Y., Fadina, A. G., Tikhonova, E. V., Troitskaya, I. Y., Fatyhova, R. M., Petrova, I. F., Tudupova, T. T., Tsiring, D. A., Panfilov, A. N., L'dokova, G. M., Aristova, I. L., Mescheryakov, B. G., Zorina, J., Yuschenkova, D. V., Fotekova, T. A., Osmina, E. V., Vavilkina, N. G., Skhorohodova, N. Y., Zernova, T. I., Dostovalov, S. G., Kadykova, S. A., Korepanova, I. A., Saharova, A., Naumov, N. D., Snegireva, T. V., Kuznetsov, I. Y., Kuznetsova, S. A., Rubtsova, M. O., Filatova, A. F., Nechaeva, T. M., Borisova, S. N., Postnikova, M. I., Gluhanyuk, N. S., Dyachenko, E. V., Fomina, N. A., Eromasova, A. A., Myshkina, S. V., Rulina, T. K., Knyazev, G. G., Ryanichenko, T. I., Demidova, I. F., Uvarov, E. A., Lopukhova, O. G., Vasyagina, N. N., Leonenko, N. O., Arnin, E. I., Lyapina, A. A., Dulina, N. V., Poyarova, T. A., Gaidar, K. M., Baranov, A. A., Kozhevnikova, O. V., Kalinichenko, O. V., Korneeva, E. E. (2011). Personality profiles and the "Russian soul": Literary and scholarly views evaluated. *Journal of Cross-Cultural Psychology*, 42, 372–389.

Allison, J., Blatt, S., & Zimet, C. N. (1968). *The interpretation of psychological tests.* New York: Hemisphere Publishing Corp/Harper & Row Publishers.

Allport, G. W., & Odbert, H. S. (1936). Trait-names: A psycho-lexical study. *Psychological Monographs*, 47, 1–171.

American Law Institute (1985). *Model penal code: Official draft and explanatory notes. Complete text of model penal code as adopted at the 1962 annual meeting of the American Law Institute at Washington, DC, May 24, 1962*. Philadelphia, PA: The Institute.

American Psychiatric Association (1952). *Diagnostic and statistical manual of mental disorders* (1st ed.). Washington, DC: APA.

American Psychiatric Association (1968). *Diagnostic and statistical manual of mental disorders* (2nd ed.). Washington, DC: APA.

American Psychiatric Association. (1980). *Diagnostic and statistical manual of mental disorders* (3rd ed.). Washington, DC: APA.

American Psychiatric Association (1994). *Diagnostic and statistical manual of mental disorders* (4th ed.). Washington, DC: APA.

American Psychiatric Association (2000). *Diagnostic and statistical manual of mental disorders,* (4th ed., text revision). Washington, DC: APA.

American Psychiatric Association (2013). *Diagnostic and statistical manual of mental disorders* (5th ed.). Washington, DC: APA.

Anderson, J. L., & Sellbom, M. (2015). Construct validity of the DSM–5 Section III personality trait profile for borderline personality disorder. *Journal of Personality Assessment*, 97, 478–486.

Anderson, J. L., & Sellbom, M. (2018). Evaluating the DSM–5 Section III personality disorder impairment criteria. *Personality Disorders: Theory, Research, and Treatment*, 9, 51–61.

Anderson, J. L., Sellbom, M., Ayearst, L., Quilty, L. C., Chmielewski, M., & Bagby, R. (2015). Associations between DSM-5 Section III personality traits and the Minnesota Multiphasic Personality Inventory 2-Restructured Form (MMPI-2-RF) scales in a psychiatric patient sample. *Psychological Assessment*, 27, 801–815.

Anderson, J. L., Sellbom, M., Bagby, R. M., Quilty, L. C., Veltri, C. O., Markon, K. E., & Krueger, R. F. (2013). On the convergence between PSY-5 domains and PID-5 domains and facets: Implications for assessment of DSM-5 personality traits. *Assessment*, 20, 286–294.

Anderson, J. L., Sellbom, M., Wygant, D. B., Salekin, R. T., & Krueger, R. F. (2014). Examining the associations between DSM-5 Section III antisocial personality disorder traits and psychopathy in community and university samples. *Journal of Personality Disorders*, 28, 675–697.

Andreasen, N. C. (2006). DSM and the death of phenomenology in America: An example of unintended consequences. *Schizophrenia Bulletin*, 33, 108–112.

Andrews, G., Goldberg, D. P., Krueger, R. F., Carpenter, W. J., Hyman, S. E., Sachdev, P., & Pine, D. S. (2009). Exploring the feasibility of a meta-structure for DSM-V and ICD-11: Could it improve utility and validity? *Psychological Medicine*, 39, 1993–2000.

Ashton, M. C. & Lee, K. (2007). Empirical, theoretical, and practical advantages of the HEXACO model of personality structure. *Personality and Social Psychology Review*, 11, 150–166.

Ashton, M. C., Lee, K., de Vries, R. E., Hendrickse, J., & Born, M. P. (2012). The maladaptive personality traits of the Personality Inventory for DSM-5 (PID-5) in relation to the HEXACO personality factors and schizotypy/dissociation. *Journal of Personality Disorders*, 26, 641–659.

Azim, H. F., Piper, W. E., Segal, P. M., Nixon, G. W., & Duncan, S. C. (1991). The quality of object relations scale. *Bulletin of the Menninger Clinic*, 55, 323–343.

Babor, T. F., Higgins-Biddle, J. C., Saunders, J. B., & Montiero, M. G. (2001). *The Alcohol Use Disorders Identification Test: Guidelines of use in primary care* (2nd ed). Geneva, Switzerland: World Health Organization.

Bach, B., Anderson, J., & Simonsen, E. (2017). Continuity between interview-rated personality disorders and self-reported DSM–5 traits in a Danish psychiatric sample. *Personality Disorders: Theory, Research, and Treatment*, 8, 261–267.

Bach, B., & Hutsebaut, J. (2018). Level of Personality Functioning Scale–Brief Form 2.0: Utility in capturing personality problems in psychiatric outpatients and incarcerated addicts. *Journal of Personality Assessment*, 1, 1–11.

Bach, B., Lee, C., Mortensen, E. L., & Simonsen, E. (2016). How do DSM-5 personality traits align with schema therapy constructs? *Journal of Personality Disorders*, 30, 502–529.

Bach, B., Maples-Keller, J. L., Bo, S., & Simonsen, E. (2016). The alternative DSM-5 personality disorder traits criterion: A comparative examination of three self-report forms in a Danish population. *Personality Disorders: Theory, Research, and Treatment*, 7, 124–135.

Bach, B., Markon, K., Simonsen, E., & Krueger, R. F. (2015). Clinical utility of the DSM-5 alternative model of personality disorders: Six cases from practice. *Journal of Psychiatric Practice*, 21, 3–25.

Bach, B., & Sellbom, M. (2016). Continuity between DSM-5 categorical criteria and traits criteria for borderline personality disorder. *The Canadian Journal of Psychiatry*, 61, 489–494.

Bach, B., Sellbom, M., Bo, S., & Simonsen, E. (2016). Utility of DSM-5 Section III personality traits in differentiating borderline personality disorder from comparison groups. *European Psychiatry*, 37, 22–27.

Bach, B., Sellbom, M., Kongerslev, M., Simonsen, E., Krueger, R. F., & Mulder, R. (2017). Deriving ICD-11 personality disorder domains from DSM-5 traits: Initial attempt to harmonize two diagnostic systems. *Acta Psychiatrica Scandinavica*, 136, 108–117.

Bach, B., Sellbom, M., & Simonsen, E. (2018). Personality inventory for DSM-5 (PID-5) in clinical versus nonclinical individuals: Generalizability of psychometric features. *Assessment*, 25, 815–825.

Bagby, R. M., Parker, J. A., Joffe, R. T., & Buis, T. (1994). Reconstruction and validation of the Depressive Experiences Questionnaire. *Assessment*, 1, 59–68. doi:10.1177/107319119400100109

Bagby, R. M., & Sellbom, M. (2018). The validity and clinical utility of the Personality Inventory for DSM–5 Response Inconsistency Scale. *Journal of Personality Assessment*, 100, 398–405.

Bagby, R. M., & Widiger, T. A. (2018). Five Factor Model personality disorder scales: An introduction to a special section on assessment of maladaptive variants of the five factor model. *Psychological Assessment*, 30, 1–9.

Bakermans-Kranenburg, M. J., & van IJzendoorn, M. H. (2009). The first 10,000 adult attachment interviews: Distributions of adult attachment representations in clinical and non-clinical groups. *Attachment & Human Development*, 11, 223–263.

Balint, M. (1968). *The basic fault*. London, UK: Tavistock Publications..

Ban, T. A. (2007). Fifty years chlorpromazine: A historical perspective. *Neuropsychiatric Disease and Treatment*, 3, 495–500.

Bandura, A. (1989). Human agency in social cognitive theory. *American Psychologist*, 44, 1175–1184.

Barlow, D. H., Allen, L. B., & Choate, M. L. (2004). Toward a unified treatment for emotional disorders. *Behavior Therapy*, 35, 205–230.

Barlow, D. H., Farchione, T. J., Sauer-Zavala, S., Latin, H. M., Ellard, K. K., Bullis, J. R., Bentley, K. H., Boettcher, H. T., & Cassiello-Robbins, C. (2017). *Unified protocol for transdiagnostic treatment of emotional disorders: Therapist guide*. Oxford, UK: Oxford University Press.

Baron-Cohen, S., Leslie, A. M., & Frith, U. (1985). Does the autistic child have a "theory of mind"? *Cognition*, 21, 37–46.

Baron-Cohen, S., Wheelwright, S., Hill, J., Raste, Y., & Plumb, I. (2001). The 'Reading the mind in the eyes' Test revised version: A study with normal adults, and adults with Asperger syndrome or high-functioning autism. *Journal of Child Psychology and Psychiatry*, 42, 241–251.

Baron-Cohen, S., Wheelwright, S., Skinner, R., Martin, J., & Clubley, E. (2001). The autism-spectrum quotient (AQ): Evidence from asperger syndrome/high-functioning autism, males and females, scientists and mathematicians. *Journal of Autism and Developmental Disorders*, 31, 5–17.

Bartholomew, K., & Horowitz, L. M. (1991). Attachment styles among young adults: A test of a four- category model. *Journal of Personality and Social Psychology*, 61, 226–244.

Bastiaens, T., Claes, L., Smits, D., De Clercq, B., De Fruyt, F., Rossi, G. & De Hert, M. (2016). The construct validity of the Dutch Personality Inventory for DSM-5 personality disorders (PID-5) in a clinical sample. *Assessment*, 23, 42–51.

Bastiaens, T., Smits, D., De Hert, M., Vanwalleghem, D., & Claes, L. (2016). DSM-5 Section III personality traits and Section II personality disorders in a Flemish community sample. *Psychiatry Research*, 238, 290–298.

Bastiaansen, L., Hopwood, C. J., Van den Broeck, J., Rossi, G., Schotte, C., & De Fruyt, F. (2016). The twofold diagnosis of personality disorder: How do personality dysfunction and pathological traits increment each other at successive levels of the trait hierarchy? *Personality Disorders: Theory, Research, and Treatment*, 7, 280–292.

Bateman, A. W., & Fonagy, P. (2000). Effectiveness of psychotherapeutic treatment of personality disorder. *The British Journal of Psychiatry*, 177, 138–143.

Bateman, A.W., & Fonagy, P. (2004). *Psychotherapy for borderline personality disorder.* Oxford, UK: Oxford University Press.

Bateman, A.W., & Fonagy, P. (2006). *Mentalization-based treatment for borderline personality disorder: A practical guide.* Oxford, UK: Oxford University Press.

Bateman, A. W., Gunderson, J., & Mulder, R. (2015). Treatment of personality disorder. *The Lancet*, 385, 735–743.

Beach, F. A. (1950). The snark was a boojum. *American Psychologist*, 5, 115–124.

Beanland, V., Sellbom, M., & Johnson, A. K. (2014). Personality domains and traits that predict self-reported aberrant driving behaviours in a southeastern US university sample. *Accident Analysis & Prevention*, 72, 184–192.

Beck, A. T., Epstein, N., Harrison, R. P., & Emery, G. (1983). *Development of the Sociotropy-Autonomy Scale: A measure of personality factors in psychopathology.* Unpublished manuscript. Philadelphia, PA: University of Pennsylvania.

Beck, A. T., Freeman, A., & Davis, D. D. (Eds.). (2015). *Cognitive therapy of personality disorders* (3rd ed). New York, NY: Guilford Press.

Becker, E. (1973). *The denial of death.* New York, NY: Free Press.

Bender, D. S. (2005). The therapeutic alliance in the treatment of personality disorders. *Journal of Psychiatric Practice*, 11, 73–87. doi:10.1097/00131746-200503000-00002

Bender, D. S., Morey, L. C., & Skodol, A. E. (2011). Toward a model for assessing level of personality functioning in DSM–5, part I: A review of theory and methods. *Journal of Personality Assessment*, 93, 332–346.

Benjamin, L. (1993). Every psychopathology is a gift of love. *Psychotherapy Research*, 3, 1–24.

Benjamin, L. S. (1996. *Interpersonal diagnosis and treatment of personality disorders* (2nd ed.). New York, NY: Guilford Press.

Benjamin, L. S. (2000). *Intrex user's manual.* Salt Lake City, UT: University of Utah.

Benjamin, L. S. (2003). *Interpersonal reconstructive therapy.* New York, NY: Guilford Press.

Benjamin, L. S., & Critchfield, K. L. (2010). An interpersonal perspective on therapy alliancesand techniques. In J. C. Muran & J. P. Barber (Eds.), *The therapeutic alliance: An evidence-based guide to practice* (pp. 97–122). New York, NY: Guilford Press.

Benjamin, L. S., Rothweiler, J. C., & Critchfield, K. L. (2006). The use of structural analysis of social behavior (SASB) as an assessment tool. *Annual Review of Clinical Psychology*, 2, 83–109. doi:10.1146/annurev.clinpsy.2.022305.095337

Bennett, C. E., & Hammond, W. A. (1902). *The characters of Theophrastus* (trans. and introduction). New York, NY: Longmans, Green and Co.

Ben-Porath, Y. S., & Tellegen, A. (2008). *Minnesota Multiphasic Personality Inventory-2-Restructured Form (MMPI-2-RF) technical manual.* Minneapolis, MN: University of Minnesota Press.

Ben-Porath, Y., & Tellegen, A. (2011). *MMPI 2 RF manual for administration, scoring, and interpretation*. Minneapolis, MN: University of Minnesota Press.

Berghuis, H., Ingenhoven, T. J. M., van der Heijden, P. T., Rossi, G. M. P., & Schotte, C. K. W. (2017). Assessment of pathological traits in DSM-5 personality disorders by the DAPP-BQ: How do these traits relate to the six personality disorder types of the alternative model? *Journal of Personality Disorders*, 9, 1–22.

Berghuis, H., Kamphuis, J. H., Verheul, R., Larstone, R., & Livesley, J. (2013). The General Assessment of Personality Disorder (GAPD) as an instrument for assessing the core features of personality disorders. *Clinical Psychology & Psychotherapy*, 20, 544–557.

Bernstein, D. P., Iscan, C., & Maser, J. (2007). Opinions of personality disorder experts regarding the DSM-IV personality disorders classification system. *Journal of Personal Disorders*, 21, 536–551.

Berrios, G. E. (1993). European views on personality disorders: A conceptual history. *Comprehensive Psychiatry*, 34, 14–30.

Berrios, G. E. (1996). *The history of mental symptoms: descriptive psychopathology since the nineteenth century.* Cambridge, MA: Cambridge University Press.

Berrios, G. E. (1999). Classifications in psychiatry: A conceptual history. *Australian & New Zealand Journal of Psychiatry*, 33, 145–160.

Berrios, G. E., & Marková, I. S. (2015). Towards a new epistemology of psychiatry. In L. J. Kirmayer, R. Lemelson, & C. A. Cummings (Eds.), *Re-visioning psychiatry: Cultural phenomenology, critical neuroscience, and global mental health* (pp. 41–64). New York, NY: Cambridge University Press.

Bers, S. A., Blatt, S. J., Sayward, H. K., & Johnston, R. S. (1993). Normal and pathological aspects of self-descriptions and their change over long-term treatment. *Psychoanalytic Psychology*, 10, 17–37.

Betan, E., Heim, A. K., Zittel Conklin, C. Z., & Westen, D. (2005). Countertransference phenomena and personality pathology in clinical practice: An empirical investigation. *American Journal of Psychiatry*, 162, 890–895.

Binswanger, L. (1958). The case of Ellen West: An anthropological-clinical study (W. M. Mendel & J. Lyons, Trans.). In R. May, E. Angel, & H. F. Ellenberger (Eds.), *Existence: A new dimension in psychiatry and psychology* (pp. 237–364). New York, NY: Basic Books.

Black, D. W., Pfohl, B., Blum, N., McCormick, B., Allen, J., North, C. S., Phillips, K. A., Robins, C., Siever, L., Silk, K. R., Williams, J. B., & Zimmerman, M. (2011). Attitudes toward borderline personality disorder: A survey of 706 mental health clinicians. *CNS Spectrums*, 16, 67–74. doi:10.1017/S109285291200020X

Blagov, P. S., Bi, W., Shedler, J., & Westen, D. (2012). The Shedler-Westen Assessment Procedure (SWAP): Evaluating psychometric questions about its reliability, validity, and impact of its fixed score distribution. *Assessment*, 19, 370–382.

Blanco, C., Bragdon, L. B., Schneier, F. R., & Liebowitz, M. R. (2013). The evidence-based pharmacotherapy of social anxiety disorder. *International Journal of Neuropsychopharmacology*, 16, 235–249.

Blashfield, R. K. (1984). *The classification of psychopathology.* New York, NY: Plenum.

Blashfield, R. K., & Draguns, J. G. (1976). Evaluative criteria for psychiatric classification. *Journal of Abnormal Psychology*, 85, 140–150.

Blashfield, R. K., & Fuller, A. K. (1996). Predicting the DSM-V. *The Journal of Nervous and Mental Disease*, 184, 4–7.

Blashfield, R. K., Keeley, J. W., Flanagan, E. H., & Miles, S. R. (2014). The cycle of classification: DSM-I through DSM-5. *Annual Review of Clinical Psychology*, 10, 25–51.

Blashfield, R. K., & Livesley, W. J. (1991). Metaphorical analysis of psychiatric classification as a psychological test. *Journal of Abnormal Psychology*, 100, 262–270.

Blatt, S. J. (1974). Levels of object representation in anaclitic and introjective depression. *The Psychoanalytic Study of the Child*, 29, 107–157.

Blatt, S. J. (1995). Representational structures in psychopathology. In D. Cicchetti & S. L. Toth (Eds.), *Emotion, cognition, and representation* (pp. 1–33). Rochester, NY: University of Rochester Press.

Blatt, S. J., Bers, S. A., & Schaffer, C. E. (1993). *The assessment of self-descriptions.* Unpublished research manual. New Haven, CT: Yale University.

Blatt, S. J., Chevron, E. S., Quinlan, D. M., Schaffer, C. E., & Wein, S. (1992). *The assessment of qualitative and structural dimensions of object representations* (Rev. ed.). Unpublished research manual. New Haven, CT: Yale University.

Blatt, S. J., D'Afflitti, J. P., & Quinlan, D. P. (1976). *Depressive experiences questionnaire.* New Haven, CT: Yale University Press.

Blatt, S. J., & Felsen, I. (1993). Different kinds of folks may need different kinds of strokes: The effect of patients' characteristics on therapeutic process and outcome. *Psychotherapy Research*, 3, 245–259. doi:10.1080/10503309312331333829

Blatt, S. J., & Ford, R. (1994). *Therapeutic change: An object relations perspective.* New York, NY: Plenum.

Blatt, S. J. & Lerner, H. (1983). The psychological assessment of object representation. *Journal of Personality Assessment*, 47, 7–28.

Blatt, S. J., Zuroff, D. C., Hawley, L. L., & Auerbach, J. S. (2010). Predictors of sustained therapeutic change. *Psychotherapy Research*, 20, 37–54.

Bleakley, A. (2017). *Thinking with metaphors in medicine: The state of the art.* London, UK: Routldege.

Block, J. (2010). The five-factor framing of personality and beyond: Some ruminations. *Psychological Inquiry*, 21, 2–25.

Bo, S., Bach, B., Mortensen, E. L., & Simonsen, E. (2016). Reliability and hierarchical structure of DSM- 5 pathological traits in a Danish mixed sample. *Journal of Personality Disorders*, 30, 112–129.

Boland, J. K., Damnjanovic, T., & Anderson, J. L. (in press, 2018). Evaluating the role of functional impairment in personality psychopathology. *Psychiatry Research.* doi:10.1016/j.psychres.2018.03.049

Bollas, C. (1989). *The shadow of the object: Psychoanalysis of the unthought known.* New York, NY: Columbia University Press.

Bordin, E. S. (1979). The generalizability of the psychoanalytic concept of the working alliance. *Psychotherapy: Theory, Research & Practice*, 16, 252–260.

Borges, J. L. (1946/1998). On exactitude in science. In *Collected Fictions* (Trans
A. Hurley) (p. 325). New York, NY: Penguin.

Bornstein, R. F. (1998). Reconceptualizing personality disorder diagnosis in the DSM-V: The discriminant validity challenge. *Clinical Psychology: Science and Practice*, 5, 333–343.
Bornstein, R. F. (1999). Criterion validity of objective and projective dependency tests: A meta-analytic assessment of behavioral prediction. *Psychological Assessment*, 11, 48–57.
Bornstein, R. F. (2009). Heisenberg, Kandinsky, and the heteromethod convergence problem: Lessons from within and beyond psychology. *Journal of Personality Assessment*, 91, 1–8.
Bornstein, R. F. (2011). Toward a process-focused model of test score validity: Improving psychological assessment in science and practice. *Psychological Assessment*, 23, 532–544.
Borsboom, D. (2008). Psychometric perspectives on diagnostic systems. *Journal of Clinical Psychology*, 64, 1089–1108.
Borsboom, D., & Cramer, A. (2013). Network analysis: An integrative approach to the structure of psychopathology. *Annual Review of Clinical Psychology*, 9, 91–121.
Borsboom, D., Cramer, A. O., Schmittmann, V. D., Epskamp, S., & Waldorp, L. J. (2011). The small world of psychopathology. *PloS one*, 6, e27407.
Borsboom, D., Rhemtulla, M., Cramer, A. O. J., Van der Maas, H. L. J., Scheffer, M., & Dolan, C. V. (2016). Kinds versus continua: A review of psychometric approaches to uncover the structure of psychiatric constructs. *Psychological Medicine*, 46, 1567–1579.
Bowlby, J. (1969). *Attachment*. New York, NY: Basic Books.
Bourke, M. E., & Grenyer, B. F. (2013). Therapists' accounts of psychotherapy process associated with treating patients with borderline personality disorder. *Journal of Personality Disorders*, 27, 735–745.
Bowlby, J. (1973). *Attachment and loss: II. Separation: Anxiety and anger*. London, UK: Hogarth.
Bray, A. (2001). The silence surrounding 'Ellen West': Binswanger and Foucault. *Journal of the British Society for Phenomenology*, 32, 125–146.
Breger, L. (2009). *Dostoevsky: The author as psychoanalyst*. Piscataway, NJ: Transaction Publishers.
Briand-Malenfant, R., Lecours, S., & Deschenaux, E. (2012). What does sadness mean to BPD patients? *Journal of Personality Disorders*, 26, 939–955.
Brown, T. L. (2003). *Making truth: Metaphor in science*. Champaign, IL: University of Illinois Press.
Brown, T. N. (2003). Critical race theory speaks to the sociology of mental health: Mental health problems produced by racial stratification. *Journal of Health and Social Behavior*, 44, 292–301.
Brunswik, E. (1955). Representative design and probabilistic theory in a functional psychology. *Psychological Review*, 62, 193.
Budge, S. L., Moore, J. T., Del Re, A. C., Wampold, B. E., Baardseth, T. P., & Nienhuis, J. B. (2013). The effectiveness of evidence-based treatments for personality disorders when comparing treatment-as-usual and bona fide treatments. *Clinical Psychology Review*, 33, 1057–1066.
Buer Christensen, T., Paap, M. C., Arnesen, M., Koritzinsky, K., Nysaeter, T. E., Eikenaes, I., Germans Selvik, S., Walther, K., Torgersen, S., Bender, D. S., Skodol, A. E., Kvarstein, E., Pedersen, G., & Hummelen, B. (in press, 2018). Interrater reliability of the structured clinical interview for the DSM–5

Alternative Model of Personality Disorders Module i: Level of Personality Functioning Scale. *Journal of Personality Assessment*. doi:10.1080/00223891.2018.1483377

Busch, A. J., Morey, L. C., & Hopwood, C. J. (2017). Exploring the assessment of the DSM-5 alternative model for personality disorders with the Personality Assessment Inventory. *Journal of Personality Assessment*, 99, 211–218.

Cade, J. F. (1949). Lithium salts in the treatment of psychotic excitement. *Medical Journal of Australia*, 2, 349–352.

Cain, N. M., Ansell, E. B., Simpson, H. B., & Pinto, A. (2015). Interpersonal functioning in obsessive–compulsive personality disorder. *Journal of Personality Assessment*, 97, 90–99. doi:10.1080/00223891.2014.934376

Cain, N. M., Pincus, A. L., & Ansell, E. B. (2008). Narcissism at the crossroads: Phenotypic description of pathological narcissism across clinical theory, social/personality psychology, and psychiatric diagnosis. *Clinical Psychology Review*, 28, 638–656.

Cain, N. M., Pincus, A. L., & Holtforth, M. G. (2010). Interpersonal subtypes in social phobia: Diagnostic and treatment implications. *Journal of Personality Assessment*, 92, 514–527. doi:10.1080/00223891.2010.513704

Caligor, E., & Clarkin, J. F. (2010). An object relations model of personality and personality pathology. In J. F. Clarkin, P. Fonagy & G. O. Gabbard (Eds.), *Psychodynamic psychotherapy for personality disorders: A clinical handbook* (pp. 3–35). Arlington, VA: American Psychiatric Publishing.

Caligor, E., Levy, K. N., & Yeomans, F. E. (2015). Narcissistic personality disorder: Diagnostic and clinical challenges. *The American Journal of Psychiatry*, 172, 415–422.

Campbell, D. T., & Fiske, D. W. (1959). Convergent and discriminant validation by the multitrait-multimethod matrix. *Psychological Bulletin*, 56, 81.

Cannon, T. D., & Keller, M. C. (2006). Endophenotypes in the genetic analyses of mental disorders. *Annual Review of Clinical Psychology*, 2, 267–290.

Cantor, N., Smith, E. E., French, R. D., & Mezzich, J. (1980). Psychiatric diagnosis as prototype categorization. *Journal of Abnormal Psychology*, 89, 181–193.

Carey, B. (2011, June 23). Expert on mental illness reveals her own fight. The New York Times. Retrieved from www.nytimes.com/2011/06/23/health/23lives.html?pagewanted=all

Carleton, R. N., Sharpe, D., & Asmundson, G. G. (2007). Anxiety, sensitivity and intolerance of uncertainty: Requisites of the fundamental fears? *Behaviour Research and Therapy*, 45, 2307–2316.

Carlotta, D., Krueger, R. F., Markon, K. E., Borroni, S., Frera, F., Somma, A., & Fossati, A. (2015). Adaptive and maladaptive personality traits in high-risk gamblers. *Journal of Personality Disorders*, 29, 378–392.

Carroll, L. (1876/1981). *The hunting of the snark: An agony, in eight fits*. London, UK: MacMillan.

Carroll, L., Holiday, H., Tanis, J., Dooley, J., Gardner, M., Mitchell, C., & Goodacre, S. H. (1981). *Lewis Carroll's "The hunting of the snark"*. Los Altos, CA: William Kaufmann Inc.

Carson, R. C. (1969). *Interaction concepts of personality*. Chicago, IL: Aldine Publishing.

Cartwright, C. (2011). Transference, countertransference, and reflective practice in cognitive therapy. *Clinical Psychologist*, 15, 112–120.

Cartwright, N. (1999). *The dappled world: A study of the boundaries of science.* Cambridge, MA: Cambridge University Press.
Cartwright, N. (2004). Causation: One word, many things. *Philosophy of Science*, 71, 805–819.
Caruth, C. (2016). *Unclaimed experience: Trauma, narrative, and history.* Baltimore, MD: Johns Hopkins University Press.
Caspi, A., Houts, R. M., Belsky, D. W., Goldman-Mellor, S. J., Harrington, H., Israel, S., Meier, M. H., Ramrakha, S., Shalev, I., Poulton, R., & Moffitt, T. E. (2014). The p factor: One general psychopathology factor in the structure of psychiatric disorders? *Clinical Psychological Science*, 2, 119–137.
Cattell, R. B. (1933). Temperament tests. I. temperament. *British Journal of Psychology*, 23, 308–329.
Cattell, R. B. (1943). The description of personality. *The Journal of Abnormal and Social Psychology*, 38, 476–506.
Cattell, R. B. (1978). *The scientific use of factor analysis in behavioral and life sciences.* New York, NY: Plenum Press.
Cattell, R. B. (1988). The data box: Its ordering of total resources in terms of possible relational systems. In J. R. Nesselroade & R. B. Cattell (Eds.), *Handbook of multivariate experimental psychology* (2nd ed.) (pp. 69–130). New York, NY: Plenum.
Chang, H. (2017). Epistemic iteration and natural kinds: Realism and pluralism in taxonomy. In K. S. Kendler & J. Parnas (Eds.), *Philosophical issues in psychiatry IV: Classification of psychiatric illness.* (pp. 229–245). New York, NY: Oxford University Press.
Chartonas, D., Kyratsous, M., Dracass, S., Lee, T., & Bhiu, K. (2017). Personality disorder: Still the patients psychiatrists dislike? *British Journal of Psychology Bulletin*, 41, 12–17.
Chmielewski, M., Bagby, R. M., Markon, K., Ring, A. J., & Ryder, A. G. (2014). Openness to experience, intellect, schizotypal personality disorder, and psychoticism: Resolving the controversy. *Journal of Personality Disorders*, 28, 483–499.
Choi-Kain, L. W., & Gunderson, J. G. (2008). Mentalization: Ontogeny, assessment, and application in the treatment of borderline personality disorder. *The American Journal of Psychiatry*, 165, 1127–1135.
Chu, J. A. (1991). The repetition compulsion revisited: Reliving dissociated trauma. *Psychotherapy: Theory, Research, Practice, Training*, 28, 327.
Cicchetti, D. V. (1994). Guidelines, criteria, and rules of thumb for evaluating normed and standardized assessment instruments in psychology. *Psychological Assessment*, 6, 284–290.
Clark, L.A. (1993). *Schedule for Nonadaptive and Adaptive Personality (SNAP): Manual for administration, scoring, and interpretation.* Minneapolis, MN: University of Minnesota Press.
Clark, L. A. (2005). Temperament as a unifying basis for personality and psychopathology. *Journal of Abnormal Psychology*, 114, 505.
Clark, L. A. (2007). Assessment and diagnosis of personality disorder: Perennial issues and an emerging reconceptualization. *Annual Review of Psychology*, 58, 227–257.
Clarkin, J. F., Cain, N., & Livesley, W. J. (2015). An integrated approach to treatment of patients with personality disorders. *Journal of Psychotherapy Integration*, 25, 3–12.

Clarkin, J. F., Caligor, E., Stern, B., & Kernberg, O. F. (2007). *Structured Interview of Personality Organization (STIPO).* New York, NY: Weill Medical College of Cornell University.
Clarkin, J. F., Levy, K. N., Lenzenweger, M. F., & Kernberg, O. F. (2007). Evaluating three treatments for borderline personality disorder: a multiwave study. *American Journal of Psychiatry*, 164, 922–928.
Clarkin, J. F., Yeomans, F. E., & Kernberg, O. F. (2006). *Psychotherapy for borderline personality: Focusing on object relations.* Arlington, VA: American Psychiatric Publishing.
Cleckley, H. (1941). *The mask of sanity: An attempt to reinterpret the so-called psychopathic personality.* Oxford, UK: Mosby.
Cleckley, H. M. (1955). *The mask of sanity: An attempt to clarify some issues about the so-called psychopathic personality* (3rd ed.). St. Louis: Mosby.
Cloninger, C. R. (1987). A systematic method for clinical description and classification of personality variants: A proposal. *Archives of General Psychiatry*, 44, 573–588.
Cloninger, C. R. (2000). A practical way to diagnosis personality disorder: A proposal. *Journal of Personality Disorders*, 14, 99–108.
Cloninger, C. R., Svrakic, D. M., & Przybeck, T. R. (1993). A psychobiological model of temperament and character. *Archives of General Psychiatry*, 50, 975–990.
Cohen, J. M., Feinstein, B. A., Rodriguez-Seijas, C., Taylor, C. B., & Newman, M. G. (2016). Rejection sensitivity as a transdiagnostic risk factor for internalizing psychopathology among gay and bisexual men. *Psychology of Sexual Orientation and Gender Diversity*, 3, 259–264.
Colli, A., Tanzilli, A., Dimaggio, G., & Lingiardi, V. (2014). Patient personality and therapist response: An empirical investigation. *The American Journal of Psychiatry*, 171, 102–108.
Committee on Statistics, American Medico-Psychological Association (1918). *Statistical manual for the use of institutions for the insane.* New York, NY: National Committee for Mental Hygiene.
Conners, C. K., Erhardt, D., & Sparrow, E. P. (1999). *Conners' adult ADHD rating scales (CAARS): Technical manual.* North Tonawanda, NY: MHS.
Conway, C. C., Hammen, C., & Brennan, P. A. (2016). Optimizing prediction of psychosocial and clinical outcomes with a transdiagnostic model of personality disorder. *Journal of Personality Disorders*, 30, 545–566.
Cooper, R. (2012). Psychiatric classification and subjective experience. *Emotion Review*, 4, 197–202.
Cooper, R. (2015). Why is the Diagnostic and Statistical Manual of Mental Disorders so hard to revise? Path-dependence and "lock-in" in classification. *Studies in History and Philosophy of Science Part C: Studies in History and Philosophy of Biological and Biomedical Sciences*, 51, 1–10.
Cooper, R., & Blashfield, R. K. (2016). Re-evaluating DSM-I. *Psychological Medicine*, 46, 449–456.
Corrigan, P. W. (2005). *On the stigma of mental illness: Practical strategies for research and social change.* Washington, DC: American Psychological Association.
Costa Jr., P. T., & McCrae, R. R. (1990). Personality disorders and the five-factor model of personality. *Journal of Personality Disorders*, 4, 362–371.
Costa Jr., P. T., & McCrae, R. R. (1992). *Revised NEO Personality Inventory (NEO PI-R) and NEO Five-Factor Inventory (NEO-FFI).* Odessa, FL: Psychological Assessment Resources.

Costa, P. T., Jr., & Widiger, T. A. (Eds.) (1994). *Personality disorders and the five-factor model of personality.* Washington, D.C: American Psychological Association.

Cox, B. J., Pagura, J., Stein, M. B., & Sareen, J. (2009). The relationship between generalized social phobia and avoidant personality disorder in a national mental health survey. *Depression and Anxiety*, 26, 354–362.

Cramer, A. O. J., van Borkulo, C. D., Giltay, E. J., van der Maas, H. L. J., Kendler, K. S., Scheffer, M., Borsboom, D. (2016). Major depression as a complex dynamic system. *PLoS ONE*, 11, e0167490. doi:10.1371/journal.pone.0167490

Crawford, T. N., Livesley, W. J., Jang, K. L., Shaver, P. R., Cohen, P., & Ganiban, J. (2007). Insecure attachment and personality disorder: A twin study of adults. *European Journal of Personality*, 21, 191–208.

Crego, C., & Widiger, T. A. (2014). Psychopathy, DSM-5, and a caution. *Personality Disorders: Theory, Research, and Treatment*, 5, 335–347.

Crego, C., & Widiger, T. A. (2016). Convergent and discriminant validity of alternative measures of maladaptive personality traits. *Psychological Assessment*, 28, 1561.

Creswell, K. G., Bachrach, R. L., Wright, A. G., Pinto, A., & Ansell, E. (2016). Predicting problematic alcohol use with the DSM-5 alternative model of personality pathology. *Personality Disorders: Theory, Research, and Treatment*, 7, 103–111.

Cristea, I. A., Gentili, C., Cotet, C. D., Palomba, D., Barbui, C., & Cuijpers, P. (2017). Efficacy of psychotherapies for borderline personality disorder: A systematic review and meta-analysis. *JAMA Psychiatry*, 74, 319–328.

Critchfield, K. L., & Benjamin, L. S. (2008). Internalized representations of early interpersonal experience and adult relationships: A test of copy process theory in clinical and non-clinical settings. *Psychiatry: Interpersonal and Biological Processes*, 71, 71–92.

Critchfield, K. L., & Benjamin, L. S. (2010). Assessment of repeated relational patterns for individual cases using the SASB-based Intrex questionnaire. *Journal of Personality Assessment*, 92, 480–489.

Critchfield, K. L., Benjamin, L. S., & Levenick, K. (2015). Reliability, sensitivity, and specificity of case formulations for comorbid profiles in interpersonal reconstructive therapy: Addressing mechanisms of psychopathology. *Journal of Personality Disorders*, 29, 547–573.

Crocq, M. A. (2013). Milestones in the history of personality disorders. *Dialogues in Clinical Neuroscience*, 15, 147–153.

Cronbach, L., & Meehl, P. (1955). Construct validity in psychological tests. *Psychological Bulletin*, 52, 281–302.

Croskerry, P. (2003). The importance of cognitive errors in diagnosis and strategies to minimize them. *Academic Medicine*, 78, 775–780.

Croskerry, P. (2009). Clinical cognition and diagnostic error: Applications of a dual process model of reasoning. *Advances in Health Sciences Education*, 14, 27–35.

Crowell, S. E., Beauchaine, T. P., & Linehan, M. M. (2009). A biosocial developmental model of borderline personality: Elaborating and extending Linehan's theory. *Psychological Bulletin*, 135, 495.

Cuthbert, B. N., & Insel, T. R. (2013). Toward the future of psychiatric diagnosis: The seven pillars of RDoC. *BMC Medicine*, 11, 126.

Daly, K. D., & Mallinckrodt, B. (2009). Experienced therapists' approach to psychotherapy for adults with attachment avoidance or attachment anxiety. *Journal of Counseling Psychology*, 56, 549–563.

Daubert v. Merrell Dow Pharmaceuticals, Inc. 509 U.S. 579 (1993).

Davidson, K. M., Obonsawin, M. C., Seils, M., & Patience, L. (2003). Patient and clinician agreement on personality using the SWAP-200. *Journal of Personality Disorders*, 17, 208–218.

Davis, R. T., Blashfield, R. K., & McElroy, R. J. (1993). Weighting criteria in the diagnosis of a personality disorder: A demonstration. *Journal of Abnormal Psychology*, 102, 319–322. doi:10.1037/0021-843X.102.2.319

Dawkins, R. (1986). *The blind watchmaker: Why the evidence of evolution reveals a universe without design*. New York, NY: W. W. Norton & Company.

Dawood, S., Dowgwillo, E.A., Wu, L.Z., & Pincus, A.L. (2018). Contemporary integrative interpersonal theory of personality. In V. Zeigler-Hill and T. Shackleford (Eds.), *The SAGE handbook of personality and individual differences. Vol. 1: The science of personality and individual differences*. Los Angeles, CA: Sage Publications.

Dawood, S., & Pincus, A.L. (2016). Multi-surface interpersonal assessment in a cognitive-behavioral therapy context. *Journal of Personality Assessment*, 98, 449–460.

Deacon, B. J., & Baird, G. L. (2009). The chemical imbalance explanation of depression: Reducing blame at what cost? *Journal of Social and Clinical Psychology*, 28, 415–435.

Debast, I., Rossi, G., & van Alphen, S. P. J. (2018). Age-neutrality of a brief assessment of the Section III Alternative Model for Personality Disorders in older adults. *Assessment*, 25, 310–323.

De Caluwé, E., Decuyper, M., & De Clercq, B. (2013). The child behavior checklist dysregulation profile predicts adolescent DSM-5 pathological personality traits 4 years later. *European Child & Adolescent Psychiatry*, 22, 401–411.

De Caluwé, E., Rettew, D. C., & De Clercq, B. (2014). The continuity between DSM-5 obsessive- compulsive personality disorder traits and obsessive-compulsive symptoms in adolescence: An item response theory study. *The Journal of Clinical Psychiatry*, 75, e1271–1277.

De Clercq, B., De Fruyt, F., De Bolle, M., Van Hiel, A., Markon, K. E., & Krueger, R. F. (2014). The hierarchical structure and construct validity of the PID-5 trait measure in adolescence. *Journal of Personality*, 82, 158–169.

Decuyper, M., De Caluwé, E., De Clercq, B., & De Fruyt, F. (2014). Callous-unemotional traits in youth from a DSM-5 trait perspective. *Journal of Personality Disorders*, 28, 334–357.

De Fruyt, F., De Clercq, B., De Bolle, M., Wille, B., Markon, K. E., & Krueger R. F. (2013). General and maladaptive traits in a five-factor framework for DSM-5 in a university student sample. *Assessment*, 20, 295–307.

de Groot, E. R., Verheul, R., & Trijsburg, R. W. (2008). An integrative perspective on psychotherapeutic treatments for borderline personality disorder. *Journal of Personality Disorders*, 22, 332–352.

De La Durantaye, L. (2005). Vladimir Nabokov and Sigmund Freud, or a Particular Problem. *American Imago*, 62, 59–73.

Depue, R. A., & Lenzenweger, M. F. (2001). A neurobehavioral dimensional model. In W. J. Livesley (Ed.), *Handbook of personality disorders: Theory, research, and treatment* (pp. 136–176). New York, NY: Guilford Press.

de Queiroz, K., & Gauthier, J. (1994). Toward a phylogenetic system of biological nomenclature. *Trends in Ecology & Evolution*, 9, 27–31.

Der-Avakian, A., & Markou, A. (2012). The neurobiology of anhedonia and other reward-related deficits. *Trends in Neurosciences*, 35, 68–77.

Dereboy, F., Dereboy, Ç., & Eskin, M. (in press, 2018). Validation of the DSM–5 alternative model personality disorder diagnoses in Turkey, Part 1: LEAD validity and reliability of the personality functioning ratings. *Journal of Personality Assessment*. doi:10.1080/00223891.2018.1423989

Dermody, S. S., Thomas, K. M., Hopwood, C. J., Durbin, C. E., & Wright, A. G. C. (2017). Modeling the complexity of dynamic, momentary interpersonal behavior: Applying the time-varying effect model to test predictions from interpersonal theory. *Journal of Research in Personality*, 68, 54–62.

DeYoung, C. G. (2015). Cybernetic Big Five Theory. *Journal of Research in Personality*, 56, 33–58.

DeYoung, C. G., Carey, B. E., Krueger, R. F., & Ross, S. R. (2016). Ten aspects of the Big Five in the Personality Inventory for DSM-5. *Personality Disorders: Theory, Research, and Treatment*, 7, 113–123.

DeYoung, C. G., Grazioplene, R. G., & Peterson, J. B. (2012). From madness to genius: The Openness/Intellect trait domain as a paradoxical simplex. *Journal of Research in Personality*, 46, 63–78.

DeYoung, C. G., Hirsh, J. B., Shane, M. S., Papademetris, X., Rajeevan, N., & Gray, J. R. (2010). Testing predictions from personality neuroscience: *Brain* structure and the Big Five. *Psychological Science, 21*, 820–828.

DeYoung, C. G., Quilty, L. C., & Peterson, J. B. (2007). Between facets and domains: 10 aspects of the Big Five. *Journal of Personality and Social Psychology*, 93, 880–896.

Diguer, L., Pelletier, S., Hebert, E., Descoteaux, J., Rousseau, P., & Daoust, J. P. (2004). Personality organization, psychiatric severity, and self and object representations. *Psychoanalytic Psychology*, 21, 259–275.

Dilchert, S., Ones, D. S., & Krueger, R. F. (2014). Maladaptive personality constructs, measures, and work behaviors. *Industrial and Organizational Psychology*, 7, 98–110.

Dillard, A. (1982). *Living by fiction*. New York, NY: Harper & Row.

Dimaggio, G., Semerari, A., Carcione, A., Procacci, M., & Nicolò, G. (2006). Toward a model of self pathology underlying personality disorders: Narratives, metacognition, interpersonal cycles and decision-making processes. *Journal of Personality Disorders*, 20, 597–617.

Dimitrijević, A., Hanak, N., Dimitrijević, A. A., & Marjanović, Z. J. (2018). The Mentalization Scale (MentS): A self-report measure for the assessment of mentalizing capacity. *Journal of Personality Assessment*, 100, 268–280.

Dinger, U., Barrett, M. S., Zimmermann, J., Schauenburg, H., Wright, A. G., Renner, F., Ailcha-Mano, S., & Barber, J. P. (2015). Interpersonal problems, dependency, and self-criticism in major depressive disorder. *Journal of Clinical Psychology*, 71, 93–104.

Doering, S., Burgmer, M., Heuft, G., Menke, D., Bäumer, B., Lübking, M., Feldmann, M., Horz, S., & Schneider, G. (2013). Reliability and validity of the German version of the structured interview of personality organization (STIPO). *BMC Psychiatry*, 13, 13.

Dowgwillo, E. A., Ménard, K. S., Krueger, R. F., & Pincus, A. L. (2016). DSM-5 pathological personality traits and intimate partner violence among male and female college students. *Violence and Victims*, 31, 416–437.

Dowgwillo, E. A., Roche, M. J., & Pincus, A. L. (in press, 2018). Examining the interpersonal nature of Criterion A of the DSM-5 Section III alternative model for personality disorders using bootstrapped confidence intervals for the interpersonal circumplex. *Journal of Personality Assessment*. doi:10.1080/00223891.2018.1464016

Drapeau, M., & Perry, J. C. (2009). The Core Conflictual Relationship Themes (CCRT) in borderline personality disorder. *Journal of Personality Disorders*, 23, 425–431.

Eaton, N., Krueger, R. F., South, C., Simms, L. J., & Clark, L. A. (2011). Contrasting prototypes and dimensions in the classification of personality pathology: Evidence that dimensions, but not prototypes, are robust. *Psychological Medicine*, 41, 1151–1163.

Edelstein, R. S. (2006). Attachment and emotional memory: Investigating the source and extent of avoidant memory impairments. *Emotion*, 6, 340–345.

Edens, J. F., & Boccaccini, M. T. (2017). Taking forensic mental health assessment "out of the lab" and into "the real world": Introduction to the special issue on the field utility of forensic assessment instruments and procedures. *Psychological Assessment*, 29, 599–610.

Edens, J. F., Cox, J., Smith, J. T., DeMatteo, D., & Sörman, K. (2015). How reliable are Psychopathy Checklist-Revised scores in Canadian criminal trials? A case law review. *Psychological Assessment*, 27, 447–456.

Egan, S. J., Wade, T. D., & Shafran, R. (2011). Perfectionism as a transdiagnostic process: A clinical review. *Clinical Psychology Review*, 31, 203–212.

Ehring, T., & Watkins, E. R. (2012). Repetitive negative thinking as a transdiagnostic process. *International Journal of Cognitive Therapy*, 45, 5–20.

Eikenaes, I., Hummelen, B., Abrahamsen, G., Andrea, H., & Wilberg, T. (2013). Personality functioning in patients with avoidant personality disorder and social phobia. *Journal of Personality Disorders*, 27, 746–763.

Elad-Strenger, J. (2013). Changing minds. *Review of General Psychology*, 17, 40–52.

Ellison, W. D., & Levy, K. N. (2012). Factor structure of the primary scales of the Inventory of Personality Organization in a nonclinical sample using exploratory structural equation modeling. *Psychological Assessment*, 24, 503–517.

Engel, G. L. (1977). The need for a new medical model: A challenge for biomedicine. *Science*, 196, 129–136.

Ensink, K., Rousseau, M., Biberdzic, M., Bégin, M., & Normandin, L. (2017). Reflective functioning and personality organization: Associations with negative maternal behaviors. *Infant Mental Health Journal*, 38, 351–362.

Evans, C. M., & Simms, L. J. (2018). Assessing inter-model continuity between the Section II and Section III conceptualizations of borderline personality disorder in DSM-5. *Personality Disorders: Theory, Research, and Treatment*, 9, 290–296.

Evans, J. S. B. (2008). Dual-processing accounts of reasoning, judgment, and social cognition. *Annual Review of Psychology*, 59, 255–278.

Exner, J. E. (2003). *The Rorschach: A comprehensive system. Basic foundations and principles of interpretation (Vol 1)* (4th ed.). New York, NY: John Wiley and Sons.

Eysenck, H. J. (1963). Biological basis of personality. *Nature*, 199, 1031–1034.

Fairbairn, W. R. D. (1949). Steps in the development of an object-relations theory of the personality. *Psychology and Psychotherapy: Theory, Research and Practice*, 22, 26–31.

Fairbairn, W. R. D. (1952). *Psychoanalytic studies of the personality.* London, UK: Routledge.
Falgares, G., De Santis, S., Gullo, S., Kopala-Sibley, D. C., Scrima, F., & Livi, S. (2017). Psychometric aspects of the Depressive Experiences Questionnaire: Implications for clinical assessment and research. *Journal of Personality Assessment*, 100, 207–218.
Falkenström, F., Granström, F., & Holmqvist, R. (2013). Therapeutic alliance predicts symptomatic improvement session by session. *Journal of Counseling Psychology*, 60, 317–328.
Farnfield, S., & Holmes, P. (2014). *The Routledge handbook of attachment: Assessment*. London, UK: Routledge.
Fazel, S., & Danesh, J. (2002). Serious mental disorder in 23,000 prisoners: A systematic review of 62 surveys. *The Lancet*, 359, 545–550.
Feeney, J. A., Noller, P., & Hanrahan, M. (1994). Assessing adult attachment. In M. B. Sperling & W. H. Berman (Eds.), *Attachment in adults: Clinical and developmental perspectives* (pp. 128–152). New York, NY: Guilford Press.
Feighner, J. P., Robins, E., Guze, S. B., Woodruff, R. A., Winokur, G., & Munoz, R. (1972). Diagnostic criteria for use in psychiatric research. *Archives of General Psychiatry*, 26, 57–63.
Fertuck, E. A., Jekal, A., Song, I., Wyman, B., Morris, M. C., Wilson, S. T., Brodsky, B. S., & Stanley, B. (2009). Enhanced "Reading the Mind in the Eyes" in borderline personality disorder compared to healthy controls. *Psychological Medicine*, 39, 1979–1988.
Fertuck, E. A., Karan, E., & Stanley, B. (2016). The specificity of mental pain in borderline personality disorder compared to depressive disorders and healthy controls. *Borderline Personality Disorder and Emotion Dysregulation*, 3, 2.
Few, L. R., Miller, J. D., Rothbaum, A. O., Meller, S., Maples, J., Terry, D. P., Collins, B. & MacKillop, J. (2013). Examination of the Section III DSM-5 diagnostic system for personality disorders in an outpatient clinical sample. *Journal of Abnormal Psychology*, 122, 1057–1069.
Finn, S. E. (2007) *In our clients' shoes: Theory and techniques of therapeutic assessment*. New York, NY: Routledge.
Finn, S. E., & Tonsager, M. E. (2002). How therapeutic assessment became humanistic. *The Humanistic Psychologist*, 30, 10–22.
First, M. B., Pincus, H. A., Levine, J. B., Williams, J. W., Ustun, B., & Peele, R. (2004). Clinical utility as a criterion for revising psychiatric diagnoses. *The American Journal of Psychiatry*, 161, 946–954.
First, M. B., Skodol, A. E., Bender, D. S., & Oldham, J. M. (2017). *User's guide for the Structured Clinical Interview for the DSM-5 Alternative Model for Personality Disorders (SCID-5-AMPD)*. Arlington, VA: American Psychiatric Publishing.
First, M. B., & Westen, D. (2007). Classification for clinical practice: How to make ICD and DSM better able to serve clinicians. *International Review of Psychiatry*, 19, 473–481.
Flanagan, E. H., & Blashfield, R. K. (2010). Increasing clinical utility by aligning the DSM and ICD with clinicians' conceptualizations. *Professional Psychology: Research and Practice*, 41, 474–481.
Flanagan, E. H., & Davidson, L. (2007). "Schizophrenics," "Borderlines," and the lingering legacy of misplaced concreteness: An examination of the persistent

misconception that the DSM classifies people instead of disorders. *Psychiatry: Interpersonal and Biological Processes*, 70, 100–112.

Flanagan, E. H., Keeley, J., & Blashfield, R. K. (2008). An alternative hierarchical organization of the mental disorders of the DSM-IV. *Journal of Abnormal Psychology*, 117, 693–698.

Fleeson, W., & Jayawickreme, E. (2015). Whole trait theory. *Journal of Research in Personality*, 56, 82–92.

Flynn, T. (1994). Foucault's mapping of history. In G. Gutting (Ed.), *The Cambridge Companion to Foucault (Vol. 2)* (pp. 29–48). Cambridge, UK: Cambridge University Press.

Fonagy, P., & Bateman, A. (2008). The development of borderline personality disorder: A mentalizing model. *Journal of Personality Disorders*, 22, 4–21.

Fonagy, P., Gergely, G., Jurist, E. L., & Target, M. (2005). *Affect regulation, mentalization and the development of the self.* London, UK: Karnac books.

Fonagy, P. & Luyten, P. (2016). A multilevel perspective on the development of borderline personality disorder. *Developmental Psychopathology*, 3, 1–67.

Fonagy, P., Luyten, P., & Allison, E. (2015). Epistemic petrification and the restoration of epistemic trust: A new conceptualization of borderline personality disorder and its psychosocial treatment. *Journal of Personality Disorders*, 29, 575–609.

Fonagy, P., Luyten, P., Allison, E., & Campbell, C. (2017). What we have changed our minds about: Part 2. Borderline personality disorder, epistemic trust and the developmental significance of social communication. *Borderline Personality Disorder and Emotion Dysregulation*, 4. doi:10.1186/s40479-017-0062-8

Fonagy, P., Steele, M., Steele, H., Moran, G. S., & Higgitt, A. C. (1991). The capacity for understanding mental states: The reflective self in parent and child and its significance for security of attachment. *Infant Mental Health Journal*, 12, 201–218.

Fonagy, P., Target, M., Steele, H., & Steele, M. (1998). *Reflective Functioning Scale manual.* Unpublished manuscript. London, UK: University College London.

Forbes, M. K., Wright, A. G., Markon, K. E., & Krueger, R. F. (2017). Evidence that psychopathology symptom networks have limited replicability. *Journal of Abnormal Psychology*, 126, 969.

Fossati, A., Borroni, S., Somma, A., Markon, K. E., & Krueger, R. F. (2017). Testing relationships between DSM-5 Section III maladaptive traits and measures of self and interpersonal impairment in Italian community dwelling adults. *Personality Disorders: Theory, Research, and Treatment*, 8, 275–280.

Fossati, A., Krueger, R. F., Markon, K. E., Borroni, S., & Maffei, C. (2013). Reliability and validity of the Personality Inventory for DSM-5 (PID-5) predicting DSM-IV personality disorders and psychopathy in community-dwelling Italian adults. *Assessment*, 20, 689–708.

Fossati, A., Krueger, R. F., Markon, K. E., Borroni, S., Maffei, C., & Somma, A. (2015). The DSM-5 Alternative Model of Personality Disorders from the perspective of adult attachment: A study in community-dwelling adults. *Journal of Nervous and Mental Disease*, 203, 252–258.

Fossati, A., Somma, A., Borroni, S., Maffei, C., Markon, K. E., & Krueger, R. F. (2016a). Borderline personality disorder and narcissistic personality disorder diagnoses from the perspective of the DSM-5 personality traits: A study on Italian clinical participants. *The Journal of Nervous and Mental Disease*, 204, 939–949.

Fossati, A., Somma, A., Borroni, S., Maffei, C., Markon, K. E., & Krueger, R. F. (2016b). A head-to-head comparison of the Personality Inventory for DSM-5 (PID-5) with the Personality Diagnostic Questionnaire-4 (PDQ-4) in predicting the general level of personality pathology among community dwelling subjects. *Journal of Personality Disorders*, 30, 82–94.

Fossati, A., Somma, A., Borroni, S., Markon, K. E., & Krueger, R. F. (2017). The Personality Inventory for DSM-5 Brief Form: Evidence for reliability and construct validity in a sample of community-dwelling Italian adolescents. *Assessment*, 24, 615–631.

Fossati, A., Somma, A., Borroni, S., Pincus, A. L., Markon, K. E., & Krueger, R. F. (2016). Profiling pathological narcissism according to DSM–5 domains and traits: A study on consecutively admitted Italian psychotherapy patients. *Psychological Assessment*, 29, 1400–1411.

Fossati, A., Somma, A., Krueger, R. F., Markon, K. E., & Borroni, S. (2017). On the relationships between DSM-5 dysfunctional personality traits and social cognition deficits: A study in a sample of consecutively admitted Italian psychotherapy patients. *Clinical Psychology & Psychotherapy*, 24, 1421–1434.

Foucault, M. (1977). *Discipline and punish: The birth of the prison*. New York, NY: Vintage Books.

Fraley, C. R., & Brumbaugh, C. C. (2007). Adult attachment and preemptive defenses: Converging evidence on the role of defensive exclusion at the level of encoding. *Journal of Personality*, 75, 1033–1050.

France, C. M., Lysaker, P. H., & Robinson, R. P. (2007). The "chemical imbalance" explanation for depression: Origins, lay endorsement, and clinical implications. *Professional Psychology: Research and Practice*, 38, 411–420.

Frances, A. (2012). Prototypal diagnosis: Will this relic from the past become the wave of the future? *World Psychiatry*, 11, 26.

Frank, J. D., & Frank, J. B. (1961/ 1993). *Persuasion and healing: A comparative study of psychotherapy*. Baltimore, MD: Johns Hopkins University Press.

Freud, A. (1946/1992). *The ego and the mechanisms of defence*. London, UK: Karnac Books.

Friston, K., Redish, A., & Gordon, J. (2017). Computational nosology and precision psychiatry. *Computational Psychiatry*, 1, 2–23.

Friston, K. J., Stephan, K. E., Montague, R., & Dolan, R. J. (2014). Computational psychiatry: the brain as a phantastic organ. *The Lancet Psychiatry*, 1, 148–158.

Frith, U., & Frith, C. D. (2003). Development and neurophysiology of mentalizing. *Philosophical Transactions of the Royal Society B: Biological Sciences*, 358, 459–473.

Fromm-Reichmann, F. (1959). Loneliness. *Psychiatry*, 2, 1–25.

Frye v. U.S., 54 Appl. D.C. 46, 293 Fed. 1013 (1923).

Fuchs, T. (2007). Fragmented selves: Temporality and identity in borderline personality disorder. *Psychopathology*, 40, 379–387.

Furnham, A., Milner, R., Akhtar, R., & De Fruyt, F. (2014). A review of the measures designed to assess DSM-5 personality disorders. *Psychology*, 5, 1646.

Gabbard, G. O. (1995). Countertransference: the emerging common ground. *The International Journal of Psycho-Analysis*, 76, 475–485.

Gabbard, G. O. (2000). Psychotherapy of personality disorders. *The Journal of Psychotherapy Practice and Research*, 9, 1–6.

Gabbard, G. O. (2009). *Textbook of psychotherapeutic treatments.* Arlington, VA: American Psychiatric Publishing.
Gabbard, G. O., & Crisp-Han, H. (2016). The many faces of narcissism. *World Psychiatry*, 15, 115–116.
Gallo, L. C., Smith, T. W., & Ruiz, J. M. (2003). An interpersonal analysis of adult attachment style: Circumplex descriptions, recalled developmental experiences, self-representations and interpersonal functioning in adulthood. *Journal of Personality*, 71, 141–181.
Galton, F. (1888). Co-relations and their measurement, chiefly from anthropometric data. *Proceedings of the Royal Society of London*, 45, 135–145.
Garb, H. N. (1997). Race bias, social class bias, and gender bias in clinical judgment. *Clinical Psychology: Science and Practice*, 4, 99–120.
Garcia, D. J., Skadberg, R. M., Schmidt, M., Bierma, S., Shorter, R., & Waugh, M. H. (in press, 2018). Learning the DSM-5, Section III Alternative Model for Personality Disorder. *Journal of Personality Assessment.*
Gardner, B. O., Boccaccini, M. T., Bitting, B. S., & Edens, J. F. (2015). Personality Assessment Inventory scores as predictors of misconduct, recidivism, and violence: A meta-analytic review. *Psychological Assessment*, 27, 534–544.
Gardner, H. (1992). Scientific psychology: Should we bury it or praise it? *New Ideas in Psychology*, 10, 179–190.
Gazzillo, F., Lingiardi, V., Del Corno, F., Genova, F., Bornstein, R. F., Gordon, R. M., & McWilliams, N. (2015). Clinicians' emotional responses and Psychodynamic Diagnostic Manual adult personality disorders: A clinically relevant empirical investigation. *Psychotherapy*, 52, 238–246.
George, C., Kaplan, N., & Main, M. (1984). *Adult Attachment Interview protocol.* Unpublished manuscript. Berkeley, CA: University of California at Berkeley.
Ghaemi, S. N. (2003). *The concepts of psychiatry: A pluralistic approach to the mind and mental illness.* Baltimore, MD: John Hopkins University Press.
Giffin, C., Wilkenfeld, D., Lombrozo, T. (2017). The explanatory effect of a label: Explanations with named categories are more satisfying. *Cognition*, 168, 357–369.
Gilbert, P., & Leahy, R. L. (Eds.) (2007). *The therapeutic relationship in the cognitive behavioral psychotherapies.* New York, NY: Routledge.
Girard, J. M., & Wright A. G. C. (2018) DARMA: Dual axis rating and media annotation. *Behavioral Research Methods*, 50, 902–909.
Giromini, L., Viglione, D. J., Pineda, J. A., Porcelli, P., Hubbard, D., Zennaro, A., & Cauda, F. (in press, 2018). Human movement responses to the Rorschach and mirroring activity: An fMRI study. *Assessment.* doi:10.1177/10731911177318131–14
Goldberg, L. R. (1993). The structure of phenotypic personality traits. *American Psychologist*, 48, 26–34.
Goldberg, L. R., Johnson, J. A., Eber, H. W., Hogan, R., Ashton, M. C., Cloninger, C. R., & Gough, H. G. (2006). The international personality item pool and the future of public-domain personality measures. *Journal of Research in Personality*, 40, 84–96.
Gore, W., & Widiger, T. (2013). The DSM-5 dimensional trait model and five-factor models of general personality. *Journal of Abnormal Psychology*, 122, 816–821.
Gore, W., & Widiger, T. (2015). Assessment of dependency by the FFDI: Comparisons to the PID-5 and maladaptive agreeableness. *Personality and Mental Health*, 9, 258–276.

Gore, W. L., & Widiger, T. A. (2016). Fluctuation between grandiose and vulnerable narcissism. *Personality Disorders: Theory, Research, and Treatment*, 7, 363–371.
Gough, H. G. (1948). A sociological theory of psychopathy. *American Journal of Sociology*, 53, 359–366.
Graf, M. C., Gaudiano, B. A., & Geller, P. A. (2008). Written emotional disclosure: A controlled study of the benefits of expressive writing homework in outpatient psychotherapy. *Psychotherapy Research*, 18, 389–399.
Greenberg, J., Solomon, S., & Pyszczynski, T. (1997). Terror management theory of self-esteem and cultural worldviews: Empirical assessments and conceptual refinements. *Advances in Experimental Social Psychology*, 29, 61–139.
Greenberg, S. A., & Shuman, D. W. (1997). Irreconcilable conflict between therapeutic and forensic roles. *Professional Psychology: Research and Practice*, 28, 50–57.
Greenwald, A. (1980). The totalitarian ego: Fabrication and revision of personal history. *American Psychologist*, 35, 603–618.
Griffin, S. A., & Samuel, D. B. (2014). A closer look at the lower-order structure of the Personality Inventory for DSM-5: Comparison with the Five-Factor Model. *Personality Disorders: Theory, Research, and Treatment*, 5, 406–412.
Grilo, C. M., McGlashan, T. H., Morey, L. C., Gunderson, J. G., Skodol, A. E., Tracie Shea, M., Sanislow, C. A., Zanarini, M. C., Bender, D., Oldham, J. M., Dyck, I., & Stout, R. L. (2001). Internal consistency, intercriterion overlap and diagnostic efficiency of criteria sets for DSM-IV schizotypal, borderline, avoidant and obsessive-compulsive personality disorders. *Acta Psychiatrica Scandinavica*, 104, 264–272.
Gritti, E. S., & Samuel, D. B. (2015). Diagnostic agreement between clinicians and clients: The convergent and discriminant validity of the SWAP-200 and MCMI-III Personality Disorder Scales. *Journal of Personality Disorders*, 29, 231.
Gritti, E. S., Samuel, D. B., & Lang, M. (2016) Diagnostic agreement between clinicians and clients: The convergent and discriminant validity of the SWAP-200 and MCMI-III Personality Disorder Scales. *Journal of Personality Disorders*, 30, 796–812.
Guloksuz, S., Pries, L. K., & Van Os, J. (2017). Application of network methods for understanding mental disorders: pitfalls and promise. *Psychological Medicine*, 47, 2743–2752.
Gunderson, J. G. (2009a). *Borderline personality disorder: A clinical guide*. Arlington, VA: American Psychiatric Publishing.
Gunderson, J. G. (2009b). Borderline personality disorder: Ontogeny of a diagnosis. *American Journal of Psychiatry*, 166, 530–539.
Gunderson, J. G., & Links, P. S. (2008). *Borderline personality disorder: A clinical guide* (2nd ed.). Arlington, VA: American Psychiatric Publishing.
Gunderson, J. G., Links, P. S., & Reich, J. H. (1991). Competing models of personality disorders. *Journal of Personality Disorders*, 5, 60–68.
Guntrip, H. (1962). The schizoid compromise and psychotherapeutic stalemate. *Psychology and Psychotherapy: Theory, Research and Practice*, 35, 273–288.
Guntrip, H. (1968). *Schizoid phenomena, object relations and the self*. London, UK: Karnac Books.
Gurtman, M. B. (2009). Exploring personality with the interpersonal circumplex. *Social and Personality Psychology Compass*, 3, 601–619.

Gutheil, T. G. (2005). The history of forensic psychiatry. *Journal of the American Academy of Psychiatry and the Law*, 33, 259–262.
Gutiérrez, F., Aluja, A., Peri, J. M., Calvo, N., Ferrer, M., Baillés, E., Gutiérrez-Zotes, J. A., Gárriz, M. Caseras, X., Markon, K. E., & Krueger, R. F. (2017). Psychometric properties of the Spanish PID-5 in a clinical and a community sample. *Assessment*, 24, 326–336.
Haggerty, G., Blanchard, M., Baity, M. R., Defife, J. A., Stein, M. B., Siefert, C. J., Sinclair, S. J., & Zodan, J. (2015). Clinical validity of a dimensional assessment of self- and interpersonal functioning in adolescent inpatients. *Journal of Personality Assessment*, 97, 3–12.
Hallquist, M. N., & Pilkonis, P. A. (2012). Refining the phenotype of borderline personality disorder: Diagnostic criteria and beyond. *Personality Disorders*, 3, 228–246.
Hare, R. D. (1980). A research scale for the assessment of psychopathy in criminal populations. *Personality and Individual Differences*, 1, 111–119.
Hare, R. D. (2003). *Psychopathy checklist – revised technical manual* (2nd ed.). Toronto, Canada: Multinational Systems.
Hare, R. D., & Neumann, C. S. (2009). Psychopathy: Assessment and forensic implications. *The Canadian Psychiatric Association Journal / La Revue De L'association Des Psychiatres Du Canada*, 54, 791–802.
Harkness, A. R., McNulty, J. L., & Ben-Porath, Y. S. (1995). The Personality Psychopathology Five (PSY-5): Constructs and MMPI-2 scales. *Psychological Assessment*, 7, 104–114.
Harkness, A. R., Reynolds, S. M., & Lilienfeld, S. O. (2014). A review of systems for psychology and psychiatry: Adaptive systems, Personality Psychopathology Five (PSY–5), and the DSM–5. *Journal of Personality Assessment*, 96, 121–139.
Haslam, N., Bastian, B., & Bissett, M. (2004). Essentialist beliefs about personality and their implications. *Personality and Social Psychology Bulletin*, 30, 1661–1673.
Haslam, N., & Ernst, D. (2002). Essentialist beliefs about mental disorders. *Journal of Social and Clinical Psychology*, 21, 628–644.
Haslam, N., Holland, E., & Kuppens, P. (2012). Categories versus dimensions in personality and psychopathology: A quantitative review of taxometric research. *Psychological Medicine*, 42, 903–920.
Hatcher, R. L., & Rogers, D. T. (2009). Development and validation of a measure of interpersonal strengths: The inventory of interpersonal strengths. *Psychological Assessment*, 21, 554–569.
Hathaway, S. R., & McKinley, J. C. (1942). *Minnesota Multiphasic Personality Inventory*. Minneapolis, MN: University of Minnesota Press.
Hathaway, S. R., McKinley, J. C., Butcher, J. N., Dahlstrom, W. G., Graham, J. R., & Tellegen, A. (1989). *Minnesota Multiphasic Personality Inventory test booklet*. Minneapolis, MI: Regents of the University of Minnesota.
Hausberg, M. C., Schulz, H., Piegler, T., Happach, C. G., Klöpper, M., Brütt, A. L., Sammet, I., & Andreas, S. (2012). Is a self-rated instrument appropriate to assess mentalization in patients with mental disorders? Development and first validation of the Mentalization Questionnaire (MZQ). *Psychotherapy Research*, 22, 699–709.
Hayes, S. C. (2016). *The ACT in context*. New York, NY: Routledge.
Hayes, S. C., Strosahl, K. D., & Wilson, K. G. (2011). *Acceptance and commitment therapy: The process and practice of mindful change*. New York, NY: Guilford Press.

Heck, S. A., & Pincus, A. L. (2001). Agency and communion in the structure of parental representations. *Journal of Personality Assessment*, 76, 180–184.

Heilbrun, K. (1992). The role of psychological testing in forensic assessment. *Law and Human Behavior*, 16, 257.

Heilbrun, K. (2001). *Principles of forensic mental health assessment*. New York, NY: Kluwer Academic/Plenum Publishers.

Heilbrun, K., & Brooks, S. (2010). Forensic psychology and forensic science: A proposed agenda for the next decade. *Psychology, Public Policy, and Law*, 16, 219.

Helle, A. C., Trull, T. J., Widiger, T. A., & Mullins-Sweatt, S. N. (2017). Utilizing interview and self-report assessment of the Five-Factor Model to examine convergence with the alternative model for personality disorders. *Personality Disorders: Theory, Research, and Treatment*, 8, 247–254.

Herpertz, S. C., Huprich, S. K., Bohus, M., Chanen, A., Goodman, M., Mehlum, L., Moran, P., Newton-Howes, G., Scott, L., & Sharp, C. (2017). The challenge of transforming the diagnostic system of personality disorders. *Journal of Personality Disorders*, 31, 577–589.

Hess, N. (2016). On making emotional contact with a schizoid patient. *British Journal of Psychotherapy*, 32, 53–64.

Hilsenroth, M., Stein, M., & Pinsker, J. (2007). *Social Cognition and Object Relations Scale: Global rating method (SCORS-G)*. Unpublished manuscript. Garden City, NY: The Derner Institute of Advanced Psychological Studies, Adelphi University.

Hofmann, S. G., & Otto, M. W. (2008). *Cognitive behavioral therapy for social anxiety disorder: Evidence-based and disorder-specific treatment techniques*. Abingdon, UK: Routledge.

Hopwood, C. J. (2011). Personality traits in the DSM-5. *Journal of Personality Assessment*, 93, 398–405.

Hopwood, C. J. (2018). A framework for treating DSM-5 alternative model for personality disorder features. *Personality and Mental Health, 12*, 107–125.

Hopwood, C. J., Ansell, E. A., Pincus, A. L., Wright, A. G. C., Lukowitsky, M. R., & Roche, M. J. (2011). The circumplex structure of interpersonal sensitivities. *Journal of Personality*, 79, 707–740.

Hopwood, C. J. & Bleidorn, W. (2018). Stability and change in personality and personality disorders. *Current Opinion in Psychology*, 21, 6–10.

Hopwood, C. J., & Bornstein, R. F. (Eds.) (2014). *Multimethod clinical assessment*. New York, NY: Guilford Press.

Hopwood, C. J., Good, E. W., & Morey, L. C. (in press, 2018). Validity of the DSM-5 levels of personality functioning scale—self report. *Journal of Personality Assessment*. doi:10.1080/00223891.2017.1420660

Hopwood, C. J., Kotov, R., Krueger, R. F., Watson, D., Widiger, T. A., Althoff, R. R., Ansell, E. B., Bach, B., Bagby, R. M., Blais, M. A., Bornovalova, M. A., Chmielewski, M., Cicero, D. C., Conway, C., De Clerq, B., De Fruyt, F., Docherty, A. R., Eaton, N. R., Edens, J. F., Forbes, M. K., Forbush, K. T., Hengartner, M. P., Ivanova, M. Y., Leising, D., Livesley, W. J., Lukowitsky, M. R., Lynam, D. R., Markon, K. E., Miller, J. D., Morey, L. C., Mullins-Sweatt, S. N., Ormel, J. H., Patrick, C. J., Pincus, A. L., Ruggero, C., Samuel, D. B., Sellbom, M., Slade, T., Tackett, J. L., Thomas, K. M., Trull, T. J., Vachon, D. D., Waldman, I. D., Waszczuk, M. A., Waugh, M. H., Wright,

A. G. C., Yalch, M. M., Zald, D. H., and Zimmermann, J. (2017). The time has come for dimensional personality disorder diagnosis. *Personality and Mental Health*, 12, 82–86.

Hopwood, C. J., Malone, J. C., Ansell, E. B., Sanislow, C. A., Grilo, C. M., McGlashan, T. H., Pinto, A., Markowitz, J. C., Shea, M. T., Skodol, A. E., Gunderson, J. G., Zanarini, M. C., & Morey, L. C. (2011). Personality assessment in DSM-V: Empirical support for rating severity, style, and traits. *Journal of Personality Disorders*, 25, 305–320.

Hopwood, C.J., Pincus, A.L., & Wright, A.G.C. (2019). The interpersonal situation: Integrating personality assessment, case formulation, and intervention. In D. Samuel & D. Lynam (Eds.), *Using basic personality research to inform personality disorders.* New York, NY: Oxford University Press.

Hopwood, C. J., Schade, N., Krueger, R. F., Wright, A. C., & Markon, K. E. (2013). Connecting DSM-5 personality traits and pathological beliefs: Toward a unifying model. *Journal of Psychopathology and Behavioral Assessment*, 35, 162–172. doi:10.1007/s10862–012–9332–3

Hopwood, C. J., & Sellbom, M. (2013). Implications of DSM-5 personality traits for forensic psychology. *Psychological Injury and Law*, 6, 314–323.

Hopwood, C. J., Thomas, K. M., Luo, X., Bernard, N., Lin, Y., & Levendosky, A. A. (2016). Implementing dynamic assessments in psychotherapy. *Assessment*, 23, 507–517.

Hopwood, C. J., Thomas, K. M., Markon, K. E., Wright, A. G., & Krueger, R. F. (2012). DSM-5 personality traits and DSM–IV personality disorders. *Journal of Abnormal Psychology*, 121, 424.

Hopwood, C. J., & Waugh, M. H. (in press). *Personality assessment paradigms and methods: A collaborative reassessment of Madeline G.* London, UK: Routledge.

Hopwood, C. J., Wright, A. C., Ansell, E. B., & Pincus, A. L. (2013). The interpersonal core of personality pathology. *Journal of Personality Disorders*, 27, 270–295.

Hopwood, C. J., Wright, A. G., Krueger, R. F., Schade, N., Markon, K. E., & Morey, L. C. (2013). DSM-5 pathological personality traits and the Personality Assessment Inventory. *Assessment*, 20, 269–285.

Hopwood, C. J., Zimmermann, J., Pincus, A. L., & Krueger, R. F. (2015). Connecting personality structure and dynamics: Towards a more evidence-based and clinically useful diagnostic scheme. *Journal of Personality Disorders*, 29, 431–448.

Horowitz, L. M. (2004). *Interpersonal foundations of psychopathology.* Washington, DC: American Psychological Association.

Horowitz, M. J. (1975). Sliding meanings: A defense against threat in narcissistic personalities. *International Journal of Psychoanalytic Psychotherapy*, 4, 167–180.

Horowitz, M. J. (1994). Configurational analysis and the use of role-relationship models to understand transference. *Psychotherapy Research*, 4, 184–196.

Horowitz, M. (2009). Clinical phenomenology of narcissistic pathology. *Psychiatric Annals*, 39, 124–128.

Horowitz, M. (2013). Disturbed personality functioning and psychotherapy technique. *Psychotherapy*, 50, 438–442.

Horvath, A. O. (2001). The alliance. Psychotherapy: Theory, Research, Practice, Training, 38, 365–372.

Horwitz, A. V., & Wakefield, J. C. (2007). *The loss of sadness: How psychiatry transformed normal sorrow into depressive disorder.* New York, NY: Oxford University Press.

Huprich, S. K., Auerbach, J. S., Porcerelli, J. H., & Bupp, L. L. (2016). Sidney Blatt's Object Relations Inventory: Contributions and future directions. *Journal of Personality Assessment*, 98, 30–43.
Huprich, S. K., Nelson, S. M., Meehan, K. B., Siefert, C. J., Haggerty, G., Sexton, J., Dauphin, V. B., Macaluso, M., Jackson, J., Zackula, R., & Baade, L. (in press, 2018). Introduction of the DSM-5 Levels of Personality Functioning Questionnaire. *Personality Disorders: Theory, Research, and Treatment*. doi:10.1037/per0000264
Hutsebaut, J., Feenstra, D. J., & Kamphuis, J. H. (2016). Development and preliminary psychometric evaluation of a brief self-report questionnaire for the assessment of the DSM–5 Level of Personality Functioning Scale: The LPFS Brief Form (LPFS-BF). *Personality Disorders: Theory, Research, and Treatment*, 7, 192–197.
Hutsebaut, J., Kamphuis, J. H., Feenstra, D. J., Weekers, L. C., & De Saeger, H. (2017). Assessing DSM-5-oriented level of personality functioning: Development and psychometric evaluation of the Semi-Structured Interview for Personality Functioning DSM-5 (STiP-5.1). *Personality Disorders: Theory, Research, and Treatment*, 8, 94.
Hyman, S. E. (2010). The diagnosis of mental disorders: The problem of reification. *Annual Review of Clinical Psychology*, 6, 155–179.
Insel, T., Cuthbert, B., Garvey, M., Heinssen, R., Pine, D. S., Quinn, K., Sanislow, C., & Wang, P. (2010). Research domain criteria (RDoC): Toward a new classification framework for research on mental disorders. *The American Journal of Psychiatry*, 167, 748–751.
Ivey, G. (2013). Cognitive therapy's assimilation of countertransference: A psychodynamic perspective. *British Journal of Psychotherapy*, 29, 230–244.
Iwamasa, G. Y., Larrabee, A. L., & Merritt, R. D. (2000). Are personality disorder criteria ethnically biased? A card-sort analysis. *Cultural Diversity and Ethnic Minority Psychology*, 6, 284–296.
Izdebska, A. (2015). Assessment of personality according to Otto Kernberg's conception. *Current Issues in Personality Psychology*, 3, 65–83.
Jablensky, A. (2007). Living in a Kraepelinian world: Kraepelin's impact on modern psychiatry. *History of Psychiatry*, 18, 381–388
Jablensky, A. (2012). Prototypes, syndromes and dimensions of psychopathology: An open agenda for research. *World Psychiatry*, 11, 22–23.
Jablensky, A. (2016). Psychiatric classifications: validity and utility. *World Psychiatry*, 15, 26–31.
Jackson, C., Davidson, G., Russell, J., & Vandereycken, W. (1990). Ellen West revisited: The theme of death in eating disorders. *International Journal of Eating Disorders*, 9, 529–536.
James, L. M., Anders, S. L., Peterson, C. K., Engdahl, B. E., Krueger, R. F., & Georgopoulos, A. P. (2015). DSM-5 personality traits discriminate between posttraumatic stress disorder and control groups. *Experimental Brain Research*, 233, 2021–2028.
James, L. M., Engdahl, B. E., Leuthold, A. C., Krueger, R. F., & Georgopoulos, A. P. (2015). Pathological personality traits modulate neural interactions. *Experimental brain research*, 233, 3543–3552.
James, W. (1890/1950). *The principles of psychology*. New York, NY: Dover.
Jaspers, K. (1912/1968). The phenomenological approach in psychopathology. *British Journal of Psychiatry*, 114, 1313–1323.

Jaspers, K. (1913/1997). *General psychopathology (Vol. 2)* (J. Hoenig & M. Hamilton, Trans.). Baltimore, MD: Johns Hopkins University Press.

Jaspers, K. (1953/1976). *The origin and goal of history.* Santa Barbara, CA: Greenwood Press.

Jaspers, K. (1957/1997). *Reason and existence: Five lectures.* Milwaukee, WI: Marquette University Press.

Jeandarme, I., Edens, J. F., Habets, P., Bruckers, L., Oei, K., & Bogaerts, S. (2017). PCL-R field validity in prison and hospital settings. *Law and Human Behavior*, 41, 29–43.

Johnson, J. A., Carroll, J., Gottschall, J., & Kruger, D. (2011). Portrayal of personality in Victorian novels reflects modern research findings but amplifies the significance of agreeableness. *Journal of Research in Personality*, 45, 50–58.

Johnson, J. G., Cohen, P., Kasen, S., Skodol, A. E., Hamagami, F., & Brook, J. S. (2000). Age-related change in personality disorder trait levels between early adolescence and adulthood: A community-based longitudinal investigation. *Acta Psychiatrica Scandinavica*, 102, 265–275.

Johnson, M. & Ferraro, K. (2000). Research on domestic violence in the 1990s: Making distinctions. *Journal of Marriage and Family*, 62, 948–963. doi:10.1111/j.1741-3737.2000.00948.x

Johnson, S. C., & Elbogen, E. B. (2013). Personality disorders at the interface of psychiatry and the law: Legal use and clinical classification. *Dialogues in Clinical Neuroscience*, 15, 203–211.

Jopp, A. M., & South, S. C. (2015). Investigating the Personality Inventory for DSM-5 using self and spouse reports. *Journal of Personality Disorders*, 29, 193–214.

Joyce, J. (1922/1986). *Ulysses.* New York, NY: Vintage.

Kagan, J. (2009). *The three cultures: Natural sciences, social sciences, and the humanities in the 21st century.* Cambridge, MA: Cambridge University Press.

Kahneman, D. (2011). *Thinking, fast and slow.* Basingstoke, UK: Macmillan.

Karpman, B. (1948). The myth of the psychopathic personality. *The American Journal of Psychiatry*, 104, 523–534.

Karpman, S. (1968). Fairy tales and script drama analysis. *Transactional Analysis Bulletin*, 7, 39–43.

Kealy, D., & Rasmussen, B. (2012). Veiled and vulnerable: The other side of grandiose narcissism. *Clinical Social Work Journal*, 40, 356–366.

Keeley, J. (2015). The background assumptions of measurement practices in psychological assessment and psychiatric diagnosis. In P. Zachar, D. Stoyanov, M. Aragona, & A. Jablensky (Eds.), *Alternative perspectives on psychiatric validation.* Oxford, UK: Oxford University Press.

Keeley, J. W., Chmielewski, M. S., & Bagby, R. M. (2015). Interaction effects in comorbid psychopathology. *Comprehensive Psychiatry*, 60, 35–39.

Keeley, J. W., DeLao, C. S., & Kirk, C. L. (2013). The commutative property in comorbid diagnosis: Does A + B = B + A? *Clinical Psychological Science*, 1, 16–29.

Kelly, G. A. (1955). *The psychology of personal constructs (Vol. 1–2).* New York, NY: Routledge.

Kelley, T. L. (1927). *Interpretation of educational measurements.* Yonkers-on-Hudson: World Book Company.

Kendell, R., & Jablensky, A. (2003). Distinguishing between the validity and utility of psychiatric diagnoses. *American Journal of Psychiatry*, 160, 4–12.

Kendler, K. S. (2005). Toward a philosophical structure for psychiatry. *American Journal of Psychiatry*, 162, 433–440.
Kendler, K. S. (2008). Explanatory models for psychiatric illness. *American Journal of Psychiatry*, 165, 695–702.
Kendler, K. S. (2009). A historical framework for psychiatric nosology. *Psychological Medicine*, 39, 1935–1941.
Kendler, K. S. (2015). Toward a limited realism for psychiatric nosology based on the coherence theory of truth. *Psychological Medicine*, 45, 1115–1118.
Kendler, K. S., & Solomon, M. (2016). Expert consensus v. evidence-based approaches in the revision of the DSM. *Psychological Medicine*, 46, 2255–2262.
Kendler, K. S., Zachar, P., & Craver, C. (2011). What kinds of things are psychiatric disorders? *Psychological Medicine*, 41, 1143–1150.
Kernberg, O. F. (1967). Borderline personality organization. *Journal of the American Psychoanalytic Association*, 15, 641–685.
Kernberg, O.F. (1984). *Severe personality disorders.* New Haven, CT: Yale University Press.
Kernberg, O. F. (1993). *Severe personality disorders: Psychotherapeutic strategies.* New Haven, CT: Yale University Press.
Kernberg, O. F. (2012). Overview and critique of the classification of personality disorders proposed for DSM-V. *Swiss Arch Neurol and Psychiatry*, 163, 234–238.
Kernberg, O. F. (2016). What is personality? *Journal of Personality Disorders*, 30, 145–156.
Kernberg, O. F., & Caligor, E. (2005). A psychoanalytic theory of personality disorders. In M.F. Lenzenweger, & J.F. Clarkin (Eds.), *Major theories of personality disorder.* (2nd ed., pp. 114–156). New York, NY: Guilford.
Kernberg, O. F., Yeomans, F. E., Clarkin, J. F., & Levy, K. N. (2008). Transference focused psychotherapy: Overview and update. *The International Journal of Psychoanalysis*, 89, 601–620.
Kidd, D. C., & Castano, E. (2013). Reading literary fiction improves theory of mind. *Science*, 342, 377–380.
Kim, N. S., & Ahn, W. (2002). Clinical psychologists' theory-based representations of mental disorders predict their diagnostic reasoning and memory. *Journal of Experimental Psychology: General*, 131, 451–476.
Kim, N. S., Johnson, S. G. B., Ahn, W., & Knobe, J. (2017). The effect of abstract versus concrete framing on judgments of biological and psychological bases of behavior. *Cognitive Research: Principles and Implications*, 2, 1–16.
Klerman, G. L. (1978). The evolution of scientific nosology. In J. C. Shershow (Ed.), *Schizophrenia: Science and practice* (pp. 99–121). Cambridge, MA: Harvard University Press.
Knight, R. P. (1953). Management and psychotherapy of the borderline schizophrenic patient. *Bulletin of the Menninger Clinic*, 17, 139–150.
Kohlenberg, R. J., & Tsai, M. (2007). *Functional analytic psychotherapy: Creating intense and curative therapeutic relationships.* Berlin, Germany: Springer Science & Business Media.
Kohut, H. (1971). *The analysis of the self.* New York, NY: International Universities.
Kohut, H. (1977). *The restoration of the self.* Chicago, IL: University of Chicago Press.

Kohut, H. (1979). The two analyses of Mr. Z. *The International Journal of Psychoanalysis*, 60, 3–28.

Komarraju, M., & Cokely, K. (2008). Horizontal and vertical dimensions of individualism- collectivism: A comparison of African-Americans and European Americans. *Cultural Diversity and Ethnic Minority Psychology*, 14, 336–343.

Konrad, N. (2002). Prisons as new asylums. *Current Opinion in Psychiatry*, 15, 583–587.

Kopala-Sibley, D. C., Zuroff, D. C., Russell, J. J., & Moskowitz, D. S. (2014). Understanding heterogeneity in social anxiety disorder: Dependency and self-criticism moderate fear responses to interpersonal cues. *British Journal of Clinical Psychology*, 53, 141–156.

Korzybski, A. (1933). *Science and sanity: An introduction to non-Aristotelian systems and general semantics*. New York, NY: Wiley.

Kotov, R., Krueger, R. F., Watson, D., Achenbach, T. M., Althoff, R. R., Bagby, R. M., Brown, T. A., Carpenter, W. T., Caspi, A., Clark, L. A., Eaton, N. R., Forbes, M. K., Forbush, K. T., Goldberg, D., Hasin, D., Hyman, S. E., Ivanova, M. Y., Lynam, D. R., Markon, K., Miller, J. D., Moffitt, T. E., Morey, L. C., Mullins-Sweatt, S. N., Ormel, J., Patrick, P. J., Regier, D. A., Rescoria, L., Ruggero, C. J., Samuel, D. B., Sellbom, M., Simms, L. J., Skodol, A. E., Slade, T., South, S. C., Tackett, J. L., Waldman, I. D., Waszczuk, M. A., Widiger, T. A., Wright, A. G. C., & Zimmerman, M. (2017). The Hierarchical Taxonomy of Psychopathology (HiTOP): A dimensional alternative to traditional nosologies. *Journal of Abnormal Psychology*, 126, 454–477. doi:10.1037/abn0000258

Kraepelin, E. (1904). *Psychiatrie. Ein Lehrbuch für Studierende und Ärtzte. 7. Auflage. II. Band. Klinische Psychiatrie*. Leipzig, Germany: Verlag Barth.

Kragh, J. V. (2010). Malaria fever therapy for general paralysis of the insane in Denmark. *History of psychiatry*, 21, 471–486.

Krueger, R. F. (1999). The structure of common mental disorders. *Archives of General Psychiatry*, 56, 921–926.

Krueger, R. F. (2005). Continuity of Axes I and II: Toward a Unified Model of Personality, Personality Disorders, and Clinical Disorders. *Journal of Personality Disorders*, 19, 233–261.

Krueger, R. F., Derringer, J., Markon, K. E., Watson, D., & Skodol, A. E. (2012). Initial construction of a maladaptive personality trait model and inventory for DSM-5. *Psychological Medicine*, 42, 1879–1890.

Krueger, R. F., Derringer, J., Markon, K. E., Watson, D., & Skodol, A. E. (2013). The Personality Inventory for DSM-5—Brief Form (PID-5-BF)—adult. Arlington, VA: American Psychiatric Association.

Krueger, R. F., & DeYoung, C. G. (2016). The RDoC initiative and the structure of psychopathology. *Psychophysiology*, 53, 351–354.

Krueger, R. F., & Eaton, N. R. (2015). Transdiagnostic factors of mental disorders. *World Psychiatry*, 14, 27–29.

Krueger, R. F., Eaton, N. R., Derringer, J., Markon, K. E., Watson, D., & Skodol, A. E. (2011). Personality in DSM–5: Helping delineate personality disorder content and framing the metastructure. *Journal of Personality Assessment*, 93, 325–331.

Krueger, R. F., Hopwood, C. J., Wright, A. C., & Markon, K. E. (2014). DSM-5 and the path toward empirically based and clinically useful conceptualization of personality and psychopathology. *Clinical Psychology: Science and Practice*, 21, 245–261.

Krueger, R. F., & Markon, K. E. (2014). The role of the DSM-5 personality trait model in moving toward a quantitative and empirically based approach to classifying personality and psychopathology. *Annual Review of Clinical Psychology*, 10, 477–501.
Kuhn, T. S. (1962/2012). *The structure of scientific revolutions.* Chicago, IL: University of Chicago Press.
Kuhn, T. S. (1979). Metaphor in science. In A. Ortony (Ed.), *Metaphor and Thought* (pp. 409–419). Cambridge, UK: Cambridge University Press.
Lacasse, J. R., & Leo, J. (2005). Serotonin and depression: A disconnect between the advertisements and the scientific literature. PLoS Med, *2*, e392.
Lakoff, G., & Johnson, M. (1980). *Metaphors we live by.* Chicago, IL: University of Chicago Press.
Lampe, L. (2016) Avoidant personality disorder as a social anxiety phenotype: Risk factors, associations and treatment. *Current Opinion Psychiatry*, 29, 64–69.
Lampe, L., & Sunderland, M. (2015). Social phobia and avoidant personality disorder: Similar but different? *Journal of personality disorders*, 29, 115–130.
Lander, T. D., & Heilbrun, K. (2009). The content and quality of forensic mental health assessment: Validation of a principles-based approach. *International Journal of Forensic Mental Health*, 8, 115–121.
Laplanche, J., & Pontalis, J. B. (1988). *The language of psychoanalysis.* London, UK: Karnac Books.
Leahy, R. L. (2008). The therapeutic relationship in cognitive-behavioral therapy. *Behavioural and Cognitive Psychotherapy*, 36, 769–777.
Leahy, R. L. (2017). *Cognitive therapy techniques: A practitioner's guide* (2nd ed.). New York, NY: Guilford Press.
Leahy, R. L., Beck, J., & Beck, A. T. (2005). Cognitive therapy for the personality disorders. In S. Strack (Ed.), *Handbook of personology and psychopathology* (pp. 442–461). New York, NY: John Wiley & Sons.
Leary, T. (1957). *Interpersonal diagnosis of personality.* New York, NY: Blackwell Publishing.
Leising, D., Scherbaum, S., Packmohr, P., & Zimmermann, J. (in press, 2018). Substance and Evaluation in Personality Disorder Diagnoses. *Journal of Personality Disorders.* doi:10.1521/pedi_2017_31_324
Lenzenweger, M. F. (2010). *Schizotypy and schizophrenia: The view from experimental psychopathology.* New York, NY: Guilford Press.
Lenzenweger, M.F. (2015). Thinking clearly about schizotypy: Hewing to the schizophrenia liability core, considering interesting tangents, and avoiding conceptual quicksand. *Schizophrenia Bulletin*, 41, S483.
Lenzenweger, M. F., Clarkin, J. F., Kernberg, O. F., & Foelsch, P. A. (2001). The Inventory of Personality Organization: Psychometric properties, factorial composition, and criterion relations with affect, aggressive dyscontrol, psychosis proneness, and self-domains in a nonclinical sample. *Psychological Assessment*, 13, 577–591.
Lenzenweger, M. F., Clarkin, J. F., Yeomans, F. E., Kernberg, O. F., & Levy, K. N. (2008). Refining the borderline personality disorder phenotype through finite mixture modeling: Implications for classification. *Journal of Personality Disorders*, 22, 313–331.
Lesko, L. J., Zineh, I., & Huang, S. M. (2010). What is clinical utility and why should we care? *Clinical Pharmacology & Therapeutics*, 88, 729–733.

Levy, K. N. (2005). The implications of attachment theory and research for understanding borderline personality disorder. *Development and Psychopathology*, 17, 959–986.

Levy, K. N., Johnson, B. N., Clouthier, T. L., Scala, J. W., & Temes, C. M. (2015). An attachment theoretical framework for personality disorders. *Canadian Psychology/Psychologie Canadienne*, 56, 197–207.

Levy, M. S. (2000). A conceptualization of the repetition compulsion. *Psychiatry*, 63, 45–53.

Lewin, K. (1936). A dynamic theory of personality: Selected papers. *The Journal of Nervous and Mental Disease*, 84, 612–613.

Lewin, K. (1943). Psychology and the process of group living. *The Journal of Social Psychology*, 17, 113–131.

Lieberman, L., Gorka, S. M., Huggins, A. A., Katz, A. C., Sarapas, C., & Shankman, S. A. (2016). Agreement between self- and informant-reported ratings of personality traits: The moderating effects of major depressive and/or panic disorder. *Journal of Nervous and Mental Disease*, 204, 306–313.

Liggett, J., Sellbom, M., & Carmichael, K. L. (2017). Examining the DSM-5 Section III criteria for obsessive-compulsive personality disorder in a community sample. *Journal of Personality Disorders*, 39, 723–741.

Lilienfeld, S. O., Sauvigné, K. C., Lynn, S. J., Cautin, R. L., Latzman, R. D., & Waldman, I. D. (2015). Fifty psychological and psychiatric terms to avoid: A list of inaccurate, misleading, misused, ambiguous, and logically confused words and phrases. *Frontiers in Psychology*, 6, 1100.

Linehan, M. (1993). *Cognitive–behavioral treatment of borderline personality disorder*. New York, NY: Guilford Press.

Linehan, M. M. (2015). *DBT Skills Training Manual* (2nd ed.). New York, NY: Guilford Press.

Lingiardi, V., Filippucci, L., & Baiocco, R. (2005). Therapeutic alliance evaluation in personality disorders psychotherapy. *Psychotherapy Research*, 15, 45–53.

Lingiardi, V., & McWilliams, N. (Eds.). (2017). *Psychodynamic diagnostic manual: PDM-2*. New York, NY: Guilford Publications.

Lingiardi, V., McWilliams, N., Bornstein, R. F., Gazzillo, F., & Gordon, R. M. (2015). The Psychodynamic Diagnostic Manual Version 2 (PDM-2): Assessing patients for improved clinical practice and research. *Psychoanalytic Psychology*, 32, 94.

Livesley, W. J. (1985). The classification of personality disorder: I. The choice of category concept. *The Canadian Journal of Psychiatry*, 30, 353–358.

Livesley, W. J. (1991). Classifying personality disorders: Ideal types, prototypes, or dimensions? *Journal of Personality Disorders*, 5, 52–59.

Livesley, W. J. (1998). Suggestions for a framework for an empirically based classification of personality disorder. *The Canadian Journal of Psychiatry*, 43, 137–147.

Livesley, W. J. (2005). Principles and strategies for treating personality disorder. *The Canadian Journal of Psychiatry / La Revue Canadienne De Psychiatrie*, 50, 442–450.

Livesley, W. J. (2006). The Dimensional Assessment of Personality Pathology (DAPP) approach to personality disorder. In S. Strack (Ed.), *Differentiating normal and abnormal personality* (pp. 401–429). New York, NY: Springer.

Livesley, W. J., & Jackson, D. N. (2000). *Dimensional assessment of personality problems*. Port Huron, MI: Sigma Assessment Systems.

Livesley, W. J., & Jackson, D. (2009). *Manual for the dimensional assessment of personality pathology—basic questionnaire.* Port Huron, MI: SIGMA Assessment Systems.
Livesley, W. J., Jang, K. L., & Vernon, P. A. (1998). Phenotypic and genetic structure of traits delineating personality disorder. *Archives of General Psychiatry*, 55, 941–948.
Lizdek, I., Sadler, P., Woody, E., Ethier, N., & Malet, G. (2012). Capturing the stream of behavior: A computer-joystick method for coding interpersonal behavior continuously over time. *Social Science Computer Review*, 30, 513–521.
Locke, K. D. (2000). Circumplex scales of interpersonal values: Reliability, validity, and applicability to interpersonal problems and personality disorders. *Journal of Personality Assessment*, 75, 249–267.
Locke, K. D. (2011). Circumplex measures of interpersonal constructs. In L. M. Horowitz, & S. Strack (Eds.), *Handbook of interpersonal psychology: Theory, research, assessment, and therapeutic interventions* (pp. 313–324). Hoboken, NJ: Wiley.
Locke, K. D., & Sadler, P. (2007). Self-efficacy, values, and complementarity in dyadic interactions: Integrating interpersonal and social-cognitive theory. *Personality and Social Psychology Bulletin*, 33, 94–109.
Loevinger, J. (1957). Objective tests as instruments of psychological theory. *Psychological Reports*, 3, 635–694.
Loevinger, J. (1966). Three principles for a psychoanalytic psychology. *Journal of Abnormal Psychology*, 71, 432.
Loevinger, J. (1976). *Ego development: Conceptions and theories.* San Francisco, CA: Jossey-Bass.
Loevinger, J. (1987). *Paradigms of personality.* New York, NY: W. H. Freeman/ Times Books/Henry Holt & Co.
Loevinger, J. (1993). Measurement of personality: True or false. *Psychological Inquiry*, 4, 1–16.
Loevinger, J. (1994) Has psychology lost its conscience? *Journal of Personality Assessment*, 62, 2–8.
Lowyck, B., Luyten, P., Verhaest, Y., Vandeneede, B., & Vermote, R. (2013). Levels of personality functioning and their association with clinical features and interpersonal functioning in patients with personality disorders. *Journal of Personality Disorders*, 27, 320–336.
Lowyck, B., Luyten, P., Vermote, R., Verhaest, Y., & Vansteelandt, K. (2017). Self-critical perfectionism, dependency, and symptomatic distress in patients with personality disorder during hospitalization-based psychodynamic treatment: A parallel process growth modeling approach. *Personality Disorders: Theory, Research, and Treatment*, 8, 268.
Luborsky, L., & Crits-Christoph, P. (1990). *Understanding transference: The CCRT method.* New York, NY: Basic Books.
Luyten, P. & Blatt, S. J. (2011). Integrating theory-driven and empirically-derived models of personality development and psychopathology: A proposal for DSM-V. *Clinical Psychology Review*, 31, 52–68.
Luyten, P., & Blatt, S. J. (2016). A hierarchical multiple-level approach to the assessment of interpersonal relatedness and self-definition: Implications for research, clinical practice, and DSM planning. *Journal of Personality Assessment*, 98, 5–13.

Luyten, P., Lowyck, B., & Blatt, S. J. (2017). Mechanisms of change through the lens of two-polarities models of personality development: State of the art and new directions. *Psychoanalytic Inquiry*, 37, 179–190.
Luyten, P., Mayes, L. C., Blatt, S. J., Fonagy, P., & Target, M. (2015). *Handbook of psychodynamic approaches to psychopathology*. New York, NY: Guilford Press.
Lynam, D. R., & Widiger, T. A. (2001). Using the Five-Factor Model to represent the DSM-IV personality disorders: An expert consensus approach. *Journal of Abnormal Psychology*, 110, 401–412.
Lynch, T. R., Trost, W. T., Salsman, N., & Linehan, M. M. (2007). Dialectical behavior therapy for borderline personality disorder. *Annual Review of Clinical Psychology*, 3, 181–205.
MacCorquodale, K., & Meehl, P. E. (1948). On a distinction between hypothetical constructs and intervening variables. *Psychological Review*, 55, 95–107.
Maltsberger, J. T. (1996). The case of Ellen West revisited: A permitted suicide. *Suicide and Life-Threatening Behavior*, 26, 86–97.
Mansell, W., Harvey, A., Watkins, E., & Shafran, R. (2009). Conceptual foundations of the transdiagnostic approach to CBT. *Journal of Cognitive Psychotherapy*, 23, 6–19.
Maples, J. L., Carter, N. T., Few, L. R., Crego, C., Gore, W. L., Samuel, D. B., Williamson, R. L., Lynam, D. R., Widiger, T. A., Markon, K. E., Krueger, R. F., & Miller, J. D. (2015). Testing whether the DSM-5 Personality Disorder Trait Model can be measured with a reduced set of items: An item response theory investigation of the personality inventory for DSM-5. *Psychological Assessment*, 27, 1195–1210.
Mar, R. A., & Oatley, K. (2008). The function of fiction is the abstraction and simulation of social experience. *Perspectives on psychological science*, 3, 173–192.
Markon, K. (2010). How things fall apart: understanding the nature of internalizing through its relationship with impairment. *Journal of Abnormal Psychology*, 119, 447–458.
Markon, K. E. (2013). Epistemological pluralism and scientific development: An argument against authoritative nosologies. *Journal of Personality Disorders*, 27, 554–579.
Markon, K. E., Krueger, R. F., & Watson, D. (2005). Delineating the structure of normal and abnormal personality: An integrative hierarchical approach. Journal of Personality and Social Psychology, 88, 139–157.
Markon, K. E., Quilty, L. C., Bagby, R. M., & Krueger, R. F. (2013). The development and psychometric properties of an informant-report form of the Personality Inventory for DSM-5 (PID-5). *Assessment*, 20, 370–383.
Marková, I. S., & Berrios, G. E. (2009). Epistemology of mental symptoms. *Psychopathology*, 42, 343–349.
Marková, I. S., & Berrios, G. E. (2012). Epistemology of psychiatry. *Psychopathology, 45*, 220–227.
Maroda, K. J. (1998). Enactment: When the patient's and analyst's pasts converge. *Psychoanalytic Psychology*, 15, 517–535.
Maroda, K. J. (2013). *The power of countertransference: Innovations in analytic technique*. New York, NY: Routledge.
Martino, D., Tanner, A., Defazio, G., Church, A. J., Bhatia, K. P., Giovannoni, G., & Dale, R. C. (2005). Tracing Sydenham's chorea: Historical documents from a British paediatric hospital. *Archives of Disease in Childhood*, 90, 507–511.

Masterson, J. F. (1981). *The narcissistic and borderline disorders: An integrated developmental approach*. New York, NY: Brunner/Mazel.
McAdams, D. P. (1993). *The stories we live by: Personal myths and the making of the self.* New York, NY: Guilford Press.
McAdams, D. P. (1995). What do we know when we know a person? *Journal of Personality*, 63, 365–396.
McAdams D. P. (1998). Coding system for contamination sequences. Retrieved from www.sesp.northwestern.edu/foley/instruments/contamination/
McAdams D. P. (1999). Coding system for redemptive sequences. Retrieved from www.sesp.northwestern.edu/foley/instruments/redemption/
McAdams, D. P. (2001). The psychology of life stories. *Review of General Psychology*, 5, 100–122.
McAdams D. P. (2002). Coding systems for themes of agency and communion. Retrieved from www.sesp.northwestern.edu/foley/instruments/agency/
McAdams D. P. (2008). The Life Story Interview. Retrieved from www.sesp.northwestern.edu/docs/LifeStoryInterview.pdf
McAdams, D. P. (2010). *George W. Bush and the redemptive dream: A psychological portrait*. New York, NY: Oxford University Press.
McAdams, D. P. (2013). The psychological self as actor, agent, and author. *Perspectives on Psychological Science*, 8, 272–295.
McAdams, D. P. (2015). *The art and science of personality development*. New York, NY: Guilford Press
McAdams, D. P., & de St. Aubin, E. (1992). A theory of generativity and its assessment through self-report, behavioral acts, and narrative themes in autobiography. *Journal of Personality and Social Psychology*, 62, 1003–1015.
McAdams, D. P., Diamond, A., de St. Aubin, E., & Mansfield, E. (1997). Stories of commitment: The psychosocial construction of generative lives. *Journal of Personality and Social Psychology*, 72, 678.
McAdams, D. P., Hart, H. M., & Maruna, S. (1998). The anatomy of generativity. In D. P. McAdams and E. de St. Aubin (Eds.), *Generativity and adult development: How and why we care for the next generation* (pp. 7–43). Washington, DC: APA Press.
McAdams, D. P., Hoffman, B. J., Day, R., & Mansfield, E. D. (1996). Themes of agency and communion in significant autobiographical scenes. *Journal of Personality*, 64, 339–377.
McAdams, D. P., & Manczak, E. (2015). Personality and the life story. In M. Mikulincer, P. R. Shaver, M. L. Cooper & R. J. Larsen (Eds.), *APA handbook of personality and social psychology (Vol. 4): Personality processes and individual differences* (pp. 425–446). Washington, DC: American Psychological Association.
McAdams, D. P., & Pals, J. L. (2006). A new Big Five: Fundamental principles for an integrative science of personality. *The American Psychologist*, 61, 204–217.
McAdams, D. P., & Pals, J. L. (2007). The role of theory in personality research. In R. W. Robins, R. C. Fraley, & R. F. Krueger (Eds.), *Handbook of research methods in personality psychology* (pp. 3–20). New York, NY: Guilford Press.
McAdams, D. P., Reynolds, J., Lewis, M., Patten, A. H., & Bowman, P. J. (2001). When bad things turn good and good things turn bad: Sequences of redemption and contamination in life narrative and their relation to psychosocial adaptation in midlife adults and in students. *Personality and Social Psychology Bulletin*, 27, 474–485.

McAdams, D. P., & Walden, K. (2010). Jack Block, the Big Five, and personality from the standpoints of actor, agent, and author. *Psychological Inquiry*, 21, 50–56.
McCrae, R. R., & Costa Jr., P. T. (1987). Validation of the five-factor model of personality across instruments and observers. *Journal of Personality and Social Psychology*, 52, 81–90.
McCrae, R. R., & Costa Jr., P. T., (2008). The Five-Factor Theory of personality. In O. P. John, R. W. Robins, & L. A. Pervin (Eds.), *Handbook of personality: Theory and research* (3rd ed.) (pp. 159–181). New York, NY: Guilford.
McCrae, R. R., Costa Jr., P. T., & Martin, T. A. (2005). The NEO–PI–3: A more readable revised NEO Personality Inventory. *Journal of Personality Assessment*, 84, 261–270.
McCrae, R. R., Gaines, J. F., & Wellington, M. A. (2012). The Five-Factor Model in fact and fiction. In H. Tennen, J. Suls, & I. B. Weiner (Eds.), *Handbook of psychology: Personality and social psychology (Vol. 5)* (2nd ed.; pp. 65–91). Hoboken, NJ: John Wiley & Sons.
McNally, R. J. (2016). Can network analysis transform psychopathology? *Behaviour Research and Therapy*, 86, 95–104.
Medin, D. L. (1989). Concepts and conceptual structure. *American Psychologist*, 44, 1469–1481.
Meehl, P. E. (1945). The dynamics of "structured" personality tests. *Journal of Clinical Psychology*, 1, 296–303.
Meehl, P. E. (1960). The cognitive activity of the clinician. *American Psychologist*, 15, 19–27.
Meehl, P. E. (1962). Schizotaxia, schizotypy, schizophrenia. *American Psychologist*, 17, 827–838.
Meehl, P. E. (1964). *Manual for use with Checklist of Schizophrenic Syndrome.* Minneapolis, MN: University of Minnesota Medical School.
Meehl, P. E. (1977). Specific etiology and other forms of strong influence: Some quantitative meanings. *The Journal of Medicine and Philosophy*, 2, 33–53.
Meehl, P. E. (1986). Diagnostic taxa as open concepts: Metatheoretical and statistical questions about reliability and construct validity in the grand strategy of nosological revision. In T. Millon & G. L. Klerman (Eds.), *Contemporary directions in psychopathology: Toward the DSM-IV* (pp. 215–231). New York, NY: Guilford Press.
Meehl, P. E. (1992). Factors and taxa, traits and types, differences of degree and differences in kind. *Journal of Personality*, 60, 117–174.
Messer, S. B., & Wampold, B. E. (2002). Let's face facts: Common factors are more potent than specific therapy ingredients. *Clinical Psychology: Science and Practice*, 9, 21–25.
Meyer, B., & Carver, C. S. (2000). Negative childhood accounts, sensitivity, and pessimism: A study of avoidant personality disorder features in college students. *Journal of Personality Disorders*, 14, 233–248.
Meyer, B., & Pilkonis, P. A. (2005). An attachment model of personality disorders. In M. F. Lenzenweger & J. F. Clarkin (Eds.), *Major theories of personality disorder* (2nd ed.) (pp. 231–281). New York, NY: Guilford Press.
Meyer, G. J., Viglione, D. J., Mihura, J. L., Erard, R. E. & Erdberg, P. (2011). *Rorschach Performance Assessment System: Administration, coding, interpretation, and technical manual.* Toledo, OH: Rorschach Performance Assessment Systems.

Mihura, J. L., & Meyer, G. J. (2017). *Using the Rorschach Performance Assessment System® (R-PAS®)*. New York, NY: Guilford.
Mikulincer, M., & Shaver, P. R. (2012). An attachment perspective on psychopathology. *World Psychiatry*, 11, 11–15.
Miller, G. A., & Lazowski, L. E. (1999). *The adult SASSI-3 manual*. Springville, IN: The SASSI Institute.
Miller, J. D. (2012). Five-Factor Model personality disorder prototypes: A review of their development, validity, and comparison to alternative approaches. *Journal of Personality*, 80, 1565–1591.
Miller, J. D., McCain, J., Lynam, D. R., Few, L. R., Gentile, B., MacKillop, J., & Campbell, W. K. (2014). A comparison of the criterion validity of popular measures of narcissism and narcissistic personality disorder via the use of expert ratings. *Psychological Assessment*, 26, 958.
Miller, R., & Hilsenroth, M. (2016). Assessing anaclitic and introjective characteristics using the SWAP-200 Q-sort: Concurrent validity with the inventory of interpersonal problems circumplex scales. *Clinical Psychology & Psychotherapy*, 24, 932–941.
Miller, J. D., Widiger, T. A., & Campbell, W. K. (2010). Narcissistic personality disorder and the DSM-5. *Journal of Abnormal Psychology*, 119, 640–649.
Millon, T. (1983). The DSM-III: An insider's perspective. *American Psychologist*, 38, 804–814.
Millon, T. (1991). Classification in psychopathology. *Journal of Abnormal Psychology*, 100, 245–261.
Millon, T. (1994). Personality disorders: Conceptual distinctions and classification issues. In P. T. Costa Jr. & T. A. Widiger (Eds.), *Personality disorders and the five-factor model of personality* (pp. 279–301). Washington, DC: American Psychological Association.
Millon, T. (2016). What is a personality disorder? *Journal of Personality Disorders*, 30, 289–306.
Millon, T., Davis, R. D., & Millon, C. (1997). *MCMI-III Manual*. Minneapolis, MN: National Computer Systems.
Millon, T., & Strack, S. (2015). An integrating and comprehensive model of personality pathology based on evolutionary theory. In S. K. Huprich (Ed.), *Personality disorders: Toward theoretical and empirical integration in diagnosis and assessment* (pp. 367–393). Washington, DC: American Psychological Association.
Modell, A. H. (1975). A narcissistic defence against affects and the illusion of self-sufficiency. *The International Journal of Psycho-Analysis*, 56, 275.
Monnot, M. J., Quirk, S. W., Hoerger, M., & Brewer, L. (2009). Racial bias in personality assessment: Using the MMPI-2 to predict psychiatric diagnoses of African American and Caucasian chemical dependency inpatients. *Psychological Assessment*, 21, 137–151.
Moore, T.V. (1930). The empirical determination of certain syndromes underlying praecox and manic-depressive psychoses. *American Journal of Psychiatry*, 86, 719–738.
Moran, P. (1999). The epidemiology of antisocial personality disorder. *Social Psychiatry and Psychiatric Epidemiology*, 34, 231–242.
Morey, L. C. (1991). Classification of mental disorder as a collection of hypothetical constructs. *Journal of Abnormal Psychology*, 100, 289–293.
Morey, L. C. (2007). *The Personality Assessment Inventory professional manual* (2nd ed.). Odessa, FL: Psychological Assessment Resources.

Morey, L. C. (2014). Borderline features are associated with inaccurate trait self-estimations. *Borderline Personality Disorder and Emotion Dysregulation*, 1, 4.

Morey, L. C. (2017). Development and initial evaluation of a self-report form of the DSM-5 Level of Personality Functioning Scale. *Psychological Assessment*, 29, 1302.

Morey, L. C. (in press, 2018). Application of the DSM-5 Level of Personality Functioning Scale by Lay Raters. *Journal of Personality Disorders.* doi:10.1521/pedi_2017_31_305

Morey, L. C., Bender, D. S., & Skodol, A. E. (2013). Validating the proposed diagnostic and statistical manual of mental disorders, severity indicator for personality disorder. *The Journal of Nervous and Mental Disease*, 201, 729–735.

Morey, L. C., & Benson, K. T. (2016). An investigation of adherence to diagnostic criteria, revisited: Clinical diagnosis of the DSM-IV/DSM-5 Section II Personality Disorders. *Journal of Personality Disorders*, 30, 130–144.

Morey, L. C., Benson, K. T., Busch, A. J., & Skodol, A. E. (2015). Personality disorders in DSM-5: Emerging research on the alternative model. *Current Psychiatry Reports*, 17, 24.

Morey, L. C., Benson, K. T., & Skodol, A. E. (2016). Relating DSM-5 Section III Personality Traits to Section II Personality Disorder Diagnoses. *Psychological Medicine*, 46, 647–655.

Morey, L. C., Berghuis, H., Bender, D. S., Verheul, R., Krueger, R. F., & Skodol, A. E. (2011). Toward a model for assessing level of personality functioning in DSM-5, Part II: Empirical articulation of a core dimension of personality pathology. *Journal of Personality Assessment*, 93, 347–353.

Morey, L. C. & Hopwood, C. J. (in press). Expert preferences for categorical, dimensional, and mixed/hybrid approaches to personality disorder classification. *Journal of Personality Disorders.*

Morey, L. C., Krueger, R. F., & Skodol, A. E. (2013). The hierarchical structure of clinician ratings of proposed DSM-5 pathological personality traits. *Journal of Abnormal Psychology*, 122, 836.

Morey, L. C., & Ochoa, E. S. (1989). An investigation of adherence to diagnostic criteria: Clinical diagnosis of the DSM-III personality disorders. *Journal of Personality Disorders*, 3, 180–192.

Morey, L. C., Skodol, A. E., & Oldham, J. M. (2014). Clinician judgments of clinical utility: A comparison of DSM-IV-TR personality disorders and the alternative model for DSM-5 personality disorders. *Journal of Abnormal Psychology*, 123, 398–405.

Morey, L. C., & Stagner, B. H. (2012). Narcissistic pathology as core personality dysfunction: Comparing the DSM-IV and the DSM-5 proposal for narcissistic personality disorder. *Journal of Clinical Psychology*, 68, 908–921.

Moskowitz, D. S. (2009). Coming full circle: Conceptualizing the study of interpersonal behaviour. *Canadian Psychology/Psychologie Canadienne*, 50, 33–41.

Moskowitz, D.S., & Sadikaj, G. (2012). Event-contingent recording. In M. R. Mehl, & T. S. Conner (Eds.), *Handbook of research methods for studying daily life* (pp. 160–175). New York, NY: Guilford.

Mulay, A. L., Cain, N. M., Waugh, M. H., Finn, M. T., Gilmore, J. E., Gordon, R. M., Hopwood, C. J., Nichols, D. S., Streiner, D. S., & Whitley, M. L. (in press, 2018). Contemporary MMPI-2 personality disorder spectra scales. *Archives of Assessment Psychology.*

Mulay, A. L., Cain, N. M., Waugh, M. H., Hopwood, C. J., Adler, J. M., Garcia, D. J., Kurtz, J. E., Lenger, K. A., & Skadberg, R. (in press, 2018). Construct and paradigm in the alternative DSM-5 model for personality disorders. *Journal of Personality Assessment*. doi:10.1080/00223891.2018.1477787

Mullins-Sweatt, S. N., Lengel, G. J., & DeShong, H. L. (2016). The importance of considering clinical utility in the construction of a diagnostic manual. *Annual Review of Clinical Psychology*, 12, 133–155.

Mullins-Sweatt, S. N., & Widiger, T. A. (2009). Clinical utility and DSM-V. *Psychological Assessment*, 21, 302–312.

Murphy, D. (2017) Philosophy of psychiatry. In: E. N. Zalta (Ed.) *The Stanford encyclopedia of philosophy*. Stanford, CA: Stanford University.

Murray, H. (1943). *Thematic Apperception Test manual*. Cambridge, MA: Harvard University Press.

Murray, H. A. (1951). Uses of the Thematic Apperception Test. *American Journal of Psychiatry*, 107, 577–581.

Nabakov, V. (1955). *Lolita, or confession of a white widowed male*. New York, NY: Random House.

Nabokov, V. (1980/2017). *Lectures on literature*. Boston, MA: Houghton Mifflin Harcourt.

Nagel, T. (1974). What is it like to be a bat? *The Philosophical Review*, 83, 435–450.

Najavits, L. M. (2000). Researching therapist emotions and countertransference. *Cognitive and Behavioral Practice*, 7, 322–328.

Nelson, S. M., Huprich, S. K., Shankar, S., Sohnleitner, A., & Paggeot, A. V. (2017). A quantitative and qualitative evaluation of trainee opinions of four methods of personality disorder diagnosis. *Personality Disorders: Theory, Research, and Treatment*, 8, 217–227.

Nelson-Gray, R. O. (1991). DSM-IV: Empirical guidelines from psychometrics. *Journal of Abnormal Psychology*, 100, 308.

Nichols, D. S. (2006). Tell me a story: MMPI responses and personal biography in the case of a serial killer. *Journal of Personality Assessment*, 86, 242–262.

Norcross, J. C., & Goldfried, M. R. (2005) *Handbook of psychotherapy integration* (2nd ed.). New York, NY: Oxford University Press.

Noser, A. E., Zeigler-Hill, V., Vrabel, J. K., Besser, A., Ewing, T. D., & Southard, A. C. (2015). Dark and immoral: The links between pathological personality features and moral values. *Personality and Individual Differences*, 75, 30–35.

Oates, J.C. (2012). *Mudwoman: A widow's story*. New York, NY: Harper Collins.

Oatley, K. (2016). Fiction: Simulation of social worlds. *Trends in Cognitive Sciences*, 20, 618–628.

Olajide, K., Munjiza, J., Moran, P., O'Connell, L., Newton-Howes, G., Bassett, P., Akintomide, G., Ng, N., Tyrer, P., Mulder, R. & Crawford, M. J. (2018). Development and psychometric properties of the Standardized Assessment of Severity of Personality Disorder (SASPD). Journal of Personality Disorders, 32, 44–56.

Oldham, J., Skodol, A., & Bender, D. (2014). *The American psychiatric publishing textbook of personality disorders* (2nd ed.). Washington, DC: American Psychiatric Publishing.

Oltmanns, T. F., Friedman, J. W., Fiedler, E. R., & Turkheimer, E. (2004). Perceptions of people with personality disorders based on thin slices of behavior. *Journal of Research in Personality*, 38, 216–229.

Oltmanns, T. F., & Turkheimer, E. (2006). Perceptions of self and others regarding pathological personality traits. In R. F. Krueger, J. L. Tackett, R. F. Krueger, & J. L. Tackett (Eds.), *Personality and psychopathology* (pp. 71–111). New York, NY: Guilford Press.

Oltmanns, J. R., & Widiger, T. A. (2016). Self-pathology, the Five-Factor Model, and bloated specific factors: A cautionary tale. *Journal of Abnormal Psychology*, 125, 423–434.

Oltmanns, J. R., & Widiger, T. A. (2018). A self-report measure for the ICD-11 dimensional trait model proposal: The personality inventory for ICD-11. *Psychological Assessment*, 30, 154.

OPD Task Force (Eds.) (2008). *Operationalized Psychodynamic Diagnosis OPD-2: Manual of diagnosis and treatment planning*. Kirkland, WA: Hogrefe & Huber.

Orcutt, C. (2018). Schizoid Fantasy: Refuge or Transitional Location? *Clinical Social Work Journal*, 46, 42–47.

Panksepp, J. (2004). *Affective neuroscience: The foundations of human and animal emotions*. New York, NY: Oxford University Press.

Panksepp, J., & Biven, J. (2012). *The archaeology of mind*. New York, NY: Norton.

Paris, J. (1993). Personality disorders: A biopsychosocial model. *Journal of Personality Disorders*, 7, 255–264.

Paris, J. (2015). Applying the principles of psychotherapy integration to the treatment of borderline personality disorder. *Journal of Psychotherapy Integration*, 25, 13–19.

Parker, G., Hadzi-Pavolvic, D., Both, L., Kumar, S., Wilhelm, K., & Olley, A. (2004). Measuring disordered personality functioning: To love and work reprised. *Acta Psychiatrica Scandinavica*, 110, 230–239.

Parnas, J., Sass, L. A., & Zahavi, D. (2012). Rediscovering psychopathology: The epistemology and phenomenology of the psychiatric object. *Schizophrenia Bulletin*, 39, 270–277.

Peebles-Kleiger, M. J. (2002). Elaboration of some sequence analysis strategies: Examples and guidelines for level of confidence. Journal of Personality Assessment, 79, 19–38.

Perry, J. C., Banon, E., & Ianni, F. (1999). Effectiveness of psychotherapy for personality disorders. *The American Journal of Psychiatry*, 156, 1312–1321.

Persius, K. I., Ekdahl, S., Asberg, M., & Samuelsson, M. (2005). To tame a volcano: Patients with borderline personality disorder and their perceptions of suffering. *Archives of Psychiatric Nursing*, 19, 160–168.

Phillips, J. J., Schurg, N. E., Smith, A. J., Walker, J. W., Wilson, K. A., & Roche, M. J. (2017, April). Using the LPFS to identify psychopathology in personality: Validity in self-report vs observation. Poster presented at the 20th Annual Laurel Highlands Undergraduate Psychology Conference, Johnstown, PA.

Pincus, A. L. (2010). Introduction to the special series on integrating personality, psychopathology, and psychotherapy using interpersonal assessment. *Journal of Personality Assessment*, 92, 467–470.

Pincus, A. L. (2005). A contemporary integrative interpersonal theory of personality disorders. In M. Lenzenweger & J. Clarkin (Eds.), *Major theories of personality disorder* (2nd ed., pp. 282–331). New York, NY: Guilford Press.

Pincus, A. L. (2011). Some comments on nomology, diagnostic process, and narcissistic personality disorder in the DSM-5 proposal for personality and personality disorders. *Personality Disorders: Theory, Research, and Treatment*, 2, 41–53.

Pincus, A. L. (2018). An interpersonal perspective on Criterion A of the DSM-5 alternative model for personality disorders. *Contemporary Opinion in Psychology*, 21, 11–17.
Pincus, A. L., & Ansell, E.B. (2013). Interpersonal theory of personality. In J. Suls & H. Tennen (Eds.), *Handbook of Psychology (Vol. 5): Personality and social psycyhology* (2nd ed.) (pp. 141–159). Hoboken, NJ: Wiley.
Pincus, A. L., Cain, N. M., & Wright, A. G. (2014). Narcissistic grandiosity and narcissistic vulnerability in psychotherapy. *Personality Disorders: Theory, Research, and Treatment*, 5, 439–443.
Pincus, A. L., Dowgwillo, E. A., & Greenberg, L. S. (2016). Three cases of narcissistic personality disorder through the lens of the DSM-5 alternative model for personality disorders. *Practice Innovations*, 1, 164–177.
Pincus, A. L., & Gurtman, M.B. (2003). Interpersonal assessment. In J. S. Wiggins (Ed.), *Paradigms of Personality Assessment* (pp. 246–261). New York, NY: Guilford.
Pincus, A. L., Hopwood, C. J., & Wright, A. G. C. (in press). The interpersonal situation: An integrative framework for the study of personality, psychopathology, and psychotherapy. In D. Funder, J. F. Rauthmann, & R. Sherman (Eds.), *Oxford handbook of psychological situations.* New York, NY: Oxford University Press.
Pincus, A. L., & Lukowitsky, M. R. (2010). Pathological narcissism and narcissistic personality disorder. *Annual Review of Clinical Psychology*, 6, 421–446.
Pincus, A. L., Roche, M. J., & Good, E. W. (2015). Narcissistic personality disorder and pathologogical narcissism. In P. H. Blaney, R. F. Krueger, & T. Millon (Eds.), *Oxford textbook of psychopathology* (3rd ed., pp. 791–813). New York, NY: Oxford University Press.
Pincus, A. L., Sadler, P., Woody, E., Roche, M. J., Thomas, K. M., & Wright, A. G. C. (2014). Multimethod assessment of interpersonal dynamics. In C. J. Hopwood & R. F. Bornstein (Eds.), *Multimethod clinical assessment* (pp. 51–91). New York, NY: Guilford.
Pincus, A. L., & Wiggins, J. S. (1990). Interpersonal problems and conceptions of personality disorders. *Journal of Personality Disorders*, 4, 342–352.
Pino, M. C., & Mazza, M. (2016). The use of "literary fiction" to promote mentalizing ability. *PloS one*, 11, e0160254.
Pires, R., Sousa Ferreira, A., Guedes, D. (2017). The psychometric properties of the Portuguese version of the Personality Inventory for DSM-5. *Scandinavian Journal of Psychology*, 58, 468–475.
Planck, M. K. (1950). *Scientific autobiography and other papers.* New York, NY: Philosophical Library.
Plomin, R., Owen, M. J., & McGuffin, P. (1994). The genetic basis of complex human behaviors. *Science*, 264, 1733–1739.
Polanyi, M. (1952). The stability of beliefs. *The British Journal for the Philosophy of Science*, 3, 217–232.
Pollock, N. C., McCabe, G. A., Southard, A. C., & Zeigler-Hill, V. (2016). Pathological personality traits and emotion regulation difficulties. *Personality and Individual Differences*, 95, 168–177.
Porcelli, P., & Kleiger, J. H. (2016). The "feeling of movement": Notes on the Rorschach human movement response. *Journal of Personality Assessment*, 98, 124–134.
Posner, M. I., & Petersen, S. E. (1990). The attention system of the human brain. *Annual Review of Neuroscience*, 13, 25–42.

Prasko, J., Diveky, T., Grambal, A., Kamaradova, D., Monzy, P., Sigmundova, Z., Slepecky, M., & Vyskocilova, J. (2010). Transference and countertransference in cognitive behavioral therapy. *Biomedical Papers*, 154, 189–197.

Premack, D., & Woodruff, G. (1978). Does the chimpanzee have a theory of mind? *Behavioral and Brain Sciences*, 1, 515–526.

Preti, E., Di Pierro, R., Costantini, G., Benzi, I. M., De Panfilis, C., & Madeddu, F. (in press, 2018). Using the Structured Interview of Personality Organization for DSM–5 Level of Personality Functioning Rating performed by inexperienced raters. *Journal of Personality Assessment*. doi:10.1080/00223891.2018.1448985

Preti, E., Prunas, A., De Panfilis, C., Marchesi, C., Madeddu, F., & Clarkin, J. F. (2015). The facets of identity: Personality pathology assessment through the inventory of personality organization. *Personality Disorders: Theory, Research, and Treatment*, 6, 129–140.

Prichard, J. C. (1835). *A treatise of insanity*. London, UK: Sherwood, Gilbert, & Piper.

Prunas, A., & Bernorio, R. (2016). Dimensions of personality organization and sexual life in a community sample of women. *Journal of Sex & Marital Therapy*, 42, 158–164.

Psychodynamic Diagnostic Manual Task Force (2006). *Psychodynamic diagnostic manual*. Silver Spring, MD: Alliance of Psychoanalytic Organizations.

Quilty, L. C., Ayearst, L., Chmielewski, M., Pollock, B. G., & Bagby, R. M. (2013). The psychometric properties of the Personality Inventory for DSM-5 in an APA DSM-5 field trial sample. *Assessment*, 20, 362–369.

Raballo, A., & Parnas, J. (2010). The silent side of the spectrum: schizotypy and the schizotaxic self. *Schizophrenia Bulletin*, 37, 1017–1026.

Racker, H. (1968/2002). *Transference and countertransference*. London, UK: Karnac Books.

Ralevski, E., Sanislow, C. A., Grilo, C. M., Skodol, A. E., Gunderson, J. G., Shea, M. T., Yen, S., Bender, D. S., Zanarini, M. C., & McGlashan, T. H. (2005). Avoidant personality disorder and social phobia: Distinct enough to be separate disorders? *Acta Psychiatrica Scandinavica*, 112, 208–214.

Rapaport, D., Gill, M., & Schafer, R. (1946). *Diagnostic psychological testing: The theory, statistical evaluation, and diagnostic application of a battery of tests (Vol. 2)*. Chicago, IL: The Year Book Publishers.

Rapp, D. N., Gerrig, R. J., & Prentice, D. A. (2001). Readers' trait-based models of characters in narrative comprehension. *Journal of Memory and Language*, 45, 737–750.

Reed, G. M. (2010). Toward ICD-11: Improving the clinical utility of WHO's International Classification of mental disorders. *Professional Psychology: Research and Practice*, 41, 457–464.

Regier, D. A., Narrow, W. E., Clarke, D. E., Kraemer, H. C., Kuramoto, S. J., Kuhl, E. A., & Kupfer, D. J. (2013). DSM-5 field trials in the United States and Canada, Part II: test-retest reliability of selected categorical diagnoses. *American Journal of Psychiatry*, 170, 59–70.

Regier, D. A., Narrow, W. E., Kuhl, E. A., & Kupfer, D. J. (2009). The conceptual development of DSM-V. *American Journal of Psychiatry*, 166, 645–650.

Reich, W. (1945/1972). *Character analysis* (3rd ed.). (V. Carfango, Trans.). New York, NY: Farrar, Straus, & Giroux.

Reichborn-Kjennerud, T., Krueger, R. F., Ystrom, E., Torvik, F. A., Rosenström, T. H., Aggen, S. H., South, S. C., Neale, M. C., Knudsen, G. P., Kendler, K. S., & Czajkowski, N. O. (2017). Do DSM-5 Section II personality disorders and Section III personality trait domains reflect the same genetic and environmental risk factors? *Psychological Medicine*, 47, 2205–2215.

Reidy, T. J., Sorensen, J. R., & Davidson, M. (2016). Testing the predictive validity of the Personality Assessment Inventory (PAI) in relation to inmate misconduct and violence. *Psychological Assessment*, 28, 871–884.

Rentrop, M., Zilker, T., Lederle, A., Birkhofer, A., & Hörz, S. (2014). Psychiatric comorbidity and personality structure in patients with polyvalent addiction. *Psychopathology*, 47, 133–140.

Rettew, D. C. (2000). Avoidant personality disorder, generalized social phobia, and shyness: Putting the personality back into personality disorders. *Harvard Review of Psychiatry*, 8, 283–297.

Richetin, J., Preti, E., Costantini, G., & De Panfilis, C. (2017). The centrality of affective instability and identity in Borderline Personality Disorder: Evidence from network analysis. *PLoS One*, 12, e0186695.

Roberts, A. L., & Coid, J. W. (2010). Personality disorder and offending behaviour: Findings from the national survey of male prisoners in England and Wales. *Journal of Forensic Psychiatry & Psychology*, 21, 221–237.

Robins, C. J., Ladd, J., Welkowitz, J., Blaney, P. H., Diaz, R., & Kutcher, G. (1994). The Personal Style Inventory: Preliminary validation studies of new measures of sociotropy and autonomy. *Journal of Psychopathology and Behavioral Assessment*, 16, 277–300.

Robins, E., & Guze, S. B. (1970). Establishment of diagnostic validity in psychiatric illness: Its application to schizophrenia. *The American Journal of Psychiatry*, 126, 983–986.

Robinson, A. H. (1958). *Elements of cartography*. New York, NY: Wiley.

Robinson, A. H. (1974). A new map projection: Its development and characteristics. *International Yearbook of Cartography*, 14, 145–155.

Robinson, A. H. (1979). Geography and cartography then and now. *Annals of the Association of American Geographers*, 69, 97–102.

Roche, M. J. (in press, 2018). Examining the Alternative Model of Personality Disorder in daily life: Evidence for incremental validity. *Journal of Personality Disorders*. doi:10.1037/per0000295

Roche, M. J., Jacobson, N. C., & Phillips, J. J. (in press, 2018). Expanding the validity of the level of Personality Functioning Scale observer report and self-report versions across psychodynamic and interpersonal paradigms. *Journal of Personality Assessment*. doi:10.1080/00223891.2018.1475394

Roche, M. J., Jacobson, N. C., & Pincus, A. L. (2016). Using repeated daily assessments to uncover oscillating patterns and temporally-dynamic triggers in structures of psychopathology: Applications to the DSM-5 alternative model of personality disorders. *Journal of Abnormal Psychology*, 125, 1090–1112.

Roche, M. J., & Pincus, A. L. (2016). Precision assessment: An individualized and temporally dynamic approach to understanding patients in their daily lives. In U. Kumar (Ed.), *The Wiley handbook of personality assessment* (pp.192–204). Hoboken, NJ: Wiley Blackwell.

Roche, M. J., Pincus, A. L., Rebar, A. L., Conroy, D. E., & Ram, N. (2014). Enriching psychological assessment using a person-specific analysis of interpersonal processes in daily life. *Assessment*, 21, 515–528.

Rodriguez-Seijas, C., Eaton, N. R., & Krueger, R. F. (2015). How transdiagnostic factors of personality and psychopathology can inform clinical assessment and intervention. *Journal of Personality Assessment*, 97, 425–435.

Rogers, C. R. (1961). The loneliness of contemporary man as seen in the case of Ellen West. *Annals of Psychotherapy*, 3, 22–27.

Ronningstam, E. (2009). Narcissistic personality disorder: Facing DSM–5. *Psychiatric Annals*, 39, 111–121.

Ronningstam, E. (2012). Alliance building and narcissistic personality disorder. *Journal of Clinical Psychology*, 68, 943–953.

Ronningstam, E. (2014). Beyond the diagnostic traits: A collaborative exploratory diagnostic process for dimensions and underpinnings of narcissistic personality disorder. *Personality Disorders: Theory, Research, and Treatment*, 5, 434–438.

Ronningstam, E. (2017). Intersect between self-esteem and emotion regulation in narcissistic personality disorder: Implications for alliance building and treatment. *Borderline Personality Disorder and Emotion Dysregulation*, 4. doi:10.1186/s40479-017-0054-8

Rorty, A. (Ed.). (1976). *The identities of persons (Vol. 3)*. Berkley, CA: University of California Press.

Rosenzweig, S. (1936). Some implicit common factors in diverse methods of psychotherapy. *American Journal of Orthopsychiatry*, 6, 412–415.

Roskam, I., Galdiolo, S., Hansenne, M., Massoudi, K., Rossier, J., Gicquel, L., & Rolland, J. P. (2015). The psychometric properties of the French version of the Personality Inventory for DSM-5. *PloS One*, 10, e0133413.

Rossi, G., Debast, I., & van Alphen, S. P. J. (2017). Measuring personality functioning in older adults: construct validity of the Severity Indices of Personality Functioning–Short Form (SIPP-SF). *Aging & Mental Health*, 21, 703–711.

Rost, F., Luyten, P., & Fonagy, P. (2018). The Anaclitic–Introjective Depression Assessment: Development and preliminary validity of an observer-rated measure. *Clinical Psychology & Psychotherapy*, 25, 195–209.

Ruiz, M. A., Hopwood, C. J., Cox, J. L., Edens, J. F., & Morey, L. C. (in press, 2018). Initial development of pathological personality trait measures using the Personality Assessment Inventory item pool. *Personality Disorders: Theory, Research, and Treatment*. doi:10.1037/per0000286

Russell, T. D., & King, A. R. (2016). Distrustful, conventional, entitled, and dysregulated: PID-5 personality facets predict hostile masculinity and sexual violence in community men. *Journal of Interpersonal Violence*. doi:10.1177/0886260517689887

Rutter, M. (1987). Temperament, personality and personality disorder. *The British Journal of Psychiatry*, 150, 443–458.

Rychlak, J. F. (1968). *A philosophy of science for personality theory*. Boston, MA: Houghton, Miffin and Company. Available at doi:10.1037/10535-000

Rychlak, J. F. (1988). *The psychology of rigorous humanism* (2nd ed.). New York, NY: New York University Press.

Sadler, J. Z. (2013). Vice and mental disorders. In K. M. Fulford, M. Davies, R. T. Gipps, G. Graham, J. Z. Sadler, G. Stanghellini, & T. Thornton (Eds.), *The Oxford handbook of philosophy and psychiatry* (pp. 451–479). New York, NY: Oxford University Press.

Sadler, J. Z., Hulgus, Y. F., & Agich, G. J. (1994). On values in recent American psychiatric classification. *The Journal of Medicine and Philosophy*, 19, 261–277.

Sadler, P., Woody, E., McDonald, K., Lizdek, I., & Little, J. (2015). A lot can happen in a few minutes: Examining dynamic patterns within an interaction to illuminate the interpersonal nature of personality disorders. *Journal of Personality Disorders*, 29, 526–546.

Sadoff, R. L. (2015). *The evolution of forensic psychiatry: History, current developments, future directions.* New York, NY: Oxford University Press.

Safran, J. D. (1984). Assessing the cognitive-interpersonal cycle. *Cognitive Therapy and Research*, 8, 333–347. doi:10.1007/BF01173309

Salekin, R. T. (2015). *Forensic evaluation and treatment of juveniles: Innovation and best practice.* Washington, DC: American Psychological Association.

Samuel, D. B. (2015). A review of the agreement between clinicians' personality disorder diagnoses and those from other methods and sources. *Clinical Psychology: Science and Practice*, 22, 1–19.

Samuel, D. B., & Bucher, M. A. (2017). Assessing the assessors: The feasibility and validity of clinicians as a source for personality disorder research. *Personality Disorders: Theory, Research, and Treatment*, 8, 104.

Samuel, D. B., Hopwood, C. J., Krueger, R. F., Thomas, K. M., & Ruggero, C. J. (2013). Comparing methods for scoring personality disorder types using maladaptive traits in DSM-5. *Assessment*, 20, 353–361.

Samuel, D. B., Sanislow, C. A., Hopwood, C. J., Shea, M. T., Skodol, A. E., Morey, L. C., Ansell, E. B., Markowitz, J. C., Zanarini, M. C., & Grilo, C. M. (2013). Convergent and incremental predictive validity of clinician, self-report, and structured interview diagnoses for personality disorders over 5 years. *Journal of Consulting and Clinical Psychology*, 81, 650.

Samuel, D. B., Simms, L. J., Clark, L. A., Livesley, W. J., & Widiger, T. A. (2010). An item response theory integration of normal and abnormal personality scales. *Personality Disorders: Theory, Research, and Treatment*, 1, 5–21.

Samuel, D. B., Suzuki, T., & Griffin, S. A. (2016). Clinicians and clients disagree: Five implications for clinical science. *Journal of Abnormal Psychology*, 125, 1001–1010.

Samuel, D. B., & Widiger, T. W. (2010). Comparing personality disorder models: Cross-method assessment of the FFM and DSM-IV-TR. *Journal of Personality Disorders*, 24, 721–745.

Sandler, J. (1976). Countertransference and role responsiveness. *International Journal of Psychoanalysis*, 3, 43–47.

Sauer-Zavala, S., Bentley, K. H., & Wilner, J. G. (2016). Transdiagnostic treatment of borderline personality disorder and comorbid disorders: A clinical replication series. *Journal of Personality Disorders*, 30, 35–51.

Sauer-Zavala, S., Gutner, C. A., Farchione, T. J., Boettcher, H. T., Bullis, J. R., & Barlow, D. H. (2017). Current definitions of "transdiagnostic" in treatment development: A search for consensus. *Behavior Therapy*, 48, 128–138.

Sauer-Zavala, S., Wilner, J. G., & Barlow, D. H. (2017). Addressing neuroticism in psychological treatment. *Personality Disorders: Theory, Research, and Treatment*, 8, 191–198.

Schafer, R. (1954). *Psychoanalytic interpretation in Rorschach testing: Theory and application*. Oxford, UK: Grune & Stratton.

Schafer, R. (1980). Action and narration in psychoanalysis. *New Literary History*, 12, 61–85.

Schmeck, K., Schlüter-Müller, S., Foelsch, P. A., & Doering, S. (2013). The role of identity in the DSM–5 classification of personality disorders. *Child and Adolescent Psychiatry and Mental Health*, 7, 27.

Schmidt, J. A., Wagner, C. C., & Kiesler, D. J. (1999). Psychometric and circumplex properties of the Octant Scale Impact Message Inventory (IMI-C): A structural evaluation. *Journal of Counseling Psychology*, 46, 325–334.

Schneider, K. (1923). *Die psychopathischen personlichkeiten*. Leipzig: Thieme.

Schneider, K. (1950). *Psychopathic personalities* (9th edn). London: Cassell.

Schneider, K. (1958). *Psychopathic personalities*. London, UK: Cassell.

Schwartz, M. A., Wiggins, O. P., & Norko, M. A. (1989). Prototypes, ideal types, and personality disorders: The return to classical psychiatry. *Journal of Personality Disorders*, 3, 1–9.

Searles, H. F. (1986). *My work with borderline patients*. Oxford, UK: Jason Aronson.

Sellbom, M., Anderson, J. L., & Bagby, R. M. (2013). Assessing DSM-5 Section III personality traits and disorders with the MMPI-2-RF. *Assessment*, 20, 709–722.

Sellbom, M., Carmichael, K. L., & Liggett, J. (2017). Examination of DSM-5 Section III avoidant personality disorder in a community sample. *Personality and Mental Health*, 11, 299–313.

Sellbom, M., Dhillon, S., & Bagby, R. M. (2018). Development and validation of an overreporting scale for the Personality Inventory for DSM-5 (PID-5). *Psychological Assessment*, 30, 582–593.

Sellbom, M., Waugh, M. H., & Hopwood, C. J. (2018). Development and validation of Personality Disorder Spectra Scales for the MMPI–2–RF. *Journal of Personality Assessment*, 100, 406–420.

Sellbom, M., Wygant, D. B., & Drislane, L. E. (2015). Elucidating the construct validity of the psychopathic personality inventory triarchic scales. *Journal of Personality Assessment*, 97, 374–381.

Shahar, G., Blatt, S. J., & Ford, R. Q. (2003). Mixed anaclitic-introjective psychopathology in treatment-resistant inpatients undergoing psychoanalytic psychotherapy. *Psychoanalytic Psychology*, 20, 84–102.

Shakespeare, W. (1599/1986/2005). Romeo and Juliet. In S. Wells & G. Taylor (Eds.). *The Oxford Shakespeare* (2nd ed.). Oxford, UK: Clarendon Press.

Shapiro, F., & Solomon, R. M. (1995). *Eye movement desensitization and reprocessing*. Chichester, UK: John Wiley & Sons.

Sharp, C., Ha, C., Carbone, C., Kim, S., Perry, K., Williams, L., & Fonagy, P. (2013). Hypermentalizing in adolescent inpatients: Treatment effects and association with borderline traits. *Journal of Personality Disorders*, 27, 3–18.

Sharp, C., Wright, A. G. C., Fowler, J. C., Frueh, B. C., Allen, J. G., Oldham, J., & Clark, L. A. (2015). The structure of personality pathology: Both general ('g') and specific ('s') factors? *Journal of Abnormal Psychology*, 124, 387–398.

Shaver, P. R., & Mikulincer, M. (2002). Attachment-related psychodynamics. *Attachment & Human Development*, 4, 133–161.

Shearin, E. N., & Linehan, M. M. (1992). Patient-therapist ratings and relationship to progress in dialectical behavior therapy for borderline personality disorder. *Behavior Therapy*, 23, 730–741.

Shedler, J., Beck, A., Fonagy, P., Gabbard, G. O., Gunderson, J., Kernberg, O., Michels, R., & Westen, D. (2010). Personality disorders in DSM-5. *American Journal of Psychiatry*, 167, 1026–1028.

Shedler, J., & Westen, D. (2007). The Shedler –Westen Assessment Procedure (SWAP): Making personality diagnosis clinically meaningful. *Journal of Personality Assessment*, 89, 41–55.

Sheehan, L., Nieweglowski, K., & Corrigan, P. (2016). The stigma of personality disorders. *Current Psychiatry Reports*, 18. doi:10.1007/s11920-015-0654-1

Shiner, R. L. (2005). A developmental perspective on personality disorders: Lessons from research on normal personality development in childhood and adolescence. *Journal of Personality Disorders*, 19, 202–210.

Silk, K. R. (2010). The quality of depression in borderline personality disorder and the diagnostic process. *Journal of Personality Disorders*, 24, 25–37.

Simms, L. J., & Calabrese, W. R. (2016). Incremental validity of the DSM-5 Section III personality disorder traits with respect to psychosocial impairment. *Journal of Personality Disorders*, 30, 95–111.

Simms, L. J., Goldberg, L. R., Roberts, J. E., Watson, D., Welte, J., & Rotterman, J. H. (2011). Computerized adaptive assessment of personality disorder: Introducing the CAT–PD project. *Journal of Personality Assessment*, 93, 380–389.

Simon, R. I., & Gold, L. H. (Eds.) (2010). *The American Psychiatric Publishing textbook of forensic psychiatry.* Arlington, VA: American Psychiatric Association Publishing.

Simonsen, S., & Simonsen, E. (2014). Contemporary directions in theories and psychotherapeutic strategies in treatment of personality disorders: Relation to level of personality functioning. *Journal of Contemporary Psychotherapy*, 44, 141–148.

Singer, M. T., & Larson, D. G. (1981). Borderline personality and the Rorschach test. *Archives of General Psychiatry*, 38, 693–698.

Singer, T., & Lamm, C. (2009). The social neuroscience of empathy. *Annals of the New York Academy of Sciences*, 1156, 81–96.

Skadberg, R., Fox, L., & Waugh, M. H. (2018, March). Mapping intra-person variability with the AMPD. Poster session presented at the Annual Convention of the Society for Personality Assessment, Washington, DC.

Skodol, A. E. (2012). Personality disorders in DSM-5. *Annual Review of Clinical Psychology*, 8, 317–344.

Skodol, A. E., Morey, L. C., Bender, D. S., & Oldham, J. M. (2015). The alternative DSM-5 model for personality disorders: A clinical application. *American Journal of Psychiatry*, 172, 606–613.

Slaney, K. L., & Garcia, D. A. (2015). Constructing psychological objects: The rhetoric of constructs. *Journal of Theoretical and Philosophical Psychology*, 35, 244–259.

Sleep, C., Lynam, D., Widiger, T. A., Crowe, M. L., & Miller, J. (in press, 2018). An evaluation of DSM-5 Section III Personality Disorder Criterion A (Impairment) in accounting for psychopathology. *Psychological Assessment.* doi:10.31234/osf.io/z48tv

Smits, M., Feenstra, D., Bales, D., Vos, J., Lucas, Z., Verhuel, R., & Luyten, P. (2017). Subtypes of borderline personality disorder patients: A cluster-analytic approach. *Borderline Personality Disorder and Emotion Dysregulation*, 4. doi:10.1186/s40479-017-0066-4

Snow, C. P. (1959) Two cultures. *Science*, 130, 419.

Soderstrom, I. R. (2007). Mental illness in offender populations: Prevalence, duty and implications. *Journal of Offender Rehabilitation*, 45, 1–17.

Soldz, S., Budman, S., Demby, A., & Merry, J. (1995). A short form of the inventory of interpersonal problems circumplex scales. *Assessment*, 2, 53–63.

Somma, A., Borroni, S., Kelley, S. E., Edens, J. F., & Fossati, A. (2018). Further evidence for the validity of a response inconsistency scale for the Personality Inventory for DSM-5 in Italian community-dwelling adolescents, community-dwelling adults, and clinical adults. *Psychological Assessment*, 30, 929–940.

Somma, A., Krueger, R. F., Markon, K. E., Borroni, S., & Fossati, A. (in press, 2018). Item Response Theory analyses, factor structure, and external correlates of the Italian translation of the Personality Inventory for DSM-5 Short Form in community-dwelling adults and clinical adults. *Assessment*. doi:10.1177/1073191118781006

Sontag, S. (1978). *Illness as metaphor*. New York, NY: Farrar, Strauss & Giroux.

Sontag, S. (1989). *AIDS and its metaphors*. New York, NY: Farrar, Strauss & Giroux.

Soto, C. J., & John, O. P. (2017). The next Big Five Inventory (BFI-2): Developing and assessing a hierarchical model with 15 facets to enhance bandwidth, fidelity, and predictive power. *Journal of Personality and Social Psychology*, 113, 117–143.

South, S. C., Krueger, R. F., Knudsen, G. P., Ystrom, E., Czajkowski, N., Aggen, S. H., Neale, M. C., Gillespie, N. A., Kendler, K. S., & Reichborn-Kjennerud, T. (2017). A population based twin study of DSM-5 maladaptive personality domains. *Personality Disorders: Theory, Research, and Treatment*, 8, 366.

Southard, A. C., Noser, A. E., Pollock, N. C., Mercer, S. H., & Zeigler-Hill, V. (2015). The interpersonal nature of dark personality features. *Journal of Social and Clinical Psychology*, 34, 555–586.

Spence, D. P. (1984). *Narrative truth and historical truth: Meaning and interpretation in psychoanalysis*. New York, NY: WW Norton & Company.

Spitzer, R. L. (1981). The diagnostic status of homosexuality in DSM-III: A reformulation of the issues. *American Journal of Psychiatry*, 138, 210–215.

Spitzer, R. L., First, M. B., Shedler, J., Westen, D., & Skodol, A. E. (2008). Clinical utility of five dimensional systems for personality diagnosis: A "consumer preference" study. *Journal of Nervous and Mental Disease*, 196, 356–374.

Spruit, J. E. (1998). The penal conceptions of the emperor Marcus Aurelius in respect of lunatics: Reflections on D. 1, 18, 14. *International Journal of Law and Psychiatry*, 21, 315–333.

Stanley, B., Perez-Rodriguez, M. M., Labouliere, C., & Roose, S. (in press, 2018). A neuroscience-oriented research approach to borderline personality disorder. *Journal of Personality Disorders*. doi:10.1521/pedi_2018_32_326

Stanton, K., Rozek, D. C., Stasik-O'Brien, S. M., Ellickson-Larew, S., & Watson, D. (2016). A transdiagnostic approach to examining the incremental predictive power of emotion regulation and basic personality dimensions. *Journal of Abnormal Psychology*, 125, 960–975.

State of New York v. Nicholas T. (2017). Retrieved from http://law.justia.com/cases/new-york/other-courts/2017/2017-ny-slip-op-27077.html

Stein, M., Hilsenroth, M., Slavin-Mulford, J., & Pinsker, J. (2011). *Social Cognition and Object Relations Scale: Global rating method (SCORS-G)* (4th ed.). Unpublished manuscript. Boston, MA: Massachusetts General Hospital and Harvard Medical School.

Stein, M., & Slavin-Mulford, J. (2017). *The Social Cognition and Object Relations Scale-Global Rating Method (SCORS-G): A comprehensive guide for clinicians and researchers*. Abington, UK: Routledge.

Stein, M. B., Slavin-Mulford, J., Siefert, C. J., Sinclair, S. J., Renna, M., Malone, J., Bello, I., & Blais, M. A. (2014). SCORS-G stimulus characteristics of select Thematic Apperception Test cards. *Journal of Personality Assessment*, 96, 339–349.
Stein, M. B., Slavin-Mulford, J., Sinclair, S. J., Chung, W. J., Roche, M., Denckla, C., & Blais, M. A. (2018). Extending the use of the SCORS-G Composite Ratings in assessing level of personality organization. *Journal of Personality Assessment*, 100, 166–175.
Sterba, R. F. (1934). The fate of the ego in psychoanalysis. *International Journal of Psycho-Analysis*, 15, 117–126.
Stern, B. L., Caligor, E., Clarkin, J. F., Critchfield, K. L., Horz, S., MacCornack, V., Lenzenweger, M. F., & Kernberg, O. F. (2010). Structured Interview of Personality Organization (STIPO): Preliminary psychometrics in a clinical sample. *Journal of Personality Assessment*, 92, 35–44.
Stevens, S. S. (1946). On the theory of scales of measurement. *Science*, 103, 667–680.
Stewart, C. T. (2012). *New ideas about eating disorders: Human emotions and the hunger drive*. New York, NY: Routledge.
Stinson, F. S., Dawson, D. A., Goldstein, R. B., Chou, S. P., Huang, B., Smith, S. M., Ruan, W. J., Pulay, A. J., Saha, T. D., Pickering, R. P., & Grant, B. F. (2008). Prevalence, correlates, disability, and comorbidity of DSM-IV narcissistic personality disorder: Results from the Wave 2 National Epidemiologic Survey on Alcohol and Related Conditions. *The Journal of Clinical Psychiatry*, 69, 1033–1045.
Stoeber, J. (2014). Multidimensional perfectionism and the DSM-5 personality traits. *Personality and Individual Differences*, 64, 115–120.
Strachey, J. (1953). The interpretation of dreams. In J. Strachey (Ed.), *The standard edition of the complete psychological works of Sigmund Freud (Vol. 5)*. London, UK: Hogarth Press and the Institute of Psycho-Analysis.
Stricker G., & Gold J. R. (2013). *Comprehensive handbook of psychotherapy integration*. New York, NY: Springer.
Strickland, C. M., Drislane, L. E., Lucy, M., Krueger, R. F., & Patrick, C. J. (2013). Characterizing psychopathy using DSM-5 personality traits. *Assessment*, 20, 327–338.
Strickland, C. M., Hopwood, C. J., Bornovalova, M. A., Rojas, E. C., Krueger, R. F., & Patrick, C. J. (in press, 2018). Categorical and dimensional conceptions of personality pathology in DSM-5: Toward a model-based synthesis. *Journal of Personality Disorders*. doi:10.1521/pedi_2018_32_33
Strozier, C. B. (2001). *Heinz Kohut: The making of a psychoanalyst*. New York, NY: Macmillan.
Sullivan, H. S. (1953/2013). *The interpersonal theory of psychiatry*. New York, NY: Routledge.
Suzuki, T., Griffin, S. A., & Samuel, D. B. (2017). Capturing the DSM-5 alternative personality disorder model traits in the Five-Factor Model's nomological net. *Journal of Personality*, 85, 220–231.
Suzuki, T., Samuel, D. B., Pahlen, S., & Krueger, R. F. (2015). DSM-5 alternative personality disorder model traits as maladaptive extreme variants of the Five-Factor Model: An item-response theory analysis. *Journal of Abnormal Psychology*, 124, 343.
Swami, V., Weis, L., Lay, A., Barron, D., & Furnham, A. (2016). Associations between belief in conspiracy theories and the maladaptive personality traits of the Personality Inventory for DSM-5. *Psychiatry Research*, 236, 86–90.

Tansey, M. J., & Burke, W. F. (1989). *Understanding countertransfrence.* Hillsdale, NJ: Analytic Press.

Tasca, G. A., Ritchie, K., & Balfour, L. (2011). Implications of attachment theory and research for the assessment and treatment of eating disorders. *Psychotherapy*, 48, 249–259. doi:10.1037/a0022423

Taubner, S., Hörz, S., Fischer-Kern, M., Doering, S., Buchheim, A., & Zimmermann, J. (2013). Internal structure of the reflective functioning scale. *Psychological Assessment*, 25, 127–135.

Tellegen, A., & Waller, N. G. (2008). Exploring personality through test construction: Development of the Multidimensional Personality Questionnaire. In G. J. Boyle, G. Matthews, & D. H. Saklofske (Eds.), *The SAGE handbook of personality theory and assessment, Vol 2: Personality measurement and testing* (pp. 261–292). Thousand Oaks, CA: Sage Publications.

Thimm, J. C., Jordan, S., & Bach, B. (2016). The Personality Inventory for DSM-5 Short Form (PID-5-SF): Psychometric properties and association with Big Five traits and pathological beliefs in a Norwegian population. *BMC Psychology*, 4, 61.

Thomas, K. M., Yalch, M. M., Krueger, R. F., Wright, A. G. C., Markon, K. E., & Hopwood, C. J. (2013). The convergent structure of DSM-5 personality trait facets and Five-Factor Model trait domains. *Assessment*, 20, 308–311.

Thylstrup, B., & Hesse, M. (2009). "I am not complaining": Ambivalence construct in schizoid personality disorder. *American Journal of Psychotherapy*, 63, 147–167.

Thylstrup, B., Simonsen, S., Nemery, C., Simonsen, E., Noll, J. F., Myatt, M. W., & Hesse, M. (2016). Assessment of personality-related levels of functioning: A pilot study of clinical assessment of the DSM-5 level of personality functioning based on a semi-structured interview. *BMC Psychiatry*, 16, 8.

Todes, D. P. (1987). Darwin's Malthusian metaphor and Russian evolutionary thought, 1859–1917. *Isis*, 78, 537–551.

Tomkins, S. S. (1978). Script theory: Differential magnification of affects. *Nebraska Symposium on Motivation*, 26, 201–236.

Tomkins, S. S. (1987). Script theory. In J. Aronoff, A. I. Rabin, & R. A. Zucker (Eds.), *The emergence of personality* (pp. 147–216). New York, NY: Springer.

Tomkins, S. S. (1995). *Exploring affect: The selected writings of Silvan S. Tomkins.* Cambridge, UK: Cambridge University Press.

Tversky, A., & Kahneman, D. (1974). Judgment under uncertainty: Heuristics and biases. *Science*, 185, 1124–1131.

Tyrer, P. (2005). The problem of severity in the classification of personality disorder. *Journal of Personality Disorders*, 19, 309–314.

Urist, J. (1977). The Rorschach test and the assessment of object relations. *Journal of Personality Assessment*, 41, 3–9.

Vaillant, G. E. (1992). The beginning of wisdom is never calling a patient a borderline; or, the clinical management of immature defenses in the treatment of individuals with personality disorders. *The Journal of Psychotherapy Practice and Research*, 1, 117.

Vaillant, G. E. (2000). Adaptive mental mechanisms: Their role in a positive psychology. *American Psychologist*, 55, 89–98.

Van den Broeck, J., Bastiaansen, L., Rossi, G., Dierckx, E., & De Clercq, B. (2013). Age-neutrality of the trait facets proposed for personality disorders in DSM-5: A DIFAS analysis of the PID-5. *Journal of Psychopathology and Behavioral Assessment*, 35, 487–494.

Van den Broeck, J., Bastiaansen, L., Rossi, G., Dierckx, E., De Clercq, B., & Hofmans, J. (2014). Hierarchical structure of maladaptive personality traits in older adults: Joint factor analysis of the PID-5 and the DAPP-BQ. *Journal of Personality Disorders*, 28, 198–211.
Van Denburg, T. F., Schmidt, J. A., & Kiesler, D. J. (1992). Interpersonal assessment in counseling and psychotherapy. *Journal of Counseling & Development*, 71, 84–90.
Van der Kolk, B. A., & Van der Hart, O. (1991). The intrusive past: The flexibility of memory and the engraving of trauma. *American Imago*, 48, 425–454.
van Geel, R., Houtmans, T., Verboon, P., & Laumen, T. (2016). Integrating adult attachment scales and vulnerability factors in depression. Int*ernational Journal of Personality Psychology*, 2, 51–63.
Verheul, R. (2005). Clinical utility of dimensional models for personality pathology. *Journal of Personality Disorders*, 19, 283–302.
Verheul, R., Andrea, H., Berghout, C. C., Dolan, C., Busschbach, J. J., van der Kroft, P. J., Bateman, A. W., & Fonagy, P. (2008). Severity Indices of Personality Problems (SIPP-118): Development, factor structure, reliability, and validity. *Psychological Assessment*, 20, 23–34.
Verheul, R., & Widiger, T.A. (2004). A meta-analysis of the prevalence and usage of the Personality Disorder Not Otherwise Specified (PDNOS) diagnosis. *Journal of Personality Disorders*, 18, 309–319.
Wachtel, P. L. (1997). *Psychoanalysis, behavior therapy, and the relational world*. Washington, DC: American Psychological Association.
Wakefield, J. C. (2006). Personality disorder as harmful dysfunction: DSM's cultural deviance criterion reconsidered. *Journal of Personality Disorders*, 20, 157–169.
Wakefield, J. C. (2012). Are you as smart as a 4th grader? Why the prototype-similarity approach to diagnosis is a step backward for a scientific psychiatry. *World Psychiatry*, 11, 27–28.
Wallin, D. J. (2007). *Attachment in psychotherapy*. New York, NY: Guilford press.
Wampold, B. E. (2010). The research evidence for the common factors models: A historically situated perspective. In B. L. Duncan, S. D. Miller, B. E. Wampold, & M. A. Hubble (Eds.), *The heart and soul of change: Delivering what works in therapy* (pp. 49–81). Washington, DC: American Psychological Association.
Watson, D., Stasik, S. M., Ro, E., & Clark, L. A. (2013). Integrating normal and pathological personality: Relating the DSM-5 trait-dimensional model to general traits of personality. *Assessment*, 20, 312–326.
Waugh, M. H. (1997, September 12). Psychiatry for the primary care physician. Lecture presented at the University of Tennessee Graduate School of Medicine Departments of Medicine and Continuing Medical Education, Knoxville, TN.
Waugh, M. H. (2014). *The PDLT-C*. Unpublished manuscript. Knoxville, TN: Department of Psychology, University of Tennessee.
Waugh, M. H., Hopwood, C. J., Krueger, R. F., Morey, L. C., Pincus, A. L., & Wright, A. C. (2017). Psychological assessment with the DSM-5 Alternative Model for Personality Disorders: Tradition and innovation. *Professional Psychology: Research and Practice*, 48, 79–89.
Wechsler, D. (2008). *Wechsler adult intelligence scale* (4th ed.) (WAIS–IV). San Antonio, TX: NCS Pearson.
Weiss, J. (1993). *How psychotherapy works: Process and technique*. New York, NY: Guilford Press.

Werbart, A., Aldén, S., & Diedrichs, A. (2017). Changes in the anaclitic-introjective personality configurations following psychoanalytic psychotherapy with young adults. *Research in Psychotherapy: Psychopathology, Process and Outcome*, 20. doi:10.4081/ripppo.2017.239

Westen, D. (1997). Divergences between clinical and research methods for assessing personality disorders: Implications for research and the evolution of Axis II. *American Journal of Psychiatry*, 154, 895–903.

Westen, D. (2012). Prototype diagnosis of psychiatric syndromes. *World Psychiatry*, 11, 16–21.

Westen, D., Ludolph, P., Misle, B., Ruffins, S., & Block, J. (1990). Physical and sexual abuse in adolescent girls with borderline personality disorder. *American Journal of Orthopsychiatry*, 60, 55–66.

Westen, D., Nakash, O., Thomas, C., & Bradley, R. (2006). Clinical assessment of attachment patterns and personality disorder in adolescents and adults. *Journal of Consulting and Clinical Psychology*, 74, 1065–1085.

Westen, D., & Shedler, J. (1999). Revising and assessing Axis II, Part I: Developing a clinically and empirically valid assessment method. *American Journal of Psychiatry*, 156, 258–272.

Westen, D., Shedler, J., & Bradley, R. (2006). A prototype approach to personality disorder diagnosis. *American Journal of Psychiatry*, 163, 846–856.

Westen, D., Shedler, J., Bradley, B., & DeFife, J. A. (2012). An empirically derived taxonomy for personality diagnosis: Bridging science and practice in conceptualizing personality. *The American Journal of Psychiatry*, 169, 273–284.

White, J. L., Moffitt, T. E., Caspi, A., Bartusch, D. J., Needles, D. J., & Stouthamer-Loeber, M. (1994). Measuring impulsivity and examining its relationship to delinquency. *Journal of Abnormal Psychology*, 103, 192–205.

White, R. W. (1959). Motivation reconsidered: The concept of competence. *Psychological Review*, 66, 297–333.

Widiger, T. A. (2001). Official classification systems. In W. J. Livesley (Ed.), *Handbook of personality disorders: Theory, research, and treatment* (pp. 60–83). New York, NY: Guilford Press.

Widiger, T. A. (2011). Personality and psychopathology. *World Psychiatry*, 10, 103–106.

Widiger, T. A. (2015). Assessment of DSM-5 personality disorder. *Journal of Personality Assessment*, 97, 456–466.

Widiger, T. (in press, 2018). Bruno Klopfer award address: Five-Factor Model personality disorder scales. *Journal of Personality Assessment*. doi:10.1080/00223891.2018

Widiger, T. A., Bach, B., Chmielewski, M., Clark, L. A., DeYoung, C., Hopwood, C. J., Kotov, R., Krueger, R. F., Miller, J. D., Morey, L. C., Mullins-Sweatt, S. N., Patrick, C. J., Pincus, A. L., Samuel, D. B., Sellbom, M., South, S. C., Tackett, J. L., Watson, D., Waugh, M. H., Wright, A. G. C., Zimmermann, J., Bagby, R. M., Cicero, D. C., Conway, C. C., De Clercq, B., Docherty, A. R., Eaton, N. R., Forbush, K. T., Haltigan, J. D., Ivanova, M. Y., Latzman, R. D., Lynam, D. R., Markon, K. E., Reininghaus, U., & Thomas, K. M. (in press, 2018). Criterion A of the AMPD in HiTOP. *Journal of Personality Assessment*. doi:10.1080/00223891.2018.1465431

Widiger, T. A., & Frances, A. (1985). The DSM-III personality disorders: Perspectives from psychology. *Archives of General Psychiatry*, 42, 615–623.

Widiger, T. A., Lynam, D. R., Miller, J. D., & Oltmanns, T. F. (2012). Measures to assess maladaptive variants of the Five-Factor Model. *Journal of Personality Assessment*, 94, 450–455.
Widiger, T. A., & Simonsen, E. (2005). Alternative dimensional models of personality disorder: Finding a common ground. *Journal of Personality Disorders*, 19, 110–130.
Widiger, T. A., & Trull, T. J. (2007). Plate tectonics in the classification of personality disorder: Shifting to a dimensional model. *American Psychologist*, 62, 71–83.
Wiegand, W. A. (1998). The "Amherst Method": The origins of the Dewey decimal classification scheme. *Libraries & Culture*, 33, 175–194.
Wiggins, J. S. (1991). Agency and communion as conceptual coordinates for the understanding and measurement of interpersonal behavior. In D. Cicchetti & W. M. Grove (Eds.), *Thinking clearly about psychology: Essays in honor of Paul E. Meehl (Vol. 2): Personality and psychopathology* (pp.89–113). Minneapolis, MN: University of Minnesota Press.
Wiggins, J. S. (1995). *Interpersonal Adjective Scales professional manual.* Odessa, FL: Psychological Assessment Resources.
Wiggins, J. S. (1996). An informal history of the interpersonal circumplex tradition. *Journal of Personality Assessment*, 66, 217–233.
Wiggins, J. S. (2003). *Paradigms of personality assessment*. New York, NY: Guilford Press.
Wiggins, J. S., & Pincus, A. L. (1989). Conceptions of personality disorders and dimensions of personality. *Psychological Assessment: A Journal of Consulting and Clinical Psychology*, 1, 305–316.
Wilford, J. N. (2001). *The mapmakers.* New York, NY: Vintage Books.
Wilkinson-Ryan, T., & Westen, D. (2000). Identity disturbance in borderline personality disorder: An empirical investigation. *American Journal of Psychiatry*, 157, 528–541.
Williams, T. (1944/2012). *The glass menagerie* (3rd ed.). New York, NY: New Directions
Williams, T. F., Scalco, M. D., & Simms, L. J. (2018). The construct validity of general and specific dimensions of personality pathology. *Psychological Medicine*, 48, 834–848.
Wills, C. D., & Gold, L. H. (2014). Introduction to the special section on DSM-5 and forensic psychiatry. *Journal of the American Academy of Psychiatry and the Law*, 42, 132–135.
Winarick, D. J., & Bornstein, R. F. (2015). Toward resolution of a longstanding controversy in personality disorder diagnosis: Contrasting correlates of schizoid and avoidant traits. *Personality and Individual Differences*, 79, 25–29.
Winnicott, D. W. (1949). Hate in the counter-transference. *International Journal of Psycho-Analysis*, 30, 69–74.
Winnicott, D. W. (1967/1986). *Home is where we start from: Essays by a psychoanalyst*. New York, NY: WW Norton & Company.
Winnicott, D. W. (1974). Fear of breakdown. *International Review of Psycho-Analysis*, 1, 103–107.
Wittgenstein, L. (1975). *Philosophical investigations* (M. Aue, Trans.). Chicago, IL: University of Chicago Press.
Wolpe, J. (1958). *Psychotherapy by reciprocal inhibition*. Palo Alto, CA: Stanford University Press.

World Health Organization (1992). *The ICD-10 classification of mental and behavioural disorders: clinical descriptions and diagnostic guidelines (Vol. 1)*. Geneva, Switzerland: World Health Organization.

Wright, A. C., Calabrese, W. R., Rudick, M. M., Yam, W. H., Zelazny, K., Williams, T. F., Rotterman, J. H., & Simms, L. J. (2015). Stability of the DSM-5 Section III pathological personality traits and their longitudinal associations with psychosocial functioning in personality disordered individuals. *Journal of Abnormal Psychology*, 124, 199–207.

Wright, A. C., Hopwood, C. J., & Simms, L. J. (2015). Daily interpersonal and affective dynamics in personality disorder. *Journal of Personality Disorders*, 29, 503–525.

Wright, A. C., Pincus, A. L., Hopwood, C. J., Thomas, K. M., Markon, K. E., & Krueger, R. F. (2012). An interpersonal analysis of pathological personality traits in DSM-5. *Assessment*, 19, 263–275.

Wright, A. G., Hallquist, M. N., Beeney, J. E., & Pilkonis, P. A. (2013). Borderline personality pathology and the stability of interpersonal problems. *Journal of Abnormal Psychology*, 122, 1094–1100.

Wright, A. G., Hopwood, C. J., Skodol, A. E., & Morey, L. C. (2016). Longitudinal validation of general and specific structural features of personality pathology. *Journal of Abnormal Psychology*, 125, 1120–1134.

Wright, A. G., Pincus, A. L., Thomas, K. M., Hopwood, C. J., Markon, K. E., & Krueger, R. F. (2013). Conceptions of narcissism and the DSM-5 pathological personality traits. *Assessment*, 20, 339–352.

Wright, A. G., & Simms, L. J. (2014). On the structure of personality disorder traits: Conjoint analyses of the CAT-PD, PID-5, and NEO-PI-3 trait models. Per*sonality Disorders: Theory, Research, and Treatment*, 5, 43.

Wright, A. G., & Simms, L. J. (2015). A metastructural model of mental disorders and pathological personality traits. *Psychological Medicine*, 45, 2309–2319.

Wright, A. G., Thomas, K. M., Hopwood, C. J., Markon, K. E., Pincus, A. L., & Krueger, R. F. (2012). The hierarchical structure of DSM-5 pathological personality traits. *Journal of Abnormal Psychology*, 121, 951–957.

Wright, Z. E., Pahlen, S., & Krueger, R. F. (2017). Genetic and environmental influences on Diagnostic and Statistical Manual of Mental Disorders (DSM-5) maladaptive personality traits and their connections with normative personality traits. *Journal of Abnormal Psychology*, 126, 416.

Wygant, D. B., Sellbom, M., Sleep, C. E., Wall, T. D., Applegate, K. C., Krueger, R. F., & Patrick, C. J. (2016). Examining the DSM-5 alternative personality disorder model operationalization of antisocial personality disorder and psychopathy in a male correctional sample. *Personality Disorders: Theory, Research, and Treatment*, 7, 229–239.

Yalom, I., & Elkin, G. (1974). *Every day gets a little closer: A twice-told therapy.* New York, NY: Basic Books.

Yam, W. H., & Simms, L. J. (2014). Comparing criterion- and trait-based personality disorder diagnoses in DSM-5. *Journal of Abnormal Psychology*, 123, 802–808.

Yeomans, F. E., Clarkin, J. F., & Kernberg, O. F. (2015). *Transference-focused psychotherapy for borderline personality disorder: A clinical guide.* Arlington, VA: American Psychiatric Publishing.

Young, J. E. (1994). *Cognitive therapy for personality disorders: A schema-focused approach* (revised ed.). Sarasota, FL: Professional Resource Press/Professional Resource Exchange.

Zachar, P. (2015). Personality disorder: Philosophical problems. In T. Schramme & S. Edwards (Eds.), *Handbook of the philosophy of medicine*. Dordrecht, NL: Springer.
Zachar, P., & Kendler, K. S. (2007). Psychiatric disorders: A conceptual taxonomy. *American Journal of Psychiatry*, 164, 557–565.
Zachar, P., & Kendler, K. S. (2012). The removal of Pluto from the class of planets and homosexuality from the class of psychiatric disorders: A comparison. *Philosophy, Ethics, and Humanities in Medicine*, 7, 1–7.
Zachar, P., & Kendler, K. S. (2017). The philosophy of nosology. *Annual Review of Clinical Psychology*, 13, 49–71.
Zachar, P., Krueger, R. F., & Kendler, K. S. (2016). Personality disorder in DSM-5: An oral history. *Psychological Medicine*, 46, 1–10.
Zanarini, M. C. (2009). Psychotherapy of borderline personality disorder. *Acta Psychiatrica Scandinavica*, 120, 373–377.
Zanarini, M. C., & Frankenburg, F. R. (1997). Pathways to the development of borderline personality disorder. *Journal of Personality Disorders*, 11, 93–104.
Zanarini, M. C., & Frankenburg, F. R. (2007). The essential nature of borderline psychopathology. *Journal of Personality Disorders*, 21, 518–535.
Zandersen, M., Henriksen, M. G., & Parnas, J. (in press, 2018). A recurrent question: What is borderline? *Journal of Personality Disorders*. doi:10.1521/pedi_2018_32_348
Zeigler-Hill, V., McCabe, G. A., & Vrabel, J. K. (2016). The dark side of humor: DSM-5 pathological personality traits and humor styles. *European Journal of Psychology*, 12, 363–376.
Zeigler-Hill, V., & Wallace, M. T. (2011). Racial differences in narcissistic tendencies. *Journal of Research in Personality*, 45, 456–467.
Zimmermann, J., Altenstein, D., Krieger, T., Holtforth, M. G., Pretsch, J., Alexopoulos, J., & Leising, D. (2014). The structure and correlates of self-reported DSM-5 maladaptive personality traits: Findings from two German-speaking samples. *Journal of Personality Disorders*, 28, 518–540.
Zimmermann, J., Benecke, C., Bender, D. S., Skodol, A. E., Schauenburg, H., Cierpka, M., & Leising, D. (2014). Assessing DSM-5 level of personality functioning from videotaped clinical interviews: A pilot study with untrained and clinically inexperienced students. *Journal of Personality Assessment*, 96, 397–409.
Zimmermann, J., Böhnke, J. R., Eschstruth, R., Mathews, A., Wenzel, K., & Leising, D. (2015). The latent structure of personality functioning: Investigating criterion a from the alternative model for personality disorders in DSM-5. *Journal of Abnormal Psychology*, 124, 532–548.
Zimmermann, J., Ehrenthal, J. C., Cierpka, M., Schauenburg, H., Doering, S., & Benecke, C. (2012). Assessing the level of structural integration using Operationalized Psychodynamic Diagnosis (OPD): Implications for DSM-5. *Journal of Personality Assessment*, 94, 522–532.
Zimmermann, J., Schwarzer, I., Masuhr, O., Jaeger, U., Spitzer, C., & Wright, A. G. C. (2016). Tägliches erleben im stationären setting: Eine tagebuchstudie zum einfluss psychoanalytisch-interaktioneller gruppentherapie. *PDP Psychodynamische Psychotherapie: Forum Der Tiefenpsychologisch Fundierten Psychotherapie*, 15, 219–232.
Zimmerman, M. (2011). A critique of the proposed prototype rating system for personality disorders in DSM-5. *Journal of Personality Disorders*, 25, 206–221.

Zimmerman, M., & Mattia, J. I. (1999). Differences between clinical and research practices in diagnosing borderline personality disorder. *American Journal of Psychiatry*, 156, 1570–1574.

Zuckerman, M., & Kuhlman, D. M. (2000). Personality and risk-taking: Common biosocial factors. *Journal of Personality*, 68, 999–1029.

Zuroff, D. C., & Fitzpatrick, D. K. (1995). Depressive personality styles: Implications for adult attachment. *Personality and Individual Differences*, 18, 253–365.

Zuroff, D. C., Moskowitz, D. S., Wielgus, M. S., Powers, T. A., & Franko, D. L. (1983). Construct validation of the Dependency and Self-Criticism Scales of the Depressive Experiences Questionnaire. *Journal of Research in Personality*, 17, 226–241.

Index

Note: Page numbers in *italic* refer to figures, those in **bold** to tables. Footnotes are indicted by a lower-case n followed by the note number.

For Product Safety Concerns and Information please contact our EU representative GPSR@taylorandfrancis.com
Taylor & Francis Verlag GmbH, Kaufingerstraße 24, 80331 München, Germany

www.ingramcontent.com/pod-product-compliance
Ingram Content Group UK Ltd.
Pitfield, Milton Keynes, MK11 3LW, UK
UKHW021502240926
475702UK00035B/220

* 9 7 8 1 1 3 8 6 9 3 1 3 5 *